Including Pupils
with Disabilities

Including Pupils
with Disabilities

Edited by

Tony Booth and Will Swann

Open University Press

Milton Keynes · Philadelphia

Open University Press
Celtic Court
22 Ballmoor
Buckingham
MK18 1XW

and
1900 Frost Road, Suite 101
Bristol, PA 19007, USA

First published 1987
Reprinted 1988, 1993

British Library Cataloguing in Publication Data
Including pupils with disabilities.————
   (Curricula for all)
   1. Handicapped children   Education   England
   2. Mainstreaming in education   England
   I. Booth, Tony   II. Swann, Will   III. Series

   371.9′0942   LC4036.G6

   ISBN 0-335-15978-8
   ISBN 0-335-15977-X Pbk

Library of Congress Cataloging in Publication Data
Main entry under title:
Including pupils with disabilities.
   (Curricula for all)
   Includes index.
   1. Handicapped children——Education——Great Britain.
   2. Mainstreaming in education——Great Britain.
   I. Booth, Tony.   II. Swann, Will.   III. Series.
LC4036.G7I53   1986   371.9′046′0941   86–23647

ISBN 0-335-15978-8
ISBN 0-335-15977-X (pbk.)

Text design by Nicola Sheldon
Typeset by Thomson Litho Ltd
Printed in Great Britain by
St Edmundsbury Press Ltd
Bury St Edmunds, Suffolk

For Adam, Lydia, Stephen and Vincent

Contents

SECTION ONE   TEACHING AND LEARNING

(a)   Life in classrooms

(b)   Using microtechnology

Introduction to the series: curricula for all
Tony Booth

Curricula for All is the general title of a series of three books. The first is entitled *Preventing Difficulties in Learning*, the second, *Producing and Reducing Disaffection*, and the third, *Including Pupils with Disabilities*. They reflect the approach to special needs in education of the special education group of the Open University and are the support material for the project year of our Advanced Diploma. Those familiar with our earlier course E241, *Special Needs in Education* will be aware of its attempt to move the concerns of special education away from a marginal esoteric segment of the education system towards the enhancement of comprehensive nursery, primary and secondary schools and further education colleges. Within that course we examined and developed a concept of integration as the foundation for a philosophy of special education. As the principle was formulated and clarified it merged with a principle of comprehensive, community education. Integration became the process of increasing the participation of pupils, families, school workers and communities in the life of mainstream schools. A focus on one group who experience limited participation, such as pupils with disabilities, naturally leads to an examination of the causes of, and possible solutions to the lack of involvement of other groups. The absurdity of finding appropriate forms of schooling for such groups viewed in isolation is emphasized by a pupil's possible multiple membership of disadvantaged groups.

We are concerned, then, to examine the ways in which schools can respond to and reflect the diversity of their pupils. We have come to see how both an integration principle and comprehensive principle can be elucidated by being linked to a principle of equality of value. In schools which operate according to such a principle attempts are made to reduce the devaluation of pupils according to their sex, background, colour, economic or class position, ability, disability or attainment. In fact it can be argued that special education exists as a distinct area of concern for educators because of a particular set of devaluations of pupils on the basis of their disability, ability, attainment or background. If, however, we are to see pupils who gain Oxbridge entry as of no greater value, as no more worthy of congratulation, than pupils with severe mental handicap, then this has far reaching consequences for what happens in schools and for how we perceive social inequalities outside them. Yet if it is the job of educators to discover and act in the interests of the pupils they serve it is hard to see how those who profess a concern for vulnerable and disadvantaged pupils should take any other view.

For us, the purpose of providing training in 'special needs in education' is to provide support for teachers and others to move away from a system in which large numbers of pupils are thought to be failures and from which pupils are selected out on the grounds of low ability or disability. We argue that the devaluation of pupils within the mainstream and selection out of it are mutually supportive. A training in special education which concentrates on those who fail to adapt to existing mainstream curricula or are excluded from them inevitably helps to perpetuate existing casualty rates. Our concern is with an approach to special needs in education which will enhance rather than undermine the development of comprehensive nursery, primary and secondary provision. We are as much or more concerned with the creation of curricula which cater for diverse groups, as with overcoming the difficulties experienced by particular pupils.

The practical implementation of a principle of equality of value is a thoroughly utopian notion; the possibility of its achievement is remote and partial as long as society and schools continue to provide areas for competing interests. In such circumstances the advancement of the participation of one group must be at the expense of the re-evaluation of another. We have tried to be clear about the principles which underly this series of books because it is our firm belief that clarity over principles is the best way to facilitate decisions about practice. But the emphasis is on practice rather than principles. We have provided a wide variety of examples of practice concerned with making curricula in schools responsive to all pupils.

The first book in the series is entitled *Preventing Difficulties in Learning*. This book takes as its starting point a definition of learning difficulty as a mismatch between pupils and tasks. Consequently, the prevention of difficulties in learning involves changing the experiences of pupils in schools so that they are more closely matched to their abilities and interests. The book looks both at the way curricula can be made more generally accessible and at the kinds of organization and support required within schools to initiate and sustain such changes. It looks at the way existing people and structures concerned with the learning difficulties of pupils can develop a concern for the nature of the whole curriculum. If the problem of learning difficulties cannot be resolved by focusing on groups of pupils who have limited ability or attainment or have disabilities then the job of special or remedial educators becomes a collaborative one and the basis of their expertise has to shift. These issues are carefully examined and exemplified. This book also provides the support material for our pack, EP538 *Teaching for Diversity: Preventing Difficulties in Learning*.

The second book in the series is entitled *Producing and Reducing Disaffection*. In that book we have explored the links between the curriculum in schools and the way pupils can become disaffected or disenchanted with school. It depicts classroom practice and the experiences and views of teachers and pupils. It looks in detail at the attitudes that are fostered in pupils towards themselves and others by the way people, their backgrounds and families are represented and valued within the overt and hidden curriculum. We have examined the processes whereby some pupils are moved out of the mainstream as a result of deviance in behaviour or emotional state and the nature of the special provision in which they are schooled. We have investigated the scope and limits for reducing disaffection through curriculum reform.

The introduction to this volume, which is the third in the series, follows this series introduction.

The great majority of the contributions are published in the series for the first time. We have tried to overcome problems of coherence created by having large numbers of contributing authors in part by providing authors with a careful list of suggestions and by negotiating chapters through a process of drafting and redrafting. Our contributors have been wonderfully persevering during these stages and our offices and homes have echoed too with cries of 'never again!' Yet we are well aware of the necessity for allowing many voices to be represented in this enterprise particularly from practising teachers and others who can tell their experience at first hand. We have also provided each chapter with an introductory paragraph and have written introductory chapters for each book. We do not expect anyone to plough straight through the books. They are a resource for learning and their use should be adapted to the needs of any particular reader. The series is the result of our efforts to reground special education in a body of knowledge which will allow practitioners to begin to implement some of the rhetoric of the last ten years. The abolition of distinctions between special, remedial and mainstream education requires a radical rethink of the work of special educators and, inevitably, new forms of training. The concepts and content of training is one way of assessing whether the rhetoric of change is serious in intent or if what is to be offered is more of the same. The way to avoid a simple backsliding into old ways is to articulate the underlying principles on which a non-selective, non-categorical approach to special education could be based.

To complete our Advanced Diploma students study E241 and a broadening education or social science course. They then produce three projects in conjunction with *Curricula for All*. The first of these is a study of learning from the perspective of pupils, the second a piece of curriculum analysis and development and the third a study of decision and policy making within a school and/or LEA. The demands of these projects have helped to determine the shape of the books and have made us attend carefully to the range of topics we need to cover to provide an adequate basis for training. Perhaps, it is in the third area that we are weakest. Partly this is because policy making was a particular concern of our earlier course but largely it is because the level of discussion about decisions and developments in schools which we would like to include is very difficult to find in already published form and very difficult to persuade others to write. It is honest reporting and discussion about practice and the many slips between policy as rhetoric or intention and its practical implementation from which others can best learn. Perhaps our course will begin to break down the formidable barriers to sharing such information which many find to be excessively threatening.

There are a few final things which have to be made clear. Firstly we do not want our ready use of the word 'curriculum' to imply that we believe what pupils are offered in school can be written down on a bit of paper and handed out or down in staffroom and classroom. Our notion of curriculum encompasses the experiences of pupils, teachers and others in school and the interactions between school and community rather than being reserved for the written intentions of departmental heads. The kind of community a school provides is as important a feature of the curriculum as the words transmitted in formal lessons. Nor do we think it is unproblematic to match curricula to the backgrounds, interests and capacities of pupils. Understanding the needs and interests of others is complex and problematic but it becomes slightly less so if we listen to the voices of those whose interests we claim to serve.

Most importantly, we do not argue that a relocation of the problem of difficulties in learning from inside the child or the child's background or culture or family to the curriculum in school can cause problems within schools to evaporate, nor that teachers can be held personally responsible for the difficulties which do arise. Teachers are under massive pressures within a shrinking education system which is in turn adapting to shrinking employment opportunities for school leavers. There is a definite danger that a new focus on the curriculum within schools will deflect attention from the handicapping social conditions outside them or even hold schools responsible for such conditions. This is a clear strand in attempts to vocationalize the curriculum in secondary schools where high unemployment is blamed, in part, on the inappropriateness of the training given to the workforce which is offered vocational training after school and prevocational training within it. Schooling is not created anew by each generation of teachers; they operate within institutional constraints not of their choosing. But having said this we would argue that viewing difficulties in learning as arising from the relationship between pupils and curricula can enhance the contribution of teachers to their own working lives, as well as to the lives of their pupils.

Introduction

Will Swann

In this book we have tried to indicate ways in which pupils with disabilities can share in the lives of ordinary schools and communities. It continues the demonstration of the practice of integration that has been a feature of our previous work and the work of others (Booth and Potts 1983, Booth, Potts and Swann 1982, Hegarty and Pocklington 1981, 1982; see Booth and Potts 1983 for a detailed bibliography of sources). Our ideal system would deny no one the right of participation in ordinary schools and in the life of the community on grounds of ability or disability. But we are aware that such a system is a remote possibility. We hope that the portrayal of some people's practice and the successes and pitfalls of their efforts will provide a source of ideas for others.

We are also aware that the theory and practice of integration entails immense complexities. We do not believe that the implementation of integration policies is at all straightforward: the contents of this book bear ample witness to this. Indeed one of the limitations of the literature in the field to date has been the distinct lack of detailed analyses of practice and policy-making. This has been most noticeable at the classroom level; published observational studies of children with disabilities learning have been all but nonexistent. One task we set ourselves in planning this book was to begin to develop and encourage studies which are based around detailed observations of individual children in their own environment. We are sure that any attempt to improve classroom practice, to be successful, requires thorough understanding of classroom events as they occur at present. Hence we have begun the book with six detailed case studies of the experience of pupils with disabilities in schools and classrooms. The same applies to studies of policy-making. Here we have tried to provide critical accounts which recognize the sizeable gap between the rhetoric and reality of decision-making, which illuminate the way decisions are taken in practice, and which analyse the forces at work. Policies which assume the world is other than it is are unlikely to have the desired effects.

Disability and the mainstream curriculum

This is a book whose existence depends on two other books. When we decided to deal with pupils with disabilities in a separate volume, we were conscious of taking a risk: that we promote the belief that the inclusion of pupils with disabilities in primary and secondary schools depends largely on specific responses to those pupils. Their involvement in ordinary schools is certainly limited by the absence of specialist resources and expertise in ordinary schools, but it is far more profoundly constrained by the ordinary failure of ordinary schools to adapt to the abilities and interests of all their pupils, and by the way some groups of pupils are valued more highly than others. We included a section entitled 'Integrating Special Education' in the first book in the series, *Preventing Difficulties in Learning*, in order to link the issues in these two books. More generally, this book should be read in conjunction with both other books in the series: *Preventing Difficulties in Learning* (Booth, Potts and Swann 1987) and *Producing and Reducing Disaffection* (Booth and Coulby 1987).

Our concern in the series as a whole is to encourage the development of an education system which responds flexibly to children's abilities, interests and backgrounds and which does not devalue pupils on these grounds. The strategies by which children with disabilities can participate in ordinary curricula should be seen as extensions of these developments. Failure to make a link between the reform of mainstream schools and strategies for including pupils with disabilities creates two dilemmas. The first concerns the relationship between ability and disability. If we see the process of integrating pupils with disabilities as no more than providing access to a system of education whose basic design we do not question, then we may simply reinforce the exclusion of other pupils. It has been often remarked by mainstream teachers exposed to the most able and least disabled sections of the population of a special school that the pupils with disabilities are 'no trouble'. 'Trouble' comes in the form of any pupil who does not fit the demands of the curriculum, especially when he or she lets it be known. Helping children with disabilities to fit curriculum demands is known as 'providing access.' Bodily impairments have become a less significant barrier to the curriculum of ordinary schools as technological aids have become more widely available (Chapters 2, 4, 7, 8, 9 and 10), as buildings have been adapted (Chapters 17 and 18), as special schools have begun to establish links with ordinary schools (Chapters 4, 17 and 18), and as specialist staff have taken on support roles (Chapters 2, 5, 6 and 9). This has been reflected in a fall in the proportion of children who attend special schools for pupils with physical and sensory disabilities (Swann 1985). But any amount of 'access' and 'support' cannot guarantee that the curriculum which is made accessible is appropriate. This is 'the bottom line' for many integration schemes and it guarantees the exclusion of some pupils. The success of those who 'make it' into an ordinary school whose curriculum remains unchanged is bought at the cost of the failure of others, whose marginal status is even more firmly guaranteed. When those who 'make it' come from the same special school as those who don't, as in Evesham School in Chapter 18, the contrast is only more visible.

The dilemma is best illustrated in the case of Andrew in Chapter 4, who is an A-level student who also happens to have a severe disability. Through careful planning and the use of microtechnology, this young man has been permitted to compete in the race for academic credentials. It is ironic that the value placed on his education should inevitably depend upon the devaluation of many others. His membership of the mainstream has helped to restructure one part of the system by which value is assigned to pupils, and reinforced another.

In the education of Samantha Hulley (Chapters 1 and 27) we perhaps gain the clearest signs in this book of a system which values pupils regardless of ability and disability. This girl began her school career in the 'special care unit' of (what we now call) a school for children with severe learning difficulties. Samantha's successful participation in her junior school has been built on both a flexible curriculum and an effective network of support. She, more than any other child described in this book, challenges the claim in the Warnock Report, continually repeated since, that special schools would continue to be necessary for children with 'severe or complex physical, sensory or intellectual disabilities (DES 1978).

The second dilemma arising from the separation of issues of disability and mainstream curricula is implicit in the first. It is tempting, in a book about pupils with disabilities to see the central issue as one of access. But the value of any strategy for access is determined in part by the experiences which it makes accessible. There is also a danger, in talking of 'access to the curriculum', that we may think of access strategies themselves in a different way from 'the curriculum'. In this series of books we have adopted a definition of the curriculum as the sum total of pupils' experiences in school. Access strategies, in this sense, are *part of* the curriculum. Some people may be tempted, for example, in reading Chapters 6 and 14 which concern the education of Ben, a deaf child whose first language is British Sign Language, to interpret the use of BSL as a means of access, whose value derives solely from its potential to promote the acquisition of literacy, numeracy and the other ordinary goals of primary education. Yet, as Lorraine Fletcher depicts Ben's education, his use of BSL has value in its own right as an integral part of his developing self-identity and self-esteem as a member of the Deaf community. Similarly, in Chapter 8, Janis Firminger tells us that some students with disabilities have rejected microtechnology as a means of access to the further education curriculum not because it technically cannot do the job, but because they find it alienates them from their work. Microtechnology, support teaching, aids and communication systems do not simply provide access to experiences, they form experiences themselves. The problem takes a final twist when we realize that the way in which pupils experience means of access to the curriculum may depend upon other aspects of the curriculum. A thirteen-year old with mild athetosis known to me has great problems in his comprehensive school because of his extremely untidy writing, not helped by his use of biro, which he smudges constantly. A simple means of access to more rewarding experiences would be a pencil, but in some subjects using a pencil is frowned upon, and so he continues to smudge. He has been offered a microwriter, which is a small hand-held microelectronic device which would enable him to make and store all the notes he needs. He rejects it because he fears it would serve to segregate him further.

For these reasons, we have tried as far as possible to avoid isolating a discussion of access strategies from their context in the curriculum. Almost inevitably, we have been seduced to some extent by the separate existence of this book and the constraints of space. Readers must judge for themselves the extent of the seduction.

The special system

Our focus in the other two books in the series is on the reform of ordinary schools as a means to reduce the devaluation and increase the participation of pupils. The emphasis of this book cannot be as single-minded, for the exclusion of children with disabilities is not only produced by the nature of ordinary schooling. It also occurs as a result of the existence of a segregated special education system. For this reason, this book does not sustain the ordinary classroom focus that is evident throughout its companion volumes. We found it necessary to examine the ways in which the special system sustains itself, and to consider the consequences of attempts to change it.

The rate of progress towards an integrated system may seem to some people to be unacceptably rapid, particularly where they believe that integration has been poorly implemented. For example, Freddie Green, who was at the time Chief HMI for Special Education, argued during a presentation to the British Psychological Society Education Section Conference 1983 that pupils were being placed, not integrated, and he feared a 'backlash'. Yet in reality, up to 1983 the special school sector overall was still growing. Only since then has the proportion of children registered in special schools begun to fall. From its high point in 1983, it fell by four per cent in the following two years (DES 1984, 1985, 1986). At this rate it would be 2011 before the special school sector lost half its present share of the child population, and 2036 before it was empty.

This overall picture obscures the more serious threats to special schools for specific groups of pupils. We have considered the particular cases of schools for pupils with hearing and visual impairments in Chapters 20 and 21, and examined the pressures on one special school for pupils with physical disabilities in Chapter 18.

The closure of special schools and the transformation of others to resource centres poses another dilemma. The development of an integrated system would satisfy the wishes of many parents (Chapter 16 and 19) and people with disabilities (Chapters 17, 21, 24 and 25). At the same time, it appears to place in jeopardy the interests of parents and people with disabilities who wish their children, and members of their community, to attend a special school (Chapter 14). In evaluating parents' wishes it is important to realize that they are often expressed in response to existing options for the education of their children. In a study of the wishes of a small group of parents of children with disabilities who had been integrated from a special school into a comprehensive school I found a common history. When their children first arrived in the special school, all were firm supporters of segregation, especially those who had found their children actively rejected by the mainstream. Not surprisingly, they were apprehensive about the prospect of a move into a comprehensive school. Yet it took only a short experience of properly supported integrated education for these parents to become firm advocates of integration, not only for their own children but for others as well (Swann 1984).

Some may see the dilemma of conflicting client interests resolved through the development of 'a continuum of provision' in which parents have the choice of placement in their own areas. Here there would still be special schools but as well there would be a range of integrated options for the same children. The dangers of such an expanded special system are by now well established. It may encourage a further shedding of responsibility by mainstream teachers and schools. In any case, financial circumstances make the continuum of provision little more than a mirage to drool at as policy-makers wander the desert. The possibility for individual responses to the wishes of those parents who have the time, expertise and energy to press for the creation of new options (Chapter 14 and 16) is strictly limited, and does nothing to satisfy the wishes of parents who accept options they regard as unsuitable, but who do not wish to engage in a lengthy fight with their LEA.

There is no prospect of devising a system in which all interests are in harmony, but we badly need one which responds positively to the wishes of many more of its clients than at present. This book, and the series as a whole, is based on the premise that a fully comprehensive system of education is most likely to hold the competing interests of its clients in balance, and to offer a fair distribution of opportunities.

From the perspective of some people working in special schools, this approach may seem negative. This is, to a degree, inevitable. It is hard to envisage any significant shift in the direction of educating pupils with disabilities in ordinary schools that will not lead to the disappearance or radical transformation of special schools. But promoting the participation of pupils with disabilities in ordinary schools does *not* entail any wholesale rejection of the expertise of teachers in special schools. It simply calls into question the manner in which that expertise is deployed, and seeks new ways to use it. Thus, for example, Tim Southgate (Chapter 7) is the head of a special school who devotes much of his expertise to supporting children in the mainstream. Andrew's education (Chapter 4) has depended for its success on close collaboration between teachers in a mainstream and a special school. Gil Parsons, who is Samantha Hulley's special teacher (Chapter 1) was originally her teacher in a special care unit.

Although several chapters describe the delivery of specialist support to ordinary schools (Chapters 2, 5, 7, 12, 17 and 18), this is an area where with more time and space we might have done more. We can perhaps take comfort in the fact that many others are also addressing this issue.

Disability in school and community

A fourteen-year-old boy from a comprehensive school was visiting a local special school for children with physical disabilities, and he discussed the experience with his teacher:

> I feel I'm treating them as if they're a bit peculiar. They don't do the work that we do – it's all easy here. You begin to realize what other people must think when they see kids at a school like this – they think there must be something wrong.

Such a comment might not be noteworthy, were it not that this boy is describing his own old school. He has a heart defect, and until he reached twelve had never been to an ordinary school. The tendency to treat people with disabilities as if they were 'a bit peculiar' might be better described as a peculiar way to treat people.

Attitudes to disability are often most clearly revealed in unguarded, or off-the-cuff remarks. Radio 4's *The News Quiz* produced a fine example, when Barry Took told the story of some Iranian Athletes at the 35th World Stoke Mandeville Wheelchair Games held during July 1986. Apparently it was discovered that several Iranians were there under false pretences when, according to Barry Took, they leapt out of their wheelchairs, 'revealing that they weren't really ill at all'. But then neither was anyone else in the arena: how could world-class athletes compete if they were ill? The idea that someone with a disability can also be extremely fit seems to be an uneasy combination, even in the face of overwhelming evidence to the contrary.

The association of disability and sickness is only one of the many such packages of ideas by which we order our responses to people with disabilities. My own neatly packaged view of people categorized as 'mentally handicapped' took a severe knock in 1982 when I visited a youth club attended mainly by young people who were ex-pupils of two special schools. All of them had been categorized as 'educationally subnormal,' either 'moderate' or 'severe'. I spent some time with a young woman called Shirley, who now attended an Adult Training Centre. Shirley told me she spent most of her time packaging 'hospital supplies' into plastic bags. I pursued my self-imposed role of interrogator:

'What kind of supplies?'
'STs.'
'Sorry?'
'Sanitary Towels.'

For this, Shirley was paid 50p per week. I asked her why she stayed there. She replied, 'Well, I suppose they're training me for a job, but I've been there two or three years and it's getting on.'

I also met Shirley's friend, Wendy, who invited me to play *Mastermind*. This is a game that requires you to deduce the composition of a hidden pattern of four coloured pegs by successive approximations. After each attempt to reproduce the pattern, the opponent tells you how many of the pegs are the correct colour, and how many are in the correct place. Wendy lost, but only just: she was only marginally less competent (or more incompetent) at this game than me.

These conversations play havoc with conventional notions of mental handicap. People so labelled are supposed to be lacking in social skills. How then could Shirley be so sensitive as to try to spare her own and my embarrassment by using the euphemism 'STs?' How could she be so aware of the contradictions of Adult Training Centres? And how could Wendy show such deductive logical capacity?

We have many ways of coping with such assaults to our category system. One method was adopted by Wendy's former deputy head. When I remarked to her that Wendy played *Mastermind* very well, she replied, 'Yes, she's an interesting case', and she told me there was 'a history' involving 'genes' and 'chromosomes'. In such discourse, there are 'cases' rather than people. 'Cases' are for investigation and explanation and possibly diagnosis: they are objects of study, rather than people whose abilities demand ordinary social responses. Another method is to recognize the achievements but to stress their exceptional status: the 'aren't they wonderful' response. Some years ago, the BBC screened a documentary about a young woman with cerebral palsy. I saw it as a portrait of a lively independently-minded person engaged in such activities as learning to drive and looking for a job. The continuity announcer, however, introduced the programme as '... and now for the story of a very remarkable young lady'. If ordinary experiences for able-bodied people are 'extraordinary' for someone with a disability, then by implication ordinary life for *ordinary* people with disabilities excludes such experiences.

Wendy denied her categorization. She lived in a group home with one other person described as 'mentally handicapped', two deaf people and two University students. She didn't mind this arrangement, except that, 'they treat me as if I'm mentally handicapped, but I'm not. I just have difficulty in reading and writing'.

The tendency to respond to people according to their disability and its stereotypic associations is not restricted to those sections of society who have little contact with people with disabilities: it is as common amongst people whose work brings them into daily contact with them. It was customary in the early 1970s when I was a research worker concerned with mentally handicapped children to refer to them as 'subnormals'. We had more specific categories like 'spinabifs' and 'CPs'. The ultimate in nonsensical and dehumanizing behaviour came when the project I was engaged in sent out a survey questionnaire which asked for the sex of pupils as male, female or 'other'. My persistent difficulty in responding ordinarily to people called mentally handicapped is perhaps revealed by the fact that I never learnt Shirley and Wendy's surnames.

Even people who are heavily engaged in the development of integrated education fall prey to perceptions of pupils which are dominated by their disability. When I visited a special school many of whose pupils spent much of their time in ordinary schools, I sat in on a discussion group for integrating secondary aged pupils. Their teacher, whose main responsibility was the integration programme, asked them to introduce themselves in turn by saying their name, and their disability. I had not asked for this information, and it seems unlikely, given the choice, that this would be the first point about themselves that they would wish to tell a stranger.

Our peculiar ideas about disability do not arise spontaneously. They are part of a framework of social institutions that keeps people with disabilities outside the ordinary stream of life. Our sense of normality has little or no place for disability. People with disabilities often find that in order to become part of the ordinary community they have to deny their oppression and the ignorance of others (Chapter 24), and keep quiet about the pain and effort that is part of everyday experience for some of them (Chapter 4). If they become angry at their treatment, they risk being further labelled as deviant (Chapter 24). These are the tests of eligibility for membership of the ordinary community. We should not be surprised if some people with disabilities seek ways to establish a sense of worth and identity through the creation of their own community. The Deaf community has a centuries old existence, built around their common language, British Sign Language (Chapter 26). There are moves amongst some politically active groups of people with physical disabilities to establish separate institutions under their own control, within which they too can build a sense of self-worth.

In devoting a substantial portion of this book to the place of disability in school and society, we seek to widen the debate about the value and purpose of the participation of children with disabilities in ordinary schools. There are times when the temptation to evaluate integration programmes according to narrow criteria of academic performance and friendship networks seems irresistible, and warnings are issued against sacrificing pupils' educational well-being on the altar of principle. Including pupils with disabilities in ordinary life involves a redefinition of what counts as ordinary. It might, some time in the future, be unremarkable to see children with multiple disabilities in ordinary classrooms (Chapter 1); it might be as unremarkable to find other children valuing their work (Chapter 27); it might be possible not only for pupils with disabilities to demand equitable treatment (Chapter 23), but for those pupils not to have to disguise their resentment at their own limitations and those imposed on them by others, for fear of accusations that they cannot 'accept their handicap'; it might be no more surprising to find BSL as a minority language on the curriculum, as to find Urdu or Gujerati, or to find that every parent who wants it can have their deaf child educated bilingually (Chapter 26). It is by changes like these, as well as the personal achievements of individuals, that we should judge our progress.

The structure and content of this book

The book is divided into three main sections.

Section One: Teaching and Learning

We start in the classroom. We have felt for some time that the level of detailed description of classroom events involving pupils with disabilities which would both provoke interest and aid reflection on current practice was largely unavailable. The first six chapters are the beginnings of an attempt to write at this level about individual pupils. We are particularly pleased that two of them have been jointly written by teachers and parents. In *Chapter 1*, Bobby and Tom Hulley, Gil Parsons, Sandra Madden and Will Swann write about Samantha Hulley, a girl who has multiple disabilities who attends a junior school. In *Chapter 2*, Terence Bailey and Doreen Furby describe the experience of Kevin who attends a comprehensive and who has cerebral palsy. Their analysis reveals the successes as well as the challenges entailed in supporting Kevin. Hasit, who is the subject of *Chapter 3*, by June Statham, may seem out of place in this book, since his only physical problem is that he is very small. But the fact that this contributes to his being out of place in his ordinary school makes the chapter a revealing one about the consequences of bodily variation, as well as many other facets of Hasit's difficulties. Andrew, whose education is described in *Chapter 4* is much more obviously disabled. With the help of careful planning and microtechnology, he has climbed high up the academic ladder. This chapter also assesses the additional difficulties thrust on Andrew by the examination system. Chapters 5 and 6 describe deaf children in two contrasting environments. *Chapter 5* by Juliet Bishop and Susan Gregory describes and contrasts the experience of two deaf children in schools which have adopted a policy of 'natural oralism'. Chapter 6, by Siân Downs, Annette Fletcher and Lorraine Fletcher portrays another deaf child, Ben, under a different regime which treats Ben as a user of a different language from the other pupils, and which offers a bilingual education.

It was obvious that microtechnology would have a substantial place in this book. Its potential to liberate people from the constraints of their disabilities and to provide access to wider educational opportunities is undeniable. Chapters 7 to 11 deal specifically with this area. Tim Southgate, in *Chapter 7*, argues that we should think of microcomputers not as replacements for teachers, but as tools for learning and communicating. He describes five children whose education has been enhanced through the use of a microcomputer. Janis Firminger, in *Chapter 8*, writes about microtechnology in further education. She shows that the way such resources are used is as important as the design of the hardware; she argues that microtechnology should be seen as a means to increase the control of people with disabilities over their own lives. *Chapter 9*, by Julian Watson and Tom Vincent, describes how a microcomputer-based workstation has enhanced the experience of blind pupils in an ordinary school and that of their teachers, especially by providing an automatic translation from Braille to print. In *Chapter 10*, Harry Cayton describes the use of hearing aids to support pupils with hearing impairments. He provides practical guidance and points out that the presence of an aid in the classroom may require many adaptations in organization and teaching method.

The final two chapters of this Section focus on mobility. Andrew Sutton, in *Chapter 11*, describes the system of education for people with 'motor disorders' known as conductive education. This method has excited much interest recently in this country in view of its spectacular successes in its native Hungary. Andrew Sutton assesses the prospects for introducing conductive education here, and looks at its implications for integration policies. *Chapter 12* is by Ann Markee, who is a physiotherapist. She describes her work and that of other physiotherapists, particularly in supporting children with disabilities in their homes and neighbourhood schools.

Section Two: Policy and Decision-Making

In this section we wanted to reflect the real lives of people in schools and LEAs, and the way decisions are actually taken in the messy world of competing interests and philosophies. This is an infinitely trickier task than accounts of official versions of policy. If people find it hard to agree, for example, about what a document like the 1981 Education Act says, what hope is there that we can reveal the goings-on of staff-rooms, class-rooms and committee-rooms? All the claims made in the chapters in this section should be tested against the evidence presented, and the location of the author. In some cases, the author is a participant in the events being described, and they are able to reveal issues and events that might remain hidden to an outsider. In other chapters the author is an outsider, although that status manifestly does not guarantee neutrality for anyone.

The first four chapters in this section are concerned with decisions about individual children. In *Chapter 13*, Ann Elsegood describes what seems like the inexorable segregation of a boy with muscular dystrophy whom she taught. *Chapter 14* recounts the background to the education of Ben described in Chapter 6. Lorraine Fletcher sets out her philosophy, the way professionals in her local authority responded to her wishes, and the series of decisions that led eventually to Ben attending his infant school.

Many key decisions about the education of children with disabilities are taken outside schools during the process of 'assessment'. Chapters 15 and 16 look at this process, and both contrast the rhetoric and reality of practice. Simon Dyson, in *Chapter 15*, analyses the many functions served by assessment and exemplifies what may be learnt by considering assessments as social practices rather than technical exercises. *Chapter 16*, by Will Swann, focuses on the preparation of statements of special need, and argues that they cannot serve the functions described for them in official documents.

Chapters 17 to 19 are about decision-making at the level of schools and LEAs. In *Chapter 17*, David Ruebain provides the double perspective of a governor of a mainstream school and an ex-pupil of a special school on the initial stages of an integration scheme. He describes its shaky start and considers how it could be on a firmer footing. *Chapter 18* contains the story of developments in an integration scheme that has been established for many years. Will Swann focuses on the conflicts and tensions inherent in the scheme as it begins to threaten the viability and well-being of the special school involved in this partnership with a comprehensive. *Chapter 19*, by Linda Jordan, vividly describes the conflicts that arose when she and others tried to introduce a policy of integration into one local authority.

The last two chapters in this section focus on national policy trends. Gordon Mitchell, in *Chapter 20*, gives an overview of the development of policy for deaf education, and Terry Moody, in *Chapter 21*, considers developments in the education of children with visual disabilities. Both chapters assess recent moves by the DES to rationalize policy at national and regional levels.

Section Three: Liberty, Equality and Disability

In this final section of the book, we have tried to reflect and consider the social position of people with disabilities and its relationship to the education system. We have given particular emphasis to the views of people with disabilities themselves, although we have not gone as far as we would have wished in giving them a direct voice. Only four chapters in the whole book have authors who have disabilities.

Chapter 22, by Jenny Corbett, tells the story of her son's epilepsy and its consequences. In the past 'epileptics' have been classified with the deviants and undesirables of society. This chapter shows how epilepsy need not define anyone's identity. *Chapter 23* is an account by David Cropp of a group of adolescents with disabilities taking some control of their school experience. Their wishes reveal both the unequal treatment they resented, and the kind of school community they wanted to be part of. Jenny Morris is a teacher with a disability, and in *Chapter 24* she recounts her experience of how her colleagues and her college responded to her. Another set of views on the responses of 'ordinary society' is given by June Statham in *Chapter 25*. This chapter describes the work of a group of people called mentally handicapped who have become 'self-advocates'. It is a story of growing political awareness, and a determination to have a stake in the society of which they insist on being a part. *Chapter 26* focuses on another group: deaf people. Mary Brennan describes their language, British Sign Language, which binds together the Deaf community in this country, and considers the implications of a respect for their language and community for the education of deaf children.

The last chapter, *Chapter 27*, steps back into the classroom, and provides a glimpse of the attitudes of ordinary children and how they might change. Will Swann presents an annotated interview with four classmates of Samantha Hulley whose education is described in Chapter 1. Their comments reveal something of their own conceptions of Samantha as a person.

References

Booth, T. and Coulby, D. 1986. *Producing and Reducing Disaffection*, Milton Keynes, Open University Press.

Booth, T. and Potts, P. 1983. *Integrating Special Education*, Oxford, Basil Blackwell.

Booth, T., Potts, P. and Swann, W. 1982. 'An alternative system: a special imagination', Unit 16 of E241, *Special Needs in Education*, Milton Keynes, Open University Press.

Booth, T., Potts, P. and Swann, W. 1986. *Preventing Difficulties in Learning*, Oxford, Basil Blackwell.

Department of Education and Science (DES) 1978. *Special Educational Needs* (The Warnock Report), London, HMSO.

Department of Education and Science (DES) 1984, 1985, 1986. *Statistics of Schools*, London, DES.

Hegarty, S. and Pocklington, K. 1981. *Educating Pupils with Special Needs in the Ordinary School*, Windsor, NFER/Nelson.

Hegarty, S. and Pocklington, K. 1982. *Integration in Action*, Windsor, NFER/Nelson.

Swann, W. 1984. 'Conflict and control: some observations on parents and the integration of children with special needs', paper presented to the British Psychological Society Annual Conference, Swansea, April 1984.

Swann, W. 1985. 'Is the integration of children with special needs happening?', *Oxford Review of Education*, *11*(1), pp. 3–18.

References

SECTION I

Teaching and Learning

1 Samantha

Bobby Hulley, Tom Hulley, Gil Parsons, Sandra Madden and
Will Swann

This chapter tells how one eleven-year-old girl, Samantha Hulley, who has quite severe impairments, attends an ordinary school on a part-time basis. It has been written collaboratively by Tom and Bobby Hulley, Sam's parents, Sandra Madden, who is Sam's class teacher at Burydale Junior School in Stevenage, Gil Parsons, who is Sam's support teacher, and Will Swann, who helped to collect some of the observations in the chapter. First, it summarizes Sam's educational background, then it describes the way Sam has learnt to communicate: this is a central part of her education. It then goes on to describe how Sam is taught with her mainstream class, inside and outside the school, and how she benefits from it. Sam is also the subject of Chapter 27 which is an edited interview with four of her classmates.

Introduction

Samantha was born, unimpaired, in July 1974. At seventeen months she was walking well, talking to some extent and understanding everything. She was bright and full of love. Suddenly, just before Christmas 1975, she caught an infection which constricted her throat and eventually led to pneumonia. On the way to hospital her breathing stopped for several minutes before she was resuscitated in the casualty unit on arrival. She was left with extensive brain injury. When Sam returned from hospital she had a severe disability. She had been tube fed but was beginning to accept a bottle. Her expression remained blank. She could not roll over and hated being handled, or even cuddled. She was totally blind and had fits. Today, at eleven years of age, Sam appears to many people who know her as an achieving person, although she is one of the least able of children. The story of how Bobby and Tom worked with a number of professionals to help Sam to learn throughout her life is told in Tom's account: *Samantha Goes to School* (Hulley 1985).

In the past Sam has been to a variety of places for teaching and therapy. These include a playgroup based at Great Ormond Street Hospital where parents and professionals work together with children with disabilities, and an integrated Opportunity Group in Stevenage, Sam's home town, where parents' and professionals' skills were also combined. Sam's full-time education began at a local special school for children with severe learning difficulties, where she was initially placed in the special care unit. Later, after some quiet persuasion by Bobby, her mother, Sam joined the newly established nursery group in the same special school, taught by Gil Parsons, who was later to become Sam's special teacher in her junior school.

By the spring of 1979, two years after starting school, Sam had made a lot of progress. She could now see and was beginning to use her vision to help her to move. She could get around the classroom unaided and was exploring toys mainly by chewing them. She was vocalizing. By December 1979, Sam was using a trundle truck, beginning to understand direction, and she could recognize forty pictures. She had begun to use signs. Her first sign was for 'toilet'.

By this stage Tom and Bobby had come to feel strongly that Sam should attend a mainstream school. Their philosophy is set out in *Samantha Goes to School*. Luckily, they found that they did not have a great fight on their hands. The head of the local Infants School, Shephall Green, invited Sam into the school on a part-time basis, beginning with one half day a week. Two terms after starting at Shephall Green, Sam stopped attending the special school.

With Bobby as her helper, Sam joined in all activities as far as possible. Many, like painting, required a joint effort from Sam and Bobby. Sam held the brush, chose the colour and made arm movements with help. The ethos of the school made Sam's inclusion possible. At any one time children would be doing many different things. Into this setting, Bobby could fit the more formal programme she had devised, aimed at increasing recognition, improving her ability to make choices and extending her vocabulary. Sam had no useful speech, just a few sounds and, at this stage, only a small number of signs, but she understood many aspects of conversation and story-telling.

For some time, the arrangement at Shephall Green had not been formalized, and involved no local education authority input. In autumn 1982, Tom and Bobby contacted the LEA asking them to commit additional resources to Sam's education. In Summer 1983, the LEA agreed to provide five hours from a home tutor and ten hours' welfare assistance. It was agreed that Sam would have half-time schooling starting in the infants school, but with a view to the overdue move to a junior school. Sam was now nine years old.

In September 1984, Sam moved on. Her schooling from then to the present has been split between Burydale Junior School and Lonsdale Special School for children with physical disabilities. She spends three half days at Burydale, and two days a week at Lonsdale. One half day at Burydale is spent swimming and the other two sessions are spent working in Sam's classroom. Gil, Sam's special teacher, supports her for one of these sessions, for the other she is supported by Ann, her welfare assistant. Each visit to Burydale includes school dinner, an important occasion for Sam. When Sam is at Lonsdale School, she spends time with the physiotherapist and speech therapist, and she makes good use of the heated swimming pool.

Sam has now been accepted at a comprehensive school. She starts at Heathcote School in September 1986. All her school-based education will take place there and she will only visit the special school for treatment sessions. There are excellent signs of willingness to co-operate in the development of Sam's integration by the staff at Heathcote. Her first year tutor group includes classmates from Burydale. Both her elder brothers have attended Heathcote and one will still be there in the fifth year. Sam applauded loudly at a meeting for new pupils when the headteacher announced a full meals service would be available from September.

Learning to communicate

Learning to communicate is the linchpin of growing up. Sam has needed a great deal of help to develop her ability in this area. Communication is central to her education.

Sam is very sociable. She tries to communicate with most people that she meets, and she enjoys the company of others. She communicates with sounds and gestures and by pointing at objects and pictures. Some of her methods have been taught by her parents and teachers; she has developed others by herself.

She began to communicate, like any other child, with smiles and tears; then she learned to get what she wanted by withholding her co-operation. When unwilling to eat or drink she turned her head away, and shut her mouth. She cried when her audio-cassettes finished or when someone played one she did not like.

By the age of five, her understanding of language had outstripped her means of expressing herself. Frustration sometimes set in, revealed by her banging her head and chewing her clothes. Some systematic attempt to extend Sam's ability to communicate was needed. Bobby and Gil attended a workshop on teaching profoundly handicapped children and from this developed the idea of communicating through pictures. Pictures, cut out from books and magazines, were chosen because of their importance to Sam. Responding to Sam's interests and respecting her wishes has been a basic principle of all her teaching. Sam quickly learnt to identify a number of pictures, and started pointing more accurately. This allowed her to make more choices and exert more control over her environment. Offering choice, and increasing Sam's control is another important basis to the way she has been helped to develop her communication. Her direct indication increased and improved. She could, for example, point to a toy she wanted or to the garden door when she wanted to go out. Her pointing was accompanied by sounds from early on.

The picture and pointing method was limited. Sam was unable, through lack of manual dexterity, to sort her pictures so she could select what she wanted. Often the pictures were not available, and if whatever she wanted was not in the room, she could not express her wishes. Bobby and Gil had rejected signing as a communication method initially, as they thought Sam's physical limits were too severe, but it was clear now that signing was worth trying. Using the Makaton vocabulary, which is derived from British Sign Language, they taught Sam a sign for 'drink'. This was done by guiding her hand rather than by imitation. She quickly understood the purpose of the sign, and soon acquired signs for 'listen' and 'look' as well. 'Look' gave her a way of asking for her pictures; 'listen' a way of asking for her cassettes. At this early stage, she began to adapt signs to her own requirements. The 'look' sign changed from pointing to her eye to a finger on the nose. Clearly, she did not want to poke herself in the eye through her poor hand control.

The range of meanings that Sam can express, and the means by which she communicates them have developed together. Sam has found it possible to use single signs for a variety of purposes. Early on, she was taught the sign for banana, which is her favourite food. This was the first sign she changed to meet a new need. Because she liked buying the bananas as much as eating them, she used the sign to mean 'buying bananas' and then to mean 'shopping'. Her use of signs to mean objects and where they are bought extends to several other shops, so that carrot and greengrocer's are expressed by one sign, cake and baker's by another, toothpaste and chemist by another, and so on.

Signs are drawn from many sources. Some continue to come from Makaton, but if the Makaton sign for something Sam wants to say is inappropriate, Amerind, another signing system, has been used, as in the case of Sam's sign for 'friends'. Some signs are shorthand versions of mimes, which are extensively modified in form and meaning. For example, a finger on the knee started as Sam's version of holding reins, and meant 'riding'. Later this came to mean horse, stables, greengrocer (who sells carrots for the pony), carrots, then woods (where she rides).

Although Sam has a much more extensive range of signs than sounds, she sometimes prefers to use her voice. She currently uses some fifteen distinct sounds, the most important of which are a soft pleasant 'uh' which means 'yes,' and a more strident 'ech' which means 'no'. In some cases, Sam seems to have great difficulty using a sign. For a number of years, Bobby tried to teach Sam to sign 'car'. This is a relevant word to her and something she would probably enjoy talking about. Attempts at signs included a steering wheel in the air, and the movement of changing gear which Sam enjoys doing in the family car. It seemed on a few occasions she had tried to make a 'c' sound. Finally Gil asked Sam, 'Do you want to say "car" with your hands or your mouth? Hands?' Sam gave her 'no' sound, 'ech'. 'Mouth?' Sam gave her 'yes' sound, 'uh'. Since then she has tried with varying degrees of success to make a sound for 'car'.

Some sounds and signs have emerged from Sam herself without any help. Sam's parents and teachers have sometimes become aware that Sam is consistently using a new form, and have then listened or watched for the occasions when she uses it. This was how the sound for 'Granny' emerged. Sam used it for some time before anyone realized what she was saying. Sam's persistence and patience were important here.

Because Sam can use the same sound or sign for several meanings, establishing what she wants to say is a joint endeavour. Conversations are necessary. For example:

Sam puts her finger on her knee.
Ask: 'do you mean 'riding?'
Sam says: 'ech' (no) or 'uh' (yes)
If no, ask: 'Something about horses?'
If no, ask: 'The greengrocers?'
If no, it must mean 'woods' or some similar meaning like going into the country.

Ambiguities are not always resolved. Sometimes, it seems that Sam compromises and accepts an available meaning, instead of what she wants to say.

Sam combines signs to make new meanings. Sometimes she does this to enable her to refer to someone or something. For example, the sign for 'school' followed by the sign for 'coffee' refers to the Head of Burydale, Jenny MacKay. Sam thinks of her as the person she likes to have coffee with at school. She uses the signs for 'school' and 'cooking' together to refer to her class teacher, Sandra Madden. The combinations are sometimes simplified by dropping the sign for 'school', but this is discouraged because it confuses other people.

With the support of her parents and her teachers listening to her and understanding the context for a conversation, she is able to combine signs to express quite complex meanings. Recent examples have included the signs for 'brother'

+ 'shops' + 'night' which Tom glossed as 'Cliff is going to get me a cream egg from the off licence. The signs for 'riding' + 'money' + 'eat' in context meant 'Don't forget to take the money and some carrots when we go to the stables'.

When Sam has changed the meaning of a sign, or altered her method of signing, or when she has developed her own sign or sound, her decisions have always been accepted. More recently, she has been encouraged to use gestures instead of signs because these can be more easily understood by others. The disadvantage of this sign system is its limited community of users, so Sam's parents and teachers have continued to develop work with pictures and with speech. Her pictures have been collected together into a plastic-covered, loose-leaf book and she has learned to turn the pages and converse using the pictures. She does not choose this way to communicate as she finds it clumsy compared to sounds and signs. Sam's parents and teachers hope to develop her picture and symbol recognition and improve her fine pointing when working on a computer. Microelectronics may offer her a means of easily understood communication. Developing these different means reflect another important aim: to enable Sam to communicate with as wide a range of people as possible rather than confining her to communication with those who know her very well.

Sam understands a great deal more than she can say. This is evident from many episodes at home. For example, Tom was listening to a Leonard Cohen record while Sam was in the room. As he sang: 'As I lay sick in bed...', Sam instantly signed 'doctor'. In the supermarket, a lady said to her friend as Tom and Sam passed: 'I went...but it was closed'. Sam said 'Ech' (meaning 'no') and signed 'open'. She doesn't like places to be closed. After stories, Tom and Bobby check Sam's understanding. One night, Tom read Sam a long and complicated Rupert story, which she found boring in parts. She is generally polite and signs 'tomorrow' when bored. There were many concepts in the story that Sam did not understand, but many others that she did. Tom asked: 'What were Rupert and his Dad doing?' Sam replied: 'Shopping'. Next, he asked: 'Where did they nearly fall?' Sam replied with 'pond'. 'What did Bill tell the man to do after the burglars had been?' 'Telephone'. Sam also understands the word 'understand'. In conversation, she is often asked 'Do you understand?' When she rejects a new story, Tom or Bobby will often say 'You can understand this', and Sam usually stops grumbling.

Sam also has some knowledge of spelling. Her Granny plays spelling games with her which involve spelling out objects in the room. Sam then touches them. When Sandra, Sam's class teacher, did a spelling test recently in class, Tom, who was helper at the time spelled out the words to Sam and she signed back. She recognized all the words which she could sign.

Sam can now sustain lengthy conversations with people who are skilled in her system of communication and who share experiences with her. Conversations are a vital part of Sam's life. Tom and Bobby talk to her far more than children are usually spoken to. Conversation provides her with a means to take charge of her life, and they occupy much of her leisure. She has few other ways of being amused. Conversations are sometimes built around play people or pictures which are in front of Sam, and sometimes they refer to events beyond the immediate context, whether past, present or future. A daily diary of events passes to and fro between home and school so everyone is aware of what topics of conversation are likely to come up. Shared experiences like school outings provide opportunities to talk to Sam about what she is doing, will be doing and has done. She likes to talk about her daily routine and forthcoming events. For example, she talks to Gil about going to have tea with her, coming in her car, knocking on the door, doing some cooking, going shopping. Sam recognizes these as future events and distinguishes them from future events which may not happen, such as going to a class-mate's house, and from past events. Sam's concept of time was first recognized when a yawn came to mean: 'in the morning'. Later on it became 'later,' then 'tomorrow', then 'next week', and 'future'. For example, when leaving the stables recently, Sam signed 'riding' and 'later'. Tom knew by checking that she understood she was not riding tomorrow but next Sunday. If she wants to ride sooner, she will say 'mo' (a vowel sound as in 'mob'), her sound for 'more'.

Many conversations around play-people or pictures take the form of stories that Sam constructs. For example, Ann (her welfare assistant) and Sam sat down to look at some picture cards of fruit and vegetables in class on one recent occasion. To an outsider it would be quite impossible to understand what was going on by watching and listening to Sam, but the nature of the conversation could be picked up from Ann's rapid running commentary which translated almost everything Sam said.

Ann began by asking Sam if she wanted to sit in an ordinary chair. Sam replied that she preferred to stay in her wheelchair. Sam wanted to do 'looking'. From then on the story was effectively dictated by Sam; Ann interpreted and clarified. It can be best presented by giving Ann's running commentary and questions. Ann's own contributions are prefixed by an 'A'; her progressive translation of Sam's contributions by an 'S'. Glosses and comments are provided in square brackets.

> A: What sort of looking? [What sort of cards do you want to look at?]
> S: Shopping looking.
> S: On the table [Sam puts her head on the table].
> S: Head on the table.
> A: You want to go to sleep? [Ann is uncertain what Sam means]
> S: The greengrocers.
> A: Who's going to the greengrocers?
> S: Ann.
> S: Daddy.

Ann lays out five cards with pictures of fruit and vegetables on them for Sam to see.

> A: I'm the shopkeeper [Sam knocks on the table].
> S: Knocking on the door.
> S: Knock again.
> S: Telephone shop.
> S: Wake up.
> S: Open your shop.
> S: At the greengrocers.
> S: One pound of carrots.
> S: Ann would like.
> S: A pound of tomatoes.
> A: Ann would like cauliflower [Sam pointed to the cauliflowers].

S: And some pears.
S: Left the money at home.
S: Go home, knock on the door.
S: Wake up at home.
S: Keep knocking.
S: Mummy comes to answer the door.
S: Money from Granny.
S: Knock on the door.
S: Knock hard.

The story continued in this vein for about five minutes: Sam decided to go to the chemist after the greengrocer and wanted to buy talc, soap, toothpaste and a toothbrush for Granny. She then went back to Granny's house and had to wake her up for the money (£4) then go back to the chemists which by this time was closed for lunch. So she went back to Granny's and had her own lunch there.

Including Sam in a mainstream class

SAM'S ABILITIES

Sam might seem a difficult child to include in a mainstream class. Although her system of communication is effective in meeting many of her needs, it is also radically different from the way in which her classmates communicate. In other ways she is far less able than most children her age. Sam finds it hard to understand new things, and can become intolerant and demanding. In frustration, she will bang her head and screech unpleasantly. She has occasional epileptic fits. She cannot walk and moves around either on her knees or bottom on the floor, or in her wheelchair. She can now get in and out of her wheelchair with little difficulty and can move it where she wants to go. Sam's ability to feed herself has developed considerably, but she still needs individual help at mealtimes.

Although Sam is no longer blind, her vision is variable. Her visual attention may have to be gained with sound. She needs to have a small number of visual alternatives to choose from at any one time. Scanning pictures can be very difficult. She may only look at part of the picture, particularly the top. If she knows what to expect she can see much more. She is better able to see with her left eye, and can track objects more easily from right to left than from left to right.

Sam is beginning to recognize and distinguish various colours by name, and Gil is working with her on various ways of counting and categorizing objects. She enjoys pretend games, as the earlier conversation makes clear. Although the games are usually based on frequently repeated stories, Sam is now beginning to introduce variations into them.

She has played with some simple jigsaws and shape sorters with some success, which have helped her ability to manipulate objects. She has started to transfer objects from one hand to another. Her ability to control a pen or brush has increased recently and she now chooses to paint or draw at times. Sam is also beginning to use and enjoy the computer. This is particularly important in encouraging the use of her vision and giving her an ability to enjoy activities on her own. The growth of her ability to use her time independently is a very important step for Sam and her family.

But for most of the time, Sam needs other people to support her involvement in the world. In the rest of this chapter, we shall describe how this happens at Sam's junior school.

SAM'S DAY AT BURYDALE

Gil or Ann usually collect Sam from home, and walk to Burydale, talking about what will happen at school that day. Sam brings some of her work with her and some is kept at school. When they arrive, the other children are usually in the middle of individual work. Sam has her own seat at one of the tables, with her own set of particular friends. Gil or Ann and Sam sit down and do some individual work with her. This might be picture or colour recognition, or playing an imaginary game. She doesn't disturb the other children, although some are curious to see what she is doing, and come to talk to her.

This time is usually used for Gil or Ann to consult Sandra, the class teacher, about what is happening after lunch. They plan ways the activity can be adapted and made meaningful for Sam, or plan activities for the following week.

Sam packs up her things when it is dinner time, and goes down to the hall. She eats with about four children each day in the dining room. She chooses her meal from the cafeteria as do other children. After, she usually goes shopping with the same group of friends she had lunch with, accompanied by Gil or Ann. After the shopping expedition, she returns to school and plays with other children for a while. This time gives Sam the chance to relate to other children without the intervention of an adult. On the days when Sam doesn't go swimming, she goes up to the class and joins the art and craft or cookery session. She will now sit and listen to Sandra as she gives instructions to the class, and then she works with a small group of children. The activity has to be personalized for Sam, but there is usually some element that Sam can do meaningfully. Any spare time at the end of the session is taken up by individual work and play before going home.

ORGANIZING FOR SAM

Sam is a member of a class of nine- to ten-year olds. Their work is based on a termly theme to which much of the language, science, topic, art and craft and some practical maths is linked.

There are few special resources or facilities provided for or needed by Sam. Her classroom is on the first floor. She has to climb the stairs on her knees which she manages well, supervised but unaided. In the room, Sam has a wheelchair but usually prefers to be independent like the other children. There is a small carpeted area where she likes to sit and play and talk with friends, a small art area with formica-topped tables and a cramped sink area. Sam's teachers improvise and arrange existing furniture to suit the activity, and she generally uses the same tools and materials as other children. Sandra has not had time to include work on the large PE apparatus in Sam's day, although she has used it, adapted to Sam's requirements, at playtime with careful supervision. With time and help Sam could participate fully in this activity as part of the normal timetable.

When Sam first joined her class at Burydale it was for one half-day a week, and the staff saw it mainly as an opportunity for her to mix with other children of her own age. It soon became apparent that Sam could be included in many class activities, and that she could use the class theme as a basis for her work outside Burydale. At the beginning of each half-term Gil and Sandra meet to discuss the theme and the way Sam can be involved. This provides a starting point. More detailed planning happens on a weekly basis. At this stage, they decide on the materials and techniques they will use with Sam. Sandra's first concern is to provide meaningful activities for all the children in her class. Through discussion she and Gil often find several aspects that Sam can work on. On occasions, Sandra has had to postpone an activity in order to devise ways to include Sam.

SHARING ACTIVITIES IN THE CLASSROOM

Sam shares most fully in the classwork in art and craft, and cookery. Sandra's general aims for the class are to develop their confidence and skill in using different materials and techniques, to extend their powers of observation and imagination and increase their awareness of texture, form, colour and pattern. Sam is able to work with these concepts at her own level. The activities Sam has participated in include painting, drawing using paint, charcoal, chalk, pencils, pastels and felt pens, print making, collage, clay work, model making and weaving. With the rest of the class, Sam has increased her concentration, awareness and manipulative skill. She usually works with a small group supported by her own teacher. Her interest can be maintained for up to forty minutes, but sometimes she finds it difficult to concentrate and the activity is cut short. While the others continue she does something else quietly.

In one recent session Sam made a collage. The term's theme was 'wood', and Sam and her group of five others made trees from wool and fabric stuck on to hessian. Throughout Sam worked very closely with Gil; it took twenty-five minutes to finish the collage, ahead of the rest of the group. Sandra introduced the activity to the whole group. Sam's first reaction was to put some wool in her mouth. Gil began by helping Sam to tear some fabric for the trunk of the tree. It tore with difficulty. All through the activity Gil kept up a running commentary, sometimes asking questions and adding comments, sometimes translating Sam's comments. She asked: 'What sort of tree is it?' Sam signed and Gil translated: 'Doughnuts' and 'Pear'. A boy joined in with 'Partridge in a pear tree'. Sam seemed to want a story to accompany the activity, something that is often necessary to keep her attention, so Gil began a commentary about Froggie and Toad who sat down at a table with all the other children to make a tree picture.

Sam chose the blue wool first for the canopy of the tree, and Gil got her to pull some from the ball. Gil cut it, and together they gathered it up into a small tangled ball, then stuck it onto the glue on the hessian. This continued as Sam chose different colours and the canopy expanded. The other children's trees were more delicate and conventional, made up of individual strands of wool glued on to form branches. They began to notice Sam and Gil's work and dubbed it a spaghetti tree. Lorraine, next to Sam was sufficiently impressed to use the same method herself, abandoning her first attempt.

Sam's attention was not fully on her collage throughout. A number of times she asked to play with her Fischer-Price toys, and was encouraged by Lorraine who wanted to play with her. She showed her displeasure at not being able to do so with a loud scream which passed seemingly unnoticed. During the session she also managed to invite two of the children for coffee at her house, and to make it clear she wanted to have coffee at Gil's house later. When the spaghetti tree was complete, Gil asked Sam to show it to Sandra, who immediately brought it back to the others to show them how Sam had effectively represented the canopy of the tree.

Sam's favourite class activity is the weekly cookery session. The other children enjoy helping her with all tasks including washing up. In a recent session Sam and two other girls made coconut rock cakes, aided by Ann. Before they could start, Ann had to strap Sam into her wheelchair and wash and dry her hands. Once Sam was in position she picked up the mixing bowl and saw it was empty. Ann pointed out to her that the oven was getting hot, and put Sam's hand on the side to feel it. The other girls weighed the flour out, and guided by Ann, Sam rubbed it through her fingers in the bowl. Sam and Ann then weighed out the margarine, and the others mixed it. Sam was eager to rub it through as well, and when Lindsey and Karen had finished, she did so. Sam felt the sugar and coconut as it was weighed out and Ann said, as each ingredient was poured out: 'Feel how rough it is'. Lindsey mixed the coconut and sugar and then said: 'Sam's turn to do the egg'. Once the mixture was ready and Sam had had several partially successful attempts to stick her hands in it and lick them, Lindsey spooned the mixture into the tray and Ann drew Sam's attention to this. Sam then went round the other side of the bench to watch the cakes go into the oven, grabbing a boy's drawing as she went. This was quickly rescued and calmly smoothed out. Sam and Ann poured out the remaining mixture and this too went into the oven, with Sam's help.

During shared activities, even if Sam is at times only partially attentive, she sees a meaningful product achieved in a short time, and she is involved at all stages. From the common activity Sam gains specific experiences matched to her ability. While the other children may learn about weight and recipes, Sam has opportunities to learn about texture in the cooking session. Sam's participation depends on others helping and guiding her, so that everything she does is a co-operative venture. In this she differs from the other children only in degree. In the cooking session, they need Sandra to write out the recipe, lay on the ingredients and occasionally guide them. Sam needs Ann to help to stir the mixture, to guide her hands to feel the ingredients, and so on. These shared activities provide many opportunities for interchanges between Sam and the other children. Sometimes other children act as Sam's supervisors, as when Lorraine prevented Sam from tearing up some newspaper in the collage session; sometimes they learn from Sam, as when they admired and in one case copied Sam's technique for the collage; sometimes, they enter into reciprocal and equal relationships with Sam, as when Lindsey passed the mixing bowl to Sam to take her turn, or when Sam invited Chris and Lorraine for coffee. A notable absence in the sessions is any talk amongst teachers and pupils *about* Sam. Talk involving Sam is talk to or with her.

SHARING ACTIVITIES OUTSIDE THE CLASSROOM

A great deal of Sam's education takes place outside the school. Shopping is one of the most important events in Sam's life. It is a time for her classmates to know her better: they usually chat to her and learn her signs. She normally goes to a different parade of shops to the one she visits from home. This allows her to meet and communicate with a wider circle of friends and acquaintances. She now visits nearly every shop in the parade, buying something and having a conversation in each.

On one day she went with four classmates and Ann. They called first at the bakers where Sam chose scones by pointing. Ann handed her the money and Sam gave it to the shopkeeper who handed her the bag of scones. Ann took the change and told Sam she had it. As they left Sam signed 'Open tomorrow' and Ann replied, 'Yes it will be open tomorrow'. They moved on and Sam steered towards the greengrocer. The other children ran around playing. Sam was not the centre of attention. In the greengrocers, Sam indicated she wanted to buy tomatoes and apples, by Ann pointing to each box of produce in turn and Sam saying 'yes' or 'no'. While Ann paid, Sam grabbed for an orange, but was stopped by one of her friends.

On the way back there was a lengthy conversation about school being closed the following day, Saturday. Sam said she was very cross and signed 'open', to which Ann replied that it wouldn't be open. Sam then signed 'telephone school':

A: Why?
S: Open.
A: See if it's open? It's the holidays.
S: Later – tomorrow – school – open – cross – Daddy – telephone.

Sam also participates in class trips and visits. As part of the 'wood' theme, the class had been visiting a local nature reserve, Astonbury Park. Sam had been to the woods with the class the previous October and talked about it a lot, so in March another visit took place. Gil, Tom and Bobby spoke to Sam about the trip for several days before, and told her what was planned. She was very excited and greeted Gil with a huge grin that morning. She bought her picnic from the local shops. She chose the food she wanted and they took it back to Sam's house to prepare.

The car park at Astonbury resembled a quagmire, but undeterred, Gil managed to push the wheelchair through the mud. They had arranged to meet the class in the hut, which was set up for indoor work, exhibits and eating. Since they were early they went down into the wood to find the class. Sam listened, and heard their voices before Gil. They all had lunch together and then split into two groups for the afternoon. Over lunch, Gil, Sandra and the Warden of Astonbury discussed the afternoon's activities and which ones were suitable for Sam. Sam was able to work with a small group of children and made a plaster cast of twigs, cones and leaves, followed by a daylight photography picture. All the children needed a lot of help, not just Sam, and Gil was fully involved in this. Sam used the time when Gil was not with her to move around and explore the room. Sam and Gil had a story about a picnic and then a friend played shopping with Sam.

The benefits of this visit were not just confined to the actual day but were discussed and used for a long time afterwards. It gave Sam the need to sign 'picnic', which she does by combining 'wood' and 'eat'. The shared experience of the trip enabled Gil and Sam to practise all the signs and noises that Sam used to describe what she did.

A regular shared trip is to the swimming baths. Sam travels to the baths on the coach, sitting with a couple of her friends. At first, she needed an adult to sit with her but experience has lent her the confidence to manage without this. In the pool she works alone and with her helper, developing her swimming, while other children practise their skills. Before she leaves the water, there is a social time when she can splash around with her friends and play her favourite game of pushing people in. When she is dressed she joins the little throng around the sweet machine to get her chocolate. Then she makes her way slowly upstairs on her bottom to sit with the others waiting until the second batch of swimmers are ready for the return journey to school.

The whole process of going swimming provides many valuable experiences for Sam. It includes travelling; swimming; getting dressed and undressed; putting money in the slot of the machine; choosing something; moving upstairs; waiting; being with other children. All the specific skills required of Sam are used within a meaningful and enjoyable activity.

Conclusion: the common stream

Sam's parents have planned her education on the basis of a philosophy of normalization[1] and the civil rights of people with disabilities. They argue that Sam must have the right of access to education available to all other children her age. She must not be segregated or treated as special. She should be seen as an eleven-year-old girl, a person beginning adolescence, not an infant forever. It saddens them when people refer to those who have a mental impairment as, for example, 'like a five-year old'. Sam's abilities range from below one-year-old level to nearly adult. It is not even possible to suggest she is 'like a five-year old' in one area, let alone her whole being. Emotionally she ranges from a child to an adult, as we all do. Sam is a complex human being, not similar to an anything 'year-old'. She should not be refused an opportunity because of any such classification, or the prejudices of people who do not accept impairments as part of normality.

Sam's educational needs are the same as other children's: to go to school; meet people; learn to live in society; improve her knowledge and understanding; develop her faculties and skills. To make progress, she needs resources which some people do not need.

Sam's education is built around teamwork, within and beyond the family. This has not meant total harmony throughout. Tom and Bobby continue to disagree about the value of Sam's time at the special school. Most of the professionals they have encountered have responded to their demands and moved at their pace. Progress has come from regular work in planned stages. They have never waited for any 'breakthroughs', but have worked steadily, even though returns may take years. They have taken risks. Some parts of Sam's education, like teaching her to eat solids, or climb stairs, have been frightening, and occasionally painful for all. Sam's eventual success has been the pay-off for the risks.

---

[1] Normalization is an idea made popular by Wolf Wolfensberger in Canada and the USA. It entails basing all services for people with disabilities in ordinary settings. As Wolfensberger presents the idea, it involves making services 'normal', as well as making people with disabilities as normal as possible. See Wolfensberger and Nirje 1972.

The pay-offs of a mainstream education for Sam have been extensive. It provides her with rich experiences and challenges. Expectations are important: no one knew that Sam could work successfully alongside other children until it was tried. Her life in the classroom is active and purposeful. She is fully accepted as part of her class, and her contact with the other children is a vital part of Sam's life. They benefit in turn. While they are working with Sam, it is easy for them to learn and accept Sam's peculiarities as part of their normal lives. Inevitably, some of the extra attention Sam gets from adults is available to them as well.

School is as important for the family as it is for Sam. Friends and neighbours have their children at Burydale, giving them common ground for everyday conversations. All the local children know Sam and she is seen by local people as one of them. She has entered the common stream of education, with resources as buoyancy aids, without which she may have submerged. But an irrational fear of drowning is no reason for depriving children of the joy of jumping into the pool.

References

Hulley, T. 1985. *Samantha Goes to School – the Battle for Mainstream Education,* London, Campaign for Mental Handicap.

Wolfensberger, W. and Nirje, B. 1972. *The Principle of Normalization in Human Services,* Toronto, National Institute on Mental Retardation.

2 Kevin

Terence Bailey and Doreen Furby

Terence Bailey and Doreen Furby describe the way Kevin is educated in a comprehensive school. Kevin has cerebral palsy and with the support of a welfare assistant and the use of a microcomputer participates in all parts of the curriculum. His school is banded and then setted within bands. Such a system may not be ideal for encouraging flexible teaching styles. Nevertheless, the persistence of Kevin and the ingenuity of his teachers and helpers are making his school days challenging and successful.

Kevin lives with his family in the London Borough of Enfield. He has an active social life, directed mainly towards sport: he is a member of a sports club for the disabled, travelling independently to the sports centre by Dial-a-Ride, and attends home matches at Tottenham Hotspur's ground as often as he can. He also watches a local Sunday league team his father trains, and joins in the social activities at the club-house.

Kevin has cerebral palsy which affects all four limbs and confines him to an electric wheelchair. He also suffers from mild disarthria (partial paralysis of the muscles of the neck and face) which causes uncontrolled changes in pitch and volume and makes it difficult for him to form sounds. Speech therapy has been discontinued because no further improvement can be expected, but Kevin perseveres and can make himself understood quite well.

Until transfer at the secondary stage, Kevin was a pupil at the Vale School for children with physical disabilities in Haringey. He began linking with a local primary school when he was nine years old; by the summer term of his fourth year, he was established there full-time, with support from a teacher from the special school and a welfare assistant, and it was suggested that he should transfer to a mainstream comprehensive the following September.

Kevin and his parents visited two possible schools and decided that Kevin should attend Salisbury School, in Enfield, which had admitted three pupils with physical disabilities the previous year, September 1982.

Salisbury School was formed by the amalgamation of three separate schools. A new two-storey building, the base for years one and two, was built a short distance from the upper school building, with integration in mind. It has a lift at each end of the main corridor, a physiotherapy room with adjacent toilet and shower, and the necessary access and specialist equipment.

The pupils with disabilities report to the specially trained welfare assistant as they arrive and depart each day and at other times according to need. Until recently, Kevin came to school by cab, and was met by the welfare assistant with his wheelchair. He has two electric wheelchairs, one at home, the other at school. He now travels to school in a tail-lift coach in his 'home' chair and is met by the welfare assistant who helps him to transfer to his school chair, which has been charging overnight in the physio gym. She then puts his home chair on charge. In this way both chairs are kept fully charged. After she has removed Kevin's coat and helped him in the toilet, she sorts Kevin's homework, under his direction, and gets the materials he needs for his lessons. He then goes to his form-room for registration and when the bell goes, makes his way to his lesson, where the welfare assistant has set up his computer.

Salisbury is not Kevin's neighbourhood school, so he knew no one when he arrived, but he quickly settled in, developing a rapport with the special welfare assistant, Mrs Rose, and his teachers, who soon 'tuned in' to his speech. He also made a firm friend, who is able-bodied and who accompanied him to lessons, and worked with him in class.

At the primary level, Kevin had used a Canon Communicator, which is not much larger than a calculator and is operated in the same way. The work produced is printed on a continuous single strip which has to be cut into lengths and stuck into a work book. The Head of Special Needs who assessed Kevin's progress felt that a typewriter would be more effective and he soon learnt to use it. The equipment was transported on a trolley and set up by the welfare assistant who filed and stored all Kevin's work for him.

The limitations of the typewriter soon showed themselves. The word just typed was hidden by the guard and Kevin's limited hand control led to his making typing errors. Constant adjustment for review and correction meant that his output was still limited. In the summer of 1985, in his second year, Kevin was provided with a BBC microcomputer with the Wordwise Plus word processor software. The Head of Computer Studies taught him to use it in the lunch hour and the improvement in his classroom performance was immediate. He was able to lay out his work more effectively, and with a printer available for his personal use he could up-date his file between sessions. Since Christmas he has had a second computer at home, to enable him to complete his assignments on time. He now has more time to socialize in school, as in order to keep up he had had to continue working into breaks and lunch hours and was missing out on contact with the rest of his form.

Kevin transferred to the upper school in September 1985. This building has been made completely accessible to disabled pupils. It is on one level throughout and has toilet facilities similar to those in the lower school. However, it is about three hundred yards away, across a busy road, which causes problems in moving between buildings in the short breaks between lessons, especially when personal needs have to be managed, or the weather is bad. Fatigue is also a factor. The LEA intends to adapt a minibus which was donated to the school by a local charity, but until a tail-lift vehicle is available, Kevin has to be lifted into the bus in his electric wheelchair. As the computer cannot safely be transported, careful timetabling has limited subjects taught in the other building to drama and music.

There were setbacks when Kevin moved into the upper school. His close friend was placed in a lower band and Kevin was left rather isolated when faced with a more adult environment and a larger building to negotiate. He seemed to be overwhelmed by the increased work-load and the need to be more self-sufficient. Security measures meant that a printer was not easily available and he got behind with his work. By half-term a larger trolley which could store all this equipment, including a specially purchased printer, was in use. This could remain permanently set-up, and some improvement resulted.

Kevin has been placed mainly in the second and third sets of the upper band. The exception is maths, where he was placed in the top set. The pace is fast and he has had to adapt to a new teacher. The first term proved difficult for them both. Early on it seemed that Kevin was coping and achieving high marks. It became obvious after a while that he was relying heavily on the welfare assistant who was unconsciously prompting or correcting him, both in class and when he was doing his homework in the lunch-hour. When he performed badly in tests, without her assistance, he became tearful and very depressed. He also found it hard to concentrate on transferring new work from the board while listening at the same time, so now the teacher gives notes on new topics to the welfare assistant who loads them onto the maths disk before the lesson, so that Kevin can read them from the VDU as the material is introduced. She also copies down his work onto file paper and he types, so that if he wants to refer back to earlier examples without clearing the screen he can consult her notes. Another change has been made to help Kevin cope with tests, which he finds stressful. He manages better if he uses the computer for some answers and dictates others. This combination of methods reduces fatigue and he is able to work faster, but it means that he has to take the test separately as his voice control is poor. Like many people with cerebral palsy, Kevin starts violently at sudden noise. This upsets Kevin and can disturb the other pupils during tests. Removing him from the classroom for tests assists Kevin's concentration, as he cannot be startled by the routine noises of scraping chairs, sneezes, dropped rulers, etc.

In a recent lesson, Kevin sat at the centre back of the room which gave him sight of everyone else and was convenient to the power supply, with Mrs Rose, the welfare assistant, at his right side. The topic, angles, had been introduced the previous week and Kevin's notes had been printed and filed. The material covered several sheets, as Kevin's maths program uses only the left half of the possible printout width, and was in a bulky ring binder. The class was given two pages of examples to work through. It was 9.15 on a Monday morning, never a good time for Kevin, who usually seems to be recovering from the weekend or adjusting to the routine of the school.

As time went on, it was obvious that Kevin's equipment needed re-organizing. He depresses the keys with his right index finger and thumb which he uses nail-to-keys, as his fingers curl towards the palm of his hand. As he worked, his body began to twist significantly to the left and his left arm moved from his side until it hung over the back of his wheelchair. He almost had his back to Mrs Rose as she sat on the right of the chair, holding the file of notes and the work sheets, so he had to turn back every time he wanted to refer to them. Kevin took no initiative during the lesson but Mrs Rose would prompt him with questions. For example: 'Have you said what angle it is?' after he worked out the answer to example 1b. Kevin typed in '(corresponding)'. Kevin completed example 2a, b, and c, paused, and looked at her. 'If you want me to turn over the page tell me'. Kevin twisted towards her and attempted to turn the page for himself.

After three examples the screen was full, Kevin printed it and fitted a similar quantity onto the next screen. If he would abbreviate, he could put six examples onto each screen, but after one example, he either abandoned the idea or forgot. When the lesson ended Kevin was not far behind the slowest of the rest of the class of thirty, but the significant difference lay in the fact that there was constant communication between the others as they chatted between-times and consulted each other. Kevin was working in isolation, even from the assistant. As the bell went, he dumped the unfinished work, switched off the disk drive, removed the disk, and left the room, while Mrs Rose removed the printout and filed it and took the trolley back to base, to load it with the appropriate file and disk for the next lesson.

The method of teaching used in this maths set is traditionally didactic and discussion is limited. So far as Kevin is concerned, he is so fully occupied in following what is going on on his monitor while listening to the teacher's explanation as she works on the board that he is not sufficiently in command of himself and the material to be able to contribute actively to the lesson. Kevin is among the slowest in the group, both in speed of work and understanding. There are times when he does answer, but the teacher does not always understand, or mishears, and this deters him somewhat. However, since beginning a new area of maths, algebra, he has become much more confident. He is answering questions verbally in class and working independently with success. We will wait to see whether this is an all round improvement, or just a topic which he finds easy, but it is a timely boost to his confidence.

Chemistry, which follows after break on Mondays requires constant adaptation as the lessons take place in at least three different rooms, owing to shortage of laboratories. One day, the class of 29 were sent to a physics lab. In addition to Kevin, there is another boy with a disability in the set. William has spina bifida and uses elbow crutches. He and Kevin sit together at a standard table placed at the end of the demonstration bench, near the door. Kevin's computer has to be placed on the other side of the lab, so as not to create an additional hazard in an overcrowded class.

After the register had been taken, the teacher recapitulated the previous lesson, and wrote the heading for the day on the board, then called the class round the front bench for the demonstration. Kevin and William moved to the front and there was some good-natured jostling for positions – the first real contact between Kevin and the rest of the class. Kevin raised his hand to answer questions four times and when called upon to describe the effect of placing a glowing tape in the test-tube replied 'there was a blue flash and the taper glowed', speaking clearly enough for everyone to understand. After some board work, involving the names and formulae for the substances being tested, Kevin and William moved to the end of the side bench nearest the door, where Kevin's chair would not impede any other group as they carried out two further tests. William collected the equipment, lit the Bunsen burner and gave an accurate running commentary on the experiments while Kevin sat observing.

The result of the second experiment did not please William, who called over the teacher. As they repeated the experiment, he gave Kevin the taper to place in the test tube which William guided towards him. William also held the test tube for Kevin to smell.

By now the rest of the class were writing up and Kevin moved over to his computer which the teacher switched on. Kevin loaded his chemistry disk and found his place. The trolley faced the window, so that the board was on his right and to the rear. As in maths, he had to twist to the right to read the notes while his body's inclination is to the left. When a suggestion by the advisory teacher observing the lesson to turn the trolley to face the board was followed, Kevin was able to speed up the transfer of information. He had very little time left as most of the class had finished writing up the lesson, using the notes taken by the member of each group responsible for recording the practical work and writing together at their tables. Kevin and William were working in isolation and without the aid of notes. Kevin's presentation was clear and accurate, but by the end of the session he had only reached the result stage of the demonstration and had to dump the contents of the screen onto the disk, remove it, switch off and ask the teacher to switch off the VDU. By Monday lunch-time, Kevin already had a backlog of work. He would also have to rely on his memory when he came to complete the work.

The greatest pressure to load large quantities of material, and the greatest need to commit class work to memory comes in history, which also presents problems with producing diagrams and maps. Kevin uses a Rotring drawing head for simple outlines, but free-hand sketching is impossible and he relies on photocopies from the teacher. Geography poses similar problems. The current solution is that others in the class who finish first make copies for Kevin. This is unsatisfactory because Kevin is so distanced from the work while it is being executed that much of its significance is lost on him. This is particularly unfortunate as geography is one of his favourite subjects.

Kevin is not self-conscious about his speech; he plays a full part in discussions and he joins in drama sessions with confidence. He does not have a lively imagination, but he has firm opinions on many current issues and his contributions to social education sessions are made quite naturally. He is happy to repeat himself if necessary. In French he is one of the best at offering oral contributions, even though it is not one of his strongest subjects. His French teacher finds it easier to understand him in French than in English.

As far as possible, all pupils at Salisbury School follow the same timetable. The only modification common to the eleven pupils with disabilities is a swimming session at a nearby sports centre on alternate Tuesdays. The lesson they miss is made up when the rest of the year are having games. Physiotherapy is timetabled for PE sessions so that the pupils can join in wherever possible or have alternative activities which the teacher and therapist can devise when full participation is not possible. The physiotherapist visits the school three times a week. She has taught the welfare assistant each pupil's programme so that when necessary additional sessions can be carried out. In the first year, Kevin had a programme which involved daily standing, walking with a rollator and knee stretching, but there were problems with replacing the standing frame when he outgrew it and teachers were concerned at the amount of time being lost while he was being strapped in and taken out. When he began using a trolley for his equipment, its height was such that he could no longer work while standing, so his parents decided that work should have priority and his therapy programme was changed. He remains in his chair for all lessons.

This year, Kevin's programme for practical subjects has also been modified. Salisbury operates a carousel system: each of the crafts is offered for blocks during the year. Kevin particularly enjoys home economics. This is an area where, so far, few adaptations have been made to specialist rooms and the groups are very large, so not only would his access to equipment be restricted, but his and others' safety might be at risk. So that he can participate more fully he has been offered the chance to work with William on a specially adapted syllabus which allows them more opportunity to take an active part in the processes of cookery and consumer education. The teacher, welfare assistant and the two boys are working together to create a programme which will increase their understanding of the activities of daily living and also broaden their experience of the area around their school, by exploring local services. This course has been very successful. The boys have cooked lunch, have invited various members of staff as their guests and have taken part in shopping expeditions to buy ingredients. This part of the course has been linked with the wheelchair proficiency programme conducted by the physiotherapist. The head of the home economics department plans to offer a course on the same lines as a fourth year option, for a small group who would benefit from a course concentrating on basic skills.

Kevin has been using his computer for only two terms and he has concentrated on establishing its acceptance in the classroom and developing his word process-ing skills. The scope of the computer in such areas as art, design and music has yet to be explored. So far it has helped to give him access to all parts of the curriculum, sometimes with modification and support. The staff are now being encouraged to think about wider uses of the computer by investigating software packages for graphics, art, music, and introducing a 'mouse' and light-pen. The advisory teacher for mathematics is taking a keen interest in finding a suitable joystick for graphics. From being rather wary of having a welfare assistant in the classroom, teachers are increasingly calling on her for assistance.

The welfare assistants who support the physically handicapped students in schools throughout the borough have good relationships with both the children and their parents and can often reassure parents through the personal nature of their relationship to the child. Additional support teachers are being introduced into the integration scheme, and when Kevin begins his courses leading to public examinations next September he may well need such assistance.

The educational psychologist makes regular visits to the school and the advisory teacher and physiotherapist make weekly visits. A termly review, one of which constitutes the annual review, is chaired by a member of the school management team. All members of staff who have contact with the pupil are invited to contribute to the report which is presented for discussion at the meeting, along with the pupil, parents and representatives from the Medical, Education and Social Services. The minutes, which are circulated to all present, record any proposed action. The regular reviews are a way of checking that actions proposed are carried out. Since Kevin has made his option choices this term, one of the proposed actions is to explore the availability of software for the maths, biology and geography courses he wishes to follow. An application is being made for an assessment at Hereward College Information Technology Unit (see Chapter 8), to see if any further aids or equipment can improve his performance. We have consulted staff at Lord Mayor Treloar College, a residen-tial school for pupils with physical disabilities, on the implications for biology and the advisory teacher and the head of biology have visited this school. The headmaster of Salisbury, who is a physicist, went with the advisory teacher to Hephaistos School, another residential school, to see how practical and demonstration sessions were organized and to look at adapted equipment. We also have to explore the regulations of the examination boards concerned.

Despite the inevitable difficulties which Kevin encounters as one of the pioneers of our integration scheme, he seems happy at Salisbury School and is achieving a fair standard of success, both socially and academically. The only doubts his parents have expressed so far about their decision to choose a mainstream school have been that his academic opportunities might be at the expense of his physical wellbeing. Kevin is highly competitive and asks no favours. He supports House competitions enthusiastically and uses his keen wit to score verbally over others. His sense of humour allows him to take and make jokes against himself. He goes abroad on family holidays, but he would dearly love to take part in a school trip. The necessary support is not available at the moment.

The integration scheme of which Kevin is a part is a continuous learning experience for all those involved. The individual problems of each child require a variety of administrative and practical solutions, but the goodwill which is the vital ingredient of any such scheme is there.

3 Hasit
June Statham

Compared to other children and young people described in this book, Hasit Patel is scarcely disabled at all. His only bodily disadvantage is that he is extremely small: he looks roughly half his age. He also finds much of the curriculum at his High School completely incomprehensible. His literacy skills are very limited. In this chapter, June Statham describes how Hasit's physical problem interacts with the difficulties he experiences in learning and with his compliant quiet, industrious personality to produce a young person who is both literally and metaphorically overlooked.

Gunners High School is a North London comprehensive, built in the early 1950s and catering for around 750 thirteen- to sixteen-year olds. Its pupils are drawn mostly from two large council estates housing predominantly working-class families, and from a sizeable Gujerati-speaking Asian community who have settled in the area over the last fifteen to twenty years. A large paper sign in the assembly hall proclaims that this is 'a school that works for everyone', and Gunners' official policy includes a commitment to anti-sexism and anti-racism. The school is also committed to mixed-ability teaching, and the thirty or so pupils in each class display a wide range of abilities. Hasit Patel, who is nearly fifteen but is in a first year class of thirteen-year olds, is one of the pupils who has most difficulty in coping with the curriculum.

Hasit came to England from Kenya with his family when he was four and a half. He is the second youngest of a family of five; an older sister and brother have already passed through the school and a younger brother is still in a feeder middle school. Hasit's learning difficulties are compounded by his physical problems. He is extremely small for his age. At fourteen, he could pass easily for an eight year old, and is described by various teachers as 'tiny', 'weak' and 'frail'. He has dark straight hair, wears glasses, and moves around the school in his over-sized uniform, 'like a little mouse'. He avoids eye contact, rarely speaks unless spoken to, and has a very quiet voice.

It is unclear whether there is any specific medical reason for Hasit's lack of growth. He goes for regular height, weight and diet check-ups at the clinic of a local hospital, where according to the doctor they are 'investigating his muscular system, but aren't sure yet if there's any particular abnormality'. She feels that although Hasit is extremely small, he 'hasn't quite fallen off his percentile yet'. However she says she has been worried about his development, 'ever since I first saw him, which was about four years ago. 'His height, his weight, his psychological state – I wasn't happy about any of them. I wanted the school to refer him, but they wouldn't.'

Other teachers at the middle school had evidently also worried about Hasit's lack of progress, particularly the ESL teacher, who reported that he didn't open his mouth in class until he was about nine. Hasit did not come to the attention of the Schools Psychological Service until his second year in the upper school. The educational psychologist then discovered that the reason she hadn't been called in earlier was 'because the headteacher of the middle school at that time felt that every school catered for its own children, and you didn't call in the psychologist'.

Hasit moved with his classmates to the upper school, but it soon became evident that he was struggling. After a month, his English teacher reported that there was 'nothing in the library easy enough for him to read; can barely copy, very retiring and say nothing'. His science teacher wrote that, 'his written work is very weak'; in art he had 'no spatial conception at all, doesn't ask for help', and in drama he was recorded as being 'very small and weak, doesn't speak very much'. On the positive side, various teachers noted that he was 'eager', 'seems happy' or 'gets help from friends.' Hasit also got help in the form of three withdrawal periods a week for learning support and three for ESL, plus some occasional support from an extra teacher in some of his classes.

Hasit struggled on for the first year, but it was obvious that his educational needs were not being met, and after a few weeks in the second year his teachers called a meeting and decided to ask the educational psychologist to make an assessment. Using standard intelligence tests, she concluded that he was a child of 'low average ability, colossally underachieving'. He was particularly weak on the verbal tests:

> His reading age was seven, his comprehension age about eight. I wouldn't have thought that his level of reading was sufficient for him to be able to cope without an enormous amount of support in an ordinary high school. I felt that given his very small stature as well, he might have been a good candidate for the learning support unit at Warwick Park.

This unit, at another high school on the other side of the borough, was originally a unit for 'delicate' children but now acted as a well-staffed support base, to enable children with a variety of special needs to manage in the ordinary school. A case conference was called in the November of Hasit's second year at Gunners, and his mother attended with his elder sister as an interpreter. The staff were at pains to stress that they were concerned with Hasit's educational progress rather than his behaviour, and that he was not a disruptive or naughty child. A special school for children with moderate learning difficulties was considered, but the educational psychologist decided to recommend a transfer to the special unit at Warwick Park. Mrs Patel was not at all keen on this idea. She did visit the school, but was very resistant to the idea of sending Hasit there, mostly because of the travelling distance. In the end it was decided that Hasit would stay at Gunners, but move down into the first year class, which he did after the next half-term break. Hasit did not want to change schools, although he knew he was likely to find it increasingly difficult in lessons: 'The work gets harder in 14s and 15s'.

Hasit has been in Jackie Davies' class for four months now, and attends most of the same lessons as his classmates, apart from the six withdrawal periods for learning support and ESL teaching. Although Hasit's spoken English is fairly fluent it is not his native tongue; he speaks English at school and often with his siblings, but says that, 'at home we speak our language'. The ESL teacher concentrates on reading and writing work, which he sees as Hasit's weakest points:

He's basically a sound kid, but he does have certain conceptual problems. He has problems relating what he sees on paper to spoken language, and great writing difficulties. I think his main learning difficulties stem from his inability to decode written words.

Hasit's spelling of words often bears little resemblance to the original, or even to a phonetic verson: 'about' is written 'unthrey', 'because' as 'beduras', 'over' as 'orethe'. This spelling test is on the next page in Hasit's exercise book to a laboriously copied out humorous poem about the inconsistencies of spelling in the English language, comparing words like 'tough', 'bough', 'cough', and 'dough'. The ESL teacher tries to get Hasit to build up words phonetically, but he obviously finds this very difficult.

Hasit's reading and writing difficulties pose particular problems for him in coping with the secondary school curriculum. Much of the work involves using textbooks or workcards, and Hasit is often at a loss to know what he should be doing, let alone how to do it. He is a very conscientious child, and has evolved various strategies for appearing to be busy and getting on with his work. In the humanities lesson, the class are studying the Industrial Revolution. Hasit is sitting on his own, a small figure at the front desk. The teacher put him there so he could notice when Hasit needs extra attention, but finds it is all too easy to look straight over his head without realizing that he is there. The class are copying the work written in white chalk on the board, and answering the questions written in yellow chalk with the aid of their textbooks. Hasit industriously copies down a large section from the board, copies out the question too, and then stops. A boy asks him for his rubber, another girl borrows his Tippex. After a while, Hasit says, 'Sir?', timidly as the teacher passes, but is not heard. Five minutes later he puts his hand up, but more noisy children are demanding the teacher's attention and again he is missed. Finally he takes his book out to the front, and asks what he should be doing next.

Later, he is copying a picture of an iron smelting plant from the book. He spends a long time perfecting the drawing, rubbing bits out and re-doing them until he is satisfied. He labels the drawing using different coloured pens, then takes a ruler out of his fancy pencil box shaped like a calculator, and carefully measures and draws in the margins on the next two pages of his book. He then appears stuck, but is temporarily saved by the teacher's decision to show some slides. Afterwards the class are asked various questions to check they have understood the iron smelting process. Hasit never raises his hand. The teacher comes over and explains the smelting process in a simplified form, and Hasit nods when asked if he has understood. The teacher writes in pencil under Hasit's drawing for him to copy over, and then points to a question on the board and tells him to read it and write down the answer. Hasit copies out the question in full, but is saved from having to answer it by the end of the lesson. He packs away his books with an air of relief.

In maths lessons, Hasit's class have an extra teacher providing additional help to those children who most need it. There are around twelve teachers in each year who spend one period a week each giving 'learning support' in another teacher's class. This is in addition to the Learning Support Unit, where children are withdrawn for sessions with Roger Lewis, who is both the head of and the only teacher in the unit. Roger would like to see the system of classroom support extended and given high priority:

> I think most of the senior staff are for the idea in principle, but sometimes it seems like learning support is just an administrative way out of timetabling problems. It's just to fill up teachers' timetables, a timetabling nicety.

Mike Lansdown, the ESL teacher, is providing learning support in Hasit's maths lessons this year. The class are using SMILE, a system of individual worksheets with regular tests, which the maths teacher says involves her in much administrative work to keep track of each child's progress:

> It's good for Hasit in some ways, because it's individualized, but it gets chaotic sometimes, they're all coming up wanting homework and its difficult to get to the ones who don't push themselves.

Hasit doesn't push himself forward. He sits looking at his worksheet for the first ten minutes, until Mike comes over to see if he knows what to do. He doesn't. His worksheet is about numbers and products. Mike gets him to spell 'product', explains what it means and what he should be doing, and moves on to help another child. Hasit counts on his fingers, looks around, taps his foot, looks at the numbers on his calculator pencil box, as if for inspiration. Another child borrows and returns his set square. Pupils are constantly attracting Mike's or the maths teacher's attention to ask for help, but Hasit just sits quietly. He starts to write when the teacher comes over, then gets out his Tippex bottle. He flips back through his book, realizes he's doing the wrong card, and gets up to find a different one from the box. By the time Mike has explained how to do this new card, it is almost time for the lesson to finish.

Hasit's learning problems are obviously not solely to do with his physical lack of growth, but his small size combined with his quiet, unobtrusive manner mean that he often fails to get attention and help when he needs it. His teachers unanimously describe him as good, hard-working and highly motivated. 'He's no trouble', was a constant refrain. Ironically, his being 'no trouble' is precisely the problem. Hasit's good behaviour interacts with his small stature to give him a low profile, both literally and metaphorically. In a class of thirty Hasit is easily overlooked, despite his teachers' awareness of his difficulties and their desire to given him extra help. His class teacher described how she sometimes forgot that she had Hasit in her class, and when it dawned on her ten minutes after the lesson had started she would go over and find he'd got some other work out of his bag and seemed to be getting on with it. Or she would be taking the register and realize when she got to Hasit's name that she had no idea whether he was present or not. With other children she almost always knew:

> He's a boy whom you miss. You miss him coming in and you miss him going out. When you look at the class as a whole you miss him. He's so small. He's lost in a group of people.

Hasit never complains, and hardly ever asks for help. More than a few of his teachers remarked that it was difficult to tell how much he had understood:

> If you ask he just nods and glazes over.

He appears so willing and keen to do well it's hard to work out how much he takes in.

A lot of his work is just copied down, it's difficult finding out how much of it he really knows.

Their suspicion that the majority of the curriculum is by-passing Hasit seems well founded. In a lesson like French, for instance, it was clear that Hasit took in little or nothing. This is hardly surprising, given his problems with reading and writing in English. French, he said, was his least favourite lesson: 'I just can't do any of it'. This year none of Hasit's withdrawal periods coincide with French lessons. Because he moved back into the first year halfway through the term, he had to fit into the withdrawal periods that had already been timetabled for his class. As Roger Lewis remarked: 'It's the wrong way around really, the kids with the most needs should get timetabled in first'.

Science is Hasit's favourite lesson. His physics teacher, Mr Lucas, had provided learning support in Hasit's science lessons in the previous year, and so knew the level of support Hasit would need:

He really needs one-to-one attention most of the time. On his own he doesn't get very far, but he's alright if you can sit with him and coax it out of him, ask him 'when you put this there, what happened next?' He's alright with the practical work, he can manipulate the apparatus and he can make simple direct observations, but I don't think he can interpret the results.

This year, Hasit has no classroom support in physics, and Mr Lucas says he 'just has to get on as best he can. If he can communicate his understanding verbally then I don't bother too much with his written work'.

Most of Hasit's teachers do their best to provide him with extra help, given the constraints of teaching a large mixed-ability class. Some use the 'dictated experience' approach suggested to them by Roger Lewis, which involves getting Hasit to say what he has understood in a particular lesson or experiment, writing down his sentences, getting him to write over the words and then to read them back. Others, like Jackie Davies, will give him a vocabulary list of key words to help him answer questions on a comprehension exercise, or write out a passage and leave blank words for him to fill in. Their attempts to offer him extra help and attention were usually constantly distracted by other pupils' requests for homework, spelling advice or further information.

The one time when Hasit does get fairly undivided attention is in the withdrawal periods he spends with Roger Lewis in the Learning Support Unit. Housed in a quiet room near the head's office, the unit is intended as a haven for children with a variety of emotional and learning problems. Roger sees his job as, 'building up each child's confidence and making them feel good about themselves.' Hasit has begun to open up in this small group, and although he is still very quiet and avoids eye contact, he has begun to talk about his family, about the 'holy house' in East London where his mother took him to see why he wasn't growing, about ancestors and spirits and demons. Roger remarks that he is a complicated, surprising child, and shows a book that Hasit has produced, using the dictated experience approach, where he describes in considerable detail his collection of twenty diaries that have belonged to various members of his family, or tells with great suspense the story of the finding of an old stamp album in a locked trunk in his attic at home.

Roger thinks that Hasit's growth problem must create difficulties for him in the school:

> I think his size must affect his self image. He's very reluctant to speak. He walks like a little mouse around the school. I shouldn't think he's got many friends.

The majority of Hasit's teachers expressed similar feelings, describing how he hardly ever spoke, never made eye contact and seemed to have few particular friends. The head of second year comments: 'He's so small, it must affect him. It must give him a complex'. In practice, however, Hasit seemed to co-exist quite happily with his schoolmates. It is true that he was often to be seen sitting or walking away from lessons alone, and that other children rarely initiated contact with him, but on the other hand he was not ostracized or bullied in the way that some other children in his class were. Although a year older than the rest of his class, Hasit seemed to be treated as a younger brother. Jackie Davies said that, 'my boys are very nice, they look after him and help him with his work. I think they mother him'. Other children could be observed telling Hasit where to stand to field in a cricket game, reminding him to hand in his book at the end of a lesson, and suggesting to the teacher that he be given a special vocabulary book to keep a record of the words he found difficult. Much of their interaction with him was in the form of borrowing things. Hasit came to school well equipped and could always be relied upon to lend a ruler or set square, or to have copied down the homework questions, even though he was unlikely to be able to answer them himself.

In games lessons, Hasit wasn't picked for a team but neither were there any complaints when the teacher allocated him to a side. He threw the ball very weakly, but managed a couple of hits with the cricket bat and smiled happily when his team did well. The only sports where Hasit's size is a particular handicap, according to the PE teacher are those involving large heavy balls, like basketball. Here he tends to back off if a ball approaches him, and is unable to throw it. His frailty and lack of stamina also make running difficult:

> Last year they all did the 100 metres race. Everyone else took 18 or 19 seconds, and Hasit came plodding up after about 25 seconds – but they were all cheering him because they knew it was hard for him.

Hasit is not particularly sought out by other children, but neither is he left out. Although other children are unlikely to name Hasit as their friend, he readily lists half a dozen boys, mostly fellow Asians, whom he thinks of as his friends, and says that 'having friends' is the best thing about being at school. Mike Lansdown, his ESL teacher, said that, 'He sees other kids as being his friends in a way that maybe we don't see them, and it's his perceptions that count'. At dinner time, Hasit is observed selecting his tray of food (a combination of chips, can of coke and two ice pops, which would have dismayed his dietician at the clinic), and joining several other boys at a table where he sits saying little but apparently accepted. From the teachers' point of view, Hasit is a popular pupil. He is well-behaved, persistent and motivated, and his small size seems to bring out the protective instincts in female teachers in particular. They describe him as 'a sweetie', 'adorable' and 'a real cutie'. Jackie Davies reacts to him this way:

> When I first saw him I just wanted to hug him. He was standing at the side in a netball class with a big rugby jumper on that came down to his knees ... sometimes he sits at a desk in the library classroom that's too big for him and all you see is this little head poking over the top. He's such an adorable little boy.

Hasit's size combined with his learning difficulties make it easy to forget that he is approaching fifteen years old.

Despite this, Hasit seems socially well integrated into the school. He appears happy, has other children he feels able to call his friends, and can often be seen on the edge of a group smiling at someone else's joke, not at the centre of things but not excluded either. Academically, the staff are aware that he is making very little progress. One or two of his teachers have wondered whether he would be better off at a special school, where he would get more individual attention than they are able to offer, but most of them feel that changing schools would have a damaging effect on his social development. Mike Lansdown feels this way:

> He'd be a lot less secure. Okay, they'd probably be able to give him more time, but I think his emotional development would be set back three or four years. He'd be scared and unhappy. I really think this is the best place for him. He feels different enough as it is without pushing him into a special unit or school.

Hasit himself definitely prefers to stay where he is: 'I don't want to go to another school. It's nice here. You're used to it. And it's near for me. I can walk to school in ten minutes'.

It seems clear however that Hasit's needs are not being adequately met at Gunners High School, from lack of time and resources rather than from lack of good intentions on the part of the staff. The educational psychologist praises the school: 'It's a school that will bend over backwards to support him, but how long he can go on without something extra I don't know'. She is not sure yet what this 'something extra' might involve: 'He may well need a curriculum that's wound down very much, or that goes at a very slow pace'. Some teachers hope that the forthcoming introduction of TVEI, involving a practical, option-based curriculum with reduced emphasis on examinations, will be particularly suited to the educational needs of children like Hasit. More opportunities to work on the computer would be another possibility, since Hasit appears very keen on this and sometimes spends hours after school playing on the school's terminal. Other teachers put their faith in more learning support in the classroom, a direction encouraged by the educational psychologist. She thinks it would be particularly good if a Gujerati-speaking support teacher could be found, so concepts could be introduced to him in both languages. The deputy head is confident that they will be able to 'sort something out' for Hasit when he gets to the end of his repeated first year:

> Perhaps he could spend two years in the second form too, since he won't be doing exams. We might be able to give him a special timetable for his last year, choosing the lessons he likes or even the teachers he likes. We couldn't do that for all the kids, but we'll slot him in somehow.

Hasit's physical growth problems make it all the more important that he is able to remain in his ordinary school. But it also makes it especially urgent that Hasit has a curriculum organized around his particular needs, since his small size makes him so easily overlooked in the hurly burly of a large comprehensive school. The educational psychologist plans to begin the statementing procedure at the end of the year, and hopes that they will then have a clearer picture of how Hasit's needs can best be met in an ordinary school.

4 Andrew

Will Swann

This chapter describes the learning experience of a student with a severe disability reaching the end of his sixth form studies. Andrew Taylor is registered at a special school, but is taught almost entirely at the comprehensive school on the same campus. His access to mainstream education has been ensured by a combination of close liaison between the two schools, the use of microtechnology and Andrew's own approach to his education. With this background, Andrew's prospects for success at A-levels ought to depend primarily on the quality of teaching he receives and his own intellectual efforts. But they are also likely to be adversely affected by the failure of the examination board involved to understand the inevitable consequences of Andrew's disability.

Priestwood High School, a comprehensive on the Western Edge of London, shares a campus with Downhead School, a special school for children with physical disabilities. For the past eight years, the two schools have developed increasingly close links that have permitted virtually all the secondary aged pupils at Downhead to receive some of their education in Priestwood. A majority of them spend more than fifty per cent of their time at Priestwood.

Andrew Taylor was one of the pioneers of this move. He came to Downhead at the age of eleven from a neighbouring Borough which has no secondary provision for pupils with disabilities, and his placement was made with an eye towards integration. At twelve he started at Priestwood on almost a full timetable. Andrew now has five O-levels to his credit and awaits the results of his two A-levels. This has been achieved by someone who has no use of his hands whatsoever. Andrew, who has athetoid cerebral palsy, does all his work using a microcomputer operated by two foot-switches. He is dependent on other people for all his personal care needs, and has depended on the extensive efforts and support provided by the staffs of the two schools in order to achieve the degree of success he has so far reached. In many other parts of the country, the facilities to educate someone with Andrew's degree of disability would not be available in a mainstream school. The only option would be a residential special school. But success has also depended on Andrew himself, on his personality and attitude towards his work and others around him.

Who's responsible?

Anyone with a disability in Britain has to contend with prejudice and discrimination – with the behaviour of other people which would be illegal if it were directed towards someone who is black, but which carries not even the threat of a legal sanction when aimed at a disabled person:

> I'll give you a good example that really made me angry. The other week I went along to a pub in my area with a friend I used to go to school with. We went out to this pub,

31

we walked up to the bar and asked for two lagers, and the girl looked at us and said, 'sorry, I can't serve you'. We said 'Why not?', and my friend was just about to get his birth certificate out to prove that he was eighteen and she said, 'Well, you'll have to see the Manager'. Anyway, we waited there for a couple of minutes. The Manager came along and said, 'I'm sorry, we can't serve you'. We said, 'Can you tell us why?', and he said, 'Well, it will be upsetting for the other customers, would you please leave'. I was just about to explode and have a go at him, but my friend said, 'It's not worth it, we'll go somewhere else', and we just walked out. But I'm going back there; I'm going back there in a few weeks to try again.

This is not a common experience for Andrew, but neither is it a rare one. Others he knows have been refused entry into cinemas and shops. To Andrew, such treatment is the moral equivalent of apartheid, and he would like to see it outlawed by an anti-discrimination act. Yet however outraged he is by the bigotry of some members of the able-bodied majority, his personal relationships with them are governed by an abiding sensitivity to their insecurity and reserve in dealings with him. He is patient and tolerant, and has been throughout his integrated schooling:

If you go into a class, you haven't seen a handicapped person, well somebody sitting there shaking about, you're going to be unnerved obviously, and you've got to gain their confidence . . . I think when you're a handicapped person, you make the first move; they're going to be wary, they're going to get unnerved and I can understand that, I really can. Maybe all the onus shouldn't be put on me, but I think most of it should.

Now, Andrew's relationships with his fellow students are mostly very positive. He is included in ordinary conversations before and after lessons as anyone else might be, despite the fact that he spent a year away from Priestwood at the end of his O-levels and so does not know his A-level group as well as they know each other. He is also hampered by living well outside the school's catchment area. In spite of the generally positive relationships with other students, Andrew knows that a few of his fellow students find it especially difficult to relate to him. One such is Amanda, a member of Andrew's A-level English class. Amanda doesn't look at Andrew in discussions; she seems almost to avoid looking at him. Andrew knows this, but attributes the problem to Amanda's natural reserve. Just how far her attitude is determined by Andrew's disability is impossible to know. She may have reacted this way had Andrew been able-bodied:

She's the sort of person that needs to know someone really well before she will talk to them and open up. She was very cold at the start. I thought I'm never going to get near her. Last term she actually opened up and started chatting to me. We get on fine now.

'If anybody was going to be laughed at', said his headteacher at Downhead, 'it would be Andrew'. He moves continually from the shoulders, and his walk is stooping and scissored. No one makes fun of him now, but they used to:

When I started I got a hell of a lot of stick. Some of it I honestly enjoyed . . . I could see the funny side of it. Actually I've got a strange sense of humour I'm afraid, and I can laugh at some of the sickest jokes around, particularly about handicapped people. But when they get really personal that's when it does affect me, and it affects everybody. Some people will say, 'Oh he doesn't bother with that person any more, he's learnt to handle it'. I don't believe it. Any human being who's got any emotion at all would be affected. I don't get it any more, because I've won over the people who have done that in the class, but in the second and third year I did get it quite a lot. I learnt to cope with it, and I think it's something good in the long run. It's toughened me up a lot.

Andrew is included in his A-level classes by his teachers on the same basis as other students. Treating pupils with disabilities appropriately does not come easily to all teachers. There is a fine balance to be made between taking a pupil's disability into account, and making unnecessary concessions. A great deal of in-service training run jointly by Downhead and Priestwood has concentrated on this issue. Andrew himself has had to contend with the uncertainty of some of his teachers. His Deputy Head at Downhead used to be a mainstream French teacher before she moved to the special school which is now Andrew's base. He was, to her, 'a completely new visual impact'. His Head of English at the comprehensive where he is taught, knows, even now, that he has to resist an intangible pressure from within not to involve Andrew in lessons:

One tends to feel, wrongly, that his speech will not be clear. I'm still fighting this one. I've got a gut reaction: don't put as many questions to Andrew; don't ask him to read parts in plays.

Involvement is vital to Andrew, and he knows the solution does not lie entirely in his hands:

I'm not going to mention any names because that wouldn't be fair, but there are some teachers that won't ask you questions. When I answer questions I shake more, my speech becomes a bit worse, so they feel, 'you don't ask him questions because it will affect him'. But it doesn't really. I like people asking me because you feel part of the system. You're part of a class team.

For Andrew, the solution lies in extra effort from him and as well as the teachers. He has made a point of answering questions to let teachers know he is willing to do so. The headteacher of the comprehensive, who taught him physics, recognized the problem and raised the issue with Andrew, as Andrew explains:

I said to him, 'You don't like asking me questions, do you?', and he said, 'No, because I think it affects you'. I said, 'Yes, you'll probably see me shaking about more, but I would like you to ask me the questions, because I feel part of the class then'. After that he seemed to go to the other extreme. He asked me most of the questions.

Perhaps, suggests Elizabeth Curtis, the Head of Downhead, Andrew's acceptance and tolerance is his weakness as well as his strength. If he passes his A-levels he will go on to higher education, and there, without the support of his family and school staff, he will need a Community Service Volunteer (CSV). An occupational therapist, not his usual one, was sent to his home by the local Social Services Department, as far as Andrew was aware to plan how this was to happen. She treated Andrew as 'a new case', asking interminable questions about him to which most of the answers were 'no': 'Can you feed yourself? Can you get dressed alone? Can you use the toilet independently? Can you wash or bath yourself?' She proposed endless adaptations and specially designed clothes, but never once mentioned a CSV. Neither did Andrew: he didn't want to upset her.

His demeanour in the face of his own disability and other people's attitudes is generally regarded as his greatest asset. According to his Head of History, who is also Sixth Form Tutor at Priestwood, he is 'never moody; he never burdens us with his difficulties; there is no hint of martyrdom. He's a cheerful, resilient chap'. Elizabeth Curtis also admires the way he never exploits his handicap, as others do.

A martyr is one who suffers the abuse of others for the sake of a belief. Andrew does not put his tolerance and suffering on show, but he has suffered for the cause. He has changed attitudes towards him by keeping his hurt to himself. Ironically, had he fought back or abandoned his *sang-froid*, accusations of martyrdom might have emerged.

His patience broke once, but on this occasion not with the teachers or pupils who couldn't react to him normally, but with those who looked on at the wonder of a boy with such a severe disability doing his work with a microcomputer. He was one of the first pupils at Downhead School to use microtechnology to support his integrated education, and there was a constant trickle of visitors to the small room in Downhead with the half-glass door where he does his private study. One morning, pinned onto the noticeboard, staff found Andrew's token of anger: 'The monkey has had enough bananas'.

Doing A-levels

The motivations to enter the sixth form at school are in most cases be a mix of the instrumental and the personal. Andrew is no different. He knows that in order to gain a rewarding job in the long term he will have to be highly qualified. No one will make any concessions for him. Indeed, he may need to be more highly qualified than able-bodied people. Primarily, education is a means to an end for him, a body of knowledge that he has to acquire in order to leap the credentials hurdle. The choices open to him have been much wider than they would have been ten years ago, or in many other parts of the country today, but they have still been limited. When he began at Priestwood, he was on a full timetable except for PE/games, heavy craft and maths. He achieved only a CSE in maths, and this has been a serious impediment to his progressing to higher education. His sixth form tutor suggested possible 'technical difficulties' and 'inter-relations in the classroom' as the reason, but averred that 'he doesn't give the feeling of a boy that couldn't cope with O-level maths'. Mary Borthwick, the Deputy Head of Downhead responsible for liaison with Priestwood, suggests that since maths involved a lot of practical activity, the staff didn't think they could give Andrew the necessary attention. Andrew recognized that he was never very good at maths, and Elizabeth Curtis suggested this may be connected with his very limited ability to manipulate concrete materials in his early childhood. Andrew was also unable to draw diagrams, since his microcomputer lacks the necessary software. He also feels that teacher attitude played a role:

> I didn't have a great deal of success with my mathematics. I had a really stubborn teacher who wouldn't move out of some huts for three years. I couldn't get my computer in that hut, so I had to sit there and take no notes. I thought I got well behind in my maths lessons.

Pressure on accommodation contributed to the original siting of the maths lessons in a hut. In fact, the two schools have recently taken a joint decision not to ask teachers to move from specialist rooms to accommodate one pupil (as has been done for David's history lessons) until the LEA instals a lift that has been promised for five years. This will give pupils with disabilities access to another floor and offer much more flexibility in room allocations.

Geography was a subject that Andrew enjoyed, and was considering for his A-level programme, but he was forced to reject it because he had no means of drawing maps and diagrams independently. In this he was handicapped by his being a pioneer in the use of microtechnology. The computer he uses, an Apple II, is not now in common use, and graphics software is unavailable. Younger pupils at Downhead now regularly use graphics software driven by a bitstick or a mouse. In class this was not an insuperable restriction. Maps and diagrams could be supplied by teachers, or other pupils could help. The exam was the real barrier. Andrew had to dictate to an amanuensis. If you doubt the difficulty of conveying complex graphic images in language, you might try it yourself. This skill is not part of the geography syllabus for any able-bodied candidate. The prospect of continued difficulties of this kind was deterrent enough to persuade Andrew to choose history instead.

He had also wanted to take Law at A-level. It was one of his five O-level passes. Here he was hampered, not by his impairment or its consequences, but by the fact that a viable group could not be created to satisfy Priestwood's staffing equations. Andrew started a correspondence Law course, but it became quickly evident that he could not cope with the workload.

This left him with two subjects: English and history. An instrumental attitude does not dominate his response to either subject, even if it is his central motivation. His feelings about history range from tedium to great emotional involvement. The history of education was 'so mechanical, unbelievable . . . a series of dates, a series of Acts'. But the growth of the labour and trade union movement provoked a very different response, that coalesced with his political attitudes:

> *Andrew:* I like to understand how that affected the ordinary person, how the working class coped with their situation, and how they formed trade unions to actually improve their situation. Now I like the emotional side of that, and there was a lot of emotion in the trade union movement. They were terribly put down by the aristocracy . . .
>
> *WS:* What's the nature of your interest in politics?
>
> *Andrew:* I see a lot of things I don't like in society, and I would like to think that it could be changed. Now for me the only way to change that at the moment is through politics . . . and again, it's emotional because I see a lot of hardships around, even see it with my own eyes, and I would like to see that changed.

Andrew was complimentary about all his history teachers. Philip Carpenter teaches part of the syllabus, and has known Andrew since he joined Priestwood. He does not feel that Andrew's disability hinders his progress, nor does it affect the way he teaches, apart from the fact that he has to teach away from his usual base. Andrew clearly can't raise his hand, and so earlier in his education, Philip Carpenter and others had to look out for Andrew in other ways. Now, in a small A-level group, Andrew poses no problem at all. Indeed, Philip Carpenter's bluff, somewhat acerbic approach is applied to Andrew as much as to anyone else.

Andrew takes this as a sign of equitable treatment: 'although you're angry at the time at him shouting at you, in a funny way it's a good thing. If he didn't I wouldn't feel part of the class'. Philip Carpenter is direct with his students: when I joined Andrew for a couple of days the post-mortem on mock A-levels was under way. 'Well,' he said, 'your papers are absolutely dire ... Andrew, you had twenty minutes extra!' In the ensuing discussion, he conceded this was probably not enough. The lesson was a debriefing on a particularly awkward exam question on Bismarck and his relationship to the papacy and the socialists. Philip Carpenter was as critical of the examiners who set the question as he was with his class. But in setting out the material, his style was positive and animated, and he was in command of the subject. He presented Bismarck as a real person, with real dilemmas. He worked hard to impress on the class the logic of the times. During such a lesson, Andrew's main task is to take notes, which he does using his micro. His working speed is much slower than other students, but his note-taking is efficient and teachers do not need to slow down for him. Like many students he uses an extensive system of abbreviations.

Later that week came another history lesson from Mark McNaughton, the Head of Department, one that Andrew later said he had thoroughly enjoyed; any half-interested spectator would have agreed. It traced the growth of democratic institutions following the Great Reform Act of 1832, and was for the most part a lecture. Although the sweep was broad and took in a fifty-year period, Mark McNaughton conveyed a sense of the manoeuvring and power-broking of the period. Events were regularly related to current political structures. To convey the nature of mid-nineteenth-century political parties, he began with a question and answer session on the class basis of twentieth-century parties, and then stepped back in time with a demonstrative: 'in the nineteenth century it was not *thus*'. The drawback of the lesson was that for the most part, the students were passive listeners. This was the outcome of both his past difficulties in encouraging this group to discuss, and the pressure of the syllabus as the exam loomed closer. With more time and perhaps, less necessary anxiety about covering the syllabus, more participatory methods might have been feasible. But in this format, Andrew was clearly on a par with all other students.

Mark McNaughton assessed Andrew's competence in history against three criteria. At A-level, students had to acquire a body of knowledge, analyse it for causes and effects, inter-relationships and patterns, and apply that in a disciplined way to questions set. On the first two, Andrew was not unduly handicapped, except by his inability to use libraries, and his missing the experience of unaided research. On the third, Andrew was not shaping up too well. In his mock exam he had answered only two of the four questions, and written far too much. In one essay he had begun 'Before we start to look at the reasons why chartism rapidly rose and fell, it's better to look at what the movement was'. There followed pages of material that should not have been there. This is a common problem at A-level (and beyond) but it was especially serious for Andrew, who could write at only half normal speed.

Problems of essay technique were much less apparent in English, where his two teachers had high praise for him. In a generally weak group, Andrew was one of the brighter students. Adrian Beaton, the Head of English, set out Andrew's strong points:

Most things really. He thinks extremely well. He writes the most superb essays. If it were not for his physical limitations which tend to set him apart from the others, he would be one of the star ones who is leading the thinking of the group.

The English staff were probably more liberal in their attitudes to students' course-work than the history department, and rarely imposed upper limits on the length of essays. Under these conditions, Andrew thrived. His essays were described as well-planned, comprehensive, long and effective. He had a distinctive style and point-of-view. But they also recognized that under time constraints, his exam technique was not good.

Most A-level English syllabuses are quite limited. Students have to study ten or so texts in depth, and marks depend on their specific knowledge of these. Andrew's list was typical: *Hamlet*, *The Nun's Priest's Tale*, *Emma*, and *The Prelude* amongst them. A broader education in English literature has to be squeezed into spare time. Andrew would like to read more contemporary works, but he has very little time. This is no mere excuse. Working at half normal speed means spending twice the normal time to complete tasks. A typical weekday evening for Andrew runs like this:

4.00–4.30 Home from school; snack and drink
4.30–6.45 Work
6.45–7.45 Supper
7.45–10.00 or 10.30 Work

With weekends added in, Andrew was working around of thirty hours per week outside school in the run-up to his exams. He took Friday night and Sunday night off. Learning to cope with the demands of such a work schedule has been a central part of Andrew's education, and one that has received systematic attention at Downhead.

The English lessons I observed were less teacher-directed than history. Annabelle Keith, who was teaching *The Importance of Being Earnest*, called her lessons organic: 'they've got a life of their own'. She and Adrian Beaton encourage a lot of discussion. Andrew participates in discussions, although his role can be constrained by his impairment, by his computer, and by some of the other students. Earlier in his career at Priestwood, Andrew's speech was difficult to understand for anyone unfamiliar with him. It has improved immeasurably but remains noticeably impaired. Some staff have no problem understanding him, and to others, Andrew's speech is an occasional minor impediment. Andrew's computer and printer is mounted on a large trolley which is transported between schools and rooms by a welfare assistant. Its position in the classroom is limited by the location of plug-points. Staff place discussion groups around Andrew's fixed position, but if the spatial arrangement of students is not conducive to Andrew's involvement he depends on the other students to re-arrange themselves. Any move of position by Andrew would be very obvious, and would mean he would lose the chance to take notes. In a small group discussion in a lesson run by Adrian Beaton, Andrew was in a group of four arranged as in Figure 4.1. Most of the conversation was initiated by Sally and took place between Kevin and Sally. Amanda and Andrew also contributed. When Sally spoke she looked at Andrew, frequently giving him the chance to join in if he wished. When Amanda spoke, she looked only at Sally and Kevin, and seemed

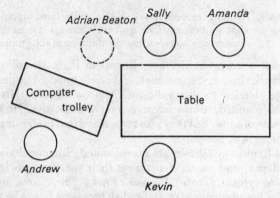

Figure 4.1   Spatial arrangement of an English discussion group

actively to avoid eye-contact with Andrew. Kevin's chair faced the table, and he scarcely turned his head at all when talking, thus rather excluding Andrew. The dynamics of the group changed markedly whenever Adrian Beaton joined them opposite Andrew, who then said much more.

One should be careful not to convey too false an impression of this group, or Andrew's relationships with his fellow-students. Kevin switched Andrew's computer off and on at the start of the lesson when a disk wouldn't load; Sally turned Andrew's copy of *Hamlet* to the correct page. He was involved in conversations at the start and finish of the lesson. Indeed he is one of the best liked students at Priestwood by staff and pupils alike.

Gaining access to education

Andrew values his membership of both schools. Attending Priestwood has not only given him access to specialist teaching at an advanced level, but it has also, in his view, contributed to the eradication of prejudice. Attending Downhead has been important as well. He spends all his private study time there, and he is in the building more often than he was during O-levels:

> It has been really important, and it still is. Sometimes I still enjoy the security of coming back here and being a bit quiet. Obviously, in a big school like that there's no place where you can go and be quiet. And also on the personal side, like toileting and things like that, they're really important.

Downhead has been the base from which Andrew's most important means of access to the curriculum at Priestwood, his microcomputer, has been established. For his first two years at Priestwood, from age twelve to thirteen, Andrew used a POSSUM typewriter driven by two foot-switches. He used a code of foot-presses to type with. The POSSUM was cumbersome, noisy, slow and inflexible. It broke down frequently because it was transported between schools on an undamped trolley. Repair and maintenance facilities were only available from Possum Controls Ltd., and could take two to three days to arrive, leaving Andrew stranded in the classroom with no means to write. At home, he had another foot-operated POSSUM, but which used a different code. As he began his O-level courses, he was given the APPLE II microcomputer, and Downhead arranged to have it programmed so that its word processing software would accept the POSSUM code. Word processing, and storage of material on disk liberated Andrew. He can now correct and edit as he goes along, accumulate notes in systematically organized disk-files, retrieve material at will, and print off copies whenever he needs them. He has not gone entirely paperless. Essays are still marked on paper, and he maintains printed copies of his notes, as well as on disk. Typed scripts to mark are a positive boon for staff.

The machine has not made him entirely independent, although without it it is hard to envisage how he would participate in his A-level classes. The human assistance he needs to support classwork and private study is minimal. Most things he can do with his feet, nose or chin; this includes finding the page in a paperback to work from, and getting material out of his zip-up bag. Andrew needs help to move his computer and written material about, and to load and unload disks. He has no extra staff to support him in class and never has had. They are not needed. Welfare assistants are needed to see to his personal care, which is done at Downhead, since Priestwood has no suitable facilities.

There is very close liaison between the two schools, conducted mainly between the two deputy heads. Both regularly monitor and review the progress of all pupils integrated into Priestwood, and are frequent visitors to each other's schools.

The future

If Andrew passes his A-levels, and staff hold out a reasonable hope that he will, he will go to either Dundee University or Lancashire Polytechnic. But if he did not have a disability, Andrew would, at least for a while, get out of education:

> *Andrew:* To be absolutely honest I've had enough of it. If I was able-bodied I would get out now after these exams and try and get a job ... If I had my choice I would honestly get out now, but education for me is a means to an end, really a means to an end.
>
> *WS:* Why are you fed up with it?
>
> *Andrew:* Being tied down night after night doing work. In our education system you're told what to do. I know basically you're told what to do when you go to a job, that's slightly different, it's a more relaxed atmosphere, I think, and it's not quite the relationship of teacher–pupil. I'd like to get out of that sort of situation, and I feel I'm working night after night, slogging away when I would like that time free, honestly.

The means to higher education is the examination system. His two schools have equipped him to enter the race, but the hurdles have been set higher for Andrew than for his fellow students who are able-bodied. Logic would seem to dictate that a student whose writing speed is materially affected by a physical impairment should be given extra time in proportion to the size of the gap between his/her own speed and normal speed. Andrew writes at dictation at 16 words per minute, and normal writing speed averages at 28 words per minute for A-level students. A proportionate time allowance would be 45 minutes for each hour: for a normal three hour paper, Andrew would be allowed five hours fifteen minutes. Up until a few weeks before he sat his A-levels, the London University Examining Board would allow only 20 minutes per hour, despite much lobbying and information from staff from both schools. After much negotiation, the Board was finally persuaded to allow 30 minutes per hour. Even with this concession, this is equivalent to giving an able-bodied candidate two hours thirty-five minutes instead of three hours.

Andrew does not want positive discrimination. He simply wants equitable treatment. In the final annual review report, he and his father both gave vent to their views on this matter. This was written when the extra time allowance was still twenty minutes in the hour. His father first:

> Andrew has had many disadvantages in life and in my view he is not being allowed anything like the additional amount of time he deserves when taking his public examinations. This only adds yet another disadvantage to those he can do nothing about. I can only assume those with the responsibility for setting the time do not appreciate the individual difficulties of some physically handicapped candidates.

And Andrew:

> All I am asking for is a fair examination, but at the moment I am at a severe disadvantage. It would be extremely sad to think that years of hard work are being jeopardized.

5 Katherine and Matthew

Juliet Bishop and Susan Gregory

In this chapter Juliet Bishop and Susan Gregory describe two children from their research into the progress of deaf pupils in ordinary schools in one Local Education Authority. The Authority pursued a policy of 'natural oralism' with deaf pupils, in which they were expected to acquire spoken English through the ordinary exchanges with their family, friends and teachers, amplified with radio hearing aids. The chapter documents the attitudes and approaches of their teachers, the support they received and the struggles they had to understand and be understood.

Introduction

Fifty years ago the notion that children with a severe hearing loss should be educated alongside normally hearing children would have been unthinkable. However, developments in the technology associated with hearing loss, together with changes in the attitudes of special educators and in the general educational climate have made such practices acceptable, and even the norm in some areas. Yet the integration of deaf children into ordinary schools is not simple, and exposure to the normal curriculum does not imply equality of access to the educational system. In this chapter we shall show some of the positive aspects of integration, together with some of the problems – both those that are inevitable, and those that are avoidable.

The two case studies presented here, are taken from a longitudinal study being carried out within the Deafness Research Group, Nottingham University, which involved twelve deaf children placed in ordinary, although not always local, primary schools.[1] The children were visited from before school entry, and followed as they passed from home through pre-school into infant schools and finally in their first year at junior school. Interviews were carried out with parents before their children entered school, with both parents and teachers after one term of schooling, and finally with the teachers when the children were six and a half years old. The children were recorded in classrooms in one-to-one conversations with their teachers, and in class groups where the teacher discussed topics with her whole class. These latter recordings were made when the children were five and a half and six and a half years old. We hope that juxtaposing the case studies of two children will give an idea of how deafness itself is only one consideration in school placement. Other less tangible factors like home and school attitudes and expectations are also important.

The children selected are both from an LEA whose policy of normal school placement of individual deaf children predates the 1981 Education Act. The closure of the School for the Deaf in the county meant that the only available special provision for deaf children was Partially Hearing Units or the occasional

The research described in this paper was supported by MRC Grant Number 337/217.

41

use of out of county special school placements. The services for the hearing impaired in this particular county pursue a firm philosophy of adopting the 'natural oral approach' to communication for young deaf children[1]. Fundamental to this philosophy is the belief that given good hearing aids and plenty of normal spoken communication experience, a deaf child, regardless of level of hearing loss, should be able to successfully develop oral communication skills.

The children

The two children to be considered in this chapter are Katherine Ashdown and Matthew Fletcher. Katherine was born in 1978, the second of two girls. Her sister, Sarah, had been diagnosed as severely deaf when she was eleven months old. Initially Katherine's parents, both teachers, felt that she could hear but by the time she was seven months they had become concerned. Katherine passed the health visitor's nine-month screening test but her mother, still anxious, contacted the local Services for the Hearing Impaired for advice. A further hearing test indicated that Katherine had a 60 db hearing loss[2] which in later years, possibly because of general deterioration, was assessed at 90–100 db. She was fitted with radio hearing aids, among the most sophisticated aids at that time. Her mother reported that in the early stages her language developed normally although slowly, and at eighteen months she could say seven words.

Matthew's history of diagnosis is far less straightforward. He, too, was born in 1978, and was an only child. When contemplating further children his parents consulted a genetic counsellor who suggested prematurity was the cause of his deafness. Initially it was thought that Matthew had a conductive hearing loss only and his failure to pass his nine-month screening test was attributed at the time to a cold and catarrh. He failed three consecutive tests and still pursuing the view that his loss was conductive, doctors suggested he underwent an exploratory operation to coincide with surgery to treat a narrow trachea. After specialists cancelled appointments and lost operation notes, investigations indicated that not only was the loss a sensori-neural hearing loss in addition to a conductive loss, but it was also severe. Matthew had a loss of over 70 db and his parents felt very bitter that having to wait until Matthew was nearly three years old before he was fitted with hearing aids had possibly unnecessarily delayed the development of his speech.

Pre-school placements

After one term in her village playgroup Katherine was placed on a part-time basis in a nursery school attached to a primary school to which she travelled several miles in a taxi provided by the local authority. The nursery staff felt that Katherine made a good initial adjustment and had coped well with the social and intellectual demands of the nursery school. Success in nursery school, educational assessments and recommendations led to Katherine being considered for

---

[1] For further details on approaches to communication with deaf children, see BATOD (1981a).
[2] For further details of classification of hearing loss, see BATOD (1981b).

ordinary school placement. When asked about Katherine's prospects her teacher had some reservations but said that she felt she would cope given a sympathetic and supportive attitude on the part of the school.

Katherine's mother put her name down at the school in their village: an open plan, single storey school in the centre of one of the village's modern housing estates. The school housed 272 four- to ten-year olds located in age-grouped bases. Katherine entered the newly formed 4+ unit staffed by a teacher and her NNEB trained assistant. There were 26 children in Katherine's base. The school, being only a few hundred yards from Katherine's home, was attended by Katherine's local friends. The peripatetic teacher approached the school before Katherine started and felt that the head welcomed the placement on the assurance that there would be specialist support. Katherine's teacher was slightly more apprehensive. She had attended a course run by the Service for the Hearing Impaired on the subject of 'The Hearing Impaired Child' and she had been left bemused by all the information. Katherine's mother was aware of her teacher's lack of experience of deafness and was anxious about how she would cope. She was also concerned for Katherine since she thought a noisy, open-plan setting might not be ideal for a deaf child.

At four and a half Matthew was attending playgroup four mornings per week and his playgroup leader described him as 'just one of the boys' and the 'sort of child who will get on well'. She was optimistic for his future in ordinary schools. Unlike Katherine's, Matthew's peripatetic teacher was not convinced at first that he should enter his local school, because of his difficulties in learning spoken English. However, despite her reservations the peripatetic teacher approached Matthew's local school, an open-plan single storey suburban school some fifteen minutes walk from his home. Matthew was to be placed in the modern infant unit of this 184 child split-site school. He entered the newly formed 4+ base of 29 children taught by an unassisted teacher. The staff seemed, according to the peripatetic teacher, to be 'very interested' and 'not at all skeptical' although concerned with the 'technical aspects of the hearing aids rather than Matthew'. Although she said she had stressed how very 'normal' Matthew's needs were, Matthew's reception class teacher was apprehensive and felt he might have special needs with which she would be ill-equipped to deal since her own experience of deafness was minimal. His mother too was anxious, especially about Matthew's communication skills.

> The only thing I am a bit worried about is the teacher asking him something and he won't understand what she wants. I'm worried that he won't be able to relate to the teacher what he has done at the weekends. I am very bothered about other children taking the mickey out of him.

PREPARING THE WAY

As with hearing children a certain amount of information exchange among parents and professionals took place. Katherine's peripatetic teacher made one visit to the school before Katherine entered and arranged for and accompanied her teacher on a visit to the nursery. Both nursery and 4+ teacher attended a one-day course together, organized by the Service for the Hearing Impaired, and took the opportunity to swap notes. Comprehensive medical and educational records were sent from the nursery to the school but the teacher felt that she preferred to get to know children herself.

Matthew's peripatetic teacher went into the school before he started but kept information exchange to a minimum. The playgroup staff regretted that although invitations were sent to the teacher and headmaster, they never visited Matthew in playgroup before school entry. Matthew's mother called in to the school several times before he started school, anxious to prepare Matthew and the school for his entry.

> He realizes something is going to happen. I've taken him twice on his own and he was frightened the second time. He didn't seem to understand. I think he thought he was being left. I've been about five times and I'm going again next week.

Communication in the school setting

KATHERINE

Before Katherine entered school her nursery teachers and parents described her spoken English as fluent though immature. Katherine would use, at most, five-word sentences like 'Daddy go in red car' and could tell her mother about events which had happened in her absence. At home her communication was mainly oral and she rarely used gesture. Her mother understood her and felt that other people would too. Inevitably school places new communication demands upon young children and this can be particularly difficult for deaf children. Moreover, many attempts to communicate by a deaf child can be difficult for an 'inexperienced' ear to comprehend and Katherine's reception class teacher said:

> I didn't really understand what she was talking about half the time but I'm getting used to her squeaks and noises now. Because she tends to gabble I ask her to repeat things and say it properly or she'll drag me along to come and explain. There's always uncertainty that I really don't know that she's understood everything I say.

Group work posed even greater problems than individual sessions, putting demands on the teacher to orchestrate and interpret:

> If she's talking to a group or if she's answering a question I've asked then I've had to try and make the conversation for her, to explain it to the other children so they don't just look at her blank and think there's something abnormal because she does make some funny noises sometimes. I just compensate for that really and just talk over what Katherine's already said.

A transcript of a classroom session when Katherine was five and a half years old exemplifies the difficulties. Katherine is asked to make her contribution for which the class has to be specially prepared by being asked to be particularly quiet. At first Katherine cannot make herself understood; she makes contributions but the teacher is unable to understand her speech, until her home-school book is used. Where possible, Katherine's contributions were transcribed by playing the tape over and over again. This should not imply that Katherine's teacher would have understood as much at the time.

> *Teacher:* Ssh can you all be very quiet whilst we listen to Katherine. Quickly, good that's much better.

Katherine: ... [very soft voice]

T: Katherine can you talk a bit louder 'cause I know you've got a much louder voice than that haven't you.

K: Yes

T: Yes. Talk a bit louder so that we can all hear you.

K: [three sentences that the teacher does not understand]

T: Do you want to go and fetch your little book so I can read to everybody what you did? It's on my...

K: [six word utterance not comprehensible]

Another child: Shall I get it her?

T: Yes it's on the chair because Katherine's mummy's written a little bit down about what you did because you had a bonfire didn't you?

One constraint operating here was the teacher's difficulty in understanding Katherine. The following piece is a further typical extract from the dialogue.

T: Let's have a look.

K: That sparkler. That... sparkler went up to the sky.

T: They went up to the sky?

K: Yes.

T: Did you like the rocket?

K: Yes the big sparkler. Round and round. Went up. Come down there.

T: Yes were they like stars?

K: Yes. Forgotten. No not stars sparklers. My little girl.

It is clear from this extract that Katherine is fluent and capable of long contributions, but these are often ungrammatical, even within the conversational context, and sometimes incomprehensible.

At five and a half and six and a half years old recordings showed her able to cope much better in an individual session, though the conversation based on the book they were looking at was better than that which was more free-floating.

However, when Katherine was six and a half years old, she still could not cope very well in the group. At one point the teacher is talking about when they were newborn babies in hospital they would have been known as 'Baby + Surname'. She goes around the class saying to each one: 'What would you have been called – Baby...?' None of them had any problem with this except Katherine, who after eight different ways of asking her, is still unable to answer and has to be told.

T: What would you have been called Katherine?

K: I don't know.

T: What's your second name?

K: [not comprehensible]

T: Baby Ash?

K: Ash.

T: What's your second name? What comes after Katherine?

K: [no response]

T: Baby who?

K: Ash

T: Ash De. Come on.

K: Ash De.

T: Ash De, I'll give you Ash De. Ash who? What's your second name? Katherine Ash?

Another child: Down.

K: Ash De.
T: Ashdown isn't it? So you would have been 'Baby Ashdown.'
K: [laughs]

With evidence of such difficulty for Katherine it seems likely that most of the rest of this group lesson would have passed Katherine by, including jokes such as the child who said he would have been called 'Baby Fox'. The teacher said, 'I wonder if they called you a Cub' – a joke which was enjoyed by the rest of the class.

MATTHEW

Matthew's mother had anticipated communication problems and was apprehensive before he started school. His English skills were less mature than Katherine's and he and his family supplemented their speech with gestures (not conventional signs) a lot of the time. He was using three-word sentences on average like 'Where you been?' and 'Mammy do it!' His mother noted that, 'his biggest problem at the moment is with understanding of what people are saying to him and making people understand what he wants to say'.

However, because of his limited speech, Matthew's mother was anxious that he would not be able to relate experiences to his teacher. This indeed proved a problem as his reception class teacher noted in interviews after Matthew's first term at school.

> Sometimes he'll come to me and try to tell me something that perhaps happened in the cloakroom – somebody may have pushed him but you see I can't understand what he's telling me. But you can tell by the tone of his, well I won't say voice . . . noise that he makes, that he's trying to get something off his chest. It's sort of indignant.

It appeared to his reception class teacher that Matthew found group sessions particularly difficult. In the recorded group session when Matthew was five and a half years old, there was no interaction between him and the teacher in the whole twenty-minute session. At the beginning of the transcript it was noted that, 'Matthew shows little concentration, stares out of the window at the other children, down at own feet, etc.'

In a nine-minute individual session there is little evidence of any shared understandings in their conversations and the only way the teacher and Matthew can develop a topic is to talk about pictures in a book, which takes up about a quarter of the session. Even in this Matthew is almost totally limited to naming the pictures in the book. Any deviation from this and he is stuck.

It is particularly important when considering transcribed excerpts of deaf children's interactions in the classroom to see whether there is a 'conversation strategy' underlying the answers they give. It is quite clear from observations of deaf children that even if they do not understand what is said to them many of them will often have devised ways of coping that will make them appear to behave as the other children, and often optimize their chances of giving the right answer even when they do not understand the question. Unusual replies or errors often give a clue to the way in which the child is coping with the classroom interaction. For example, in freer discussion, Matthew's conversational strategy appears to be to work out whether to say yes or no by looking at the teacher's face.

Sometimes this works and a pseudoconversation takes place. The problematic nature of these sessions can be seen by examining those examples when communication actually breaks down, such as in the following extract:

T: What did you do? Did you stay in bed all day?
M: [nods yes]
T: In bed all day?
M: [nods yes]
T: You didn't stay in bed all day did you? [She shakes her head]
M: No.

Matthew's strategy here seems based on working out what reply pleases or satisfies the teacher when he cannot understand the question she is asking. In this dialogue there is a further example where the teacher tries for eight separate turns to elicit a fact she herself already knows, that the mother had brought the child to school in a pushchair.

T: What did mummy bring you in this morning? How did you come to school?
M: [no response]
T: Come on. What did you have a ride in this morning?
M: [no response]
T: Was it the car?
M: [no response]
T: Was it, it wasn't was it?
M: [no response]
T: What was it?
M: Mummy.
T: Mummy had to push you didn't she?
M: Yes.
T: So what did you have a ride in?
M: [no response]
T: Pushchair, was it the pushchair?
M: No.
T: It was wasn't it?
M: [nods]

The most extreme example of Matthew trying to satisfy the teacher was where he said yes but actually shook his head to indicate no, thus one way or the other he would be right.

The recorded one-to-one session when Matthew was six and a half years old showed him to be more competent. However it is not totally clear whether they as a pair are better at managing to make it look like a conversation or whether he is actually understanding a lot more. The session is a discussion of a set of picture cards. The very first few turns of dialogue show that it is not possible to assume, without doubt, that Matthew understands what is going on.

T: What can you see what is happening in the picture?
   [points to picture cards]
M: That little boy's fell in the water.
T: The little boy's fallen in the water?
M: [nods]
T: Yes. What do you think he was doing?
M: Fell in the water.

T: Why was he near the water?
M: Little boy go in the water.

Matthew's first response is totally reasonable. However, in the light of his next two replies, which fail to answer the teacher's questions but just reiterate a description of the picture, it is not clear whether his first response was a reply to a question he had understood, or just based on an understanding that if someone points at a picture the best thing to do is to say something about it. It would, however, be wrong here to paint too negative a picture of Matthew's performance, as there is a vast improvement over the recording made when he was five and a half years old.

Teachers' attitudes to communication problems

Both reception class teachers felt that their approach with the children was individualized. However, whereas Katherine's teacher felt that this was very much part of her 'normal' repertoire, Matthew's teacher felt that this was something special she had to introduce as a concession to him. Of Katherine,

> I try to bring her forward when we're sitting in groups but I find that she can pick up what we're saying. I don't really teach them in groups in the class – I try to take them individually or group them into small groups. I usually take Katherine on her own and read on her own rather than read in groups or do activities on her own, unless it's something where I want her to benefit from other children. So whatever I do with Katherine I don't necessarily do with the rest of the children.

Of Matthew,

> Every night I go home and think, 'Will Matthew be able to do this or am I to think of some alternative'. You've got to find time really. You've got to treat him as an individual. I mean when you've chatted to the whole class about a robin or whatever you have to go over it with Matthew.

As his mother had feared before Matthew went to school, in the reception class he did not talk freely about things that had happened at home either spontaneously or even when questions were directed to him. He did not talk about school when he was at home either. It was felt by both Matthew's peripatetic teacher and his mother that a home-school diary would have been valuable, but that because his teacher seemed to resent any 'special' activities associated with Matthew they should not request it. This illustrates a further problem that can arise. The parents often feel that they are fortunate in that their child has been allowed to attend an ordinary school and therefore are reluctant to 'push their luck' and ask for any extra help. The school is told that the child is basically normal, and this is the basis on which the child is accepted. This makes it all the more difficult for requests for extra allowances to be made because of the child's disability.

Fortunately, in his second year in school, Matthew's new teacher recognized the need for a greater than average contact with his parents and she welcomed classroom door discussions with his mother.

Relationships with classmates

Before school entry both children were described as being outgoing and friendly towards other children, they had friends in their own neighbourhood who would not only attend the same school but also share in the same classrooms.

Once in school Katherine proved to be a very popular child having a number of friends with whom she shared playground and classroom activities. Katherine's teachers made a particular attempt to explain the nature of deafness to her classmates and the rest of the school, such that when Katherine took a key part in a play in assembly a special request was made of her schoolmates that they should listen carefully and be patient.

Katherine's English was felt to be understandable for the most part by other children and her teacher commented that if anything the children could understand Katherine better than she could. She also felt that there were positive aspects for other children of having Katherine in the class.

> A few of the older ones have been quite good for Katherine and good for them too, to explain things to Katherine, and get her to understand. They've actually used the microphone to help explain to Katherine.

Matthew's reception class teacher was more reserved. No special attempt had been made in school to explain Matthew's disability to the school. His teacher felt that the other children had a 'charitable' attitude towards him, expecting praise for playing with him. However, at six and a half Matthew's second teacher was more enthusiastic saying that Matthew had a special friend in the classroom, a 'motherly' figure – Janey – who 'sort of protects him' but out in the playground 'he tends to charge around with the boys!'

Educational attainment

The high expectations expressed for Katherine when she left nursery school were borne out in her first two years at school. She was described as a good reader:

> She can read and put expression in, she's very good, she obviously reads ahead enough to put expression into what she's reading and obviously does understand it very well because she talks about it afterwards. Odd sounds, the sound 's' is still a problem – it is only her pronunciation. She doesn't know the meaning sometimes and we have to go over what it means, but she will stop and ask this. I sometimes find where you've got the words that have a double meaning she perhaps knows one meaning but not the other. On the whole I would say that her reading is far better than the majority of her class – an above average reader.

Her teacher, however, expressed some fears that as she encountered more complex reading demands, especially those involving phonic skills and the comprehension of more complex vocabulary, she would have more problems. While deaf children are often able to build up a large sight vocabulary, they frequently have difficulty in building words up from individual sounds and their knowledge of the language makes guessing words from the context more difficult. Thus while they may succeed in the early stages of reading, they may have problems later on.

In Katherine's written work her teacher felt that she wrote as she spoke, missing out words in a telegraphic way, and omitting sounds that she could not hear.

If she is writing 'Mummy took me to the shops' she would write 'Mummy took to shops.' You read it and you're not quite sure what she meant.

Matthew's reception class teacher felt that his mother had emphasized written activities rather than 'actually talking to him', leading to his having gaps in his vocabulary which hampered reading, writing and number work in school. Despite this she felt his reading was quite good, although 'slightly behind.' However, when he was six and a half years old his new teacher felt that he was above average and ahead of his chronological age. She, too, felt that phonic work would produce problems.

On written work, however, as one might expect, his limited knowledge of spoken English impeded his progress.

He's behind his peer group in writing and reading although he's making big improvements. He's beginning to get meaningful sentences now, rather than just odd words here and there. He had to copy, 'If I was old enough I would like . . .' and then add on. He wrote [gets book out] 'I was old enough I would like to my motorbike going in'. That *is* poor for him. He understands what is said but he gets all the words in the wrong order.

In special schools for the deaf little use is made of television and radio programmes, but in normal schools these are widely utilized. At six and a half years old, Katherine watched two television programmes per week with her class and took part in one radio programme on music and movement. Katherine joined in with both. Matthew's class also watched the programmes and had a music and movement session. Both found great difficulties in concentrating and seemed to understand some programmes but switch off in others. Television and radio programmes accentuate the problems the children experience in group sessions especially since, unlike in a teacher-led group, it is not easy to check to see whether the children have understood, and also teachers are unable to modify the demands of the programme.

When the children were six and a half years old their teachers were asked if they had had to make any real changes to their classroom routines and curriculum to accommodate their deaf children. Katherine's teacher said,

I can't honestly say there's anything I do for her that I don't do at some point for the others.

Matthew's teacher said,

No nothing special. It's carried on quite normal. The only problem is when we're trying to explain what something means because when he first came to me I found his knowledge of the world, if you like, almost limited. He didn't even know the names of simple things in the kitchen. So we used to go on walks around the school and have little chats – that's all really.

Support given to the schools

At the start of their schooling Katherine and Matthew were visited once a week by a trained teacher of the deaf. Both Katherine's reception and subsequent teachers were happy with this degree of support.

Matthew's reception class teacher, however, felt that the degree of support she had received was insufficient, especially as she had no classroom assistant. She felt herself to be 'groping along', 'frustrated' and 'poorly prepared'. She didn't have the time to spend with Matthew on an individual basis which she felt to be necessary:

> I think he's going to need more help, extra help, I mean because the teacher's got to ask herself how much time you can spend with just Matthew when you've got 29 other children in the class.

Matthew's subsequent teacher was also frustrated, feeling that he needed more individual time than she could give. However, she seemed very pleased with the peripatetic help which she now received two sessions per week.

Conclusion

The comparison between Matthew and Katherine highlights two of the possible attitudes that schools can take. For Matthew's reception class teacher, integration was seen as synonymous with treating him as the other children, making few allowances, and the family were reluctant to request even small favours. In Katherine's case the school made a number of changes and saw the maintenance of daily contact with the family as essential. The class and school were told about Katherine and she was made a special case.

Even if the situation is ideal, however, it does seem that there remain inevitable problems, some of which have been indicated in this chapter. At a simple level, the child's deafness means it is actually difficult for him or her to hear what is being said. In addition, the effect of the deafness on the child's speech means that he or she is often difficult for the teachers to understand. At a more complex level the child's linguistic competence in English is restricted and he or she is less able than other children to describe and discuss experiences. It is also clear that a child can develop strategies to cope with the demands of communication in the classroom which can, in fact, serve to make it appear to both teacher and observer that he or she understands more than is actually the case.

While in discussion of specific issues with the teacher many problem areas were highlighted, it is interesting to note that in a more general sense the teachers expressed the feeling that all in all things were going well and that by the time they were six and a half the children had made an enormous amount of progress during their short time in school. When discussing her feelings about taking a deaf child into her class, Katherine's teacher admitted that she had been apprehensive but her fears had quickly dissipated. She felt that Katherine was well placed in a school and that for her own part she would not hesitate to take another deaf child if asked.

Matthew's teacher said that she would be quite happy to 'have another as nice as Matthew' and that her advice to another teacher taking him would be:

Take it slowly and as casually as you can and as normally as possible. Be sympathetic but don't treat him any different from the others. Don't make him stand out as something special.

References

BATOD, 1981a. 'Methodology in the education of hearing impaired children. Proposed policy statement', *Journal of the British Association of Teachers of the Deaf*, 5, pp. 8–9.

BATOD, 1981b. 'Audiological definitions and forms for recording audiometric information', *Journal of the British Association of Teachers of the Deaf*, 5, pp. 85–89.

6 Ben

Siân Downs, Annette Fletcher and Lorraine Fletcher

Ben is profoundly deaf and his first language is British Sign Language. This chapter tells how he has been educated at an ordinary primary school, aided by a signing interpreter. It has been written jointly by Siân Downs, his class teacher, Annette Fletcher, his sign language assistant, and Lorraine Fletcher, his mother. Lorraine writes about the background to Ben's education and her philosophy in Chapter 14. Ben began at his local school, Birdsedge, supported by Judith Collins, a deaf person whose first language was BSL. Shortly afterwards. Annette Fletcher, whose first language is English, but who is also a fluent user of BSL, took over. The chapter tells how Ben began to read, write and participate in all aspects of the curriculum through the medium of his own language, which in turn has given him access to English.

Preparations for Ben

Birdsedge is a village first school, which caters for approximately fifty pupils, aged from four to ten years, in three classes. During the last half-term of the academic year in which Ben was to start there, he and Judith began to visit the school every Friday afternoon with the other September starters. This was a good introduction; it gave Siân and Judith a chance to discover likely difficulties. None of the people involved at that stage thought that the situation would be easy. In June, Lorraine made some observations in the classroom on an ordinary day, hoping to pinpoint some of the likely problems and, perhaps, to arrive at some solutions.

OBSERVATION OF CLASSROOM ACTIVITIES: TUESDAY 18 JUNE 1985
1. *Pre-9.10*   Children arrive. Informal relaxed time, lots of social interaction between Siân and children and amongst the children. No problems.

2. *9.10*   Assembly. Usual format.
   Problem: suggest assembly is inappropriate for Ben; may be a good time for computer work with Judi.

3. *9.30*   (a) Children return. Preparation for TV: *Let's Go Maths*. Children sit round TV, teacher-led discussion about light and heavy. Lots of ideas emerge; all participating.
   Problem: Extremely difficult to include Ben and Judi here. Suggest good preparation essential. The teacher's booklet contains a brief summary of content of the programme plus very useful ideas for activities and further reading. Judi needs to be very familiar with the content of the programme and ideas behind it before the class watch it.
   Solution: Judi sees resource material in advance and discusses

it with Siân. Children watch the second transmission.
Lorraine records the first, takes notes for Judi, and watches
the programme with Ben at home before he sees it at school.
(b)   Siân explains activities planned for after TV. A lot of
instruction given orally.
Problem: Instructions are quite detailed and complex.
Solution: Judi has her own copy of the timetable and lesson
plans, with explanation of the aims of the activity.

4.   *9.44*   TV. The programme contains songs, a story as well as
mathematical experiments. No problem if adequately
prepared as outlined above.

5.   *9.58*   Siân directs children to activities. Discussion between Siân
and children to make sure all know what to do. No problem if
Judi is familiar with activities.

6.   *10.00*   Activities carried out in groups:
  • pictures of light and heavy things
  • working with a balance, finding out what balances 100 g
    weight, estimating first, with pre-printed charts to fill in;
    children work in pairs or together
  • weighing everyone in the class and making up a bar chart
    of the results
Children very busy and active. Lots of talk about what they
are doing.
Problem: Only that Ben would miss out on the very productive
chat between children.
Solution: Plenty of discussion with Judi about what he is doing
and everyone else is doing and why.

7.   *10.15*   Siân walks around groups. She supervises and chats with
children about their work. No problem: easy to check that
Judi and Ben are OK.

8.   *10.20*   Milk. Two children serve milk while the others are still
working. People are finishing, chatting, helping each other,
talking about what they've done, going round to see what
others are doing. Maybe this would be an opportunity, as
children finish their work, for Ben and Judi to talk to them
about it, to encourage communication between the children
and Ben and to make sure that Ben understands as much as
possible of what has been happening.

9.   *10.40*   Playtime.

10. *11.00*   Same activities, different children: groups rotate. Siân hears
reading.

11. *11.40*   Five minute warning. Children advised to finish off work. No
problem: this is easy for Siân to sign.

12. *11.45*   Tidying. Children ask to tidy up. All participate happily. Important Ben tidies up for himself. He mustn't see Judi as his personal slave.

13. *11.48*   Talk. Siân displays bar chart and talks about it with the class. *Problem*: Yes, but Judi can explain and discuss it with Ben at the same time.

14. *11.53*   Story.
Problem: Yes. See *Stories* below.

15. *12.03*   Dinner.

16. *1.05*   (a)   Children return, group chat, Siân talks about the afternoon's activities on the topic of *the sun*. Children discuss: 'What would happen if there was no sun?' etc. Children participate very actively.
Problem: Yes. See *Discussions* below.
(b)   Explaining activities. The plan: to plant cress in different lighting conditions to see how growth is affected. Each child also to plant a sunflower seed. Judi will have seen the lesson plan beforehand so can explain to Ben at the same time.

17. *1.27*   Activities. All groups working, rotating activities.
- copying from blackboard
- planting cress
- planting sunflowers
- drawing pictures of sunflowers

Again, a good chance for Judi to talk a lot to Ben about what is happening and the topic in general.

18. *1.30*   Computer. Siân offers use of computer. Two children volunteer. Two more take over, etc. Easy for Ben to participate here, using Judi only if necessary.

19. *1.45*   Temperature taking. Two children ask to record indoor and outdoor temperature using thermometer.

20. *1.53*   Recording. The children return and record the temperatures on the class chart. One draws a picture of the weather on another chart.
Problem: Need to compensate for lack of auditory information.
Solution: Ben and Judi are alerted when this sort of activity is happening so they can see for themselves and talk about it.

21. *1.54*   Instructions. Siân tells children not to disturb cress boxes. Make sure Ben receives the same instructions!

22. *2.08*   Choosing. First person finishes all set tasks and is allowed to choose what to do next. Ben's 'choose-time' might be a good time for Judi to leave him to mix and play with other children. Judi could perhaps use this time to get to know the

plans for the next day's work, look over the story for story time, look through topic information books etc.

23.   *2.15*   Playtime. Siân tells children to leave unfinished work for morning and explains that she won't be with the class after play. Siân can sign these simple instructions to Ben and Judi.

24.   *2.30*   Another teacher takes the class for music.
Problem: In general, unsuitable for Ben and Judi. May be a good time for teacher of the deaf or speech therapist to work with Ben, or for computer work.

GENERAL COMMENTS: FOR DISCUSSION AND DEVELOPMENT There are obvious areas of difficulty if we want to be sure that Ben has access to the same information and experience as the other children in the class.

1   DISCUSSIONS

A lot of interesting and important information gets passed between the children themselves and between teacher and children. Judi can lipread the teacher quite easily, but a group of chattering children is difficult to keep pace with.

Suggestions

(a)   Make, say, the first five minutes of any discussion a strictly one-at-a-time event, where all the comments are transmitted to Judi and to Ben either by signing or writing.

(b)   After this, let the discussion take its course normally, with Judi and Ben picking up what they can and the teacher signing important points or writing them down.

(c)   When the discussion has been planned in advance, Judi should be very familiar with the topic. This can be achieved by:

Lesson Plans. Judi will have a copy so will know what is likely to crop up.

Books. For each topic Siân will have selected appropriate books for the children to look through. Judi can borrow these so that she is very familiar with the information *before* it comes up in discussion and so that she will know how to get the information over to Ben.

Resources. There are also teachers' handbooks so that Judi can read up on the aims and ideas behind the topics.

Notebook. Ready access to a notebook will enable the teacher to get over information more quickly than signing, when it has to be conveyed quickly.

This will become less and less appropriate, as Siân's signing skills improve!

Good preparation in advance by Siân, Judi and Lorraine will make a lot of difference in the amount of information it is possible to get over to Ben and to the extent he will be able to benefit from being in an ordinary infant classroom.

2   STORIES

Again, good preparation is the key, but this time Judi is the best person to do it. Siân will make sure that Judi has the stories beforehand, in plenty of time to work out a BSL version for Ben to be signed to him at the same time as the story is read. Similarly with stories in TV programmes: Lorraine will prepare English version for Judi to translate.

The observations were copied and circulated, then discussed fully between Siân, Judith, the educational psychologist, Ben's peripatetic teacher and Lorraine, in plenty of time to arrive at a working strategy before the summer break. A copy of the Maths scheme teacher's manual was given to Judith; the peripatetic teacher offered to formulate a plan for the introduction of reading; Lorraine took responsibility for making the TV programmes accessible to Ben. Siân visited a nearby PHU to observe the work of the infant department there, because she had no previous experience of how the deaf were educated, and she wanted to see for herself what sort of work the teachers of the deaf at the PHU were doing with children of a similar age to Ben. She was also interested in observing how the integration of these children was achieved, within the school in which the PHU was located.

First days

Ben's start at school was trouble-free. He had the example of his big sister to follow; he went confidently and settled in well. Events and achievements were chronicled in a home/school book which we still fill in daily and which enables home to follow up, reinforce, extend and talk about school events and vice-versa.

There were a few social problems and a few discipline problems: something which hearing parents of deaf children find hard to come to terms with, and even harder to handle, is the 'three wise monkeys option': deaf children, by closing their eyes, can cut themselves off completely from the outside world. It is impossible to reason with a deaf child if he/she will not look at you, and during the early weeks at school Ben made some use of this option to avoid attempts by Siân and Judith to explain to him some of the niceties of social behaviour when he had failed to conform. He is naturally lively and enjoys boisterous physical play. This need was catered for at nursery school by the constant availability of large apparatus and wheeled toys, but within the confines of a small classroom, and when conversation is limited, it must be tempting to go for a more tangible form of contact, especially one certain to gain attention. It took Ben a while to learn that some of his new classmates were upset by it and that it was unacceptable behaviour in an infant classroom.

Although 'rules' were explained to him (when he would look), he never heard them being explained to other children. When we realized that this might make him feel 'singled out', Siân began to sign when explaining the principles of acceptable classroom behaviour to other children too. Ben became less defensive and more inclined to conform. Another aspect of life in an infant classroom which was different from his previous experience was freedom of choice. When he makes his own choice of activity, Ben's concentration is phenomenal and his skill in the execution of tasks remarkable. When set activities did not capture his imagination his concentration was poor and dedication to the task at hand virtually nil; he would perform a slaphappy attempt and sit back, unwilling to make any further effort. Here again, part of the problem may have been lack of access to peer group conversation and opinions. He did not hear Siân when she praised other children's work and he was missing out on the motivation provided by competition. But these problems were temporary. They subsided as he settled in and became more familiar with school life.

When Ben had been at school for about ten weeks, Annette Fletcher[1] took over from Judith as Ben's classroom assistant, and she is still with him at the time of writing (May 1986). Although no hearing person can bring to the job the native signing skills and instinctive understanding of a deaf child which a born-deaf adult can offer, Annette does have other skills: she can act as interpreter, making available to Ben as much as possible of what is going on in the classroom. Because her interpretation is silent (BSL cannot be accompanied by speech) her commentary is not disruptive, and at storytime the expressiveness of her interpretation actually enhances what Siân is reading. Ben is included in discussions; he knows what the other children are saying and he can make contributions without being restricted by his limited English. The programmes can be interpreted as they are broadcast. Although technically a classroom assistant, and always under Siân's direction, Annette can, and does, draw on her own experience as a reception class teacher; she knows what to expect from Ben and she knows how to motivate him into producing his best. Some examples, drawn from one 'news' book illustrate how this has been done with writing.

Bilingualism in the classroom

When he first started school Ben seemed willing enough to label his pictures (i.e. to copy the simple English sentences provided by Siân), as the other new starters were doing. He made some progress in the 'look and say' method of teaching reading advised by the teachers of the deaf. Nevertheless, progress was very slow and Ben seemed uninspired. He would talk about the pictures in his reading books with Judith, and he definitely enjoyed these and any other stories he came across, but the written word seemed to hold little interest for him. At the suggestion of Miranda Llewellyn-Jones[2] when Annette started work we took the opportunity of introducing Ben to literacy in his own language via a system of sign reading. Ben enjoyed the new approach, and took to it readily. Soon afterwards, the Service for the Hearing-Impaired decided that Ben was now getting adequate support, and the peripatetic teacher, who had been visiting Birdsedge on a weekly basis, after consulting with the staff, gave up her weekly commitment, though she remained involved in an advisory capacity. Over the next few months, we were able to observe several stages in the development of Ben's literacy and his own preference for the language and method of notation.

In November, the family had been to see a new baby, Kate (Ben's sign: KK, Figure 6.1). Kate and her parents live in Haworth, where there are still steam trains running. Ben told his news at news time in BSL, with Annette interpreting. Afterwards, Annette discussed his visit with him again, attempting to draw him out and extend the conversation for, at this time, Ben's contributions were relatively brief. She drew the signs he had used, and provided an English gloss,

---

[1] See Chapter 14 of this volume for details of Annette's background.

[2] From September 1985, Ms Llewellyn-Jones will co-ordinate the changeover to total communication by the Service for the Education of the Deaf in Leeds. Mary Brennan refers to her work at Derrymount School in Chapter 26 of this volume.

saw   trains   had

ice cream Ice cream

Figure 6.2   Story from a visit to Haworth.

Figure 6.1   Kate, a new baby.

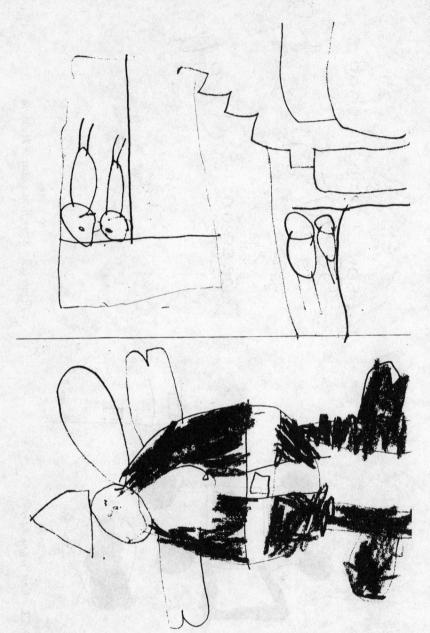

Figure 6.3 Christmas pictures.

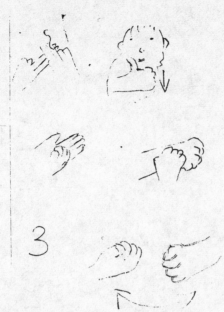

Figure 6.4 'Father Christmas present three car'.

which he copied (Figure 6.2), then read back the signs to Annette.

Towards Christmas, Ben drew the pictures in Figure 6.3, then told his story to Annette in sign, who again talked[1] with him at length, then drew the signs he had used in the conversation (Figure 6.4). At this stage, Ben, now accustomed to the routine, was co-operating by holding his hands still for Annette while she drew the signs. No English gloss was added for copying because a lot of time had been spent chatting; this activity was, and still is, considered very valuable in itself. The gloss would read: *Father Christmas present three car*. Ben read the signs back to Annette, then to Siân.

Having talked about activities at home at the weekend, Ben drew the picture in Figure 6.5, then himself chose the signs he wanted Annette to draw in his book, performing each for her to copy. Annette provided the English gloss; Ben copied, and read back the signs to Siân.

About two months later, having listened to his news, which by this time regularly consisted of a lengthy, expressive monologue in BSL, and interpreted it for the class, Annette was prepared to draw signs as usual, but Ben wanted to skip that stage and go straight to writing. Annette provided the words for him on a separate sheet as he signed phrases. Ben copied, a phrase at a time, and read the resulting story to Siân, in sign, at this stage remembering, rather than reading the words as such (Figure 6.6).

This stage coincided with his 'taking off' with reading. Following the recommendation of the Advisory Service, Siân had begun Ben's introduction to reading by aiming to establish a fairly limited sight vocabulary of nouns, gradually

---

[1] We use the word 'talk' here to mean 'have a conversation', not in its literal sense. Conversations between Annette and Ben are always in sign.

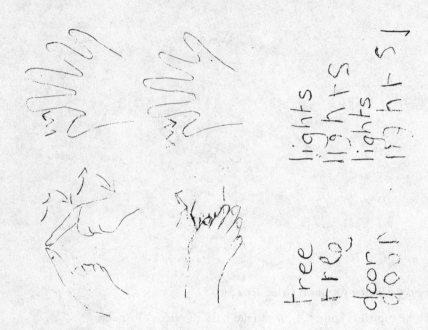

lights
lights
lights
lights

tree
tree
door
door

Figure 6.5 The Christmas Tree.

Figure 6.6 'Rope ladder I climb up and down made with wood and rope'.

adding colour names and making workbooks so that Ben could draw, acting on what he had read, 'a green car,' 'a red house', etc. Taking his interests into consideration, she had then borrowed a new reading scheme for Ben: *Crown Readers*, accounts of how a 'royal' family renovate their ramshackle castle. Again, the 'look and say' method was used; Ben learned all the main characters and words from the first book using flashcards and lots of varied word–word and word–picture matching games. After a few weeks he was thoroughly enjoying reading the books, and was working vigorously through them with Annette and Siân.

At the same time, he was developing an awareness of English, his second language. We made it clear to him that the books were written in English, 'hearing people's language', and hence that some of the words might be unfamiliar to him. He could be told that BSL ('your language') does not use – does not *need* – such words as *the, is, a*, but that English does. He was told that he could fingerspell these little words, or he could say them, but he must include them or the English would not make sense. The speech therapist worked on these little words with him in her weekly sessions, and on vowel sounds and easy consonants so that he could start to build words for himself. When he wrote his next story (Figure 6.7) he was already recognizing and saying the little function words in his reading.

After much discussion with, and agreement from, Ben about what they were doing and why, and accepting that he was trying to write English, Annette helped him to include the little English words she knew he could read. When he read this story back, he included *a, is,* and *the,* and used his voice to express them.

Before Ben wrote the story in Figure 6.8, the family had been for a very long walk in bitter cold up onto a nearby moor. It was too much for Ben, who became exhausted and had to be force-fed hot soup and a roll before he could stop crying and walk back the way they had come. He told the story at news time in a flood of BSL, then repeated it in 'points', which Annette helped him to note down. He took great delight in the resulting appearance of his story, and read it back to Siân as it appeared on the page, in BSL.

Figure 6.9 shows Ben's picture of a train going over the viaduct near Ben's house, on its way to Sheffield, where his 'Nanny' lives. Ben has a dictionary, which contains only those English words which he uses. At this stage he was starting to use the dictionary independently, finding 'train' in the *t* section, and checking on the spelling of 'the'. His 'English-consciousness' was growing; it was at this point, we think, that he began properly to understand that he has two languages, which can be used for different purposes. Although his story was told at news-time in BSL, and interpreted for the rest of the class as usual, when he sat down to write he seemed consciously, for the first time, to change mode and aim for English.

The only 'teacher interference' in the igloo story (Figure 6.10) was to suggest the insertion of 'an', and 'it is', and to translate Ben's modified sign into 'very big'. Again, a lot of checking and double-checking was done. No amendments are ever made without consultation with Ben and without Annette being absolutely sure that he understands the reason for the structure which finds its way onto the page. Ben was, at this stage, remembering which words were to be found in his dictionary, and asking for new words to be fingerspelled.

Figure 6.7   Story with English 'function words'.

Ben has made a start on independent writing. The only stumbling block is remembering spellings. Unlike a hearing child, he does not have any phonic clues (he cannot say to himself, for example, that 'car' must begin with the letter *c*), so he has to rely on his visual memory, even when he has internalized a lip pattern with an obvious start such as: 'farm'. Arthur Dimmock, a very accomplished, non-oral deaf person, writes: 'As for myself, words are seen in the mind as printed or finger-spelt... (Dimmock 1985).

In the beginning, this must be very hard work, but Ben is now remembering many more initial letters of words, so that he can be much more independent in the use of his dictionary, and he can write without consultation several very short words, including the first exclusively English ones he met in his early reading books. Because he now comes across the printed form of words so often as he reads, and in this context is remembering so many words without effort, his mental recall of the appearance of whole words should continue to improve.

Because he is learning English as a second language without hearing it spoken and internalizing rules of grammar, we are having to teach him rules as he comes across them in reading. He knows, for example, that there are two kinds of 'like', one of which means 'the same', the other... (This is far easier to explain to sign than in English: there are two different signs!) He understands that *-s* often

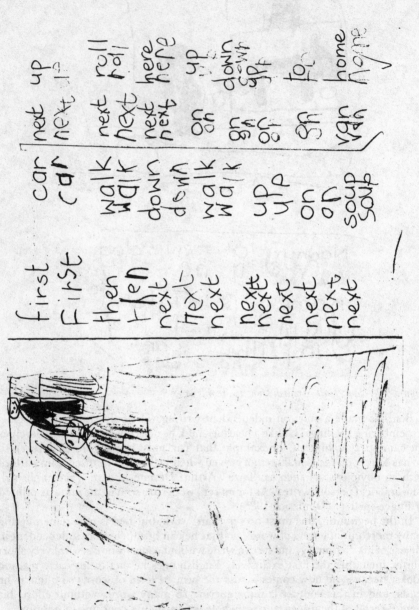

Figure 6.8   A walk on the moors.

I wenton the
trainNannys
d longWithyTitch

Figure 6.9 'I went on [to] the train Nanny's along with Titch'.

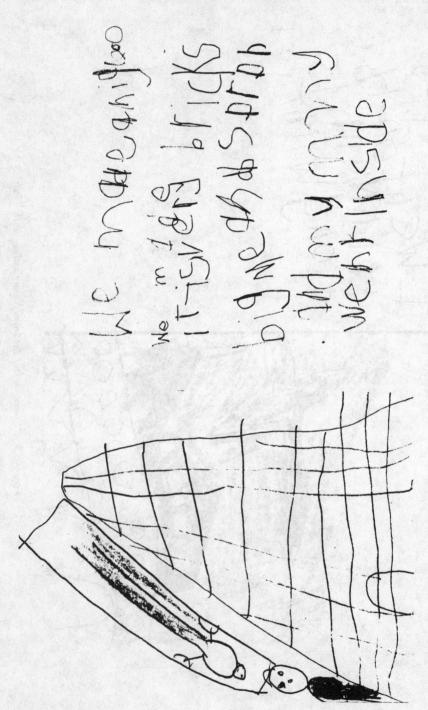

We made an igloo
We made
it is very bricks
bigneadsprob
and my mummy
weht inside

Figure 6.10 'We made an igloo we made bricks it is very big me and Sarah and Mummy went inside'.

indicates a plural and that *'s* is the possessive form. He knows that 'will...' indicates the English future tense and he is in the process of learning the difference between different past tenses, as in 'painted' and 'have painted', with the help of nuances in BSL which make the difference clear. Similarly, he knows the difference between the verb forms of, for example, 'run' and the continuous 'is running', again easily demonstrable in BSL[1]. Ben knows that English has a form 'I am, it is' etc, which is not used in BSL. We have made special booklets to reinforce the rules; we have provided illustrations from his own experience to make them more interesting for him. The *Ben book* has: 'I am Ben... I am 5... I am happy... I am a boy... I am sad... I am reading... I am building... I am strong... I am a witch... I am Superted' (He loves to dress up). The *like book* has an illustration of one sign on the front cover, with the word 'like' in red; if he opens the book this way he will find: 'I like Ben... I like dogs... I like swimming... I like ice cream... I like the baby', each time with 'like' in red. From the back, with the other sign and the word 'like' in blue, he will read: 'Like, like, like... This tree is like this tree... This house is like this house...' etc.

Ben is currently reading, competently, Book 4 of the *Crown* scheme. He understands what he reads and is enjoying the humour in the stories. If the words have signed equivalents they are signed, but Ben now adds voice or lip patterns to many of them, and where there are no signed equivalents other than fingerspelling he says the words. Hence, we see:

> *The* (spoken)
> *Queen* (signed)
> *said* (sign + lip pattern)
> *'I* (sign + speech)
> *have* (sign + speech)
> *the* (spoken)
> *paint.* (sign + speech)
> *We* (signed)
> *will* (sign + lip pattern)
> *paint* (sign + speech)
> *this* (sign + speech)
> *little* (signed)
> *window* (sign + lip pattern)
> *yellow.* (sign + speech)

This is how Ben has chosen to read. There has been no pressure on him to vocalize or to add lip patterns, simply an explanation, in his own language, of the differences between that language and the one he is now meeting in his books. English is not presented to him as superior, only different.

A full curriculum

Ben's progress in English has not been achieved at the expense of any other subject area, and language work has not been given extra priority for Ben, though of course it has required more preparation and back-up work from the teachers.

---

[1] We needed the help of experts here, and we are very grateful to Miranda Llewellyn-Jones and Syd Stone for helping us to clarify these differences.

English is used in reading, writing and at flashcard time, and during the weekly half-hour speech therapy session. Every other aspect of the curriculum is taught in BSL. Hence what Ben gets out of, and what he puts into, environmental work, Maths, TV follow-up and project work, is as far as possible the same as the other children in the class. Experiments are discussed thoroughly in BSL, before they are 'written up' in English, so that even if Ben does not understand the precise meaning of every word he writes, he does have thorough understanding of the meaning of the sentences.

There is no attempt to scale down the curriculum for Ben. Siân consciously aims for him to receive the same quality of teaching as the other children in the class. By and large, his language is adequate for this, and by making the full curriculum available in this way, we find that the gaps which still exist in his use of language are filled in: at nursery, for example, Lorraine was aware that Ben was a little confused about the signs for 'in front of' and 'behind'. At school, a few weeks' exposure to the concept-building activities of a well-thought-out Maths scheme sorted out this problem. Ben had little idea of his own position in relation to the rest of the world; topic work first on hot countries, then on cold, now on transport, have begun to enlighten him; his vocabulary is also expanding as his knowledge of the world widens.

The television programmes used by Siân in the classroom are *Thinkabout* and *Words and Pictures*. These are usually prerecorded for Ben at home and watched there before they are shown at school. Deaf people do not hear TV, radio, or other people's conversation, and many of them cannot read, so their general knowledge is often limited to situations within their own experience. TV can bring wider experience, but only if programmes are interpreted or properly explained. We find that the more often Ben sees them, the more likely he is to take in and retain the information they offer. He is not bored by repeated showings of *Words and Pictures*. As he becomes familiar with the story, and as his reading improves, he takes more notice of the script, and signs or mouths familiar words. Co-operation with home in this way means that the extra time does not have to be found during the school day at the expense of other subject areas.

Ben shows no sign of being overwhelmed by the amount of information or the number of different activities offered at school, and is extremely keen to learn. Siân finds that it is impossible to go too fast for him or to give him too much to do.

At a recent concert given by the school, Ben participated competently in the Maypole dancing, gave a mime of the nursery rhyme 'Jack and Jill' with a friend, performed a beautiful signed version of 'Hey Diddle Diddle' with his class, watched as three little girls performed 'Mary, Mary, Quite Contrary', in sign, and enjoyed two (largely visual) short mystery plays. The rest of the performance was interpreted for him.

He sometimes insists on participating in events which, on the face of it, are not much use to him, such as singing. Lorraine maintains that, if it is his free choice, he should be allowed to join in. He now occasionally accompanies the pop groups he sees on TV and has added a manic punk rocker to his repertoire of 'other beings'. In Assembly, which he still insists on attending, the story is interpreted for him, and the hymns if he seems interested. Sometimes he would rather have a conversation with Annette; because this is in sign, the singing is not disrupted. He is aware of the uses of sound and hearing, and is slowly building up a picture of the way life is for hearing people and the way it differs from his own.

Social relationships

Some concern was expressed by Ben's peripatetic teacher and the Special Education Adviser that having his own helper might give Ben an exaggerated feeling of self-importance. For a while, that was the case. To alleviate this, when Ben is able to, or would benefit, from coping on his own, Annette works elsewhere in the school. Wherever possible, she works with a group of children including Ben rather than with Ben alone, although she is always available if he wants to chat.

Ben is expected to behave as the other children do. The one exception to this is tolerance of his 'noises'. Some concern was expressed, again by the teachers of the deaf, that his natural, and unsuppressed, vocalizations might disrupt the class. In fact, the children have got used to them; everyone knows which sounds are for Ben's benefit and which expect a reply or a response, and Ben now accepts that there are some situations where it is inappropriate to use his voice.

The other children are learning various ways to relate to Ben. In his class there are several who now sign quite well; others get through using gesture and mime plus a few signs they have picked up from Ben, Annette, Siân or other children. Some, and Ben has now learned who they are, enjoy just the kind of rough physical play that he does, and relate to him that way. Watching him at a mixed-age table at lunchtime it is possible to see several strategies in operation, plus a lot of signing: the other children accept that this is Ben's language; they enjoy learning from him and from each other and use their lunchtime contact with him to practise what they have learned. Their parents report increased interest in deafness itself and in sign language: they ask to watch the few TV programmes which include signing.

Siân feels that it is essential that she is skilled enough in sign language to make herself understood to Ben; Annette makes it her duty to take every opportunity to improve her skills in BSL; the other staff choose to communicate with Ben in their own way. The lunchtime supervisory staff, for example, felt that they wanted 'to know some signs' before Ben started school. Lorraine taught them some, but also pointed out to them that they possessed quite a few non-verbal communication skills already; they were able to list mime, facial expression and gesture. Ben is very quick to respond to these techniques; he realizes that some people do not sign but still have interesting and important things to communicate. Conversations without 'proper signs' are commonplace now, both within and outside the school.

Conclusion

Despite everyone's efforts, Ben's linguistic environment is still restricted, and we feel that this will inevitably slow down his learning as it did at preschool level before Judith came to work with us. Education means more than the three Rs and the learning of facts and skills. It should comprise an introduction to the whole spectrum of experiences, social as well as intellectual, that children need to prepare them to make a useful contribution to society as they grow up. Talking with other people is one of the surest ways of developing a wider knowledge of them and of their needs and values. For as long as Ben is educated with hearing children only, no matter how good that education is on the face of it, he will be missing out on those aspects of education which require widespread complex communication. Only an environment where there are many more people especially children, who can communicate fluently in his language, can provid this, and this is why we do not see Birdsedge as a realistic long-term answer t Ben's educational needs. The Advisory Service for the Hearing Impaired i Kirklees does not appear to approve of Ben's presence at Birdsedge. It is unlikel that any more deaf children will be placed there, so before long, Ben will transfe to a special school or unit. We hope that one will be found which will continue t exploit, as we have, British Sign Language as a language of instruction an communication in the classroom.

Reference

Dimmock, A. 1985. 'Thought processes: introspections on the mind of the deaf', paper presented t the International Congress on the Education of the Deaf, Manchester.

7 Tools for learning and communicating: microcomputers and children with disabilities

Tim Southgate

In this chapter, Tim Southgate describes the way that microcomputers can be used to enhance the learning experience of children with disabilities, by describing work with five individuals. Some children use them mainly as a means to write, and thereby participate in an ordinary curriculum. For other children, microtechnology offers a means to communicate with a wide range of people. For others again, it provides a way to understand and overcome difficulties in learning of a kind that would be hard to envisage a few years ago. For all these children, microtechnology has been a liberating force.

Introduction

Microtechnology has, in recent years, become all-pervasive in most economically advanced societies. The lives of all of us, even those who have never touched a computer are affected in many ways by this new technology. Microelectronic devices appear in many guises, controlling anything from washing machines to jumbo jets, checking library books and producing instant bank statements. In offices, they inhabit word processors and are widely used for accounting and stock control. Recently, the telephone directory enquiry system too has become computerized. In these examples, and in many others that could be given, the computer is used because of its ability to handle information more effectively and reliably than other systems.

It is primarily because computers are so effective at handling information that they are of such potential benefit to the education of children with special needs. Every child with special needs is different and has different problems. However, probably the most common factor to be found among them is that the ability to handle information is in some way impaired. A physical impairment may make writing or speech difficult or impossible; a sensory impairment may prevent a child from receiving visual or auditory information. Those with moderate or severe learning difficulties may have difficulties in processing information. Even some severe behaviour problems may in part be due to an impaired ability to receive and respond appropriately to social information.

Much of the early experience of microtechnology in special education was gained in schools for children with physical disabilities. Many of these schools had, for some time, used mechanical devices to help children communicate and write. When the mass production, and the consequent falling cost, of microcomputers brought them within reach of schools, it was schools for children with physical disabilities with their often greater financial resources which were able to invest earliest in this emerging technology. A number of imaginative teachers began enlisting the help of computer programmers to use computers for the benefit of their children. As the earliest motor cars imitated the horse-drawn carriages that preceded them but then rapidly developed to offer liberation and an enormous range of new opportunities to the user, so the application of microtechnology initially tended to emulate the functions of those devices and aids already in use. Very quickly, however, they were developed to offer opportunities for communication and learning that would not have been imagined only a few years earlier.

The past few years have demonstrated that the learning experiences of children with physical disabilities can be greatly enhanced by the skilled and sensitive use of computer technology. Initially, some saw computers taking on the role of an instructor or teacher's assistant. In this role, the computer sets tasks and the child is expected to respond. Successful responses are usually rewarded with flashing lights or exciting noises, ticks or smiling faces. Incorrect responses may receive rude noises, crosses or unhappy faces. Much early excitement over the use of computers resulted from claims that computers could go on indefinitely providing these tasks with unfailing enthusiasm; the child would receive a consistent response every time. There is undoubtedly some value in providing children with stimulating and consistent rewards. However, it is this very consistency of response that makes such use of the computer largely inappropriate for children with special needs (or for that matter, for those without!). Eliciting responses from a child often requires great sensitivity and subtlety on the part of the teacher. There is no way in the foreseeable future that computers will come to possess the qualities necessary to take over the teacher's role.

Computers can, however, emancipate the learner by removing or alleviating blocks to performance. The task of writing a story, for example, involves the co-ordination of a number of quite complex skills. Holding a pen or pencil, letter formation, spelling, sentence construction are all required in addition to the actual creation of the story itself. A deficit in any of these skills may impair success in the others. For some children with physical disabilities the main need may be for some form of written output which will permit participation in the curriculum. Before the arrival of computers, many children with physical disabilities used electric typewriters as writing aids. A range of options such as keyguards, 'jumbo' typefaces, expanded keyboards, magnifiers and switch systems were available for those who found the ordinary keyboard too difficult to operate or the output hard to see. However, these devices were frequently unreliable and inflexible and the limited output rate and control that children could achieve meant that their efforts were often frustrated.

It was soon apparent that using a microcomputer as a word processor could help overcome many of the limitations of the earlier mechanical writing aids. The ability to work on a screen instead of paper resolves many frustrations and helps increase motivation. A number of special word processor programs have been developed to enable those with physical handicaps to write using a computer. The most sophisticated of these is Patrick Poon's MAC Apple.[1] This program is designed to improve the communication rate of people with severe physical impairments. It is immensely adaptable and so can be closely personalized to the

---

[1] Enquiries about MAC Apple may be directed to Patrick Poon, ACCESS Centre, Hereward College, Bramston Crescent, Tile Hill Lane, Coventry CV4 9SW.

needs of the user. Output rate is increased by the use of personalized wordlists that enable whole words or phrases to be entered into the text which, when required, can be saved on a disk. The system can be operated using only a single switch, two switches or an eight-way switch, by using the ordinary keyboard or a special keyboard.

In the first three of the examples that follow, the use of this program by children in school is described. However, a word processor program is not suitable for the many children with physical disabilities who have additional learning or sensory disabilities. The two other examples illustrate how the microcomputer can help overcome blocks to both learning and communication.

Jennifer

Jennifer's hand function is severely affected by athetoid cerebral palsy. At the age of thirteen she could use an electric typewriter with an expanded keyboard, but this was frustratingly slow and, since she could not load the paper herself or rub out her mistakes, it gave her little independence. Although Jennifer attended a special school she had the ability to benefit from the curriculum offered in a local ordinary school. However, she needed a more effective means of writing if she was to gain access to that curriculum and if she was to keep pace with the work.

A national charity was persuaded to buy Jennifer her own MAC Apple system consisting of an Apple computer, a disk drive and monitor, a printer and the MAC program on a disk. The computer was fitted with a keyguard. This, as well as the program's facility for one-handed use, made it possible for Jennifer to use the ordinary keyboard. For the first time, she was able to correct her mistakes and edit her work before she committed herself to paper. In addition, she was able to edit the wordlists to include names and words she used most often and these could be added whole to the text whenever she wished.

MAC Apple enabled Jennifer to progress so that eventually she was ready to move to an ordinary school. Unlike a special school, the timetable in the comprehensive school meant that she would be involved in a good deal of moving about for different lessons. Her whole MAC Apple system was mounted on a trolley which could be wheeled around the school and, on her MAC disk, Jennifer created separate files for each subject. Thus, she had files of work for maths, for English, for science and for various other subjects. Once a file was loaded, she could look back through her previous work by moving the cursor just as other children turn back through the pages of their books. At the end of a lesson Jennifer saved the work she had been doing on the disk and when she arrived at her next classroom, she loaded the subject file appropriate to that subject. A classroom assistant pushed the trolley around and connected the computer to the electricity supply at each location. The reliability of this new technology is such that the system continued to operate without difficulty for two years in spite of being trolleyed along corridors, carried up and downstairs and moved over rough terrain between different classroom blocks in all weathers.

Although Jennifer could handle the writing tasks she was faced with in school, there remained the problem of how she was to do her homework. To overcome this problem, a second Apple system, again provided by a charity, was installed in Jennifer's room at home. All she needed to take home were her textbooks and her MAC Apple disk.

The computer has made it possible for Jennifer to benefit from the much broader curriculum offered by a large comprehensive school. In making it possible for her to attend a mainstream school, this technology has also enabled her to share in the much richer social experiences on offer there. By the age of sixteen, she had made sufficient progress to be able to move on to further education. She now attends a college of further education and her computer is with her, helping her maintain her progress.

Sally

Like Jennifer, Sally, who is seven, has athetoid cerebral palsy although her movements are more severely affected and she needs help with feeding and many other activities. Sally, too, needs a means of writing so that she can practise and develop her language skills. This is particularly important as her speech is very difficult to understand and the written word may eventually provide her with an important means of general communication. Sally's movements ruled out the use of an ordinary keyboard, even with a keyguard and so an enlarged or 'expanded' keyboard was constructed. Incorporated into this is a variable delay on the keys so that Sally must maintain contact with a key for a set period before it activates the computer. The delay helps reduce accidental key presses and so Sally gains greater satisfaction from her work. Such a satisfying outcome is highly motivating. This is perhaps one of the most important contributions of the computer to the education of children with severe and multiple disabilities. Sally has now moved from the special school into her local primary school where her computer and expanded keyboard are in the classroom with her.

John

For both Jennifer and Sally, the computer made possible the development and greater use of language. This has been particularly important for John because, in addition to his physical disability, he is profoundly deaf. John is twelve. He can write but his athetoid movements make writing laborious and the results disappointing to one with such ability.

When he was very young, John's mother began teaching him to sign in order that they should communicate. At the special school he attended, his language was developed through individual signing work. The signs John learned are those of the Paget Gorman Sign System. Unlike British Sign Language, which has its own syntax, PGSS is a signed translation of written English. Since the use of this sytem is not widespread, its use brings with it the major disadvantage of limiting communication with the majority of deaf signers. However, because of his writing difficulties, it seemed likely that John would need to use an aid for communication and writing. For this, he would need to develop his use of language and, in particular, written English.

Before the arrival of the computers, John's teachers had tried a number of ways to enable him to produce more written work. He used magnetic letters and he had an electric typewriter. However, he found these methods uninspiring and his output remained very disappointing. His enthusiasm developed quickly, however, when he was introduced to the MAC Apple system. In part, his eagerness to work on the computer was due to his interest in the technology itself. He loved putting the bits and pieces of the system together and getting everything ready for use although a few disks suffered as a result!

John worked with his teacher, discussing through sign what he would write. He became skilful in the use of the wordlists and his reading age stayed closely in line with his chronological age. At the age of nine, his future placement was considered. It was felt that he needed more stimulation and a broader curriculum than could be provided in a small special school. A residential school for the deaf was proposed but this had no experience of children with physical disabilities. He would also have to change his sign system and, worst of all for John, be away from home. Instead, a third course was adopted. John now attends a local middle school and is in a class of children of his own age. He has an Apple computer with him on a trolley and uses this for most of his written work. For much of the time he has a signing classroom assistant who interprets the lesson content for him. In six months at his new school John has produced enormous quantities of written work. The computer has become an important element in his education. He has made many new friends and some of these are even learning to sign.

Sara

Sara's history was quite normal and she was making progress in her local primary school until, at the age of seven, she was devastated by a severe brain injury which left her in a coma for several weeks. She emerged very handicapped both physically and intellectually. She could still walk although very unsteadily but she was unable to sit unaided and frequently missed the chair as she tried to sit down. She could hold a pencil and bring it into contact with the paper. However, she found it impossible to organize her movements into writing and at best produced random marks and squiggles. She could, however, point quite accurately and so, after some practice, was able to press the keys on an ordinary computer keyboard without too much difficulty. A program was produced that enabled Sara to write words on the computer screen in very large letters. As she pressed a key the corresponding letter was drawn very large on the computer screen. Words of up to ten letters could be written and, by pressing the space bar, added to a sentence that was built up at the bottom of the screen. Sara could print out this sentence to provide a permanent record of what she had written.

Initially, Sara needed a considerable amount of help with this task. She could not recall letter names and was unable even to spell her own name. Having agreed with her what was to be written, her teacher would point out the appropriate keys for her to press. In this way, she began very slowly to rebuild a sight vocabulary. To help her progress further, the program was modified so that words she did not know could be displayed at the top of the screen to be copied. The keys on the computer keyboard were covered with self-adhesive labels bearing lower-case letters of a similar style to those on the screen. Without help, Sara had great difficulty in copying the letters of the word displayed in the correct order. She usually included all the letters but in what seemed to be a random sequence. Further assistance was therefore provided in the form of a small cursor which appeared under the letter to be copied. As the correct key was pressed, the cursor moved along to the next letter. Unfortunately, this visual indication did not improve Sara's ability to copy letters in the correct sequence and, indeed, sometimes its presence appeared only to confuse her further. She might ignore the cursor altogether or she might copy the letter immediately following the one indicated. On occasions, she appeared to see the cursor as part of the letter to be copied and so 'u' became 'y' and 'o' might become 'g'. It was apparent that Sara's ability to relearn was being constrained, not only by her impaired movement but also by her difficulty in handling visual information.

To try to overcome this block to learning, the program was developed further to incorporate electronically produced speech. A number of options were provided so that the teacher could elect to have each letter spoken as it was typed, each word spoken as it was added to the sentence or both letters and words spoken. The quality of the speech was not good and this dictated that letter names and not letter sounds be spoken. But it was clear enough for this program, where its purpose was to reinforce the child's own language and not to provide a means of communication. As Sara pressed a key she heard the corresponding letter name spoken and it was hoped that this auditory feedback would help her to make a correct choice. If she was right, she would be rewarded by hearing the intended letter spoken and, if she made an error, she would immediately be made aware of this so that she could delete the letter and try again. However, since it might be that she had intended to copy the letter spoken even though this was not the next letter in the word, Sara was not greatly helped by speech used in this way. Instead, a further option was added to the program so that, after a key was pressed, instead of speaking the corresponding letter, the computer would announce the name of the next letter to be copied. Sara found this much more helpful; it was apparent that she had far less difficulty with auditory than with visual information. To give her as much success as possible, the program was set so that, when copying, a letter would be written on the screen only when the correct key was pressed. This helped Sara to build up confidence and, as she progressed, it was possible to withdraw this support gradually. Eventually it became possible to reduce the amount of auditory assistance that was provided and her confidence then received a further boost from the knowledge that she can succeed alone.

Sara is now nearly fourteen. Her progress has been very slow but she has built a sight vocabulary sufficient for her to write some sentences of her own. There has been some natural recovery from her injury, but it is clear that her progress, and perhaps her recovery, have been promoted by the skilled and sensitive use of the computer. The computer helped Sara in three ways. First, it enabled her to write and to have the satisfaction that building up a book of written work can provide. Second, it revealed something of the nature and extent of the learning disabilities that were the result of her injuries. Third, it made possible teaching strategies that could not have been attempted using traditional technologies.

Peter

Peter was born with severe athetoid cerebral palsy and has spent all of his thirteen years in a wheelchair. He has no speech and communicates by making noises and gestures and by pointing at a variety of symbols, pictures and words on a board attached to his wheelchair. Although these enable him to convey his basic needs and some ideas, his communication is greatly restricted.

Over the years, a number of communication devices and systems had been tried with Peter. None of them proved very successful. Sometimes, there were too few staff to provide the individual attention he required. Sometimes the equipment was unreliable. Often he lacked the skills or maturity necessary to operate it. When microcomputers became available, Peter was seven and another effort was made to provide him with an effective means of communication.

It seemed likely that if Peter was to communicate he would do so in writing and, for this, he would need to become literate. Attempts had been made to teach him to read using flashcards and other such devices. However, none of these gave him any written output and so his learning remained largely passive.

To accommodate his motor difficulties, Peter was provided with a very large keyboard with a built-in variable delay. As he was a virtual non-reader, the large-letter writing program developed for Sara was used. Peter did begin to recognize some letters and he made great efforts to copy words. However, although the keys were large and spaced widely apart, he had the greatest difficulty in controlling his hand sufficiently to reach most of them unaided. He was also still very immature and the length of time he could concentrate on this task was very limited. He seemed to derive most satisfaction from the effects of pressing the full stop at the end of the sentence which caused the sentence to be printed out.

It was apparent that Peter was not ready either physically or intellectually for the task of constructing words and sentences letter by letter. If he was to build sentences he needed a means of doing so which enabled him to use whole words that he could recognize. One computer program that can be used for this is Prompt 3. Prompt 3 is a simplified, large-letter word processor which can either be operated from the keyboard or using a Concept Keyboard.[1] In the latter mode, children press areas on a paper overlay covering the Concept Keyboard and whole words appear on the screen. The teacher can make the areas to be pressed any size and any vocabulary can be included. Pictures, symbols and colours as well as words may be used on the overlay so that the program may be set up to match the child's physical and intellectual abilities. Files on words to match different overlays can be saved on disk.

Although Peter found it easier to reach some areas of the Concept Keyboard, he was still limited to using only a very few words. Although direct selection is clearly preferable to other methods of choosing words and letters, in Peter's case there seemed no alternative but to provide him with a program he could operate with a single switch. After some trial and error, it was found that he performed best with a foot-operated switch attached to his wheelchair. A program was devised in which a number of words in large letters were displayed on the screen. A large cursor scanned down the side of these words at a speed determined by the

---

[1] The Concept Keyboard is a touch-sensitive pad, either A4 or A3 size, divided into a large number of individual cells. The programmer can allocate any value he/she wishes to each cell or group of cells. The surface is overlayed with pictures, symbols or words, so that, for example, touching a picture will produce the same picture on the computer monitor, or indeed anything the programmer wishes within the computer's capabilities.

teacher. When the cursor was alongside the word he wanted, Peter had to press his switch. The word was then added to a sentence which was built up at the bottom of the screen. Peter became quite proficient at selecting words but clearly did not find the activity very exciting. Although the teacher would try to ascertain what he might like to write about, Peter had no direct control over the very limited vocabulary from which he was asked to choose. The one aspect of the program that he did find exciting, however, was when the speech synthesizer was used to speak out the completed sentence. In particular, he was highly motivated when asked to build up a sentence or 'message' which was to be spoken out to someone elsewhere in the room.

Peter was so keen on this activity that a new approach was tried using the Concept Keyboard. Instead of building up sentences on the screen, words and phrases were spoken out directly as he pressed them. To increase the vocabulary, a layering system was used so that one area could be used to produce up to six different utterances. By pressing a special square, different layers were selected. Peter was thus provided with a voice. Of course, it was an electronic voice and the range of utterances remained limited, but nevertheless it enabled him to speak directly to others for the first time.

Since the computer had to be connected to the mains electricity supply, people had to come to Peter in order for him to communicate with them. Peter had by this time been supplied with a powered wheelchair and a special switch had made him independently mobile. This made it possible for him to take his 'voice' with him as he moved around the school. A portable computer was obtained and mounted with a speech synthesiser in a strong box on the back of Peter's wheelchair. Speakers were fitted underneath his seat and power for the system was provided by re-chargeable batteries. A large A2-size expanded keyboard was mounted in front of Peter on his wheelchair in place of his communication board. To prevent him pressing the Concept Keyboard unintentionally, this was covered by a guard made of plastic sheet in which holes had been cut. Equipped with this transportable communication system, Peter can now go where he chooses within the building and, by pressing on his board, he can speak to those he meets. This system has several advantages over his communication board. He can communicate over some distance and with those who are unable to read or who cannot see the words and symbols on his board. Originally, both parties had to look at his board, so that the non-spoken elements of the interaction were missed. Now he can communicate face-to-face.

A powerful and flexible tool

In different ways and to different degrees, the computer has enabled these children to overcome both physical and intellectual blocks to learning and communication. The computer is not, and probably never will be, a replacement for the teacher. But used with skill and sensitivity, it can provide the teacher and the learner with a powerful and flexible tool for learning and can greatly enhance the learning opportunities of children with physical and communication difficulties. It can provide access to a wider curriculum and so encourage the greater integration of children with disabilities into mainstream education.

The computer by itself can do none of these things. It is the combination of good computer software and the skills of the teacher that make these developments possible. In order for software to meet the needs of children with disabilities it must be very flexible so that it can be closely adapted to the abilities of the individual. To exploit such software teachers need training.

To realize the potential benefits of the computer a number of requirements must be met. First, a continuing programme of software development is needed with programmers working in close co-operation with teachers. Secondly, teacher must have the opportunity to acquire and develop the skills necessary to apply the technology appropriately. Training in the use of good software takes more time than has perhaps been appreciated. Thirdly, children must have the hardware. Much has been done in the past few years to ensure that all children have access to computers. However, many children with disabilities need their own machine tailored to their particular requirements. Many need another at home as well. The cost of quite powerful computers continues to fall and there is now no reason why any child with a disability who needs a personal computer system for communication and learning should not be provided with it. Finally, every handicapped child has different communication needs and it is important that these should be carefully assessed. Multi-professional assessment provides an opportunity for this but the professionals concerned should be familiar with communication handicaps and the contribution that alternative systems can make to their alleviation.

Further reading

Behrmann, M. M. 1985. *Handbook of Microcomputers in Special Education*, Windsor, NFER/Nelson.

Goldenberg, E. P. 1979. *Special Technology for Special Children*, Baltimore, University Park Press.

Goldenberg, E. P. 1984. *Computers, Education and Special Needs*, London, Addison Wesley.

Hawkridge, D., Vincent, T. and Hales, G. 1985. *New Information Technology in the Education of Disabled Children and Adults*, London, Croom Helm.

Hogg, R. 1984. *Microcomputers and Special Educational Needs: a Guide to Good Practice*, Stratford upon Avon, National Council for Special Education.

Hope, M. (ed.) 1986. *The Magic of the Micro*, London, Council for Educational Technology.

Perkins, W. J. (ed.) 1983. *High Technology Aids for the Disabled*, London, Butterworth.

Ridgeway, L. and McKears, S. 1985. *Computer Help for Disabled People*, London, Souvenir Press.

Rostron, A. and Sewell, D. 1984. *Microtechnology in Special Education*, London, Croom Helm.

Saunders, P. 1984. *Micros for Handicapped Users*, Whitby, Helena Press.

Southgate, T. N. 1986. *Equipment for the Disabled – Communication*, Oxford, Mary Marlborough Lodge.

8 Microtechnology and students with disabilities in further education: the Hereward Project

Janis Firminger

Opportunities for people with disabilities to learn after school have increased in the last few years, although they are still severely limited, and often available only in segregated settings. In this chapter, Janis Firminger discusses the way in which microtechnology can further extend these opportunities. She cautions against the attractions of concentrating all one's attention on technology. It can only emancipate people in an environment more generally committed to equalizing opportunities for people with and without disabilities, and committed to giving them control over the choice and use of the technology. Solutions foisted on people against their will are no solutions. But carefully designed and planned, microtechnology can help people with disabilities to build autonomous, fruitful lives for themselves.

Introduction

Hereward College is a national college, offering a range of further education courses to residential and local day students who have disabilities, alongside care, medical and physiotherapy services. Some students follow ordinary FE courses, based at the college or elsewhere in the city-wide consortium. Study and communication difficulties are supported through the work of the Foundation Studies Department and the ACCESS Centre, which grew out of a Department of Trade and Industry funded project at the college between 1983 and 1985. This project was to evaluate the contribution of information technology in increasing students' access to mainstream courses. Today, apart from supporting the third (thirty-seven) of the Hereward student population who now use micro-based study aids (compared with three in 1982), the centre also offers short courses to non-residential students to help them to manage their studies more effectively in mainstream colleges, using new technology where appropriate. The centre also offers courses and workshops on the use of technology to staff in mainstream colleges. The Keyboard Aids Unit at the centre provides modifications to equipment to improve access to hardware and software.

In this chapter, I shall discuss some aspects of our work on the two-year DTI project, particularly our approach to assessment and our students' experience of using technology on their courses and since leaving FE. Later in the chapter I shall discuss what is required if new technology is to make a continuing contribution towards students' independence and to their ability to control their own study.

Students involved in the project were following a range of ordinary further education courses, including City and Guilds Foundation, Certificate in Prevocational Education and Training, a Manpower Services Commission Modern Office Skills course, B/Tec Diploma courses, GCE 'O' and 'A' levels. The majority had little in the way of formal qualifications when they entered further education. One-third were following City and Guilds Foundation courses.

Students tended to have quite severe disabilities: cerebral palsy was the most common impairment, but also represented were spina bifida, Still's disease, post-operative brain tumour, brain damage, muscular dystrophy, Friedrich's Ataxia, tetraplegia and osteogenesis imperfecta (brittle bones).

During the first year of the project, we equipped fifteen students with mobile microcomputer-based workstations for their personal use within Hereward. Their progress was monitored and, in the second year, we extended assessment, awareness and training facilities to students in mainstream colleges. In some cases, equipment was loaned out for periods of up to one year.

For those lecturers initially involved with the project, past experience of innovations and of working with students with more severe disabilities made them highly suspicious of technology as a way of solving educational problems. Everyone involved felt that a critical approach was essential. The work should be not only student centred but also student led. The purpose was to improve students' access to the ordinary curriculum, using the most efficient means available; it was not simply to introduce new technology. To guard against promoting technology as the cure-all, we had to keep three key issues in mind:

Is technology *relevant* to the student and his/her needs?
If it is relevant, which configuration would be most *appropriate*?
What steps will be taken to ensure its continuing *effectiveness*?

A critical, student led approach

Most students with disabilities confess themselves 'assessed' more times than they care to remember. Our aim was not to assess individuals in isolation, but to assess them in the context in which they were studying and to consider the extent to which technology might reduce the handicapping effects of that context. Assessment was not intended to prescribe solutions. It aimed to increase students' and teachers' awareness of difficulties that might arise on a course, and to find ways of overcoming them. In this way we might develop strategies that improve the quality of an individual's FE experience.

There is a considerable temptation in work with students who have more complex difficulties, particularly in their speech, to draw conclusions about their needs based on observation, and not on talking about their needs with them. Conclusions drawn on this basis will often be wrong, and resources wasted trying to solve problems that do not exist. But most important, the value of new technology resides in its potential to increase students' control over their lives. If this is to occur, then people with disabilities need to be fully involved from the outset. In the long term, they will need both the information and confidence to enable them to identify changing requirements, to recognize where technology may be used and to tap the resources available in the community to ensure that the technology remains effective. Unless students participate fully in decisions from an early stage, new technology may come to be regarded as complicated, boring and, ultimately, irrelevant. Like such gadgetry before it, it is welcomed by the professionals and discarded at the earliest opportunity by the users, such as the student who said: 'technology is boring. You don't see what you're creating and it's not personalized . . .'.

The relevance of technology

Attention to the finer points of technology is pointless if other more basic needs are not met. As one student pointed out:

> How can we ever become independent if we always have to ask people to do things for us? . . . Like, you can be stuck on the loo and not able to reach the loo roll . . . care staff come back and ask if you're ready and you have to say, 'I couldn't reach the loo roll'. You feel really stupid.

A low-tech aid may be all that is required to effect a considerable improvement in students' college lives.

Students' wider expectations of FE also need to be considered. Regardless of the degree of their disability, their perceptions are unlikely to differ significantly from those of any other student. They are likely to value the opportunity to take courses and obtain qualifications, particularly in areas not available at school. Also important is the chance to study in a more adult, less restrictive environment where, 'you get treated more as an equal'. Less emphasis on past achievements and failures, new friendships and greater independence all figure prominently. Many also complain of what they perceive as the 'fussing' they experienced in school. Study support services must take account of student expectations of 'unexceptional' provision. Special provision should not be a barrier to their participation in an ordinary experience. This is the case, for example, if study aids provided are so complicated that lengthy training is required to allow students to use them, if equipment is unreliable, or if proposed modifications will be months, or even years, in development.

It is only worth evaluating the possible contribution of technology to a student's work when you know that he or she is following a relevant course. It is not unusual to find students following courses, not because of any interest in the subjects or because they reflect future goals but rather because more appropriate options were not available. In some instances, for example, computer studies classes were impossible since they were not on the ground floor; typing was not available to students who were unable to use all fingers; modern languages were considered unsuitable for students with speech difficulties; geography was closed to students unable to draw diagrams and science was closed on account of the practical requirements. It is important to establish the right of access to any course, regardless of disability. Students themselves may also need encouragement to overcome their own prejudices about what is possible.

The limited curricula in some special schools may have adversely affected students' ideas about what is possible. Some students are simply not aware of the range of available subjects. They often believe that they need some background in languages, science, arts or commercial subjects to join an FE course. Such misconceptions need to be cleared up by giving students full information about courses and content to enable them to make informed decisions on course choice. New technology may open up subjects where it can provide an alternative means of access. Science experiments, for example, can be computer-simulated for students who are unable to handle equipment; courses which use diagrams extensively can be opened up with graphics software. Engineering, an option long considered closed to students with more severe disabilities, has now become a possibility through developments in CAD/CAM (Computer Aided Design/ Computer Aided Manufacture). One student, for example, was able to follow a mainstream CAD/CAM course, accessing the system linked to the Keymaster[1] college computer via his footskate[2] encoding device, developed at the college.

It may also be necessary to check that students are working towards the minimum entry requirements to allow them to follow their chosen career or to go on to higher education. Such matters may be obvious for other students but can be missed for a student with a severe disability. Technology in this context may be particularly effective, as was the case when several students who needed 'O' level English for university entrance were provided with word processing facilities, which enabled them to make corrections, redraft and produce neat copy. This contributed to their eventual success in passing 'O' level six months after obtaining the equipment; for two of them, at their fifth attempt.

Study difficulties we encountered on the project varied considerably, and were not closely related to the students' impairments. They included: slow writing or typing speeds (frequently below 10 w.p.m. and, in some cases, down to 2 w.p.m.); fatigue; problems with legibility; the storage and organization of paper materials; notetaking in lectures and from books; overdependence on memorizing information; difficulty with the production of graphs, diagrams and special symbols; and examinations.

Students who used technology described some of the benefits of micro-based study and communications equipment in overcoming difficulties as: increased enjoyment of the work; quicker and less tiring work; presentation, spelling and grades improved; disk storage was an advantage; and correction and editing facilities which were said to be 'brilliant'.

Some of the remaining difficulties were less obvious, especially where technology was being used with some measure of success. Even though some students doubled their writing speed (in some cases from 4 w.p.m. to 9 w.p.m.), notetaking remained a serious problem for some. We have explored the possibility of using a speed writing system but, as yet, we have not identified a viable method that can be quickly learned and is compatible with use of the standard QWERTY keyboard. In some cases, students have used their own means of abbreviation. One, for example, took 'A' level sociology on the computer using this approach, and was able to increase her output significantly. Other possibilties include the use of word lists stored in the computer, where only one or two characters may be required to access a word from the stored list. A word anticipator program, developed at Dundee University for use on the Epson PX8 portable micro, is also being tried by some students. None of the developments that are currently

---

[1] The keymaster is a modular system consisting of a keyboard emulator and a user interface, enabling the user to operate the BBC from a range of input devices. Available from Clwyd Technics Ltd, Antelope Industrial Estate, Rhyddymwyn, Mold, Clwyd, CH7 5JH.

[2] A footskate is a foot-operated alternative input device (currently offers 2, 4 or 8 switch input). Available from SB Systems, Unit 2D, Jefferson Way, Thame Industrial Estate, Thame OX9 3UJ.

available, though, seem significantly to effect speed, although the effort required may be less.

A combination of abbreviations and closer attention to the techniques of notetaking may be a better solution. Much notetaking by students in the normal course of events is not only redundant but probably unhelpful as a means of learning. It may be more valuable in the long term to work with students to develop more efficient notetaking techniques so they can use nine words when ninety might otherwise be used than to provide extensive and complex software.

Examinations remain equally difficult for students whose writing is slow. Even where special arrangements have been made, they are a marathon for many students. Alternative means of assessment, particularly course work assessment, can be more appropriate and may give a clearer indication of students' capabilities. Frequently, though, the traditional examinations treadmill remains the only available option. Arrangements need to be assessed carefully with students if they are not to be disadvantaged. It should not be assumed that the computer will be the solution. A number of students involved with the project, particularly from mainstream colleges, had been working to examination arrangements that were wholly inadequate. One student, who had left mainstream school without having had the opportunity to take any examinations, because of his 'learning difficulties', had completed a YTS course and was taking 'O' levels and an 'A' level in computer science at college. His success to date had been in 'O' level computer studies, where he had used a computer, but his performance was marred in other subjects by his illegible script. Five minutes extra time and large print examination papers did not give him an equal chance.

What technology is appropriate?

If technology is relevant to a student, the next stage is to decide what equipment is needed. The course requirements, the student's abilities and learning style, their perceptions of, and their attitudes to, technology are all important.

The course may simply require word processing facilities but more may be involved. Maths, science or modern language courses may call for special symbols and presentation. In some subjects, like accounts and business studies, diagrams or graphs may be essential. These needs affect the software or equipment that is required.

Close attention to the effects of a student's physical condition on the mechanics of studying is important. A first priority must be to ensure that the student is comfortably seated for communication and study. The advice of a physiotherapist or seating technician may be needed. In some cases, students may be seated well and have good posture but find that they have to adopt a different position to write or type. Some positions are not viable in some environments. Lying or sitting on the floor or across a desk should be avoided if possible. Before he got a footskate system, one student found that his only viable typing position was to sit on his knees on the floor and to hit the keyboard with a wooden spoon. Another student, with brittle bones, who had taken all her CSE examinations from a prone position in bed, found that sitting in a conventional position at a desk caused acute backache. She was able to overcome this problem by using an adapted microwriter.[1] She has subsequently taken 'O' and 'A' levels, and is studying for a degree with the Open University.

Physical conditions may remain stable or deteriorate. This may be uncertain, as in the case of one 'A' level student with osteoarthritis. Two months after entering further education, she lost the use of her writing hand, as the bones fused, and use of the hand became extremely painful. Within a week of using the other hand to operate a microwriter, she was able to produce neat, printed copy at 14 w.p.m. But by the end of the year her 'microwriting hand' was also deteriorating. Since her condition continues to fluctuate, she is currently keeping three options open: the use both of left- and right-handed microwriters and, on occasions, the use of a pen. She has been able to continue her studies without interruption. This had not been the case in school, where she lost much time. She hopes now to continue to higher education.

Some students are unable to use a keyboard, in which case alternative devices and switching systems will be needed. The number of switches a student can use will determine whether he or she should use a scanning matrix or an encoding device: the more switches, the quicker the writing speed. One of the most efficient input systems available at the college was devized by Patrick Poon at Charlton Park School. This consists of a footskate with the Mac Apple[2] system for writing. In college, the skate has also been linked with the keymaster for computer programming on the BBC microcomputer. More recently, it has been linked to a computer system in a neighbouring mainstream college, to enable the student to join a computer aided design course there.

It is for the student to decide whether an alternative input device is required. In some cases, students prefer to work with a standard system, even though their speed remains slow. This choice must be respected. Such devices do not always improve speed greatly; it may be more important to make the user more comfortable and reduce the effort needed.

Some students find that, for reasons which cannot fully be explained, they simply do not make progress using computer-based equipment. Their approach to learning and their individual requirements may be more effectively served by a lightweight electronic typewriter, with limited correction facilities. On occasions, students find that a large handwritten scrawl is preferable to any kind of equipment. One accomplished computer user, for example, said that he preferred his untidy handwriting any day to the 'anonymous' work created on the computer.

In a number of cases, even where careful attention has been paid to assessment and training and where students have persevered with micro-based aids over some months, these have been abandoned, not because the system is difficult to

---

[1] The Microwriter is a portable, rechargeable battery-operated word processor with 6 keys on the keyboard capable of producing all the characters of a typewriter keyboard, plus additional technical symbols. Available from The Foundation for Communication for the Disabled, 25 High Street, Woking, Surrey, EU2 11BW.

[2] Mac Apple is a communicator which allows the user to write and make corrections, draw pictures and diagrams on an Apple microcomputer by using switches or a keyboard. Enquiries to Patrick Poon, ACCESS Centre, Hereward College, Bramston Crescent, Tile Hill Lane, Coventry, CV4 9SW. The use of Mac Apple in schools is described in Chapter 7.

use but because the student feels 'further away from the work' or they do not get quick enough feedback from the machine. The equipment causes some students to feel alienated from their work. One student with a spinal injury who had learned to operate an Epson PX8 portable micro using wrist sticks, apparently very successfully, abandoned the system after several months for a portable typewriter. She preferred a low-tech approach and the immediate print-out from the typewriter. The option of a portable printer did not appeal to her because it still did not give her the immediacy that was otherwise possible.

Another cause of occasional frustration is the storage of information on disk in environments that are still entrenched in paper-based methods. One student commented that the whole object of using technology to study was defeated by the fact that lecturers marked print-outs and not disks. He could see little purpose in retaining uncorrected material on disks, so he did not use disks as his main means of storage, despite severe difficulty in using standard files and in organizing paper.

Ensuring technology remains effective

Both students and staff in FE need to be aware of the current applications and the potential of technology, Introductory training is important to increase their understanding of the role of the equipment and to ensure that they do not feel at a total loss when something goes wrong. Students also need to feel that they have staff support. If they are already struggling with 'unfriendly' manuals, on occasion losing work, meeting the kind of frustrations involved in learning any skills and at the same time trying to keep up with coursework, it can be particularly dispiriting if staff treat the system as, at best, an irrelevance and, at worst, an invasion.

Some staff in Hereward remain sceptical of the value of micro-technology. Several felt that technology had been imposed without consultation and regarded it as a hindrance. In their view, students had coped in the past without hi-tech. Several students remarked on this:

> Some lecturers thought I could write perfectly well and asked me not to use the computer. Initially, I used it every day for word processing, then things got more difficult.

> The lecturer really hated the computer, wasn't happy about me using it and objected to me bringing it into lectures when I could write.

In retrospect, staff should have been more involved. The opportunity to make micro-technological aids available to more students when we could already see it working successfully for several seemed too good to miss. We went ahead on the assumption that if it was demonstrably useful then staff in the college would accept it. We did not appreciate how the degree of success could be affected by staff attitudes. Where staff were enthusiastic and encouraging, students were more likely to persevere and succeed, particularly with more complicated equipment.

Mainstream colleges were not very different. Where staff felt involved, then they worked with and supported the student, often putting in extra time. For those less involved, and where the students' difficulties were regarded as an individual rather than an institutional problem, students sometimes felt that they had to tread warily. One commented, with evident relief, that some of the teachers at her comprehensive 'did not mind' her using a microelectronic typewriter in conjunction with a home-based BBC workstation. Throughout her education, this student had had no effective means of producing her own written work. She wrote extremely slowly and had not been able to use a typewriter or a tape recorder in class. A part-time amanuensis had been the main solution for her difficulties. Another student, with hand/eye co-ordination difficulties, was convinced of the value of a microwriter but, in practice, did not regard this as a feasible proposition. His school career had been seriously affected by his teachers' lack of understanding. As far as he was concerned, the microwriter could only serve to handicap him further by drawing attention to his difficulties, when his main aim was to be unobtrusive.

So staff need to be acquainted with the use, benefits and pitfalls of technology. Otherwise it may be seen as yet another demand on time that is already limited by the presence of a student with a disability, who runs the risk of being regarded ultimately as a source of disruption in the lecture room.

Students also need a broad awareness and training programme that will extend horizons beyond their immediate needs, and encourage them to explore the use of technology in their future lives. They need to know that equipment provided is not fixed. It can be developed and replaced as needs change. The majority of students who have used equipment expect to continue using it in their future studies or employment. A number have moved on, and are now operating successfully in new environments. New technology has given some of them a marked boost to their confidence. One student who uses a head pointer and is severely disabled by cerebral palsy, left with an A and B at 'A' level to his credit. He intends to do a Ph.D. in computer studies, eventually, and all the indications are that he will succeed. Another student who produced illegible, very slow, hand-written work before she used the microwriter, got a part-time job at the Milk Marketing Board within six months of leaving further education and established her own word processing agency for small businesses. Another was rejected by mainstream further education and spent a year in an Adult Training Centre before arriving at Hereward. She has since used a micro to organize a complicated move to a house in a new area where she lives independently. She joined a part-time diploma in higher education course and organized all the benefits and services she required. The micro, obtained through the COMET Award Scheme[1], carried her progress beyond further education and gave her the impetus she needed to organize her own life. One student with severe cerebral palsy was destined for residential care after further education. He decided not to return to his home area but to work towards becoming self-supporting and independent. After an MSC course in computing, he became involved in the Companies' Training Scheme. Three years later he has become one of the directors of a computer training centre.

COMET is a bursary scheme which makes awards to people who need microcomputers for studies and training. Organized by the Sunday Times and VNU Business Publications. Administered by NBHS, 336 Brixton Road, London, SW9 7AA.

A final example is a mature student who learned to type when she was fifteen, despite 'considerable hostility' from her headmaster at the special school she attended. She has been typing for twenty-five years. During the last ten years she has slowly taken GCEs and obtained several Open University credits towards a degree. After moving into residential care, she became demoralized and gave up her studies. She joined the Modern Office Skills course, jointly run by Hereward and the neighbouring mainstream college. Within two months of using technology, she had increased her speed from 6 w.p.m. to 10 w.p.m. and intends to double that within the next four months. For the first time in her life, she feels that she can think realistically about finding a job and becoming economically independent. She may also continue her studies, particularly as she too has obtained equipment through the COMET Scheme.

The policy and financial framework

The Hereward project was funded through the IT Awareness Programme of the Department of Trade and Industry. This pump-priming strategy meant few administrative controls and more chances to innovate. But there are penalties, not least the lack of permanent funding, although the college is committed to provide resources to allow the work to continue. MSC funding has also enabled complementary activities to develop on the same financial basis. The assessment, training and awareness facilities provided by the ACCESS Centre for people not resident at the college have no regular external sources of funding, although the centre is nominated by the Department of Education and Science to provide assessment and consultancy in the use of new-tech study aids in FE. Fees are charged, but these do not pay for the facilities available nor for the further skills which should be brought into the centre, particularly in electronics, speech therapy and occupational therapy.

The co-ordination of activities between centres is not formalized in any way. Whilst they are linked informally and share skills and experience, we need resources to consolidate and disseminate our achievements. Exchange between centres is vital for the development of the skills of centre workers and the continued provision of training and awareness courses for staff and students in ordinary colleges and other training agencies. It has also been possible to seek solutions to student difficulties through collaborative work. The University of Warwick has been particularly important in this respect. For example, joint work on the BEN project (the BBC Electronic Notepad) has produced a program for the BBC micro which enables students to carry out several study activities within a single program (Stevens and Pickering 1984).

A national policy to co-ordinate current activities and arrangements is needed, to consolidate achievements and to clarify the pattern of services. This policy should include the full involvement of students. Current arrangements for the provision of personal equipment demonstrate the dangers of a prescriptive approach to study and communications support that I discussed earlier. Students who need equipment are obliged to apply through various agencies, including charities, the COMET award scheme, local authorities and the Education Support Grant funding. There is no way to ensure that what is rapidly becoming essential equipment for many people will be made available to them.

The success of applications through the various agencies depends less upon individual need than upon access to professionals who are in a position to channel their applications. In the case of Education Support Grant funding, arrangements are such that equipment might be organized for a student without any consultation. There are no controls to ensure that individuals will see the equipment before they receive it, even less have an opportunity to determine what might best meet their needs.

We lack effective evaluation, assessment, training and equipment. The use of new technology to support people with disabilities is still at a relatively primitive stage. If the role of centres like Hereward is to be developed effectively, then future policy needs to take account of this. Facilities available at the ACCESS Centre, for example, depend on the ability to pay. Many people interested in using technology to support their return to education are not eligible even for discretionary grants from local education authorities. Some young people may not be able to persuade their authorities of the value of new technology. In any event, a 'payment by results' system is unnecessarily restrictive and cannot sustain development work in a flexible and responsive service. On the contrary, it may encourage a rehashing of the tried and tested and quick, glib solutions to difficulties that need, above all, time and commitment to resolve. We need continued investment to ensure that technology enhances quality of life and creates previously unimagined opportunities for education, training and employment.

Reference

Stevens, G. and Pickering, J. 1984. 'The electronic notepad: an integrated tool for writing, drawing and calculating,' in *The Computer as an Aid for Those with Special Needs*, Sheffield Active Conference Proceedings.

Further reading

ACE Centre Publications, ACE Centre, Ormerod School, Wayneflete Road, Headington, Oxford.

BARD – British Database on Research into Aids for the Disabled, Handicapped Persons Research Unit, Newcastle-upon-Tyne Polytechnic, No. 1 Coach Lane, Coach Lane Campus, Newcastle-upon-Tyne, NE7 7TW.

CALL Centre Publications, CALL Centre, University of Edinburgh, The Annexe, 4 Buccleuch Place, Edinburgh, EH8 9JT.

Communication Outlook, available from the Artificial Language Laboratory, Michigan State University, 405 Computer Center, East Lansing, MI 48824-10942, USA.

Hawkridge, D., Vincent, T. and Hales, G. 1985. *New Information Technology in the Education of Disabled Children and Adults*, London, Croom Helm.

SEMERC (Special Education Microelectronic Research Centre) Newsletters available from:
Bristol SEMERC, Faculty of Education, Bristol Polytechnic, Redland Hill, Bristol, BS6 6U2.
Newcastle SEMERC, Newcastle Polytechnic, Coach Lane Campus, Newcastle-upon-Tyne, NE7 7XA.
Manchester SEMERC, Manchester College of Higher Education, Hathersage Road, Manchester, M13 0JA.
Redbridge SEMERC, Dane Centre, Melbourne Road, Ilford, Essex, IG1 4HT.
With a Little Help from the Chip, BBC TV Publications, 1985.

9 Microcomputing and the education of children with visual disabilities in an ordinary school

Julian Watson and Tom Vincent

In 1982, a national project, Computing and the Blind, *was established with Government funding to explore the potential use of new technology in schools where pupils with visual disabilities are taught. Both special schools and ordinary schools were involved. The project introduced a microcomputer-based workstation into eight schools and developed software to meet their needs in conjunction with the teachers. This chapter describes the experience of one of the schools, Castlecroft Primary School, Wolverhampton. It is written by Julian Watson, the Head of Castlecroft, and Tom Vincent, who directed the project.*

The context

Some nine years ago Wolverhampton Education Authority were seeking to provide education for blind and partially-sighted children within the Borough. It was felt that such children would benefit both from living at home within their own community and from integrated provision for their education. A decision was made to develop such a resource at a mainstream primary school.

Castlecroft Primary School was selected for a number of reasons. The school contained both junior and infant children and was next to an area comprehensive school where similar resources might be developed. The catchment area has a good social mix; there are no other severe educational problems, and the school has a supportive and interested parent body. The highly committed headteacher and staff were already operating a system of team teaching which would assist the integration of both specialist staff and children.

This organization meant that children were often taught in small groups, and an atmosphere which allowed a considerable degree of individual learning was encouraged. The team-teaching approach meant that staff were quite used to working with other adults in the classroom and did not feel inhibited as a result. Children with a particular disability, and the staff to support them, could be incorporated into such an ethos without changing the nature of the school radically.

Setting up the resource

A new wing comprising two teaching areas and two small withdrawal rooms was added to the school, together with a mainstream nursery classroom. Sufficient funds were provided to allow the purchase of specialized equipment such as a thermoform machine, a closed-circuit television system and a good selection of lenses and tactile aids.

Throughout, there was a conscious effort on the part of both headteacher and staff to avoid the creation of a separate 'unit'. The area was named the 'resource area' and that was what it was to be – a resource for the whole school. Both parents and children were involved in discussions on the nature of this new project. Assembly and meetings involving children, parents and teachers played an important part in this process.

The most important element was undoubtedly staffing. The school has a policy of taking established members of the mainstream staff and sending them on secondment for specialist training at Birmingham University. This process has continued to the present. The school is now used as a placement for students on the same Special Needs (Visual Handicap) course.

Staff numbers have grown gradually. There is now a complement of five specialist staff and approximately twenty children, within a total of thirteen teaching staff, six nursery nurses and two-hundred-and-sixty children. In addition a peripatetic teacher of the visually handicapped is based at the school, supporting children with less severe disabilities in their own neighbourhood schools, making home visits and generally strengthening the links between home and school.

The present position

The school continues to use team teaching methods which allow the inclusion of a specialist teacher of the blind and partially sighted into each team. The normal pattern is for some 60 to 70 children to be taught by a group of three mainstream teachers, together with one teacher who has an extra visual handicap qualification, who is there, not to undertake all the teaching of the children with special needs but to act as consultant to the team and be responsible for the success of those children. Individual learning programmes are developed as required, but emphasis is placed upon all children sharing the same curriculum. Each visually handicapped child's progress is discussed in detail at six-monthly assessment meetings attended by educational psychologists, the Medical Officer of Health, mobility officer and Social Services representatives.

Children in school vary considerably in terms of their degree of disability and learning needs. These needs can be classified to some extent into those who have some useful sight and those who are totally blind.

Blind children are taught by tactile methods from the age of three when they enter the nursery for half-time education (either a morning or afternoon session). Braille[1] is taught from five years onwards with the work dovetailed into the mainstream reading organization. Considerable use is made of tape recorders as the child progresses, particularly in topic and project work, but there is inevitably a large amount of preparation required to braille the necessary texts.

---

[1] Braille is a sequence of cells (each cell is a 3×2 matrix of raised dots) which can represent words, numbers or punctuation. It is similar to speed writing, with wordsigns and contractions of symbols being commonly used to cut down bulk and increase efficiency. Grade 1 braille includes the letters of the alphabet, 5 special signs for common words (and, for, of, the, with) and punctuation. Grade 2 braille has, in addition, wordsigns (single braille letter of the alphabet representing a word e.g. 'c' for 'can'), abbreviations (2 or more letters representing a word (e.g. 'rcv' for 'receive'), and contractions (a letter preceded by a contraction sign to represent initial or final parts of words e.g. there is a contraction for 'ence').

The blind children normally produced their own work on a Perkins Brailler[1] until the introduction of computers. Both blind and partially-sighted children are taught touch typing in the junior department. An understanding of the QWERTY keyboard is a most useful skill for the blind, and typing assists with perhaps the greatest problem for partially sighted pupils – producing written work.

All of this work continues at Smestow, the neighbouring comprehensive school, which now has similar provision for children in the secondary age-range.

Specific teaching problems

Each of the teams within the school consists of four staff, one of whom is a visual handicap specialist. This organization means that in any one team three of the staff may not be able to read or write braille. Until recently this meant that work produced by blind children sometimes had to be overwritten in normal text for the benefit of other members of staff – a time-consuming operation which diminished time available for preparation. Mainstream teachers also felt that their supervision of blind children would be greatly improved by an immediate translation of all braille rather than waiting for the specialist teacher. Some form of automatic translation device would obviously prove useful.

Children working on the Perkins Brailler could become isolated from their peers even though they were working in the same classroom. The use of a totally different recording medium seemed to contribute to this.

The needs of the partially sighted children differed somewhat. They were concerned with their speed of recording and with the legibility of text they had produced. Even a typewriter producing 'jumbo' size print was not wholly satisfactory: correcting mistakes caused a particular problem. The school's language policy encourages the drafting and re-thinking of work for all children. It seemed possible that a word processor would be a useful alternative to other recording methods if the output could be made clearly visible.

The needs of particular children

Before the introduction of microcomputer technology there were three particular problems that concerned us. First, in the upper junior team, an intelligent blind boy, Darren, was producing large amounts of braille text, much of which required overwriting. In the same team were six other partially sighted children and this was stretching the specialist staffing considerably. Secondly, in the infant team blind twins were being introduced to braille. The school encourages all parents to participate in the reading programme, reading bedtime stories to their children, hearing them read short pieces and employing such techniques as shadow reading. The parents of the blind twins found much of this work difficult because of the braille code. They were learning braille themselves but this is a

---

[1] The Perkins Brailler is a brailling device first produced in the 1940s. It has main keys for the braille dots plus paper feed, back space and space keys. As keys are pressed (one cell at a time) the braille is embossed on heavy grade paper.

fairly complex task. Some form of translation system was required which would enable them to know more of what their children were doing in school. Third, the peripatetic member of the visual handicap team reported that a blind child with severe learning difficulties at another school was in need of some extra stimulus to extend her limited periods of concentration.

A workstation for pupils with visual disabilities

In 1979, the *Computing and the Blind* project at the Open University developed a 'talking' microcomputer for blind students. This development formed the basis for a workstation which was later used in schools. The workstation is made up of relatively low-cost hardware (BBC microcomputer, disk drive, monitor and printer) as widely used by mainstream schools. Other devices are added to provide alternative input and output facilities: a speech synthesizer, Perkins Brailler (for braille input) and a touch-sensitive Concept Keyboard[1] (to be used with embossed overlays). The total cost of the workstation is between £1300 and £2000 depending on choice of storage capacity (disks) and type of speech synthesizer.

SOFTWARE FOR THE WORKSTATION

A range of computer programs was developed by the project with the guidance of teachers. This included awareness programs to introduce pupils to the technology, braille teaching, transcription of braille to text, word processing and programming. It was not expected that all eight schools would use every program but they were all made available, together with guidance notes to allow individual schools and teachers to make appropriate selections.

The software packages made available to each school were:

1 *Introduction to braille:* Three programs that give a spoken feedback when the braille alphabet, simple words or numbers are brailled using the Perkins Brailler or embossed braille character overlay on a Concept Keyboard. A musical response is provided as an alternative, 'fun' introduction to both the technology and braille.

2 *Grade 2 words:* A facility for a teacher to construct vocabularies of words which could be used by the computer to provide an interactive test of a pupil's knowledge of braille (typing or touching). A spoken feedback is provided to help with spelling.

3 *Talking BASIC:* A version of the computer language BASIC that could be used for programming with the aid of spoken feedback and the production of programs with a speech output.

4 *Talking dictionary:* Speech synthesizers can mispronounce words. This can be overcome by changing the spelling of a word or breaking it up phonetically

---

[1] The Concept Keyboard is a flat keyboard with touch-sensitive areas. Typically, it is the size of A4 or A3 paper in order that overlays printed or embossed on paper can be used with patterns that match the touch-sensitive areas.

(e.g. 'an sir' for 'answer'), or by using codes that give direct access to phonetic sounds that can be combined to represent a word. This program gives an opportunity to experiment with alternative spelling of words and phonetics until the best pronunciation is achieved. This information can be saved in a dictionary on disk and called for use in specific programs (e.g. Grade 2 words), or, in some cases, added to the speech synthesizer dictionary that contains exceptions to the rules of translation from text to speech.

5 *Talking typewriter:* This enables each letter to be heard when typing. In addition, the resulting text can be read back either by character, word or sentence. At any point in the text, editing changes can be made deleting or adding characters or words. Finally, the corrected text can be printed. The choice of typing, editing or printing is made from a spoken menu by pressing the first letter of the option (e.g. 'p' for 'printing').

6 *Grade 2 braille translation:* A program to translate braille from a Perkins Brailler which is simultaneously displayed on a monitor, spoken at the end of each line, and printed when required.

SYNTHETIC SPEECH

All of these programs use synthetic speech output. This has been made possible by the emergence of low-cost speech synthesizers which can easily be added to a microcomputer. Three types of speech synthesizer are available that can be added to a microcomputer to make it 'talk':

1 Unlimited vocabulary, with codes input for the individual sound units.
2 Unlimited vocabulary, with the direct input of text. The text is translated into sounds on a rule basis together with look-up tables for exceptions to the rules.
3 Limited vocabulary, with human speech that is digitized, compressed, stored and recalled by simple codes.

Although the quality of the 'human speech' synthesizer is higher than the other systems, the limitation on vocabulary prevents it being used with programs such as a talking typewriter unless the typing vocabulary is severely restricted. As the talking typewriter also requires an immediate response to any word, then a 'real time' translation from text to sound is necessary (type 2 above). However, this does result in a lower quality of speech than digitized human speech. In practice, most children soon adjust to the unnatural voice. Many responses are anticipated from the context of particular programs and how they are used. The problem is greater if, for example, this type of speech is used for 'reading' an unknown text.

Introduction of microtechnology

It was after the headteacher attended a CET residential course (Microcomputers and Special Education) that the school agreed to join the *Computing and the Blind* project. The workstation was installed (see Figure 9.1) and the project gave initial instruction in its use. Although some staff had experience of a cassette-based computer system, the sight of the workstation initially proved somewhat offputting. The large trolley seemed to be crammed with unfamiliar equipment.

Figure 9.1   The workstation in the classroom.

The system was based around the BBC microcomputer which was not the one in general use in the local authority. One teacher commented:

> I was wary at first, fearing that my extremely limited knowledge of computer technology would either lead to inefficient use of the workstation or result in expensive or fatal damage to the 'works'.

The resource team of visual handicap staff met after school on a number of occasions to become more familiar with the equipment. Several members of staff were still unconvinced and uneasy about such equipment, but agreed to introduce it to the children.

The member of staff based in the upper junior team agreed to begin work with a blind boy. Within days, Darren was happily using the equipment and enjoying explaining to all who would listen the details of 'his' computer. The transfer was easy since the major means of input for Darren was still the Perkins Brailler. The voice output was a particular delight which provoked a great deal of laughter in the early stages.

Careful design of the software had made the programs very easy to use. Initially one was presented with a simple menu from which to choose functions. The choice was made with a single letter input from the keyboard. Project staff were available by telephone when problems did occur and this was most helpful in the early stages. The equipment has been very reliable – not even routine maintenance is normally required. Most problems have been the result of human error.

Staff were rapidly impressed with the translation program which gave immediate benefits to both Darren and themselves. Overwriting was never a popular task and it was a great relief to have some of the pressure removed. Other staff also felt much more confident when left to supervise Darren, since they could always observe his work via the monitor screen. Indeed Darren had to increase his work rate and accuracy considerably, since it was now clear exactly what he was producing, even from the far side of the classroom!

An unexpected development was the way in which Darren often became secretary to the group with whom he was working. Children are often asked to discuss some matter and record their thoughts. The workstation proved to be an excellent 'group noticeboard', with the monitor screen clear for all to see.

For example, Darren and a group of some sixteen other children were involved in a poetry writing session. The teacher presented the task, to record reactions to a visit to a river. The children were divided into groups and asked to collect words and images which would be appropriate. These were to be collected by one member of the group who would later report back to the whole teaching group. Because of the size of the workstation a group was formed around Darren, who was then able to record the ideas of the whole group via his Perkins Brailler and onto the monitor. These words and images were then shared with all the groups before individuals started to produce their own personal reactions. In so doing they would draw upon the collected ideas as and when they felt them to be appropriate. Darren was able to work independently at this stage, using his Brailler just as everyone else would use paper and pencil.

Before very long, partially sighted children were using the word processing program, enjoying the exceptionally clear screen display and the voice output which both motivated and gave extra security for those who found the screen difficult to see. Within a few weeks we bought a typing practice program which was put to good use during break and lunchtimes. Other commercial programs have also been used from time to time; the word processor program *Mini-Office* proved to be a useful tool. This program produces large letters on the screen and gives a very large type output when required – something missing from the original talking software, developed by the project.

We have also extended the word processing with four microwriter[1] keyboards to be used by both sighted and visually impaired children. These have been used extensively and have resulted in some excellent discussion of work in progress as output from all four microwriters appears on the same screen (Figure 9.2). The microwriter code has proved easy to memorize and it has been delightful to see both partially sighted and mainstream children sharing the same equipment and discussing their work in an animated fashion.

With only one workstation available it was necessary, initially, to timetable the equipment. Emphasis was given to times when children were producing creative work. The speech synthesis was less successful in phonic work attempted by the infant children. Fortunately, from the point of view of resources, Darren was in his final year at the school, so that more recently the workstation has been continuously available to the infant team.

The blind twins in the infant department rapidly named the workstation the 'Growly Bear' – a reflection of the sound made by the voice output device. They were introduced to the equipment via a program which turns the Perkins Brailler into a simple electric organ. This was a delightful toy initially; since that time they have both made excellent progress in braille. They were recently writing about a dragon, having heard about the Chinese New Year celebrations. One of them, Jennifer, aged six, wrote:

> my dragon is sandy
> my dragon is eating all the sand on the beach
> he has one leg too
> his tail is two feet long
> he is spiky too
> his horns are sharp

The machine means that these children are much more part of their peer group. Their work is commented upon and read out by the teacher or themselves as the lesson progresses. Very often they use the speech synthesis to review what they have written so far – indeed sometimes they have to be restrained from too much repetition.

A machine may soon be purchased for use at home, which will greatly help their parents' contribution to the learning process. Two other blind children have

---

[1] The Microwriter is a hand-held word processor that has six keys. Combinations of these keys produce letters, numbers and editing commands. The text produced can be viewed on a single line screen and printed. There are four Microwriter keyboards (without word processing and memory facilities) that can be connected to a BBC microcomputer. They can be used simultaneously with the computer with the aid of a program that includes a facility to split the computer screen into segments.

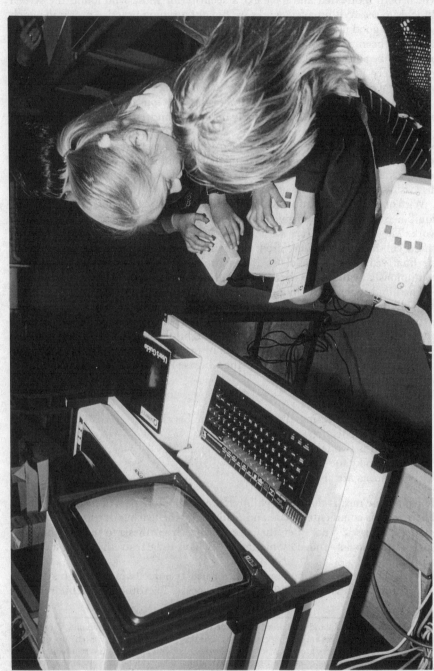

Figure 9.2 Microwriters in use.

now joined them in the infant department and they are also using the equipment regularly. Craig, one of the other visually impaired children, was recently able to post his letter of thanks, composed and written on the workstation, after a visit to the Black Country Museum.

Both staff and children can now provide interest and praise, which is so essential to any learning process, by reading the braille translation from the screen. We can now keep a record of all written work produced by the children merely by printing a second copy. This has proved a most useful guide to progress and forward planning.

The Concept Keyboard has been used in the search for a stimulus for the child with severe learning difficulties. The keyboard and the voice output have fascinated this child. The peripatetic teacher has produced a variety of textured overlays which the little girl has enjoyed using. It is now hoped to install similar equipment in her own school so that it can be used on a more regular basis.

What lessons have been learned

The introduction of a workstation into the school did create some initial tensions. As confidence in using the system grew and staff came to recognize its contribution, it became an accepted, and welcome, feature in the classroom. One teacher comments:

> Despite its size [the workstation] has been quickly accepted as part of the furniture. It in no way dominates or intrudes upon the area in which it is being used. Other staff have been encouraged to use the equipment as they see it in operation daily.

It is clear from experience at the school that simplicity of use for computer programs is essential in a classroom, together with simple and clear documentation. Nevertheless, it is surprising how quickly use of the equipment leads to further possibilities and, ideally, software needs both an initial and a more sophisticated version available.

The most successful application of microtechnology at Castlecroft Primary School has been the transcription of braille to text. This was identified earlier as a major problem for teachers who could not read braille – the majority – and, hence, could not immediately read a child's classwork. It is now commonplace to see children's braille notebooks with text printouts added that have been produced simultaneously with the braille (Figure 9.3).

In addition to braille transcription, the workstation has been used for word processing with partially sighted children where large characters are produced both on the microcomputer screen and the printer. It has also provided a stimulus for children learning braille, and for one child with severe learning difficulties.

The workstation proved so successful that it soon became indispensable. The equipment has become another tool for learning. This means that the workstation is often required in at least two places at once. The size and lack of portability proves to be a problem on occasions. Certainly a similar device within a package the size of the more recent lap-held computers would be most useful, particularly in the secondary school context. The stand-alone microwriter would

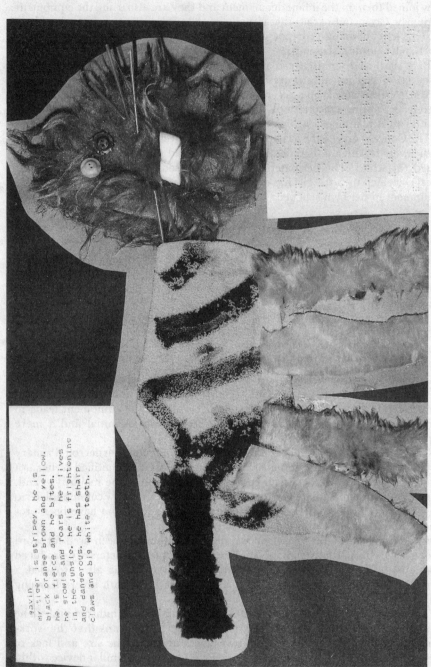

gavin is stripey. he is
my tiger.
black orange brown and yellow.
he is fierce and he bites.
he growls and roars. he lives
in the jungle. he is frightening
and dangerous. he has sharp
claws and big white teeth.

Figure 9.3   Gavin's tiger story, printed and brailled.

seem to have possibilities here, but the display is both too small and lacking in contrast at present. We also need a reasonably priced braille embosser. Connection of such a device would allow staff to type at a normal keyboard but produce both braille and normal text simultaneously.

The introduction of microtechnology into this integrated setting has undoubtedly made the process of catering for children's special needs easier. It has enabled children with a visual disability to learn more efficiently alongside their sighted colleagues with the minimum of disruption to existing practice. In some cases it has actually improved the learning experience of all children within the school. A great deal of development remains to be done but the success of the enterprise so far makes the future seem hopeful.

Further reading

Carroll Centre for the Blind 1983. 'Voice output for access by the blind and visually impaired', *Aids and Appliances Review*, 9 and 10.

Flanagan, J. L. and others 1970. 'Synthetic voices for computers', *IEEE Spectrum*, 7, pp. 22–45.

Goodrich, G. L. and others 1980. 'Preliminary report on evaluation of synthetic speech for reading machines,' *Journal of Visual Impairment and Blindness*, 74, pp. 273–75.

Hawkridge, D., Vincent, T. and Hales, G. 1985. *New Information Technology in the Education of Disabled Children and Adults*, London, Croom Helm.

Spragg, J. 1984. 'Interfacing a Perkins Brailler to a BBC Micro', *Microprocessors and Microsystems*, 8, pp. 524–27.

Vincent, A. T. 1983. 'Microcomputers and synthetic speech', *Journal of Blind Welfare*, 67, pp. 225–227.

Vincent, A. T. 1983. 'Talking BASIC and talking braille: two applications of synthetic speech', *Computer Education*, No. 45, pp. 10–12.

Vincent, A. T. and Turnbull, S. D. 1984. 'Wordprocessing for blind people', *Microprocessors and Microsystems*, 8, pp. 535–538.

10 The place of hearing aid technology in the education of deaf children

Harry Cayton

Harry Cayton describes the wide range of aids that are now available to support the education of children with hearing impairments and assesses the contribution they can make in the classroom. This contribution depends upon their effective use by teachers. The presence of a child using a hearing aid may call for significant changes in the organization of a classroom and the teacher's methods. Teachers need to understand in detail how the aid works, how it affects the child using it, and how it affects them. They need adequate support and training for this reason. Equally important, they need to take into account the wishes and views of the user, so that the aid becomes part of a collaborative effort aimed at promoting learning. Under these conditions, technology can expand and enhance education.

Introduction

The applications of new technology still retain unwarranted glamour. This applies as much to aids for people with disabilities as it does to the latest car telephones. Media coverage of disability focuses disproportionately on electronic aids and equipment, and often gives the false impression that the latest 'bionic ear' for deaf children will solve the problem of deafness forever. Against this background non-specialist teachers working with disabled children in ordinary schools might be forgiven for thinking that the appropriate hardware is the solution to the educational difficulties of such children or at least for having greater confidence in its efficacy than is reasonable.

We need to place new technology in perspective. Aids exist to serve the hearing-impaired child, not the other way round. They need to be carefully selected, in good working order, cosmetically acceptable to the child; they need to be accepted and understood by other children and the adults who work with them. New technology is not the solution to the difficulties arising from deafness, but it is an enormously valuable tool in alleviating them. It provides teachers with a whole range of ways of extending children's abilities, bypassing their disabilities and compensating for deficiencies. Technical aids must always remain the servants of the child and his or her teachers, they must be part of the curriculum not a substitute for it.

Technical aids for hearing impaired children may be divided into three groups: personal hearing aids, educational hearing aids and communication aids. The first two groups are auditory, their function is to assist the child in making use of his or her residual hearing. The third group is primarily visual, using written language as a means of bypassing oral/aural difficulties. It should not be imagined any of these aids in itself replaces lost hearing.

Personal hearing aids are those which are worn entirely by the child, they include post-aural (behind the ear) aids of which the child may wear one or more usually two; body-worn aids, which are nowadays worn only by young children and cochlear implants, an electrode implanted by surgery into the ear. This last is an experimental operation which has not yet been carried out by surgeons in this country, but a small handful of children with cochlear implants are educated in British schools.

Educational hearing aids are those in which part of the aid is worn by the child and part by the person working with them. These hearing aids are sometimes called 'aids not worn entirely on the person'. This group includes radio hearing aids and FM systems in which a transmitter is worn by the teacher, also group hearing aids and auditory speech trainers.

Communication aids include deaf communicating terminals for use with the telephone, computer mail boxes (which are not specifically designed for deaf people), and a range of computer assisted printers, desk-top or hand-held, which may be used by children with a combination of physical disabilities and severe speech impairment. Teletext television and, particularly, the provision of subtitles is invaluable in education. Do-it-yourself subtitling equipment is now also available so that schools can subtitle recorded programmes or their own videos for themselves. Communication aids in this group depend on literacy for their effectiveness, but they should not be seen as unusable with children who are not yet literate. Subtitles for example, can be a powerful tool to assist literacy and encourage reading.

One purpose of integrated education is to give disabled children access to the full curriculum in the ordinary school. New technology is a means of assisting that integration. The use of aids, therefore, needs to be seen as a part of the curriculum, and not as something added on for a hearing impaired child. All teachers working with such a child need to be able to control and use a radio aid transmitter effectively and to know when the child's own hearing aid is not working. Subtitled schools programmes can be used with the whole class, pre-recorded or live. Aids need to be seen to be helpful to the teacher as well as to the child, an extra resource for both to extend the opportunity for learning. Aids will never entirely compensate for the difficulties arising from deafness and never replace good teaching as a means of overcoming disability.

Personal hearing aids

Hearing aids, unlike glasses, do not correct hearing. What they can do, and they can do this increasingly effectively as designs improve, is boost a child's residual hearing. Hearing aids can be selected and set to boost those sounds which can be perceived. With modern high-powered aids practically no child can be described as totally deaf. There is, however, a world of difference between being able to hear a few bumps and rumbles or knowing when someone is speaking or not speaking, and being able to identify the patterns of speech. Because good hearing aids are highly effective for partially hearing children, it is easy to assume that all a deafer child needs is a more powerful aid.

Hearing aids are only as effective as the ear mould which introduces sound to the child's ear. The ear mould is the plastic plug which fits into the outer ear. There needs to be a close acoustic seal in order to ensure that the sound from the hearing aid is received as clearly as possible. Good ear moulds are notoriously difficult to make, especially for young children; if they are badly made they are uncomfortable, they fall out, they fail to make an acoustic seal. The most obvious sign of a badly fitting mould to a hearing teacher is a high pitched whistle coming from the child's aid. This is caused by feedback from the aid's output into the microphone. This may be simply remedied by asking the child to re-insert the mould, but if it is a regular occurrence a new mould should be obtained. Turning down the volume on a hearing aid may also eliminate feedback, but unless the volume has been set unusually high the need to do this indicates problems with the mould. Moulds are available in a range of different plastics, soft and hard, and in different colours to suit children's needs.

The most usual type of hearing aid which teachers in ordinary schools come across is the 'behind-the-ear' or post-aural aid. A number of models is available from the National Health Service, and ear, nose and throat consultants may prescribe commercially manufactured aids for children who need them. Commercial aids are usually more powerful and more adjustable to a child's particular hearing loss. Because of the way the Health Service is funded, the cost of prescribing manufactured aids is borne by the Local Health Authority. This means that there is financial pressure on health authorities only to provide National Health Service aids. In recent years, one or two health authorities have refused to provide commercial aids prescribed by a consultant, and others have asked parents to take out insurance policies to cover loss or damage. This practice has been officially discouraged by the Department of Health and Social Security after prolonged pressure from parents and voluntary organizations. Although this is of no direct concern to classroom teachers, their role in promoting good practice in this area is important. Classroom teachers working daily with a hearing impaired child have the best chance amongst professionals of observing whether a child's hearing aid really seems effective, and whether ear mould problems are persistent. It is important for a teacher of the deaf with overall responsibility for the child to have regular feedback from other teachers.

In some areas small profoundly deaf children may be given body-worn, rather than post-aural hearing aids. The power of these aids can now be matched by certain post-aural aids and for school-aged children the latter are certainly more practical and unobtrusive.

In rare circumstances a child with a slight hearing loss may wear an in-the-ear hearing aid. These aids are designed to fit inside the outer ear, and take up as little space as the ear mould in an ordinary aid. They have severe limitations, especially for children: their power is restricted by the closeness of the microphone and the amplifier. It is likely that such an aid will have been obtained for cosmetic reasons. Teenage deaf children can become very conscious of, and embarrassed by, their hearing aids to the extent that they regularly refuse to wear them, except when adults insist. It is crucial with hearing aids as with other prostheses, that an atmosphere is generated in a school which integrates able bodied children and children with disabilities where aids are totally accepted by staff and children and are neither objects of derision nor wonder. The social and emotional pressure on children who are unhappy about the aids they have been given should not be underestimated.

It is appropriate at this point to mention cochlear implants, although it is unlikely that many teachers in ordinary schools will have contact with an implanted child. A cochlear implant involves the placing of an electrode or electrodes either in, or on, the entrance to the inner ear. The electrode is connected to a receiver which is implanted under the skin behind the ear. The external part of the cochlear implant consists of a second processor about the size of a small cigarette packet which connects by a wire to the receiver in the child's ear. The function of the cochlear implant is to stimulate electronically the auditory nerve in those people who have no residual hearing, but can be reached by acoustic means.

There are many complex issues which arise from this still experimental operation, particularly in relation to children. Organizations for the deaf, many doctors, teachers and parents think that the ethical problems raised are more important than the, as yet unproven, benefit. Implants are being developed in Britain with post-lingually deafened adults. It is unlikely that children will be operated on in the immediate future. Implants have, however been carried out on children in the United States and some other parts of the world.

Very little information is available about the educational management of a child with a cochlear implant. Even if effective, the implant is unlikely in a school setting to give much more than a general awareness of noise and possibly some information about the patterns of speech. A child with an implant remains a profoundly deaf child and needs to be worked with accordingly.

Educational hearing aids (hearing aids not entirely worn on the listener)

A fundamental problem in the integration of children with hearing impairments into ordinary schools is the creation of an environment which does not render their hearing aids almost entirely useless. In order to make use of their residual hearing, deaf children need optimal listening conditions as well as the most suitable aids. A child with a hearing impairment has to construct spoken language from an incomplete jigsaw of pieces. Changes in the acoustic environment which to a hearing person would be minimal, can be severely disruptive. The factors which adversely affect hearing aids are background noise, reverberation and the distance between the child and the speaker to whom they are trying to listen.

Background noise and the external environment is considerable even in the most apparently silent classroom. In a classroom where there are group discussions, project work, or children playing, background noise may reach levels which make auditory speech discrimination virtually impossible for a hearing-impaired child. Reverberation describes the way in which the sound persists in a room, reflecting off walls, floor, ceilings and objects in the room and increasing the noise levels. Reverberation increases the unwanted background noise, and makes it even more difficult for a child to sort out the meaningful speech sounds. The problem of noise can be tackled in a number of ways, by acoustic treatment of the room, by the use of hearing aids which provide a direct link between the speaker and the child, and by changes in classroom management. All too often none of these techniques is used, and a deaf child is placed in an ordinary classroom and expected to cope. When educational progress is not made the child's failure is blamed on levels of hearing loss, intelligence, motivation, parents, anything, except bad educational management and lack of resources.

When properly used, radio microphone hearing aids, which provide a direct link between the speaker and the child combined with unrestricted mobility, have proved invaluable in the integration of children with hearing impairments into ordinary classes. They have had more impact on their education than any other single kind of equipment since the invention of hearing aids themselves. They should be available to every child with a hearing impairment and should not have to be bought by parents or by charities as many are at present.

The key to their importance however, is proper use, and this is notoriously difficult to achieve. Adverse environmental factors have already been mentioned, but there is also the quality of the equipment itself and its maintenance. Battery life and recharging require systematic management. Aids need to be checked once, perhaps twice daily for younger children to ensure that they are working properly. A qualified teacher of the deaf or audiologist needs to keep a regular check on equipment of this kind. The relationship between the classroom teacher and the qualified teacher of the deaf is crucial in monitoring the proper working of children's aids.

The use of such aids requires some description. They consist of a radio transmitter and microphone worn by the teacher, parent or other child, and a radio receiver worn by the user. The receiver may be built into a hearing aid itself, and therefore act as a replacement for personal hearing aids, or it may be linked to the child's personal hearing aids by a direct audio input lead, or through a neck induction loop. The former type provides more power than the latter, but means that the child either has to wear a cumbersome body aid all the time, or have a different listening experience when he or she changes from radio aids to personal aids. The neck loop system, while easy to use, particularly for older school and college students, results in significant loss of power. Direct audio input leads are not available for all post-aural hearing aids, and create an additional link in the sound chain where something may go wrong.

Radio hearing aids may be either stereo or mono. They usually have an environmental microphone as well as the receiver microphone, and may have facilities for a plug-in lapel microphone so that a child may more easily monitor his or her own voice.

Recently, a similar system has become available which uses infra-red waves rather than radio waves for the transmission of sound. This has the advantage of being free from interference from other radio signals, and of not passing through walls, thus avoiding the necessity of operating several interchangeable frequencies when more than one hearing-impaired child is being taught in school. A disadvantage of the infra-red system is that it cannot be used out of doors or in bright sunlight.

The primary use of these systems is to enable the child to receive a clear voice signal and to eliminate or reduce confusing background noise. A number of other systems have been developed to provide this facility. The loop induction system is used primarily in schools for the hearing impaired, in cinemas, churches, halls, and other meeting places. It may be used in a partially hearing unit in an ordinary school. The system consists of a microphone connected to an amplifier and a loop of wire which encircles the room. It uses the principle of the electromagnetic coil, which enables the signal from the microphone to be transmitted by a magnetic field within the loop of wire to the induction coil within the child's hearing aid. The system allows good auditory contact between teacher and child, but limits the movement of the teacher who is connected by a wire to the amplifier. There may also be a loss of power within the loop and variations in the strength of the signal within the loop. The same principle is used in the personal neck loop as part of a radio hearing aid system.

Group hearing aids may also be used in partially hearing units. A group hearing aid may be fitted into a moveable trolley, or may be permanently wired to the children's desks. As with other systems the teacher speaks directly into the microphone, the children have head phones and microphones of their own. The system provides very clear signals, allows the children to speak and listen to each other, and does not interfere with other systems. Its disadvantage is that the children are effectively tied to their desks. It thus severely limits the teaching techniques which can be used with the equipment.

Children with hearing impairments in ordinary classes often have great difficulty when television programmes are being used. Subtitled television will be dealt with later, but there are a number of ways in which the sound from a television may be boosted to help a deaf child without distracting others in the class. A television can be connected to a loop system, an amplifier may be attached to the television speaker with a volume control and lead to the child, or a television adapter may be bought which plugs directly into an output socket on the set, if it has one. The disadvantage of these systems for school use is that the child is physically linked to the television and is not using his or her own hearing aids.

Television tuners with hi-fi systems can be adapted for use for hearing-impaired children. The tuner is connected directly to the television signal from the aerial, splits off the sound signal and can be connected to a radio hearing aid transmitter to feed television sound direct into a child's own radio hearing aid. This system is ideal for children who are using radio hearing aids in ordinary schools.

The central purpose of all these educational radio hearing aid systems is to reduce the extent to which noise interferes with the voice the child is trying to make sense of. Each provides a direct link with a sound source and it is this feature, together with its mobility, that has made the radio hearing aid system so valuable. Recent research by Nolan and Tucker has suggested, however, that radio hearing aids are often being used in ways and in situations which severely limit their usefulness, and result in what they call 'auditory fatigue' in children. Nolan and Tucker (1986) stress the importance of a short distance of less than six inches between a teacher's mouth and the transmitter microphone. If the teacher wears the microphone casually and too low down there is a significant loss of power. In order that children can monitor their own voices they may themselves be wearing a microphone – their radio hearing aid has environmental microphones, so have their personal hearing aids if they are wearing them. Children in noisy classrooms may be totally swamped by sound from the very system designed to reduce such problems. The kind of educational hearing aid which is used has significant implications for the teaching techniques which are possible in that class and with that child. There are occasions, particularly in group discussions, when a child with a hearing impairment is seriously disadvantaged. Teachers must be alert to the fact that these children need visual as well as auditory information and that phrases and discussions may need to be repeated and reinforced for their benefit. The position a child sits in may be crucial for both looking and listening, but again teachers need to be aware of the sensibilities of the child when treating them differently from other children in the class.

Other communication aids

The development of microcomputers has brought about great improvements in communications technology with many exciting implications for deaf people. Not only are some of these communication aids of direct value to teachers as educational tools, they should be part of the environment in which children with hearing impairments grow up. Deaf children should have the same right of access to the television and to the telephone as hearing children. They also need to learn to use the new technology to be familiar with it and for it to be part of their lives.

Television subtitles can be very valuable in providing access to schools programmes and other television. Subtitles may be 'open', that is, on screen for all viewers or 'closed' – only visible to viewers with Teletext receivers built in or added to their television. Teletext subtitles are provided for deaf viewers on a limited but growing number of programmes by both BBC and ITV. At present, school programmes are not subtitled on Teletext. In recent years, the BBC has experimented with open captioning with a number of repeated schools broadcasts. Transcripts of the captions and teachers' notes have been available from the National Deaf Children's Society. The response to this by teachers has been disappointing. Subtitles do not limit hearing children's appreciation of the programme, and there is no reason why subtitled versions of programmes may not be used with a mixed group of hearing and deaf pupils. Even more recently, researchers at the University of Southampton have developed a do-it-yourself subtitling system which links to a BBC microcomputer called the Possum/Mountbaten Subtitling Unit. The system enables teachers to record programmes of their own choice and subtitle them in a way that is suitable for the children that they are teaching. The National Subtitling Library for the Deaf provides subtitled education videos on loan to schools in three different language levels and reading speeds.[1]

Communications technology has also enabled profoundly deaf people to have access to the telephone by visual means. Deaf communicating terminals consist of a visual display unit, a keyboard and a connector which allows signals to be sent and received by the telephone handset. Two systems at either end of the telephone line are, of course, needed. In the United States a large number of relatively cheap, compatible, systems are available. In Britain only an expensive (£400 plus) and not entirely reliable system called Vistel is currently approved by British Telecom. A much cheaper system called Minicom is seeking BT approval. A much less sophisticated system which allows 'yes' and 'no' answers to questions has recently been launched.

There is obviously not enough space in an introductory chapter of this kind to deal with all the supportive aids that are available in the communications sphere.

---

[1] Further information is available from the National Subtitling Library for Deaf People, Town Hall, Stockport, SK1 3XE.

Worth mentioning as an example, because of its usefulness with hearing-impaired children with cerebral palsy which effects their ability to speak or sign, is the Cannon Communicator[1], a small electronic typewriter which enables messages to be printed to a continuous paper tape.

At the other end of the scale in sophistication and expense, is the Possum Pallantype Computer Aided Transcription System[2]. This enables trained pallan-type operators to provide an instant verbatim transcript of a speaker's text which is projected on to a screen to be read. This equipment is most unlikely to be used in schools, but will be seen increasingly at conferences, courses and meetings where deaf people are present.

Equipment not designed for deaf people may have useful applications, computer mail boxes for instance, are a valuable, if expensive way for deaf people to communicate and to leave messages for each other. Systems of this kind are increasingly used in the workplace. The Microwriter[3], a fast electronic notetaker designed for business might be invaluable for a deaf student following an 'A' level or college course. Lipreading and note taking at the same time are very difficult tasks for a deaf student. Once the technique has been mastered, the Microwriter enables the student to concentrate on the lecturer or the discussion and to take notes with one hand.

A range of other, simple environmental aids is available to help hearing-impaired people. Many of these are for home rather than for school use, such as vibrator or flashing-light alarm clocks, flashing-light doorbells and so on. Many of these systems work on the basis of converting auditory signals of various kinds into visual form.

Hearing aids, teachers and children

Different kinds of aids have very different functions. Teachers in ordinary schools who really mean to make technology work for them and for their children need to do a great deal more than just have it available. New technology needs to be seen as part of the curriculum. Viewed in this way it will follow that changes in curriculum objectives and content will require thought about appropriate aids in appropriate situations. Moreover, the presence of a child with a hearing impairment in a class changes the method by which that class may be taught. Sometimes only small changes are necessary; the provision of the appropriate aid may be enough. In other situations the whole approach may need to be altered.

Teachers faced with technical aids need to be familiar with them, and above all confident in their use. Teachers who gingerly hang a radio aid transmitter around their necks and refer to it as 'that deaf child's hearing machine' are unlikely to understand its strengths and its weaknesses, and are conveying to the children in the class, deaf and hearing alike, a negative attitude both to the aid and to the deaf person.

---

[1] Available from Cannon (UK) Ltd, Cannon House, Manor Road, Wallington, Surrey, SM6 0AJ.
[2] Available from POSSUM Controls Ltd, Middle Green Road, Langley, Slough, Berkshire, SL3 6DF.
[3] Available from the Foundation for Communication for the Disabled, 25 High Street, Woking, Surrey, GU21 1BW.

Of course, classroom teachers cannot be expected to be experts in hearing impairment. The supportive role of the specialist teacher of the deaf and the special needs advisory teacher is crucial here. Classroom teachers should ask, indeed they should demand, information, support and equipment if they are to have hearing impaired children in their classes. The integration of disabled children into ordinary schools is not an end in itself. It is the means to an end: that is, access to the ordinary school curriculum and to their home community. If because of lack of resources deaf children are unable to benefit from that lack of access then their placement in an ordinary school is ineffective and should be enhanced.

Aids exist for children not teachers. On one level this may be obvious but it needs to be stated that while technical aids should make life easier for children, they will often make life more difficult for their teachers. Equipment needs to be selected and used with sensitivity towards a child's feelings, wishes and evaluation of the aid. Small children in particular need to learn to use hearing aids; they may find them uncomfortable and restrictive at first, just as many of us find the glasses which later become second nature to wear. We should not deliberately inflict on children the discomfort of large body-worn aids in situations where they are not appropriate or useful.

The wearing of a hearing aid marks the deaf person as deaf. It is a badge of their disability. Wearing an aid changes you. If a teacher who feels awkward about wearing a radio aid transmitter is aware of that change and discomfort only slightly, think of its force to the child who knows that the aid is both a burden and a help. With teenage deaf children this conflict can often be very apparent. The cosmetic qualities of equipment become extremely important at this age and teachers need to be aware of a child's difficulties and if necessary help in finding something more accept[able]. Coming to terms with wearing a hearing aid for a young deaf person is part of coming to terms with being deaf, and children need help and encouragement to that end. It is an absolute scandal, therefore, that black children in this country are not commonly offered skin tone hearing aids. Any teacher with any commitment to anti-racist and multi-cultural education should insist that skin tone aids and earmoulds are made available to those children who want them.

Teachers should also be ready to listen to what children with hearing impairments have to say about their aids. If children have been brought up actively to use and understand their own equipment, then they would be best able to say when it is working properly and to choose what suits them best in a particular environment. We should see children with disabilities as active partners in their own education rather than as passive recipients of help.

Effective integration is not a matter of making a deaf child behave like a hearing one. It requires a fundamental recognition of people with disabilities as people, and changes in the way schools are run to provide them with equal access. Ultimately, integration in school should lead to integration in the work place. An integrated classroom should lead in due course to an integrated staff room. Anyone who has not contemplated the implications of teaching staff with disabilities, has not thought through the philosophy of integrated education. In this context, educating ordinary children about others with special needs is central. Opportunities to handle, use and understand technical aids will demystify them and help remove the stigma attached to their use. Information and openness about disability for other children is an important part of integration. It is pointless to pretend that a child wearing a hearing aid is not different and can be treated like any other. The hearing aid itself marks out and symbolizes that difference.

It may seem that I have implied in this chapter that new technology is as much a burden as a liberation. This is obviously untrue, but I have wanted to stress the way in which the use of technical aids changes people and people's attitudes; to highlight what might be called the 'hidden curriculum' of technical aids. Aids badly maintained and badly used are not helpful. They do not expand lives.

Using technical aids well in the ordinary classroom requires the right equipment, specialist support and advice, and understanding of aids as part of the curriculum, not simply part of the child. It also requires a lot of hard work. Given this – and it undoubtedly exists in many schools – the use of new technology to aid children with hearing impairments can undoubtedly expand their lives, and indeed also, expand the lives of fellow pupils and their teachers.

Reference

Nolan, M. and Tucker, K. 1986. 'The auditory environment of hearing impaired children in modern educational practice: the need for short teacher microphone distance', *Journal of the British Association of Teachers of the Deaf, 10*, pp. 70–79.

Further reading

Gray, R. F. 1985. *Cochlear Implants*, London, Croom Helm.
Montgomery, G. (ed.) 1981. *The Integration and Disintegration of the Deaf in Society*, Scottish Workshop Publications.
Tucker, I. and Nolan, M. 1984. *Educational Audiology*, London, Croom Helm.
Webster, A. and Ellwood, J. 1985. *The Hearing Impaired Child in the Ordinary School*, London, Croom Helm.

11 The challenge of conductive education

Andrew Sutton

Conductive education is a system of education for children and adults with 'motor disorders' which originates in the work of András Pető in Hungary. It is based on the theory that individuals with disorders of movement that originate in the central nervous system can learn new ways to control their movement and thus become independent. The practice entails the merging of the Western roles of teacher and therapist in one distinct profession: the conductor. Conductive education has had remarkable results in Hungary, but its results in the UK have to date been less spectacular. Andrew Sutton argues however, that as practised in the UK, it has so far been a significantly different system. The challenge now is to see how conductive education can be fully implemented in this country.

Introduction

On 1 April 1986 BBC 1 screened a one-hour documentary film called *Standing Up for Joe* which showed the first few months of a young South London boy with severe cerebral palsy at the Institute for Motor Disorders in Budapest. One hour is a long slot for a documentary film on BBC 1. Despite a competing Bank Holiday feature film, five million people watched this programme and it achieved one of the highest interest ratings for any film shown on television. Over ten thousand written enquiries subsequently arrived at the BBC from people with motor-disordered children, from those who wanted to train and from those who simply wanted to express how moved they were by what they had seen – and to register their distress that this work was not available for British children. Yet the Hungarian work shown in the film had been vaguely known in relevant professional circles in this country for at least twenty years.

The film's impact was partly due to its placing this work firmly in the public domain, especially to the potential consumers of such a service, and partly to its superiority over other media in portraying movement and emotion. The film was about *conductive education* (*kónduktiv pedagógia* in Hungarian). In no small degree as a result of that film, considerable attention is now being given both in Britain and overseas to the problems of extracting this complex system of pedagogy from its country of origin and establishing it in altogether different contexts.

This chapter offers a summary and introductory account of this system, its context, development, practice and theory, and looks at some of the practical problems and implications of its possible establishment in this country. At the time of writing there exists only one, preliminary overview of the field in English (Cottam and Sutton 1985), though the one published Hungarian textbook is currently being prepared for translation (Hári and Akós 1971). Much basic investigation of the history, theory, sociology and politics of conductive education in Hungary, even by Hungarian scholars, remains to be done and the problems of setting it up in this country will only be fully defined and worked out in practice.

The social and historical context

Hungarian education had its earliest roots in the Christianization of the country and the associated need for literate priests in the secular administration of the state. The subsequent history of the country during the later Middle Ages, the Renaissance and the Enlightenment, particularly the foreign and cultural dominations of the Turks and the Austrians, with major linguistic diversity and the development of a top-heavy gentry class, did not make for an indigenous educational tradition. Under the Dual Monarchy (1867–1918), industrialization, urbanization and political autonomy allowed the realization of some of the liberal aspirations of 1848 and elementary education began to develop in parallel with trends in other advanced countries. Progressive forces were opposed, however, by the use of education as a repressive tool against non-Magyar minorities. Following the overthrow of the short-lived *Republic of Councils* (i.e. of Soviets) in 1919, reactionary forces initiated a process of retrenchment which, in education as elsewhere, resulted in increased social discrimination and curtailment of specialist services.

Special education for handicapped children had begun in Hungary in the nineteenth century and was brought under the Ministry of Education at the turn of the century, reflecting general trends in the countries of Western Europe and North America. Development of the system was halted by the Great War, after which, under the fascist regime of Admiral Horthy, it contracted further. By 1938 only 78 per cent of the country's school-age children entered school at all, and there were less than five thousand pupils attending only 48 special schools. The training of special educators had altogether ceased. The Second World War caused even further disruption.

Following the liberation from fascism, the education system as a whole had to be built up from a very low base. In August 1945 the Provisional National Government replaced the previous divisive system with a universal, compulsory elementary education, the 'general school' (*áltanalános iskola*). A system of special education was also established and by 1980 over thirty-seven thousand pupils were attending 167 special schools and 407 special classes attached to general schools.

Special education in Hungary is provided for the moderately and severely mentally handicapped, the deaf and the partially hearing, the blind and the partially sighted, the speech impaired and the motor-disabled. For all but the first of these categories provision is residential except in particular cases.

András Pető and conductive education

András Pető (1893-1967), the originator of conductive education, appears a mysterious character. He had been born into a Jewish family in a German-speaking area in Western Hungary. He went to medical school in Vienna where he graduated in 1916 and worked as a physician in hospitals in and around Vienna till 1938. During this period he mixed widely in intellectual circles, knew the founders of psychoanalysis (and of the rival school of sociodrama), wrote poetry, plays and philosophy in German and edited a natural healing magazine. He was a Marxist and joined the party in 1919: he was also interested in ancient religions and meditation. In 1938 he went first to Paris, then moved to Budapest, where he eked a living recycling waste-paper and making *ersatz* coffee. Immediately following the liberation of the city he asked the authorities whether he could educate motor-disordered children and was given a group of thirteen pupils and the use of basement rooms in the College of Special Education. Resources initially were very scarce. The Pestalozzi Foundation provided blankets and medical students volunteered to help. But within a couple of years about half his pupils could walk and he was made a professor at the college. In 1952 he was able to open his own National Movement Therapy Institute.

Over the course of the fifties Pető appears to have been in considerable conflict with the special education establishment and with the Ministry of Health which was responsible for his Institute. In 1963 the Institute was transferred to the Ministry of Education, where it remains. Conductive education was made the official provision for all Hungarian children suffering from relevant conditions. Pető, now in poor health, continued to work himself, his staff and pupils at the same intense rate as he always had and died at his desk in 1967.

He had published virtually nothing on the theory and practice of conductive education. The system and its methods existed implicitly in the organization and the work of his Institute and its 'conductors'.

Mobility and school

To attend school in Hungary a child must be able to walk. This general requirement applies not only to the general schools and the kindergartens but also to *all* special schools. Children who cannot fulfil this requirement, or for some other reason (e.g. incontinence) offend the normal requirements of school, are entitled only to home tuition, six hours per week. Such a requirement is not of course unique to Hungary.

There are two schools for the motor-disabled in Hungary. Even in these two schools the same requirement holds: children who cannot walk cannot attend. Pető's Institute is *not*, however, part of the special education system: it is separately administered. Relations with the wider special education system, which tends to educate children for the whole of their school careers, rather than returning them to normal schools, are not warm.

The Institute and its network

Since shortly after Pető's death, the Institute that he founded has been under the direction of Dr Mária Hári, a medical student volunteer from 1945 who never left. Since April 1984 the Institute has been housed in a magnificent and prestigious building in the Buda hills. The new building houses outpatient departments for children and adults, the Conductors' College (now a major undertaking which accepted ninety-two new students on its four-year course in September 1985), library and archives and four floors of residential facilities for kindergarten and school-age pupils. Additionally, the current five-year plan requires the Institute to establish satellite units in eleven out of Hungary's nineteen counties.

Before the move to the new premises the Institute housed two hundred residential pupils, there were some eighty day pupils and over one hundred children and their parents attending 'mother-and-baby' sessions. Over five hundred children attended under various sessional arrangements and another hundred-or-so received guidance in various settings around Budapest. There were some three hundred adult outpatients in regular attendance and around five hundred children were receiving help through what appeared a somewhat *ad hoc* and skeletal provincial network. Additionally, a very large number of cases (some four thousand in 1983) were seen for assessment, consultation and review at the Institute itself and in hospital and rural clinics. The Institute now houses four hundred residential cases. No figures are available for other activities but these also seem to have increased and will certainly do so with the establishment of a formal provincial network.

In a country of ten million inhabitants this represents a considerable national effort. This effort is directed towards a category of need, 'motor disorder', not recognized in special education in the English-speaking West. Motor disorders are problems of controlling movement due to disease or damage to the brain or central nervous system. In childhood they include cerebral palsy (spastic, athetoid and ataxic children) and spina bifida (with apparently excellent results with the vexing problem of incontinence); in adults, Friedreich's ataxia, multiple sclerosis, strokes, paraplegia and Parkinson's disease. As a very general rule, children and adults suffering from these conditions are eligible for conductive education as long as their conditions are not complicated by additional mental problems such as profound mental handicap in children, or serious depression in adults. It is also important in childhood conditions that the work begins in the early years, preferably before school age, before particular mental sets and secondary physical deformities are established.

The group of people towards whom the Institute and its network direct their provision is not therefore the same as the British 'physically handicapped'. In childhood the motor-disordered population includes some (though not all) of the children who would attend a British school for those with physical disabilities, plus some of the children in schools for severe learning difficulties (especially those in their 'special care units'), some in schools for 'delicate' pupils, some in long-stay hospitals and also a few integrated into normal schools. In adulthood it includes the victims of chronically disabling conditions with onsets from adolescence right through to extreme old age. Medically, therefore, the motor disordered are a heterogeneous population: their common bond is to be found at a higher level, in the proposition that their motor control can be greatly enhanced to establish normal everyday functions, through pedagogic means.

Taking children and adults together, the motor-disordered constitute a significant minority in the developed countries (conventional wisdom is that cerebral palsy afflicts two school-age children per 1000 live births and that Parkinson's disease afflicts one in 100 people over the age of 60). In Hungary more than twenty years have passed since conductive education was decreed the official provision for all motor-disordered children and an adequate and universal provision for all in need has still to be achieved. Only a very small proportion of the adults eligible receive this form of help.

Outcome

The development of conductive education has been unique to Hungary. Its claim for international attention is not its uniqueness, however, but the apparently extraordinary results that it routinely achieves.

There are no formal scientific research results to corroborate the success of conductive education. Partly this is because statistical research in education has been late coming to all the Socialist countries. Even though the rest of special education in Hungary has incorporated testing, the Institute maintains a vigorous distrust of non-qualitative evaluation. It should be remembered that the lack of evaluative research is a general feature of established special educational or physiotherapeutic approaches in the West. In default of formal research, quantitative information on the effectiveness of conductive education in Hungary is restricted to the detailed official returns submitted to the Ministry each year and published in its annual report, and to information from the Institute's own routine follow-up of previous cases.

The Institute's criterion for success is 'orthofunction' (the opposite of *dys*function). It does not aim to help children and adults cope with the limitations of funtion that result from a motor disorder. Thus conductive education eschews mechanical aids (such as wheelchairs), adaptations to the environment (ramps), aids (special writing and eating implements), physical interventions (severing tendons) or personal and social accommodations (helping the sufferers and those around them 'accept' or 'come to terms with' their disability). Rather it aims to teach sufferers to master their disordered movements to the degree to be able to function in the world despite their underlying physical disorders.

The spastic child may learn to walk and write neatly with a pen, the child with spina bifida may learn continence, the stroke patient may regain the use of an arm and of speech, the elderly person with Parkinson's disease may 'unfreeze', walk and write again. It means more, however, than just the acquisition of individual motor skills, but also the ability to function in the material and social world without the limitations and allowances that betoken handicap. Orthofunction in childhood is most conveniently indexed in Hungary by the ability to attend school.

School attendance for the motor-disordered Hungarian child involves something both broader, and narrower than some Western notions of integration. It means that the child is able to participate in the life and curriculum of the school, not just motorically but also psychologically, academically and socially. The standard of handwriting attained by school-age pupils at the Institute is the only such achievement yet to have been investigated by outsiders. A minority proved still unable to write; the rest could and on the whole wrote well (Aubrey and Sutton 1986). In most cases the school involved will be a kindergarten or general school. If the child is mentally handicapped as well as motor-disordered it will be in a special school.

The official statistics available do not by their very nature make it certain how many motor-disordered children slip completely through the net and never come to the attention of the Institute. Some certainly do, as was evidenced by the Hungarian parents who identified themselves following a recent report on conductive education on the national TV network, indignantly asking why this service had not been offered to their children. The Institute's own figures for 4,534 previous cases up to the end of 1983 indicate that 10.7 per cent of known cases had been closed without receiving a complete course of conductive educa-

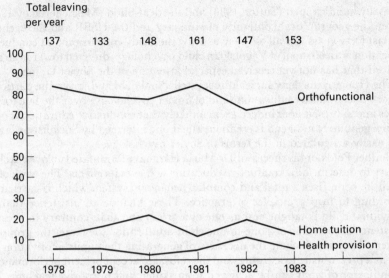

Figure 11.1 Immediate placements of children leaving residential education at the Institute, 1978 to 1983

tion. Shortage of facilities within the network appears to have been a major factor in this. Of the remainder, 7.2 per cent were being educated at home (or, if adults, were not working) and 9.1 per cent had proved unable to benefit from conductive education, usually because of profound mental handicap. The remaining 83.7 per cent were reported to be orthofunctional.

These figures are less than satisfactory in a number of respects. For example, they refer to a variety of conditions and to a mix of children and adults. Moreover, the criterion of orthofunction is not clearly defined. Differing sets of figures available, however, do show the same general pattern (and should be read with the same reservations). Figure 11.1, for example, refers to recent residential pupils.

Orthofunction, even loosely defined, for around two-thirds or three-quarters of motor-disordered people represents an advance over our own expectations for this population of such a magnitude as to be regarded as a qualitative leap.

It should be noted that orthofunction is in no way a 'cure' for the underlying condition. People remain spastic, hemiplegic or whatever, but they are nevertheless able to walk, maintain continence, and do school work.

Practice and principles

Conductive education is not a 'therapy' but a pedagogy aimed at creating new skills and mental structures out of social interaction in the material world. The basic theoretical position is very closely allied to the theory of human development proposed by L. S. Vygotskii and his successors, particularly A. N. Leont'ev, in the Soviet Union. Conductive Education presents close theoretical parallels with many areas of Soviet defectology, especially with Soviet work with the mentally handicapped (Sutton 1980) and the deaf-blind (Meshcheriakov 1979). Given the geographical contiguity of Hungary and the USSR and the events of the last forty years it is all too easy to draw the ready conclusion that conductive education is an offshoot of Vygotskian child psychology, directed towards an area of need that has not yet received especial attention in the Soviet Union.

The Hungarians deny such a direct intellectual debt and, given the particular history of conductive education (and of Soviet psychology) over the late forties, fifties and sixties, it does indeed seem unlikely that conductive education is other than a genuinely indigenous creation, albeit one informed by Socialist pedagogy and easily articulated in the terms of Soviet psychology.

Neither Pető nor his successor Dr Mária Hári have formulated an over-arching theory to describe how conductive education achieves its effects. The work of the Institute comprises a total and complex pedagogic system which is carried out according to firm principles of practice. These include an insistence that the individual child is taught best as one of a group and that, contrary to Western insistence of the value of a one-to-one child-adult ratio, 'the larger the group the better'. They also include the necessity of generating the pupils' motivation and will as a prerequisite to learning, and the refusal to accept present performance as an indicator of what can be achieved from skilled and purposive teaching. The work reflects the principle of 'plasticity', now well accepted in Western neurology, which holds that the human brain may adopt alternative means of achieving a given function.

Elaborate scientific theory notwithstanding, conductive education is essentially good teaching. It has a special emphasis on the teaching of movement but it is concerned of necessity with the development of the whole personality. It may be likened, for example, to the teaching of dance, in which non-intuitive movements (all normal motor acts are non-intuitive in the motor-disordered) are taught in a disciplined and orderly fashion with skilled attention to the learners' attitudes, motivation, persistence, morale, rate of learning, and skills. Rhythm, music and verbal instructions play an important part in the creation and internalization of new skills and abilities.

The Institute trains its own conductors. It insists that the four-year training should be 'on the job' from the outset so that there should be no separation of theory from practice. Similarly there is a determination that the intellectual aspects of the pupils' work are not separated from the emotional, and their performance and progress are not considered in isolation from their social and material context.

The way that this approach works in individual cases varies enormously. As a cardinal principle, individual pupils must form their own goals and devise their own paths to achieving them. Each different condition demands its own particular emphases and different age-stages demand different approaches. Very young children attend for short daily sessions with their parents (which may be all that is needed to attain orthofunction in some cases), older children may be admitted residentially, but there is also a day school. Adults attend sessionally, usually every other day.

Time to orthofunction varies. Thus, on average, a two-year-old child with spasticity, beginning conductive education at two years, may attain orthofunction in a year or so; a child with athetosis in three or four. If conductive education were not to start till four years it could take a year or so longer, and if the child proved mentally handicapped as well then maybe a year or two on top of that. On the other hand, the recent experience of British Parkinson's disease sufferers at the Institute indicate that noticeable changes may be apparent in this condition within a few weeks,[1] though maintenance afterwards may prove a problem.

Developments in the UK

Pető started his work in Budapest in 1945. The first child from this country to undergo his treatment was the English daughter of German-Hungarian parents, who went out to Budapest in 1947 (Savage 1986). She was his first foreign patient from any country. Pető's contact with the West over the nineteen-fifties remains as yet undocumented but German accounts of his work were published in the early sixties and the first English-language paper describing his work appeared in 1965 (Cotton 1965). This was written by Esther Cotton, a physiotherapist who had visited Pető's Institute and returned a convert to his approach. Though the paper was published in a major international journal it appears to have aroused little general interest and, perhaps in part because the journal was medical and Cotton a physiotherapist, it stimulated virtually no interest amongst special educators and the educational psychologists who worked with motor-disordered children.

Cotton set to with remarkable energy over the next twenty years to implement what she had seen in Hungary and win converts amongst others willing to adapt their work as she did. She worked for the Spastics Society and, though she never won the wholehearted support of that organization and its schools, this provided her with a base from which to spread the word, to teach and to publish. Though one of the first schools in this country to attempt to remodel itself on conductive education lines was a local authority day school for the physically handicapped (Claremont School in Bristol, which sent a number of staff to Budapest to see for themselves in the early seventies), it was largely in Spastics Society and associated schools that the approach won supporters. In one of these schools, Ingfield Manor in Sussex, the Society opened a purpose-built 'Pető Unit' in 1966, which became the flagship of Esther Cotton's movement.

Conductive education remained largely unheard of, and there were few further published accounts of the work in Budapest and its outcomes. As the seventies progressed the idea of conductive education in this country seems to have been increasingly identified with children with cerebral palsy and the work at Ingfield Manor School. Apart from the enthusiastic adherents, few seemed to have any notion of it as a possible major breakthrough, and its wider applicability to the motor-disordered as a whole seems to have been almost unknown.

By the end of that decade the concept of integration was being increasingly discussed, if not practised in this country. Partly this reflected dissatisfaction with special schools for pupils with physical disabilities. For some, particularly physiotherapists working in such schools in the state sector, this led to an interest

---

[1] For the first published extracts from adults' experience of conductive education see 'From the viewpoint of three of our members...,' *The Parkinson Newsletter*, No. 57, pp. 10–11, May 1986.

in Cotton's work as a means of giving a point and purpose to the children's schooling. By the early eighties, therefore, there was a small but growing band of converts, mostly physiotherapists but including some teachers and others, working in special education to adapt Cotton's teaching to a range of settings. One such setting, where there was also growing dissatisfaction with the content and purpose of the education provided, was the special care unit in schools for children with severe learning difficulties which cater for profoundly and multiply handicapped children. Though the interest in conductive education arose in a minority of those working with physically and multiply handicapped children, their numbers were sufficient in 1983 for Cotton and her close associates, still mainly in the Spastics Society, to form the Conductive Education Interest Group to encourage and co-ordinate the spread of this work.

Conductive education, UK-style

Esther Cotton's teachings on Conductive Education have been published in a series of booklets published by the Spastics Society (Cotton 1975, 1980, 1981). This knowledge base has been variously operationalized in the UK and abroad as what has been called 'Conductive Education, UK-style' (Lancaster-Gaye 1985). In 1984 the Conductive Education Interest Group, published a list of 'Schools and Units using Conductive Education'. At the end of 1985 an attempt was made to gain a picture of the 22 educational establishments represented on the list to identify what precisely constitutes conductive education UK-style (CEUKS for short) in our national system of special education.

The method was to enquire of the 17 principal educational psychologists of the local education authorities within which the 22 schools are situated. The intention was to gain a somewhat more independent response than might be obtained from the schools themselves, though in the event many respondents simply passed on information supplied by the schools themselves.

Only a brief summary of the findings of this survey will be given here. Two of the establishments surveyed were pre-school units, the remaining twenty were schools for children ranging in age from under three to 19: eight of these schools were listed as 'PH', five as 'ESN(S)' and one as 'Spastic ESN(S)', the populations of the remaining six were not stated. The majority lay within the state sector.

CEUKS is in fact a misnomer; all 22 establishments were in England. Though subsequent enquiries have identified other schools claiming to practise 'according to the principles of Conductive Education', no establishment has emerged in parts of the UK other than England.

The principal educational psychologists were asked for information on three basic questions about the establishments that lay in their areas:

1 Is there in fact a scheme that considers itself Conductive Education?
2 What precisely is being done: methods, hours per week, type of pupil etc?
3 Has any case of orthofunction, defined loosely in the British context by successful admission to ordinary school without aids or aides, ever been achieved?

Responses were received on sixteen establishments, revealing a very wide range of practices. At one extreme were four establishments where there was no involvement with conductive education at all. In a further eight establishments a variety of carefully qualified statements were made about conductive education. For example:

> ... the staff are adamant in their view that the title 'Conductive Education' should only be applied if Pető's prescriptions are followed to a significant extent.
>
> (State PH school with nine-years' experience of CEUKS)

> In common with other schools, what we have done is to take some of the basic concepts of conductive education ... in what we prefer to call 'Peto-style classes'.
>
> (Voluntary PH school)

> In the general inspection the HMIs counselled us against describing what we were doing as 'Peto' or 'conductive education' as it couldn't be implemented here with the purity and rigour of the system in Hungary.
>
> (State PH school)

Only four out of the sixteen schools regarded themselves as actually doing conductive education. In two cases this too was not without a certain qualification:

> ... turned the school over to conductive education in 1971. Since that time the principles of conductive education have been used as a framework throughout the school ...
>
> (State PH school)

The other schools were quite categoric. In one of these the principal psychologist merely passed on the terse information provided by the school itself: 'Conductive education is provided at this school' (Hospital ESN(S) school). In the other the psychologist provided a copy of a magazine article describing the work of the physiotherapy department at the school:

> This approach has led to a method of 'conductive education', which involves a constant 'swapping of roles' between teachers and therapists, which in turn enhances the 'symbiotic' union of community health and the local education authority.
>
> (State ESN(M) school)

In his own reply the psychologist remarked:

> I have been in touch with the psychologists working with these schools and they have attempted somewhat exhaustively to find out what is actually happening with them ... At present within [the school described in the magazine article] the physiotherapists and speech therapists do wish to be closely involved with children in the classroom; however, they remain largely separate from teaching and generally work in parallel to the teachers rather than together. There is not an emphasis on merging the role of activities offered with the teacher's role.

Of these sixteen establishments, therefore, a quarter were affirmatively not involved in such work, half had been influenced by Pető s system and only a quarter actually claimed to be doing conductive education, with varying justification.

The voluntary schools provided solely for children with cerebral palsy, the state schools for a wider range of physical disabilities. Frequent mention was made of varying degrees of mental handicap amongst the children provided for. In two cases the whole school was given over to or influenced by the attempt at conductive education, at the other extreme were single groups of around half-a-dozen children. Similarly, staff involved ranged from complex groups of teachers, therapists and assistants to a single therapist working alone. Staff–pupil ratios, where mentioned, tended to be high, as high as six 'conductors' to six children in one case. Group size was low, from five to eight pupils. The duration of the provision made ran from the whole of the school day down to 20 minutes daily.

There was little specific detail of teaching methods. Here is an exception:

> ...some of the basic philosophy of conductive education, i.e. task analysis, verbal regulation of behaviour, group participation and repetition
>
> (Voluntary PH school)

And only two schools mentioned academic work, though in an oblique way:

> All the children in this group can hold a pencil and write.
>
> (Voluntary PH school)

> In the top junior class, the children's educational needs tend to take predominance over their physical needs. Consequently conductive education takes on a modified format.
>
> (State PH school)

A number of features of conductive education in Hungary were noticeably absent. For example, the word 'group' was frequently used to describe teaching units. There was no indication, however, that the group was used as a pedagogic tool. Music only received one very brief mention and there was no mention of the development of the mental sphere, attitude, orientation, adjustment and intellectual factors.

There was no report of any formal evaluation of the work. Orthofunction was not the general criterion for success, indeed in all but three of the establishments surveyed the achievement of orthofunction was either not mentioned at all or specifically denied. Improvements in the pupils in the remainder, where reported, were quantitative rather than qualitative, for example:

> ...staff are confident that several children have been able to transfer to the mainstream [of the special school] rather than being confined to Special Care as a result of conductive education...there was a definite wide-ranging enhancement factor.
>
> (State PH school)

Three schools *did* claim orthofunction. The first of these was a state day school for pupils with physical disabilities which had been turned over to conductive education since 1971. At least four of its present staff had been to Budapest to see the Institute's work and, though the school's intake was not selective, 'there are less of the severely mentally handicapped'. Its headteacher reported as follows:

> It is hard to cite exactly in how many cases orthofunction has been achieved over the years although there are undoubtedly several cases which immediately came to

mind...There are, at present, several children from [the school] working well within the primary school next door using neither 'aids' nor 'aides.'

The second, also a state day PH school had run 'Peto groups' for two years and three of the children from these groups transferred subsequently to ordinary schools. The third was a state day PH school too. A 'cross classroom' group had been running for about four years. Two particular successes were cited, including

...one young lady who graduated from the group and whom we are now contemplating integrating into mainstream...[She] was a wheelchair-bound quadriplegic who is now independently mobile on foot with balance aids and completes her recording skills in traditional manner with pencil/pen.

It is immediately noticeable that all three schools are day schools in the state sector, not the residential voluntary schools that have provided the canonical image of CEUKS, and who tend to admit the more seriously and multiply disabled. All three were schools for pupils with physical disabilities. Two of the three schools made careful qualifications to their reports of orthofunction. The first school cited reported that 'only about 25 per cent of the children admitted actually go right through [the school]', whilst the second pointed out, with respect to its group for spina bifida children with self-help, mobility and spatial problems:

I must here emphasize that some children with spina bifida and without such problems went through our 'ordinary' classes into mainstream schools and units.

Orthofunction is not then a general feature of CEUKS, though a few children in local authority day PH schools have gone on from such programmes to function independently in normal schools. Obviously, without comparative evaluation with children who do *not* receive this help the question of 'spontaneous recovery' must remain open. The work of such schools nevertheless merits much more serious attention than has hitherto been the case.

The Spastics Society's flagship provision, Ingfield Manor School, is not included in the above account, since it lies within the local authority of one of the principal educational psychologists who made no return. Before the opening of the Peto Unit at Ingfield Manor in 1976 a careful evaluation by the London Institute of Education[1] compared the progress of children at Ingfield Manor with that of pupils at another, comparable Spastics Society school which did not attempt conductive education. The results were in favour of the comparison school. Subsequently, the first twenty children to complete two whole years in the Peto Unit were followed up (Jernqvist 1980). There was no comparison group, but a statistically significant improvement was discerned in aspects of the children's development over this period. Even so, the researcher concluded:

The two years have, in spite of the statistically significant progress, meant little towards normality in terms of schooling. In fact it has meant the opposite for the group as such, as one child who was a weekly boarder at the Unit, is now a full boarder farther away from home. One child has gone to a non-Society provision,

---

[1] This research was never published. It is written up as a series of Masters dissertations, concluding with McCormack (1976).

offering 52-weeks boarding, albeit nearer to home, giving the family the opportunity to meet for shorter but more frequent periods. The only day pupil has become a boarder.

The failure to establish orthofunction as a routine outcome for a substantial proportion of pupils is a sharp pointer to the major distinction between conductive education as developed and practised in Hungary and CEUKS as developed in England over the last twenty years and widely disseminated overseas. This might be summarized in the following terms: conductive education aims at qualitative change in its pupils, CEUKS merely quantitative changes which, desirable though they might be, are at best an improvement on current British practices, not the breakthrough that appears to have been achieved in Budapest.

Conductive education and integration

Opponents of the introduction of conductive education to this country sometimes argue that it would offend current British thinking on integration. Conductive education demands that a considerable proportion of the children's working day should be directed to learning to master specific effects of their motor disorders on mental and motor functions. Conductive education in Hungary is provided separately from the mainstream of education.

Whilst conductive education is not a direct outshoot of Soviet developmental psychology, the developmental and pedagogic principles involved are readily articulated by Vygotskian developmental theory, with the notion of the Zone of Next Development particularly relevant here (Vygotskii 1978). From this viewpoint human mental development is founded on the material base of the child's physiology but it can only emerge out of social interaction. In special cases, where the physiology is in some way impaired, then special interaction will be required. Children's development has to be seen as a *process*, never simply as a *product*, and decisions about their educational needs should never be made on the basis of what children are *now* but upon what they *might* be brought to be through the optimal adult intervention.

In the case of motor disorder one may conceive of, say, a five-year-old child with cerebral palsy admitted to a normal infant school, given the provision of an electric wheelchair, ramps and other adaptations at school and the part-time assistance of a non-teaching helper. In Vygotskian terms, this is integration at the child's actual or present level of development, accepting the child's current functioning for what it is and leaving further developments, motoric, orthopaedic, social, affective and intellectual, to be built upon this *status quo*. Or one might conceive of the same child in quite other circumstances, undertaking a course of conductive education *and then* admitted to normal school, without such facilitating (but limiting) impedimenta and with a quite different basis for future development. This would be integration of an altogether different order, based upon a strategy that emphasized the child's potential rather than present level of development as a means for long-term planning of educational provision. This strategy accepts a period of separate development as a step towards achieving a level of integration in the long term that has greater substance than simply placing handicapped children amongst their peers.

There has been little recognition of Vygotskii's Zone of Next Development in the West, as a fundamental concept linking education and development. Recent thinking on integration in the United States has begun to regard integration as a process and to recognize the possibility of a preliminary period of separate provision as one option in a range of strategies to achieve the goal of the fullest possible integration of children with disabilities into the social world.

From this stance the distinction between conductive education as practised in Budapest and the CEUKS developed over here is cardinal. Conductive education appears to offer a developmental strategy leading ultimately to a level of integration that for many of its pupils might call into question their continuing 'special needs'. In contrast, however much of an improvement CEUKS may offer, it results for most of its pupils in continuing separate placement (Sutton, in press).

The challenge

There appears to have been developed to a highly complex degree a system of educating people with motor disorders to a level of independence and autonomy quite beyond what was previously thought possible. In the context of special education this would amount to a breakthrough, a paradigm shift, with profound implications for how we conceive of considerable numbers of children whom we currently consider fated to be physically handicapped for life. This breakthrough implies a corresponding revolution in how we provide for them.

A small band of devotees in this country has known of the promise of conductive education for more than twenty years, yet was unable to attract the support and resources required to transpose the work of Pető and his successors from the Hungarian education system to the British. Now perhaps, when at least the wishes of parents are recognized in official rhetoric as a legitimate contribution to deciding the special educational provision made for their children, a wider public recognition of conductive education may generate the political will to create the radically new practice which alone can resolve the problems of this transposition.

References

Aubrey, C. and Sutton, A. 1986. 'Handwriting: one measure of orthofunction in conductive education', *British Journal of Special Education*, 13 (3), pp. 110–114.

Cottam, P. and Sutton, A. (eds.) 1985. *Conductive Education: a System for Overcoming Motor Disorders*, London, Croom Helm.

Cotton, E. 1965. 'The Institute for Movement Therapy and School of Conductors, Budapest, Hungary', *Developmental Medicine and Child Neurology*, 7 (4), pp. 437–446.

Cotton, E. 1975. *Conductive Education and Cerebral Palsy*, London, Spastics Society.

Cotton, E. 1980. *The Basic Motor Pattern*, London, Spastics Society.

Cotton, E. 1981. *The Hand as a Guide to Learning*, London, Spastics Society.

Hári, M. and Akós, K. 1971. *Kónduktiv Pedagógia*, Budapest, Tankonyvkiado. (To be published in translation by Tavistock Press).

Jernqvist, L. 1980. '*Preliminary evaluation of conductive education: the progress of twelve children with two years attendance at the Conductive Education Unit at Ingfield Manor School*', unpublished report, London, Spastics Society.

Lancaster-Gaye, D. 1985. 'Conductive Education, UK style', *Disability Now*, September 1985, p. 5.

McCormack, A. 1976. '*Conductive education reassessed*', MSc Dissertation, University of London.

Meshcheriakov, A. I. 1979. *Awakening to Life*, Moscow, Progress.

Savage, J. 1986. 'Memories of Budapest', *Special Children*, *1* (1). p. 12.

Sutton, A. 1980. 'Backward children in the USSR', in Brine, J., Perrie, M and Sutton, A. (eds.) *Home, School and Leisure in the Soviet Union*, London, Allen and Unwin.

Sutton, A, (in press). 'Conductive Education: a challenge to integration?', *Journal of Child Psychology and Psychiatry*.

Vygotskii, L. S. 1978. *Mind in Society: the Development of Higher Psychological Processes*, edited by Michael Cole, Cambridge, Mass., Harvard University Press.

12 Touch, movement and learning: the role of physiotherapy in the education of children with disabilities

Ann Markee

Ann Markee works as a physiotherapist with children with disabilities in their homes and schools, as well as in medical establishments. In this chapter she describes her own work, against a background description of the work, training and organization of physiotherapists generally. She stresses the need for close co-operation with parents and teachers, and describes the ways in which physiotherapy can be built in the ordinary life of children to aid their learning, with minimum disruption. She argues for a profession that shares its skills and knowledge with others, and which is open, in turn, to others' expertise.

What is a physiotherapist?

Ask people in the street what a physiotherapist is, and they may wave their hands about vaguely, imitating massage. Tell people you are a physiotherapist and they frequently pretend to have a bad back and rub the painful spot, but they may be unable to offer an articulate definition. Whilst indicating that the general public may be largely ignorant of the scope covered by the profession, these two rather crude examples do nevertheless highlight one important part of the job: touch.

Physiotherapists use their hands in almost every aspect of their work, not only to massage or manipulate. They often need to make physical contact with their clients, and this contact may create a communicating link, a 'therapeutic resonance' (Mason 1985), which has more far reaching effects than are measurable. They are not, however, simply 'healers by touch'; they may also be enablers, restorers of function, observers, advisors, teachers and 'normalizers'. They work in hospitals, health clinics, private clinics, in industry and sport, for charitable bodies such as the Spastics Society, in child development centres and in people's homes. In general practice they use a variety of different skills and techniques to treat people with a wide range of conditions all involving some sort of impaired function.

The working day of a physiotherapist based in a hospital might include the treatment of someone who has been involved in a road traffic accident, a child with a broken leg, a bronchitis sufferer, a person with an arthritic knee, a woman who has recently had a baby, or a sports player who has had a cartilage removed. Home or domiciliary treatment is increasingly used especially for those who have difficulty getting to hospital. In a working day, the domiciliary physiotherapist could visit people suffering from strokes, multiple sclerosis, arthritis or post-operative disability.

Working with people with such conditions requires a variety of therapeutic techniques such as electrical or manipulative ones and the use of exercise. It would also involve communication with, or advice to, families or other involved professionals or agencies, reassurance and encouragement to the client, and information about practical aids or other sources of help.

The Chartered Society of Physiotherapy has no formal definition of the profession, which is described as one 'allied to medicine'[1] – an improvement on the former 'supplementary to medicine'. 'Too rigid a definition', it says, 'might impose restrictive boundaries on the further development of a still growing profession'. Nevertheless, it offers the following description as currently acceptable:

> A systematic method of assessing musculoskeletal and neurological disorders of function, including pain and those of psychosomatic origin, and of dealing with or preventing these problems by natural methods based essentially on movement, manual therapy and physical agencies.

The change to 'allied' from 'supplementary' has implied greater professional autonomy, and has begun a shift away from the medical hierarchy and control by doctors, whose training included little or no formal study of physiotherapy, but who were able to prescribe particular treatment for patients in the same way as they prescribed drugs. This frequently led to ill-feeling and the need for negotiation. Doctors (of whom 78 per cent are men) may find it difficult to accept that the professions allied to medicine (in the case of physiotherapy, 93 per cent women) have expertise which they do not possess. A multidisciplinary approach, which is increasingly used to address the problems of disability, will help to dissipate the restrictions of medical hierarchy; it has also the advantage of breaking down professional barriers and providing a more creative forum for discussion.

All 22,000 members of the Chartered Society have completed a three- or four-year full-time vocational course, usually in a hospital, but increasingly linked with a polytechnic, college or a university. They have obtained a diploma equivalent to a degree, examined by the Society, or otherwise a conventional degree. The number of degree courses available is increasing: there are currently five on offer. As well as including physiotherapy firmly in the field of higher education, this will necessitate a careful look at the nature of the curriculum and improve the long-term possibility of achieving parity with other professions (such as teaching) and attaining more realistic pay conditions.

The current curriculum includes such subjects as anatomy, physics, physiology, pathology and applied behavioural sciences.[2] The study of child development is included, with particular emphasis on movement; and also the study of disabling conditions in children and their therapeutic management. As with some other areas of specific interest, post-initial training is necessary if sufficient expertise is to be acquired in pathology and treatment systems.

Paediatrics has for a long time been a speciality within the profession. The Association of Paediatric Chartered Physiotherapists was founded in 1972 and has become one of the biggest specific interest groups.

---

[1] *The Orthodox Alternative*, leaflet available from the Chartered Society of Physiotherapy, 14, Bedford Row, London, SW1.
[2] *The Core Curriculum*, leaflet available from the Chartered Society of Physiotherapy, 14, Bedford Row, London, SW1.

Involvement with children with disabilities

For many children with disabilities there is no medical cure for their condition, and the role of the physiotherapist may be central when physical handling and management are of great importance, not only to the child but also to family, teachers and others.

PRE-SCHOOL CHILDREN

REFERRAL A physiotherapist may be asked to see any child who has a significant delay or deviance in the development of movement. Systems of referral vary; in some areas it is exclusively through a paediatrician; in others the request might come from the child's parents, the health visitor, the GP, or a teacher. Ideally, referral should happen as soon as a problem is identified – any time from birth onwards, in fact – since it is usually preferable that treatment be started as early as possible. Intervention can, however, happen at any time.

ASSESSMENT Comprehensive and continuing assessment of movement and function is essential for effective treatment planning, both for the therapist concerned and for others involved in the child's welfare. More formal annual assessment may also be required for the statementing procedure following the 1981 Education Act, or if the physiotherapist is working in a multidisciplinary assessment centre, for example. It will cover such things as hand–eye skills, gross motor ability, balance reactions, joint range, muscle tone, and reflexes. What it reveals may vary from a simple movement delay which will catch up and may need no treatment, to a severe disorder of movement and posture caused by, for instance, cerebral palsy, which needs careful continuous management and treatment.

TREATMENT Treatment or advice from a physiotherapist may be appropriate wherever movement and function are significantly impaired, although involvement may, in practice, be limited by circumstances or liberty of action. Contact between child and therapist may happen in the child's own home, in a hospital physiotherapy department or maybe in the hospital school, in clinics, child development centres, special or normal nurseries, playgroups, special or ordinary schools, and colleges of further education.

Practice varies considerably in different parts of the country and even between adjacent health districts. In one Midlands county, flexibility is such that treatment may happen wherever it is most appropriate and beneficial for the child and the family, with parents taking an active role as co-therapists. Nearly all pre-school treatment takes place in the home and regular advice is offered to playgroups where necessary. Therapists working in this area say that parents seldom miss appointments and the expertise they acquire means that formal treatment need not happen quite so often, so that professional time is spread further. Both parents and children seem more relaxed and confident on their own ground, and learn skills and contribute their own ideas with more readiness. Therapists do not wear uniforms, which promotes this informality and pushes clinical notions further away.

In a nearby inner city health district the 50 per cent of pre-school children who are not treated in hospital are seen in clinics or health centres; only a small percentage are seen at home. Although parents are nearly always involved, many, particularly those making journeys to the hospital perhaps with other children to manage as well, would prefer to have their children treated at home if given the choice. Therapists working this system feel that it is more cost-effective and efficient, and prefer it.

In East Anglia, therapists who are based in a large hospital department assess and treat young children with disabilities at home until the age of two or two-and-a-half. After that they go to the hospital and are seen in groups, gathered according to motor ability level. At this stage parents sometimes go off to do their shopping and so on during the session, but are still kept closely in touch with treatment and progress.

Although the emphasis and the venue may be different in these three districts, parents are always involved to a greater or lesser extent. This seems to be the case all over the country now. It is possible, however, that the degree of their involvement with both therapy and therapist, and their acquisition of expertise, are increased if they are seen in their own home. The story of Lydia bears this out.

Lydia was referred to me by the local paediatrician when she was ten months old. At that time she was neither sitting alone nor rolling over; her development was at a five-month level and seemed delayed in all aspects. She also had convulsions. The possibility of 'mental retardation' was suggested at about this time by doctors. But without a definite diagnosis her parents, like many others in this situation, found it difficult to come to terms with something so nebulous, and they did not immediately get the careful support which would have made things easier for them.

The offer of some practical help for Lydia's delayed movement was eagerly accepted and I began visiting Lydia at home once a week. Together, her mother and I planned a treatment programme, basing it on normal development and emphasising the goals we would be aiming at. We used equipment available in the home: pouffes for rocking on, to train balance, and washing-up bowls to sit on and in and later step on and off. We tried to spread treatment over a whole day, except for the more concentrated hour every week when I visited. All kinds of everyday activity can be exploited, such as learning to roll in a towel after a bath, or bouncing on the bed to improve muscle tone. Once parents have learned techniques, and have planned aims in mind, they can stimulate movement by adapting everyday activities appropriately and incorporating them with play. Thus the young child can enjoy an ordinary family life.

Whilst the treatment described for Lydia was based on a normal sequence of motor development with some modifications, that planned for a young child with spina bifida and hydrocephalus may need much more detailed support for the parents. There follows a sample guide to the treatment of a baby with spina bifida up to the age of twelve months.

First 2–3 months
1 Positioning during sleep:
    (a)   Change from one feed to another to prevent deformities or reduce existing ones.

(b) For tight hip flexors [the muscles that bend the hips] lie on tummy with a weighted band on his bottom.

(c) For excessive abduction [movement of the legs to the side away from the midline] strap legs together.

(d) To improve the shape of the head, the baby must not always lie with the valve uppermost [to prevent hydrocephalus, fluid is drained from the brain through a valve in the neck into the stomach cavity].

2 Passive movements of all 'paralysed' joints. Stretch anything tight, e.g. feet.

3 Explain in detail about loss of sensation, poor insulation, and pressure sores.

4 Warn about the risk of fractures.

5 Begin to encourage head control.

6 As always, continue discussion about the condition. Make sure doctors' explanations are understood.

3–8 months

1 Encourage and work on any active movement in the legs.

2 Develop arm and hand skills.

3 Use range of positions – prone over a wedge, side-lying for play, 'sitting' in reclining chair – all with toys.

4 Continue passive movements, stretching and positioning.

5 Start using padded night splints if necessary on the feet.

6 It may be necessary to encourage improved breathing patterns.

7 Train balance reactions in lying and later in sitting.

8–12 months

1 Encourage floor sitting with suitable support, e.g. foam ring.

2 Use an upright chair if possible.

3 Train saving reactions in arms.

4 Encourage rolling.

5 Develop forward prone locomotion on low trolley with wheels.

6 Give advice on weight gain.

12 months onwards

1 Train rise to sitting from lying.

2 Start baby standing in swivel walker or standing frame.

3 Baby begins wearing shoes. Teach parents about position in them: straight toes are very important; make sure socks aren't too tight.

4 Continue training sitting balance: low stool against the wall; free stool sitting with lots of arm counter-balancing.

5 Introduce Shasbah Trolley (a low, wheel-driven, 'sit-in' trolley).

Therapy sessions, which in my area are normally weekly, are a mixture of treatment, advice and working with parents. Treatment aims to facilitate normal movement patterns by using various skilled techniques. Often the work is achieved through play. Children normally develop activity by experimentation and by exploring the environment. But children with a motor disorder may need to be taught how to sit and roll and crawl, in short, to be given the experience of mobility. Several effective systems of treatment have been developed (Levitt 1982), some of which manage to maintain the continuity of family life more successfully than others. Whilst some therapists may choose to stick to one method, many prefer a broader, more eclectic approach. Treatment includes selection and provision of appropriate equipment and furniture and other aids to improve mobility, quality of life, or comfort.

In my own experience, shared touching and handling of the child, and shared planning and goal-setting, creates an unusually close and enduring bond between parents and therapists. There is the opportunity for this partnership, which is an excellent example of fruitful co-operation between parents and professionals, to become 'client-orientated'. It is well illustrated in this account written by Lydia's mother:

> My daughter is now six years old. She has severe developmental delay. Since she was ten months old, she had been visited at home each week by a physiotherapist. This has been a very informal session, the physiotherapist wearing no uniform and being addressed by her Christian name; both parent and professional have a mutual respect for one another and a desire to help the child reach her full potential, working together with honesty, optimism where possible and with realistic aims.
>
> Such informality might be considered wrong as it might encourage disrespect, but respect is earned, it is not something automatically given because of our position ... The benefits to my child of being visited at home have been enormous. She is more relaxed in familiar surroundings and therefore has co-operated during her treatment. The same physiotherapist visiting each week has gained the child's confidence and trust, thus breaking down the barriers that can exist. My child's vocabulary is very limited, but after 'Mummy' and 'Daddy' the third word she learned to say was 'Ann' – her physiotherapist....
>
> Because the treatment has been done at home our other children have been involved where possible and they have displayed very little jealousy because their handicapped sister has been receiving all the attention. A close relationship has developed between the physiotherapist and all the family. We have shared our anxieties, tears and also laughter, giving immense benefits in maintaining the stability of the family unit as a whole.

FORMAL EDUCATION: NURSERIES AND SCHOOLS

Before 1971 physiotherapists were employed by Local Education Authorites to work in a variety of special schools helping children with disabilities. From 1971, the employing agency became the Local Health Authority, and physiotherapists in schools were now also required to cover holidays, whether visiting schools or being based in them during term time. Many schools did not have, and still do not have, enough cover. Even ten years ago domiciliary physiotherapy was rare, and a child with a disability in an ordinary school would, as a rule, visit a hospital for treatment. Children with disabilities are increasingly seen by physiotherapists in ordinary schools.

Special schools often have physiotherapists based in them, sometimes with their own small department. This is found most frequently in schools for children with physical disabilities. Some have therapists visiting regularly; some, for example many schools for children with moderate hearing difficulties, may have no formal cover at all. Where treatment is available, children are often withdrawn from lessons: this can disrupt their school day and may cause some degree of ill-feeling among staff. In this system, parents could quickly relinquish their contribution since therapy happens in school. Therapy might thus be necessary more often. Home visits for communication and advice could, and often do, happen in the holidays. Desirable facilities like hydrotherapy pools are often available in special schools, as are regular medical check-ups and doctors' clinics, and the quick availability of other professionals. Buildings should be specially designed, though this is not always the case.

Carl is a child with spina bifida. He had spent two years in a nursery attached to a special school before I met him at the age of five. He had learned to walk with a swivel walker, and later to manage calipers of the conventional type, first balancing in them and later walking with the help of a Rollator (a push-along walking aid). He was learning bowel and bladder management. His physiotherapist, based in the school, had treated him once a week, and had communicated regularly with his parents.

Carl is now eight. He wears special hip guidance calipers which facilitate the most efficient reciprocal gait for him, with the use of elbow crutches. The aim has been to develop independent function and to strengthen arms and the shoulder girdle. We have tried to ensure that all equipment was up-to-date and as efficient as possible, and when the most suitable was not on offer by the Health Service we found other means of provision.

Carl now attends the local primary school about four hundred yards up the road from his home. His friends and one of his sisters go to the same school. He has a Speedy Swedish wheelchair (the sort designed for Olympic sportspeople), because his 'therapists', that is his mother and his physio (me) decided that any other form of transport was too unathletic for him. It was provided for him by a local charity. In school, Carl's teachers and classroom helper have been quick and imaginative in responding to any problems encountered in school or brought to their notice by his mother. He gets through his day with a minimum of extra equipment. He stands at an ordinary school table with two small six-inch supports (quickly fixed by a local carpenter) to stop him falling sideways, and two broomstick clips to hold his crutches when he doesn't need them. He is in a class of 32 children.

Carl is accepted as an ordinary member of his school community. He takes PE in his . . . well, not quite in his stride, perhaps, for he joins in mostly in a jazzy bright blue shiny leotard which allows him to slide more easily on his tummy. He is quite fearless and terrifies his classroom helper. Carl can also swim 400 metres – he learned at school – and he attends an ordinary swimming club.

The success of this first phase in Carl's school life will surely be reflected in the middle school where he is due to start in September, and where his prospective headteacher has already made a very positive beginning by arranging to meet his mother, his physiotherapist and his outgoing headteacher.

In an ordinary school, teachers and other staff may be unused to disability, possibly even fearful of it. Other children could be wary of seeing, touching or communicating with children with disabilities. This may be especially difficult when the disability is not immediately or entirely obvious. Large classes do not easily accommodate extra equipment or furniture, and teachers wilt at the thought of spreading their already overstretched resources still further; they need long-term support, practical help and explanation. Mainstream schools are seldom designed for people with disabilities in mind, and adaptations, especially if requested through statutory channels, take time; equipment may not be readily or quickly available. Compare the speedy provision of Carl's horizontal supports, done overnight with minimum fuss, with the meeting (attended by headteacher, class teacher, parent, helper, education officer, schools surveyor . . .) to plan a toilet adaptation for another child. The outcome was that the old-fashioned concrete floors and walls in the lavatory would need dynamite to blast a fixing hole to take a screw, and that it could not be done. We eventually got a free-standing frame which was better than nothing, but which sometimes falls over!

Therapists conventionally based in special schools, hospitals or clinics may find that their brief lacks the flexibility to extend to mainstream schools; thus the parents' role as co-therapists becomes very important. One therapist working for part of the time in an ordinary school whose roll includes children with a variety of disabilities, and some with multiple disabilities, has a formal working brief which requires her to visit only special schools. She is thus in the ironic situation of almost inventing a 'physically handicapped unit' in order to justify her visits. She treats the children in school, sharing expertise and ideas with teachers so that they can provide continuity when she is not there.

While I continued to treat Lydia at home, she spent a year in the nursery of a special school before her parents decided that an ordinary, mainstream setting was the one she would do best in. They therefore transferred her to an 'opportunity playgroup' which offered a range of play experiences to a wide variety of children. I offered advice and taught nursery teachers and helpers, putting particular emphasis on improvement of balance, muscle tone and hand skills.

Lydia is now six years old and still attends the same playgroup because her parents have rejected the special school provision offer by the LEA. Lydia walks steadily, is beginning to trot, and is able to manage uneven terrain and steps. There is little doubt that the more vigorous movement of normal children has stimulated her towards greater experimentation and achievement. It is worth noting that during this 'grey period' since her parent's rejection of the provision offered, no other professionals, such as home teachers, have been involved in helping Lydia and her family.

Combining therapy and education

Physiotherapy is aimed at finding ways of replacing missed experience, of achieving maximum function, and of minimizing the disadvantage of disability so that education may be more effective.

Until school age, a child's treatment has often been shared with parents and with others involved in helping or caring. The benefits of this partnership may now be extended to teachers, classroom helpers and others at school. Treatment can still happen at home, and this continuum can be reassuring to the child and can avoid the possible stigma and inconvenience of withdrawal from lessons. The co-operative approach is still vital, however; regular co-worker meetings in school are essential to discuss treatment aims, goal setting and progress, and the substance of such meetings can usefully be recorded. Parents should always be ncluded, although often they are not. In one First School where a pupil was uddenly severely disabled, meetings are held once a month and include head-teacher, class teacher, classroom helper, health visitor, parent and physiotherapist.

Physiotherapists need to explain in detail to teachers and others a disabled child's abilities and problems with movement, and to make suggestions about positioning, seating, special equipment, feeding, toilet training, dressing, adaptation and mobility. They may dispel the fear of disability by explaining specialist handling to all concerned. Touch has been and will continue to be the communicating link.

In any setting, but particularly important where treatment happens away from school, the therapist may work through PE or music and movement lessons, and suggest activities specifically good for the child concerned but beneficial to and fun for all. This system of working is particularly useful for children who are very clumsy and who besides having problems with movement, may have difficulty with spatial skills and body image. It was also useful for a child I treat who has mild cerebral palsy. I spent half a morning in her primary school recently watching the class prepare for and do PE. I was able to suggest and demonstrate various suitable activities for the child and for the rest of the class, and afterwards to make observations about other activities like dressing and writing. The class teacher made notes and has built on my suggestions.

Classroom helpers are increasingly being appointed to normal schools to help children with movement disorders and associated problems. The choice of the right person is vital to successful integration, for the helper needs to be a surrogate parent and therapist during school hours. In one health district helpers join in periodic treatment sessions in the child's own home, so as to get a further understanding of the therapeutic aims and to promote maximum function in school. Physiotherapists in that area wrote to the LEA with a suggested list of qualities which might be expected in prospective helpers and of possible tasks that might be expected of them. The letter ran as follows:

Re: Helpers for handicapped children in normal schools
As Community Paediatric Physiotherapists we are obviously very involved with the care of the handicapped children being admitted into normal schools.

We are fully committed to the idea of integration and we are anxious to provide the schools with as much support as possible to enable this to happen successfully.

We feel that the role of the helper is absolutely vital to enable the child to participate in all activities and to ensure that the regime of each child corresponds as far as possible to that followed by the other children in the class. For these purposes, the relationship between the child and his/her helper must be a good one.

We assume that as integration progresses, more helpers will need to be employed and we thought it might be helpful for us to set out in writing some of the tasks which we know they will have to perform, and then for us to identify some of the qualities which we think these helpers will need in order to perform these tasks with maximum benefit to each child...

A helper may be required to do any of the following:
1 Change nappies.
2 Catheterize an incontinent child, i.e. use a tube to empty the child's bladder.
3 Take the child to the toilet or pot (encouraging independence wherever possible).

4 Clean the child up after painting, plasticine sessions etc.
5 Help with feeding and cutting up food if this is needed.
6 Dressing and undressing the child and helping him/her to learn to do this alone.
7 Putting on special boots and appliances, such as calipers and standing frames, if these are used (physiotherapist or parent will advise initially).
8 Helping to train the child to organize himself/herself as far as possible without help, e.g. getting up and down from chairs, moving about the classroom, getting from one room to the next.
9 Lifting where necessary.
10 Accompanying the child outside at play-times so that he/she can be with other children. (Most will want to be outside even when it is cold).
11 Accompanying the child on school trips and being prepared to take responsibility for the child without a parent being present.
12 Taking the child to school swimming and, if necessary, getting into the water with the child.

We will work closely with the school and helpers so that the goals set for the child to achieve physical independence can be realistic.

We think that the main qualities needed for these tasks to be carried out in the most subtle and sympathetic way are energy, enthusiasm, imagination, sensitivity and flexibility. (It may be necessary for a helper to be prepared to take different coffee and lunch breaks from other staff, and it may be necessary for her to take on different tasks from those required initially as the child grows up.)

It is also necessary for the helper to be fit and healthy. One of the problems which has already arisen is what happens to the child if the helper is off sick. (Some schools cope, others send the child home).

These are some of the thoughts which have come to mind as the first children go on into their second or third years of normal schooling.

We feel that teachers, schools, physiotherapists, helpers, parents and children are all learning together about what integration really is, and that it is important to discuss all ideas and problems so that as time goes on, we will all get better at it.

If it would be helpful, we would be very happy to meet you to discuss this letter further.

They also asked if they might be present at interviews in order to improve the chances of employing the most suitable person. The suggestion was tested at one interview and worked successfully. The candidates for employment as helpers spent part of the morning in the classroom 'helping' and talking to children, to the parent of the child concerned and to the teacher. They were then interviewed singly and informally in the headteacher's room by a panel consisting of the headteacher, an education officer and the physiotherapist, who then discussed and made the appointment.

Stigmatization and lack of understanding might also be overcome by the introduction of 'disability awareness' programmes in normal schools. (Should there be 'normal awareness' programmes in special schools?) In America these are often run by parents and volunteers (Vaughan and Shearer 1985). Physiotherapists might usefully be involved in their planning and implementation. They would do much to further the acceptance and demystification of disability.

Conclusions

It seems likely that increasing numbers of children with the sort of movement disorder that needs treatment or advice from a physiotherapist will be attending schools in the coming years. Luckily this coincides with a trend in many Health Districts to offer domiciliary treatment to young disabled children, thus increasing the flexibility of the physiotherapist's brief. In areas where the 'medical model' is still strong, however, and rooted firmly in hospital systems, physiotherapists may have to make more radical decisions about how best to meet the needs of their young clients, and then convince their employers of the need for change.

How best, then, could physiotherapy be involved in schools? What changes could be made in the future by building on present provision?

The eight suggestions which follow are in no particular order of importance.

1   There must be regular meetings in school of all those directly involved with the 'special' child, including parents, to assess progress, plan goals, and share aims.
2   Physiotherapists must be prepared to teach their special skills in handling and in management of the child with a disability to all those involved, remembering always that others may be unsure or fearful of holding and touching, and may need frequent encouragement and reassurance.
3   Physiotherapists could involve themselves in planning disability awareness programmes in all schools, thus furthering the demystification of disability.
4   Physiotherapists' participation in the appointment of classroom helpers suited to handicapped children's particular needs and their subsequent close co-operation with them could bring about the creation of another co-therapist and thereby increase the likelihood of correct physical management throughout the day, and also of learning.
5   The example of physiotherapists' informal and close 'professional partnership' with parents, acquired during pre-school years of shared treatment of the child, could overflow into schools and break down barriers of communication.
6   Participation in interdisciplinary courses is vital if professionals are to share knowledge and expertise. Physiotherapists might promote further understanding of disorders of movement where an efficient multidisciplinary approach is essential if the child is to learn effectively and enjoyably.
7   Where formal treatment is not indicated but some training in mobility or co-ordination or improvement of body image is desirable, physiotherapists might consider working through PE or music and movement lessons, offering useful and structured motor and perceptual experiences to a group of able-bodied children as well as to children with disabilities. Preparation of informative and practical leaflets might also be useful.
8   Finally, physiotherapists must regularly assess the need for their involvement. They must also recognize when it is important to stand back and become an advisor, co-ordinator or observer instead of a therapist.

Carl's mother has kept a diary. Here is one entry:

January 3rd 1986. Carl got up (having stayed dry all night), did his own catheter into a jam jar and came downstairs head first as usual. He got into his wheelchair and went for a shower while Sarah (his sister) got his breakfast. He also did his piano practice. He then put on his calipers; he needed a bit of help with his shoes. He walked to school. It was a cold and windy day. At lunch time the dinner lady did his catheter in the toilet so that he wouldn't need to take his calipers off. His teacher said he hadn't done enough sums! He walked home.

Where is the physiotherapist in this story? The answer is that Carl hardly needs her now, except as an adviser and a friend who can help in solving some problems. He keeps fit and strong with weight lifting and press-ups. His 'physio' visits him at home or at school once a month.

References

Levitt, S. 1982. *Treatment of Cerebral Palsy and Motor Delay*, Oxford, Blackwell Scientific.
Mason, A. 1985. 'Something to do with touch', *Physiotherapy Journal, 71,* No. 4, p. 167.
Vaughan, M. and Shearer, A. 1985. *Mainstreaming in Massachusetts,* London, Centre for Studies on Integration in Education/Spastics Society.

Further reading

Levitt, S. 1982. *Treatment of Cerebral Palsy and Motor Delay*, Oxford, Blackwell Scientific.
Levitt, S. and Pearson, P. H. (eds.) 1986. *Paediatric Developmental Therapy*, Oxford, Blackwell Scientific.
Scrutton, D. and Gilbertson, M. 1975. *Physiotherapy in Paediatric Pratice*, London, Butterworth.

SECTION TWO

Policy and Decision-making

13   Daniel: the segregation of a child with muscular dystrophy

Ann Elsegood

Ann Elsegood was Daniel Robinson's first class teacher when he started at primary school. When Daniel was three, his parents had learned that he had muscular dystrophy. This chapter tells the story of the attempts by Daniel's parents and ordinary school to obtain the necessary resources for him, and of his eventual removal to a special school. There is in it an element of the inevitability of a Greek tragedy. In fact, none of the confusion and bureaucratic failure was inevitable, and there are obvious pointers to the way Daniel could have continued successfully in his ordinary school. His teacher, Ann Elsegood, was left by these events with a sense of anger, and powerlessness.

Daniel, born in June 1977, has an older sister Karen, and a younger sister Lisa. The family live in a privately owned bungalow with a large well-kept garden, in semi-rural surroundings. When Daniel was a baby his mother took him to the clinic and asked the doctor to examine him, because she had a feeling that something was wrong:

> I couldn't put my finger on anything in particular. The doctor checked Daniel over and told me he could find nothing wrong. I also took him to our GP on several occasions because when he fell down, he always fell on his head and once cut it badly and needed a suture. Another time Daniel had such a large bump on his head that we were sent to the hospital so that he could be X-rayed. I did mention to the doctor that Daniel was falling down a lot but he said that children are always falling over.
> When Daniel was two and a half he had a cough and a cold. We went to the GP and while we were there he asked me if I had any other problems. I said I was worried about his speech and the doctor made an appointment for us to see a paediatrician at the hospital. At the hospital we mentioned about Daniel falling over and after blood tests and a muscle biopsy, muscular dystrophy was diagnosed. This was in May 1980. The specialists at the hospital were very good. They made an appointment for a week later so that we could go back and ask any questions. After the first shock my husband and I couldn't really talk about it. We didn't really talk about anything for fear of upsetting each other.
> The family has been very good, my sisters help out when they can. Some acquaintances avoid us – people tend to shy away, but this is possibly because to begin with, I found it very difficult to talk about it and I used to get very upset when telling anyone what was wrong with Daniel. I felt that if I didn't actually have to say the words 'muscular dystrophy' then it didn't exist, because as far as anyone else could see, Daniel was a very normal little boy.

> (Mrs Robinson)

Daniel started having physiotherapy at the hospital every three months, and was given appointments for speech therapy. Every time the Robinsons took Daniel for speech therapy they saw a different person and had to explain again what was wrong with him. The speech therapy clinic was so quiet and unattractive that

Daniel said 'sh' when they went through the door. 'He thought it was a place where you shouldn't talk. We only went three times, and he didn't talk once' (Mrs Robinson).

The Health Visitor came to the Robinsons' home when Daniel was three, and told them that he would be able to go to the local school. Daniel began attending the local playgroup where Mrs Robinson was (and still is) a helper and committee member. He settled down quite well, mixing with the other children, but the Robinsons were aware of the need to plan ahead. They applied for a grant from the district council to modernize the bathroom and adapt the bungalow, and in January 1982 received £600. The total cost of the conversion was £3,000, even though Mr Robinson did much of the work himself.

> As well as having the bathroom done, we widened most of the doors so it would be ready when Daniel needed a wheelchair. We thought it important to get these things done before we needed them rather than after. We took out a separate loan, which we are still paying back.
>
> (Mrs Robinson)

The foresight shown by the Robinsons was not matched by the preparations made by the LEA for the start of Daniel's full-time schooling.

> Before Daniel started school, and even when in school, we saw nobody from the education authority. The only person we did see before he started was the school doctor. We didn't find out until later that she had come to see if Daniel would go to the special school or the local school. We hadn't thought about special school.
>
> (Mrs Robinson)

Very little consultation had taken place between parents, the school doctor and the teaching staff before September 1982, when Daniel entered the first class of the local primary school. It was built as a traditional classroom school in the 1960s, with extensions over the years reflecting open-plan educational ideas. The single-storey building is large, with wide corridors, providing good circulation and access throughout. The site is flat with a large field and playground, and would present few problems of access to a child in a wheelchair.

I had been appointed to the school at the end of the previous term, but was only told that I would have a child with muscular dystrophy in my class when my appointment began in September 1982. I would have liked to have been informed earlier. I feel very strongly that school holidays are often an excuse for poor communication. I would have been more than happy to meet the parents or the school doctor during this time. I was entirely ignorant of Daniel's condition, found out what I could but still felt inadequate.

Daniel started school, and I kept notes on his physical condition and his social, emotional and intellectual progress:

> *October 1982* (School Comment): Daniel is small and walks stiffly. He is very appealing with a clear complexion and very large blue eyes. He finds sitting on the floor difficult but is determined to be like the other children. He is very determined not to do as he is told – have to be prepared for a battle of wills when insisting he carries out certain activities. Telephone call from school doctor – Daniel must be kept mobile – will have normal intellect but probably below average IQ – will experience lack of fluency (auditory memory) – must take care with colds – staff must watch for problems with toilet, extra help will be provided when necessary.

Firm handling is the best approach especially as an improvement in his behaviour has been apparent lately. Mrs Robinson seems surprised that Daniel enjoys school.

Indeed, as Mrs Robinson later remarked:

> I was apprehensive when he started school. I wasn't sure how he would settle in. We didn't know about the IQ or about what he would be able to do academically. I wish someone had told us.

> *December 1982* (School Comment): Daniel's behaviour much better. Joins in readily and is happy to complete set tasks. Has difficulty gripping a pencil – felt tip pen helps. Daniel is less steady on his feet on cold days – has been falling more. He falls heavily and without warning.

After the Christmas holiday, Daniel's falls became more frequent. The school doctor, who had visited the Robinsons before Daniel started school, had given them to understand that a welfare assistant would be made available to help Daniel with any problems he encountered in the local school. I was worried about the safety aspect of Daniel's increasing lack of balance, and telephoned the school doctor who said she would pursue the possibility of assistance for part of the day. With hindsight, I wished I had obtained written confirmation of this promise.

Mr and Mrs Robinson were very keen for Daniel to stay at the local school. Mrs Robinson offered to help Daniel in school, but we felt that would not be desirable at the time:

> I would have been quite happy to help in school but I didn't feel that Daniel would want his mum there helping him – I think it would have made him feel even more different than he was already feeling.

> (Mrs Robinson)

> *February 1983* (School Comment): Bumps on head quite usual. Daniel refuses to stay in at lunchtime even on cold days. Rest of class very aware of Daniel – he does not appreciate 'help' from certain members of the class who are apt to fuss over him. He continues to be very independent. Some progress being made with reading/writing. Can count to and understands numbers 1–10 and is beginning to recognize words. Copy writing has improved and he can concentrate for longer periods. Daniel is not a great talker.

> *March 1983* (School Comment): Daniel is much slower physically than when he began school in September. He has always joined in drama and movement and large climbing apparatus (with an extra adult to himself) but these activities are becoming more difficult. His determination is tremendous and he will not be left out of anything. Daniel is now unable to dress and undress for PE and sometimes has difficulty with his shoes.

At the end of March the educational psychologist visited the school and watched Daniel through the classroom door. He offered little support or advice, but did suggest seven and a half hours of welfare assistance per week, and Daniel's transfer to a named special school in due course.

During April, Mr and Mrs Robinson came for an interview to the school. Meetings between teachers and parents were fairly frequent and were particularly appreciated by the Robinsons. 'As well as the main yearly interview at school there were many informal interviews and we found these very helpful'

(Mrs Robinson). Discussion at the April meeting focused on Daniel's behaviour at school:

April 1983 (School Comment): Formal interview with parents. Daniel has been spiteful since before the Easter break. There has been no evidence of this at home. Mr and Mrs Robinson agreed that Daniel's condition is worsening but are hoping that his mobility will improve with the warmer weather. They are hopeful that Daniel will stay at this school, but are concerned that staff and other children should not suffer. Mr and Mrs Robinson are sensible caring people.

May 1983 (School Comment): Daniel is enjoying school more and more. Mrs Robinson is beginning to come to terms with the situation. Daniel's physical deterioration is tremendously upsetting. He has begun to tease his older sister.

The dilemmas Daniel's parents faced were made clear by Mrs Robinson:

I do try and tell Daniel off although it does upset me. His dad does discipline him and even that upsets me if it's a real telling off. But I know that it is necessary because we both agree that we don't want him spoilt. To let him get away with too much would not be fair on his two sisters.

The promised welfare help had still not materialized, and the school found itself involved in an unpleasant battle to obtain this long-awaited support. Mrs Robinson was 'very upset that it was such a struggle to get any help for Daniel in the classroom, as we were led to believe it would be there when he started school'. School governors and a local councillor put pressure on the LEA. Another educational psychologist visited and spent some time watching Daniel in the classroom. He considered that I was 'making a fuss over nothing' and that the class appeared to be running smoothly with Daniel in it. I thought it ironic that the effort that the other pupils and I had put into integrating Daniel into the ordinary classroom meant that he did not appear in obvious need of help. In fact, with 34 children in the class and Daniel's deteriorating physical condition, it was becoming increasingly difficult to manage the classroom without regular extra help. The promised seven and a half hours of welfare help finally materialized, just three days after the involvement of school governors and councillors. By now Daniel was becoming aware of his physical limitations:

We think Daniel is beginning to feel different to his friends – he realizes that he cannot do the things they can do. He has also started to ask questions like 'Why don't my legs work properly?' We have always tried to explain as best we can that his muscles are not as strong as other children's and that is why he cannot always do what they can do.

If Daniel has friends round after school, he tries so hard to keep up with them and gets very hurt when they rush around the garden, ride their bikes and generally play around when he has difficulty just walking up the garden. I try and push him on his bicycle and take him anywhere he wants to go but with a small baby and all the other things like cooking dinner, it's not always possible to do just what he wants when he wants.

We did join the Muscular Dystrophy Society but as yet have only met one other family with a little boy slightly older than Daniel. They seem to get on very well together. We have been involved in quite a lot of fund-raising events but at the moment do not wish to get too involved in anything else. We feel we can cope with Daniel but it could be upsetting to meet other children in varying stages of muscular dystrophy. We think it best to cope with things as they occur rather than worry about things that might happen some time in the future.

Daniel has great difficulty in expressing himself. He often knows what he wants to say, but cannot get out what he means, which ends with him getting cross and upset and quite often us getting cross and upset because he often screams and shouts as well. We know it is only frustration.

(Mr and Mrs Robinson)

In July 1983, I noticed that Daniel was much more settled and less aggressive. He could concentrate for longer periods, although he was making little progress academically. At the time we were unable to offer individualized learning programmes. Daniel was talking much more freely, both individually and in groups. His team won the mat race in the school sports, to the delight of the whole school.

At the end of the summer term the physiotherapist from the special school visited Daniel's school. The reason for the visit was not altogether clear, but she had only that week learned of Daniel's presence in the school. She also visited the Robinsons at home, and Mrs Robinson found her 'very helpful and easy to talk to as she realized what problems we were facing'.

In September 1983 Daniel moved with his peer group to the next teacher.

October 1983 (School Comment): Daniel doesn't warm easily – gives the impression of having formed a tough coating around himself. Positively resists any physical advances towards him like taking his hand. He copes extremely well within the class. He strives desperately to be like others but he unfortunately draws attention to himself especially at quiet times. Other children have a good attitude towards him and they cope with disruptions calmly and sensibly. He told his mum that he didn't want to go out at playtimes, but at playtimes refuses to stay in. It seems that Daniel is trying to communicate something which he can't really express.

At around the same time Mrs Robinson commented that 'Daniel hates being made a fuss of – he always has – which is not easy in his situation. He so desperately wants to be "one of the boys"'.

During December 1983 yet another educational psychologist visited the school and made several recommendations: that Daniel should stay at his present school for the time being; that his teachers should continue to help with pre-reading and reading skills; that a close eye be kept on signs of deterioration so that adequate preparation could be made for future education; and that the case be kept under review.

In January 1984 the school, in consultation with Mr and Mrs Robinson, decided to go ahead with the official Statementing Procedure, in the hope of gaining more resources for Daniel.

March 1984 (School Comment): Noticeable deterioration. Daniel no longer climbs up his legs with his hands to get himself up. A child will always help him. He can put on his coat but cannot manage his shoes. He has one particular loyal friend who helps him whenever he can. He rejects any physical contact except when it is an offer of help, but even then he is very selective in allowing people to help. When he falls down, which is at least once a day he fights extremely hard to avoid crying and when he does cry he hurriedly brushes away the tears. He is showing signs of aggression – perhaps a resentment of other children's normality. Despite this the other children are delighted if he receives praise, and support him whenever possible. Daniel has made little progress academically. He needs constant supervision and changes of occupation. He has however shown signs of good imagination expressed verbally, in a mature way.

Mrs Robinson wondered whether the aggression was because she had started bringing him into school and changing his shoes. 'No other mum comes in and perhaps he resents us being different each morning before school starts'. I felt that a member of staff should have collected Daniel from the playground and attended to his needs instead of his mother, but this did not happen because it 'was not school policy'.

> *April 1984* (School Comment): Daniel is now neither completely independent or totally dependent. Daniel's concession in coming into school early has meant other children taking advantage. The use of a wheelchair has been suggested for the playground and for the September term.

During April 1984, Mr and Mrs Robinson received a letter from the LEA informing them of the proposal to make formal assessment of Daniel's special educational needs under Section 5 of the 1981 Education Act. The letter was impersonal and its implications not fully understood:

> We understood that our son needed a formal assessment but the letter made us very angry and upset. It was so impersonal – it was our child they were talking about. We didn't want to be threatened with court action. Why couldn't it be explained in plain English exactly who would be coming to see us and what for? We sent the first letter back to the education authority with comments on the back complaining of the wording of the letter.
>
> The second letter ended up in the kitchen bin. I was so upset. We got it out later because we thought we ought to keep it. It's got tea stains on it.
>
> We made it very clear to the education authority that we wanted to be in on any decisions or discussions concerning Daniel, but we have not been informed or anything.
>
> (Mrs Robinson)

In June 1984, an educational welfare officer visited the home, because Mr Robinson had not immediately replied to the third letter from the LEA about the assessment of Daniel. He suggested an out-of-county placement:

> He (the EWO) mentioned different schools in different counties and I told him we did not want our son to be educated outside the county. We realized that at some time in the future Daniel would have to go to a special school, but certainly not to a boarding school hundreds of miles away.
>
> (Mrs Robinson)

The School Medical Officer made an assessment of Daniel's needs. The examination took place at home, and the doctor told Mr and Mrs Robinson that Daniel was high on the list for increased ancillary help at school. Mrs Robinson grew increasingly uneasy with the progress of events:

> People kept coming to the house – we got so confused as to why they had come. The doctor who visited to examine Daniel was talking about all sorts of things in front of him. When Daniel went to school that afternoon he was rude to the staff. I made Daniel apologize the next day for his rudeness, but I think he had been pulled about and questioned and talked about by so many people it really was no wonder he

reacted in such a way. Another child can get rid of his anger and frustration in other ways – Daniel can't!

Despite this, the school's comment on Daniel in July 1984 was that he seemed much more settled within himself and more co-operative.

July 1984 (School Comment): He seems to be accepting his handicap and is developing self-confidence. Sports Day – Daniel started ahead of the others in his race and won. Daniel played the part of Baby Bear in the end of term production of Goldilocks very confidently. Mr Robinson had made a wooden ramp for the play to enable Daniel to move more easily.

Intellectual and academic progress has been made – more than his written work would suggest.

By the end of summer term 1984, it had been agreed through the appropriate channels to increase the amount of ancillary help offered to Daniel from seven and a half hours to fifteen hours per week, starting in September. Mr and Mrs Robinson were not officially told of this. Mr Robinson had said that they would only send Daniel to school during the hours that welfare help was there for him.

Daniel stopped walking immediately term finished. Mr and Mrs Robinson later commented:

We felt we should have been told that Daniel was very near the time when a wheelchair was needed. We thought he would be walking for another six months. It was a bit of a shock.

They then received a letter from the LEA informing them that the formal Statementing procedure was complete and they could expect to hear of the outcome in due course. Four days after the end of term a fourth educational psychologist, a stranger to Mr and Mrs Robinson, visited them at home. No one seemed quite sure where she had come from. She told the Robinsons that fifteen hours was the absolute maximum for ancillary help for Daniel and that they could face legal action if they did not send him to school full-time, and that she would suggest that Daniel attended a special school, although she made it quite clear to Mr and Mrs Robinson that is was entirely their decision. She also offered some information about the special school, telling them that it would provide physiotherapy, a special chair, adjustable tables, swimming and horse riding, and that the headmaster had a policy whereby children were admitted before they were in a wheelchair, or must otherwise wait until twelve months after they could no longer walk. The rationale was that acceptance of a wheelchair could be traumatic for some children:

We were shattered and angry over this visit. We had six weeks to try and decide what to do. We couldn't get in touch with either of the schools – we hadn't even been to see the special school. We took the caravan to Yorkshire for a fortnight, but even the holiday was spoilt. Why couldn't this all have been sorted out before the end of term? We could have prepared Daniel and ourselves for the change.

(Mr and Mrs Robinson)

I was angry too. I felt that the Robinsons had been got at, that they were seen by far too many different professionals, and that they were forced to make decisions at a time when schools were closed and there was no one to consult. I was keen for Daniel to stay with us in an ordinary school.

During the holidays, and unknown to either the staff or Mr and Mrs Robinson, the school building surveyor was contacted by the AHA and asked to provide ramps for two doorways at school to accommodate Daniel's wheelchair. No one appeared to know where Daniel was going to be at the start of the following term. My colleague, Daniel's teacher, telephoned Mr and Mrs Robinson the day before the start of the autumn term, and discovered that they had made an appointment to visit the special school the next day. A wheelchair ordered for Daniel had arrived by post at the beginning of August, and Daniel's feelings about this had influenced their decision about special schooling.

> Daniel said that he did not want to be the only one in a wheelchair at the local school. This helped us to make our decision about the special school. Daniel took to the wheelchair very well, but was worried about being different. He has always tried so hard to be like other children. In the end we visited the special school on the first day of term and had to make a decision the same day. The decision was not easy – we hope for Daniel's sake that the decision for special education was the right one.
>
> (Mr Robinson)

The decision upset me; I was sure that the wheelchair problem could have been overcome and was disappointed that Daniel would not be coming back to continue his schooling. But I felt it would be wrong to try to get the Robinsons to reject the special school now that they had made up their minds. Daniel started at the special school.

Mr and Mrs Robinson meanwhile applied for financial assistance to provide ramps in the garden. The district council had no more funds available until 1985, so Mr Robinson did the job himself. They also had to find a source of funding for a motorized wheelchair. 'He has one at school which he can bring home for the holidays but he mustn't use it outside. The cost of a suitable one is about £1,800' (Mr Robinson). The Muscular Dystrophy Society, together with the local Round Table Association raised the money for the chair. In September, the Robinsons received the mobility allowance for Daniel which they had applied for seven months earlier. It took longer still – nine months – for them to receive the report from the LEA informing them of the outcome of the formal assessment of Daniel's special needs. The letter arrived in the second week of October, a month after Daniel had started at the special school. It recommended that he attend a special school as soon as possible.

Daniel seems to have settled in happily at the new school. He is collected each morning at 8.00 a.m. by taxi, and arrives home at approximately 4.15 p.m. The change of school has meant that he now sees very little of his peers, and so spends a lot of the time when he isn't at school either alone or with his sisters' friends. There has also been little contact with his former school or teachers. We sent reports of his development and progress, but I feel we were cut off from that moment. Our sense of alienation was not helped by a visit, two weeks into the autumn term, from an educational psychologist. She had come to see Daniel.

Although Daniel appears to be happy at the special school, I feel that the handling of his case left a lot to be desired. The fight for adequate support for Daniel in the ordinary school had been stressful for the Robinsons; neither they nor we at school had had much say in Daniel's educational future. The LEA didn't always seem to act in the child's best interests. The parents needed someone to talk to, an unbiased personal counsellor, someone who might even have tried to get the professionals working together. The last twelve months had been a great strain on Mr and Mrs Robinson. We fought for help and fought to keep him in mainstream. Yet it seems it had been decided long ago by the powers that be that he would eventually attend special school.

14   Deaf child, deaf language . . . education?

Lorraine Fletcher

This chapter is an account by the mother of a profoundly deaf boy of her and her husband's educational philosophy and how it was translated into action. Lorraine Fletcher is committed to an education for her son Ben which is based on a respect for Deaf culture and a recognition of the status of British Sign Language as the fully-fledged language of the Deaf community. She was also committed to offering Ben a lively, active and stimulating early education based on the principles she herself used as a nursery teacher. These considerations together led her to arrange for Ben a bilingual education in the local infants school. The detail of Ben's progamme is provided in Chapter 6. However, had an appropriate educational environment which also gave Ben access to the Deaf community been available, he would be there. Lorraine Fletcher is optimistic that such an environment will soon become available.

The first years

My son, Ben, was born in November 1980. We suspected that he might be deaf when he was about six months old; official diagnosis of 'very severe deafness' came at twelve months. Testing stopped at 100 decibels; since then Ben has responded to tests at 125 db; his deafness, then, is profound, almost total.

The first books and magazines we read about deafness, and the first professionals we consulted, led us to believe that the best way forward was to concentrate our efforts on teaching Ben to speak. When he was sixteen months old a peripatetic teacher of the deaf from the Local Education Authority arrived and began to work on his speech and to train his 'residual hearing' (that little bit of usable hearing which, we were told, all deaf children possess). To facilitate this, she lent him a phonic ear, a very high-powered hearing aid with a separate radio microphone. Later, at her recommendation, the local Round Table presented Ben with his own radio aid; later still, this was passed on to another deaf child when the Area Health Authority actually prescribed one for Ben.

Ben now had the best form of amplification available, but he did not seem to appreciate this at all. It took us some months to get him accustomed to wearing the aid, and at times the tension and unhappiness created in the family were unbearable. With our hearing daughter Sarah, two years older than Ben, my husband, Ray, and I relied on explanations and persuasion whenever there were disagreements about anything, but with Ben this was impossible: there was no communication to explain or persuade with. Aiming for speech, as we were, until he wore his hearing aid there was no possibility of explaining to him why he should be wearing it. Since he did not take to it readily, we had to resort to the sort of techniques normally reserved for animals or for older, 'difficult' children; we had to 'condition' Ben into accepting his aid by a system of rewards and punishments. All day long, I worked on him. For as long as he wore his aid he would have my complete attention. If he rejected the aid I would ignore him. I despised this kind of behaviour in myself; it was not the way I wanted to treat my baby at all, but I believed that it was necessary and so we persevered, despite the unhappiness it caused in all of us. Constantly, we were on the lookout for situations when we could slip it in unnoticed: when he was asleep, when he was eating, when he was absorbed in play. The aid ruled our lives.

We were also beginning to feel uneasy all round about the ethics of what we were doing. Ben was deaf, we accepted that, but this was not reflected in the way we were dealing with him. By concentrating on speech we were asking him to do what he was least well-equipped to do. As teachers ourselves, we were deeply unhappy with this strategy. We knew that the way to help a young child to learn was to focus on strengths rather than weaknesses, so that the child experienced success and satisfaction as quickly as possible, and thereby developed self-confidence, a sense of self-worth, and a positive attitude to learning. To subject an eighteen-month-old baby to training routines in which the expectations of him were so ill-matched to his capabilities might well instil in him a sense of failure from which he might never recover, especially if he did not achieve the intelligible speech we were working towards.

Progress seemed intolerably slow. Ben was already starting to fail. Even wearing his aid, his responses to sound were unreliable, his own vocalizations neither increased nor decreased, and the amount of information we were able to convey to each other via speech and hearing was minimal; if we really wanted to get through to him we had to resort to gesture.

'Resort to gesture'... this little phrase conveys a negative attitude to a very useful function, yet it is heard a lot in deaf education. From the very beginning, it had been made clear to us that speech and hearing should be our goals, that these were acceptable means of communication whereas gesture was not; it was second-best, to be used only when absolutely necessary. Yet gesture resulted in instant communication, whereas speech, even grossly amplified, did not. We realized that *communication* mattered most to us, not speech.

We were worried that our insistence on speech might be damaging Ben's developing self-image. We could see that it was slowing down his intellectual development. We needed to be able to communicate with him *now*, not at some unspecified time in the future, so that he could start to learn as all children do, not only from his own experience but from meaningful linguistic interaction with other people.

We learned about sign language from a little pamphlet, produced by Gallaudet, the American University for the Deaf. We read of a college full of deaf people, who were receiving as high a standard of education as their hearing counterparts in ordinary colleges, in a different language: American Sign Language. Reading this pamphlet filled us with optimism, so much so that we decided to ignore the advice of the professionals that an approach other than pure oralism would inhibit Ben's speech, and go for signing so that at least his education – from now – would not be inhibited. We would not abandon speech and auditory training work, but we would use signs as well, not as a last resort, but in conjunction with speech and with due respect for their value.

Once we told her that we wanted to sign, the peripatetic teacher supported us. Departmental policy meant, then, as now, that parents' wishes as to method of communication would be adhered to *if expressed*. The teacher had been prevented from suggesting signing to us, but once we had found out for ourselves that an alternative to 'oralism' existed, she was delighted to help. She found courses for us to attend and she established one in our home town so that we would not have to travel so far; she revealed that she could sign a little and she began to sign with Ben. But this was not enough. We were quick to learn signs, but slow to be able to combine them with speech and use them comfortably with Ben.

Meanwhile, we were continuing our reading. We came across a newly-published manual on deafness which was unlike any we had encountered before (Freeman, Carbin and Boese 1981). We gained information in plenty from the book, but its major influence on us was philosophical. Chapter one was headed: *Deafness: A Difference to be Accepted, or a Defect to be Corrected?* Ray and I were in no doubt as to which view suited us. We learned about, and we came to respect, deaf culture, deaf language, '*deaf pride!*' We visited the Centre for the Deaf in Bradford and we saw deaf culture for ourselves. We took Ben to the club, and watched how easily he fitted into this culture, how well the deaf people related to him and how fascinated he was by signed conversations, which he could actually see taking place. Here, for a short while, Ben had the same opportunity for linguistic and social development as a hearing child who is growing up in a hearing family. Here, he was not disadvantaged by his deafness at all.

During visits to the club, and as we continued our reading, we began to see signing as a language in its own right; we learned that sign language is as different from English as French, or German, or Russian. Trying to match British Sign Language sign for word to English is like trying to speak two languages at once: the result is a linguistic jumble (see Chapter 26 of this volume). At the deaf club we watched deaf people conversing; gradually we gained enough confidence to be able to join in; we became more fluent, signed more easily with Ben, and could see him making progress. This was not at the expense of speech: because we could see Ben forming the right signs, it was far easier for us to notice and support his attempts at speech than previously: because he was signing 'CAR', for example, we could be certain that he really was trying to say the word 'car'. The ability to make himself understood in sign released a lot of tension in him, so that he would use his voice naturally and freely at the same time as he signed.

Formal education

By the time Ben was ready to begin his formal education, we had established a reasonable amount of signing; Ben was not frustrated and he was starting to learn about his world through language, to make observations, to request information. For his nursery education we were looking for an environment rich in language and in exciting experiences, where he would have the opportunity to develop his sign language by contact with fluent signers, as at the deaf club.

When we began to look at the local provision for the deaf, however, we discovered that this environment did not exist. The schools and units for the deaf, at nursery level, offered training in speech and hearing in abundance, but there was little signing, little respect for deaf culture and a disappointing disregard for the principles of nursery education. The foremost consideration of the teachers was language, but by this they meant English. One school tried to attain it by discouraging signing altogether, bestowing lavish praise upon tiny children's attempts at speech, and blatantly ignoring any developing signs. The other advocated signing, but not BSL. It encouraged English, signed and spoken. None of the nurseries provided a signing environment; where signing was allowed the children's level of competence in it was minimal. I saw no conversations, no chit-chat of the kind nursery-age children love, except amongst the hearing children, who 'had been imported in vast numbers for the benefits of 'integration'.

This meant that the dominant language was spoken English and that the few deaf children were trying their best to conform, struggling to speak, straining to lipread, and squashing their natural language in the process. The deaf nursery-age children in these schools were, unquestionably, language deprived. For the sake of English their teachers were missing out on the opportunity to give them language competence at the time when children are most easily able to acquire it: during the preschool years. The only environment which provided anything like a rich input of language was the playground. Here, the children had unrestricted access to older deaf children, and probably benefited more from five minutes' signed conversation there than from five hours' of exposure to English in the classroom.

Ben's developing capacity to express himself in his own language would not be nurtured here. At home, with a different, non-signing peripatetic teacher now, Ben was directing much of his energy into avoiding the work she was offering. It was becoming harder and harder to get him to wear his phonic ear. The new teacher, relying entirely on oral methods and unhappy with Ben's lack of response using the phonic ear, was attempting to use an auditory trainer with him. This piece of equipment allows sound input of up to 135 decibels, which is about the volume of a jet engine at six feet. It damages hearing. It is the sort of volume which causes actual pain in certain individuals, including deaf people. Ben was resisting it, as only a two-year-old can, with absolute and inventive determination. He hated it, as he hated the attempts at 'speech work' which accompanied its introduction. Yet he would have to undergo training using this kind of equipment daily, in all the schools and units we visited, as a matter of course.

At the time we were looking for a suitable placement for Ben, his sister Sarah was attending the local nursery school. I trained as a nursery teacher and I have never seen a better or a more well-equipped nursery. Sarah was getting an excellent education there. Every day when we delivered her to nursery it was difficult to persuade Ben to leave this magic place and come home. Ray and I were angry and sad that, just because Ben was deaf, he would be subjected to a method and philosophy of education so ignorant of a preschool child's need for freedom of choice, for opportunities to develop self-confidence, self-esteem, inde-pendence, for fun, for excitement, for *play* – for real play, not the thinly disguised formal training that we had come to see as the hallmark of the deaf education we had encountered.

Eventually, Ray and I decided to ask if the staff at the local nursery would be prepared to take Ben. They were, and they decided to learn to sign. Their open-mindedness, their willingness to adapt, and the cheerfulness and enthusiasm with which they took to such hard work will remain one of my most treasured memories.

Ben enjoyed himself at nursery. But as time went by it became obvious to all of us that his experience was missing an essential ingredient: richness of language. Like us, the nursery staff were now able to communicate with Ben at a basic level, but we were all conscious that the preschool years are a time when children are ripe for language input, and that Ben was unable to make progress as quickly as hearing children do because of the inadequacy of the input we were able to provide.

In the autumn of that year I visited Derrymount School in Nottingham, where a profoundly deaf man, Sydney Stone, was working with profoundly deaf teenagers, all of whom had failed in the oral system.[1] His relationship with the children was delightful to see, and their progress in sign language and in general self-confidence and self-esteem was phenomenal. These were the sort of achievements I wanted for Ben – but he needed them at three, when hearing children are gaining them, not at sixteen in a unit set up as a last resort for 'ineducable' children. And Syd had shown me that it might be possible. In February 1984 I sent a letter to the LEA as our contribution to Ben's assessment for his Statement under the 1981 Education Act. Part of it read as follows:

> Thanks to sign language, Ben is having, as far as is possible, a 'normal' upbringing, in that he can communicate with his parents. But despite all our efforts, the standard of that communication is quite low in terms of content. At best it can be termed 'functional', simply because we are not yet fluent and we are not deaf; we are not native users of his language. We are the models from which, in the main, Ben is learning his language, and at present his language can go no further than the level at which we are using it. Yet his potential for learning language is at its peak. He takes all that we can give him but he is ripe for more input...
>
> We ask that Kirklees provide a model from which Ben can learn his language properly, that is, a native user of British Sign Language, to work with Ben at the nursery. We would argue that the employment of a deaf non-teaching auxiliary would be of immense benefit, not only to Ben but to his teachers, his friends and their parents. A deaf person in the nursery would be able to make available to Ben what the hearing children gain almost incidentally. A deaf person's perception of the world would be so much closer to Ben's; his or her communication would be natural, efficient, spontaneous as opposed to the slow, laboured, cumbersome efforts of the hearing signer, so that Ben would have the opportunity of picking up his language from a perfect rather than a highly imperfect model. The signing capabilities of both children and staff would improve dramatically. Everyone would benefit indirectly from contact with a severely handicapped adult; maybe they might discover that deafness in itself is not such a severe handicap at all – it is only hearing people who make it so by refusing to accept the language of the deaf. For Ben, far from the blind leading the blind, it would lead to a better understanding of the world 'as it sounds through deaf eyes', and to a better chance of his functioning sucessfully alongside his hearing contemporaries...
>
> The step which we suggest would... enable Ben to gain from these precious preschool years what any hearing child of normal intelligence gains as a matter of course: his first language. Please give him this chance *now*. In two years it will be too late.

---

[1] From September 1986, Sydney Stone will be employed full-time by Nottinghamshire Education Authority to work with deaf children who need help with communication in sign. He will be based at The Ewing School for the Hearing-Impaired and will work with teachers at three schools and the College of Further Education who have requested his help.

The letter, combined with the support of sympathetic professionals, worked. In September of the same year Judith Collins started work at the nursery school. She is the profoundly deaf daughter of deaf parents; her signing is fluent and graceful, her personality delightful. During the year she worked at the nursery the effect on Ben, on us as a family, on the nursery staff and on the community, was universally positive. The signing group already established in the village trebled in size as she took it over, and the people who participated gained valuable insights into deafness. The signing of the nursery staff improved; our horizons were widened as Judith introduced us to her family and friends and we began to meet them socially; our signing improved tremendously. We began to feel at ease as a family, as Ben's ability to communicate began to catch up with his chronological age; we could have discussions, explain, argue, tell him stories, read him poetry, as we do with Sarah. Ben's communication really blossomed: people with no signing skills commented on his delightful sense of humour, and now he was also able to express his humour in language: real joking! Ben's peripatetic teacher was thrilled at the interest he had begun to show in oral communication: within a week of Judith starting at nursery he was repeating series of lip patterns. The speech therapist reported improved concentration on people's faces and more interest in learning to speak. All this had been achieved almost 'by the way', because of Ben's contact with Judith, and without constant pressure. At the same time his general education had progressed normally: his understanding of time and number, his fine and gross motor control, his ability to predict – both in practical situations and when following a story – showed tremendous improvements. He was more than adequately equipped to begin his primary education. It was a wonderful year, unquestionably successful.[1]

Towards the end of that year, however, stress began to creep back into our lives as we faced the next decision: what to do about Ben's full-time education.

Full-time education

At the end of his time at nursery Ben had, thanks to Judith, a language with which he could learn. Also thanks to Judith, we were more aware of the importance of deaf culture to deaf people, and of the fundamental role played by the schools for the deaf in that culture. During Ben's time at nursery school, he was missing out on the company of other deaf children. His conversation with hearing children, despite those children's efforts, was still very basic by the end of the year, even with his closest friend. As the single deaf child among hearing children, he was being deprived of a very important aspect of the culture into which he would grow up: he was being prevented from making deaf friends of his own age. In considering the next step in his education, this thought was always in our minds, and in Judith's. At this stage, a deaf child should be educated with his deaf peers.

---

[1] For reasons of space, I am unable to go into much detail here, but the events of that year were filmed by a crew from Tyne Tees Television. For further information about the resulting documentary, *A Language for Ben*, contact Sheila Browne, Community Education Officer, Tyne Tees Television, City Road, Newcastle upon Tyne, NE1 2AL.

The situation in the local schools for the deaf had not changed. There was still a preoccupation with the English language, still a blatant disregard and lack of respect for the value of BSL in the education of very young children, still no sign of a deaf adult at infant level even in an establishment which prides itself on employing deaf people further up the school. There was much language work in English, an overwhelming preoccupation with reading and writing, but little maths and science. Instead of classes full of competently communicating children, experiencing a varied curriculum taught by adults fluent in sign language, children's learning was being systematically restricted because the language of instruction was the English they were struggling so hard to learn. In the infant classes I observed there was much talk from the teacher, with laboured responses from the children, who were under no illusions: they knew that speech was the major requirement in any interaction with the teacher. The classes were teacher-controlled, teacher-dominated, 'language' centred. This was not education, it was 'dummification' (Ladd 1978).

Comparison with the teaching of children from non-English speaking ethnic minorities is useful here. In that field teachers are coming to realize the importance of mother tongue teaching and the usefulness of bilingualism, and are employing native speakers of minority languages to work in their classrooms. These teachers are wisely accepting and welcoming other cultures. Teachers of the deaf and schools for the deaf which refuse to recognize and make use of the natural culture and language of the children they teach are exhibiting a form of prejudice. Schools and education authorities which deny adult users of sign language the right to teach young deaf children are being unjust in the extreme, and they are depriving themselves of an excellent resource.

If Ben went to one of the schools for the deaf, the content of what he would learn would be gravely restricted because it would be taught in what amounts to a foreign language. Teaching strategies in schools for the deaf are clearly not working: senior departments still regularly turn out scores of illiterate (Conrad 1979), innumerate and ill-educated sixteen-year olds, lamentably badly equipped for the world of work and without the self-reliance necessary to improve themselves in their leisure time (Kittel 1985). Written English is still a mystery to many of these children, and a huge number of them cannot make themselves understood orally either, despite their twelve or thirteen years of speech training and despite their teachers' preoccupation with English. Many schools for the deaf are failing the children they were set up to help.

This might possibly be forgivable if it had always been the case, if the deaf had always been ineducable. But before the infamous Congress of Milan, which in 1880 decreed that, henceforward, oralism would be the only acceptable method of teaching the deaf, deaf children had been educated *in their own language*, by deaf teachers and by hearing teachers fluent in sign language, and it had been successful. There were deaf academics, deaf professionals, and the great majority of those teaching the deaf were deaf themselves (Lane 1984).

With this in mind, we had to make our choice. We had persuaded Sarah's headteacher that it might be possible to educate Ben at his school; in anticipation of this possibility the reception class teacher at the school had been learning BSL at Judith's classes for a year and had undergone an intensive weekend of training. The school was small, a busy place, where children were treated as individuals, following a wide and full curriculum in a family atmosphere. Children at this school were blossoming, both emotionally and intellectually. But we were conscious that by placing Ben there we would be contradicting our own beliefs about the importance of deaf culture, and we felt that we were in some way being disloyal to our deaf friends by turning our backs on the schools at which they were educated. We rather shamefacedly put our case to Judith, knowing that, if she were employed, Ben would not lose touch with the deaf world. Apart from the educational aspects, we reminded Judith that Ben would have long distances to travel daily if he were to attend a school for the deaf: twenty-five miles can mean up to two hours in a local authority taxi, which would amount to fifteen or twenty wasted hours in a week, and a great deal of tiredness. Judith faced a similar journey herself every day; even though it was undertaken in her own car she found it exhausting. Surely she would not want that for Ben? She did not. Though feeling very torn herself between concern for deaf people in general and concern for Ben in particular, she agreed to follow him to Birdsedge School, on the understanding that he would transfer to a school for the deaf in the near future.

Having observed Ben over the past year, having visited Birdsedge and spoken at length with the class teacher and the headteacher, the nursery staff and the educational psychologist also agreed with our choice. The teachers of the deaf concerned with Ben did not. Much of their concern, like ours, hinged on the fact that Ben would continue to miss out on the company of other deaf children whilst at school. Another area of concern, desperately important to them, was amplification. Ben had decided to abandon his phonic ear, we had respected his decision, and we also refused to force auditory training sessions on him when he was obviously not interested. Like us, they suspected that this state of affairs would have to change if Ben were at a school for the deaf; unlike us, they were delighted at the prospect; you can't prepare a deaf child for life in a hearing society if he insists on staying deaf. Also, of course, by choosing a mainstream school we were rejecting their expertise and a system of education for and in which they had been trained, and we were disregarding their professional advice. After much discussion, however, and in view of the unanimity of opinion of the other professionals involved, they had to give way to our wishes; at Ben's review they reluctantly agreed that he should attend Birdsedge.

Ben started full-time school, with Judith to help him, in September 1985. But it soon became clear that Judith would not stay at Birdsedge. In November, she resigned from her post. The reasons behind her resignation are many and complex, and in consideration of the feelings of the people involved we shall not go into those reasons here; some are very personal and we are all still too close to the situation to be able to give an objective account of why it broke down.

We have come to believe that the most stressful aspect of having a deaf child is making the decisions about his education. Now, only months after the last one, we were faced with another choice. Judith was to leave Birdsedge. Ben was to lose his role model, his language model, his daily link with his culture. Without Judith, Ben's situation at Birdsedge would be very different. Did the benefits of being educated close to home using methods we approved of still outweigh those of being educated with his deaf peers?

We checked with the LEA, who confirmed that they would be prepared to replace Judith with another deaf person. Our friend and neighbour, Anette

Fletcher, a former reception class teacher with very good signing skills and an excellent relationship with Ben, agreed to step in until the appointment was made. In the meantime, we would increase Ben's social contact with deaf children out of school hours and would see Judith and her family regularly, so that the break was not too painful, for Judith or for Ben, and so that he would stay in touch with the culture that remains so important for all of us.

But we were still worried. Over the past few years, we had gained a lot of respect from deaf people because of the way we had, in a sense, forgotten our hearing origins and approached the education and upbringing of our son in the way deaf people have approached it, with due respect for his cultural needs. We could honestly say that we were respecting Ben's right to be deaf.

Now, it appeared that we were blatantly ignoring that right, by supporting *integration*, which, it must be said, is a dirty word in deaf circles. Some deaf people would say that the integration of deaf children into mainstream schools was organized deliberately by educators fearful of the growing deaf culture emanating from the schools for the deaf, and to prevent the acquisition of manual communication by deaf individuals. The practice of integration in other countries has indeed seriously undermined deaf culture in those countries. In general terms, it has had the worrying side-effect of producing many deaf adults who are unable, because of poor speech, to function as hearing people, but who have learned to despise their deafness and fear what they have come to see as the 'deaf ghetto' (Denmark 1972, 1973). Were we contributing to the genesis of such a disaster here by continuing to educate Ben at Birdsedge?

We hoped not. Although we were open to criticism for neglecting our son's need to be educated with other deaf children, we were certain that he was not suffering. He was settling down to work well; he had begun to form amicable relationships with other children and he seemed very happy. We were not educating him in a mainstream school in the hope that he would deny his deafness and struggle for recognition by a hearing society on its terms; we were not separating him from his culture so that he would strive to fit into ours. We were educating him at Birdsedge because it was the only place locally which would provide a full infant curriculum, taught in his own language, ideally with the help of a native signer, precisely *without* pressure to speak.

Annette Fletcher duly took over from Judith, on a temporary basis. She has known Ben since he was a baby and over the last two years she has been attending classes and courses in BSL. She very rarely has difficulty in communicating with him.

In the spring of this year interviews were held for Judith's replacement. There was not a lot of response from the deaf world, possibly because of the controversial nature of Ben's situation, possibly – and quite understandably – because of the low pay. We live in a rural area with a scattered population; any deaf person employed to work at Birdsedge would have long distances to travel, and despite the undoubted significance and importance of the role the LEA will not pay on anything other than a non-teaching assistant scale, without travelling expenses. Two deaf people were called to interview; one did not arrive, the other had heard between applying and being interviewed that she might be accepted for a teacher-training course the following September. Both candidates' main language was English; neither had had the advantage of being brought up in a deaf family with

BSL as a first language; each had learned to sign as a teenager. The school and the LEA representative, after much deliberation – for they understood the importance to Ben of a role model and link with his culture – decided, in the end, to offer Annette the post. She was very happy to accept.

At the time of writing (May 1986), we are delighted with Ben's progress at Birdsedge. He is receiving a good, broad infant education; at five and a half years old he is reading English, an achievement which we had not dared to expect. His mathematical knowledge is wide and sound; his general knowledge increases daily. He is vocalizing as he reads, an indication that, later, he might wish to learn to speak. But he is no high-flyer. Any deaf child of normal intelligence could have achieved what Ben has achieved in the way he has achieved it, *no matter how deaf*, because it has been achieved without the acquisition of speech and without the use of hearing. Ben has proved that you don't need to speak in order to think, that you don't need to hear in order to learn, that you can fit into a hearing world without disguising your deafness, that you can grow up normally and happily, *without pressure*. Ben knows that you don't have to pretend to be a hearing person in order to succeed.

The future

Before long, it will be time for Ben to make the transfer to a special school or unit. But, hopefully, by that time, an approach to deaf education will have evolved which differs greatly from that which I have so roundly criticized in this chapter.

Schools for the deaf are called, rightly, the cornerstones of the deaf community. For this reason, deaf people have patiently supported them, though privately expressing grave doubts as to their effectiveness, particularly where they have insisted on oral policies. The schools for the deaf have placed the adult deaf population in an intolerable position over the last hundred years or so: committed to support, desperate yet powerless to change. Now, at last, the change is beginning.

In deciding how best to design and implement a new policy on total communication, Leeds Education Authority conducted a piece of research aimed at ascertaining the educational needs of deaf children. They consulted all interested parties: teachers, parents, educational psychologists, speech therapists, and the adult deaf community. At an open forum, deaf adults were given the opportunity to challenge conventional educators and teachers of the deaf regarding the observable effects of the oral system on the deaf community, in the presence of the Leeds policy-makers. The resulting policy document specifies a programme of education for deaf children which will cater for their needs *as the deaf themselves see them*. If the policies outlined in this document are implemented, we shall have arrived at a turning point not only in the education of the deaf, but in the whole philosophy of attitudes towards deaf people of all ages, in that they will have been accepted as a cultural and linguistic minority – a people with something of great value to offer to the hearing community.

Some of the proposed changes are already taking effect. Leeds Education Authority has taken on its first deaf adult sign language instructor, who will be paid, not as a classroom auxiliary, but as a lecturer. In the appointment of

Miranda Llewellyn-Jones (the teacher at the Derrymount unit) to a key position in its reorganization, the Authority clearly recognizes the validity of her belief in the fundamental importance of British Sign Language and the need for a strong deaf presence in the education of the deaf. In units for preschool deaf children, deaf adults are already involved in an informal way: they have been invited in to tell stories and generally encourage the children's BSL, by teachers who are committed to a philosophy of total communication which is wide enough to include it.

Within six years, deaf children in Leeds will be taught by teachers of the deaf who have acquired fluency in BSL from properly trained, qualified *and paid* deaf people. Where appropriate, and particularly with very young children, teachers will be accompanied in the classroom by signing deaf adults, whose pay will reflect the equal status and respect accorded to them by their employers. Young profoundly deaf children's use of BSL will not only be accepted, it will be extended and developed as part of a bilingual teaching programme. These children will be able to follow the same curriculum, at the same level, as their hearing contemporaries, because their learning will be geared to their intelligence, and not to the level of competence which they have reached in English or the effectiveness of their oral comprehension and expression. Just as their hearing contemporaries do, these children will be able to benefit from an approach which is geared to their real needs, as children. The preschool years will no longer be wasted in frenetic attempts to train deaf children to use hearing people's language: these children will be able to acquire their own language, naturally and at their own pace – a language which properly trained teachers and deaf adults can then help them to use in acquiring English as a second language.

Hearing children in Leeds will have the opportunity to learn BSL in their own schools, from deaf adults, as part of the normal curriculum, so that, when deaf and hearing children mix, it will no longer be expected that the minority culture use the majority language: the hearing children will learn the deaf children's language, and vice-versa: the partnership will be equal, not one-sided.

Our dream for Ben is about to come true, in Leeds. If such a system had been available a year ago, this is what we would have wanted for him. We would never have contemplated 'mainstreaming'. We are deeply grateful to Birdsedge and to Annette for giving Ben such an excellent start, but they are under no illusions either.

Our commitment is to deaf language and culture. One Local Education Authority now appreciates the immense value of a system which nurtures both the language and the culture of the deaf, and wants to provide, for all its deaf children, the sort of experience we would want for Ben. In a system such as this, Ben would receive an education appropriate to his needs and preferences, in the company of other deaf children. I would be happy that his rights, as a child, to a meaningful education, and as a developing deaf person, to a meaningful culture, were being respected.[1]

---

[1] The full story of Ben's education is in my forthcoming book from Souvenir Press.

References

Conrad, R. 1979. *The Deaf School Child: Language and Cognitive Function*, London, Harper and Row.

Denmark, J. 1972. 'Surdophrenia', *Sound, 6*, pp. 97–98.

Denmark, J. 1973. 'Psychiatry for the deaf', *Hearing, 28*, pp. 208–214.

Freeman, R., Carbin, C. and Boese, R. 1981. *Can't Your Child Hear?*, London, Croom Helm.

Kittel, R. 1985. 'Employment is more than merely having a job', paper presented to the International Congress on the Education of the Deaf, Manchester.

Ladd, P. 1978. 'Communication or dummification: a consumer viewpoint', in Montgomery, G. (ed), *Of Sound and Mind: Deafness, Personality and Mental Health*, Edinburgh, Scottish Workshop Publications.

Lane, H. 1984. *When the Mind Hears*, New York, Random House.

15 Reasons for assessment: rhetoric and reality in the assessment of children with disabilities

Simon Dyson

This chapter is based on research carried out by Simon Dyson in the early 1980s into the problems facing the parents of children with mental handicaps, particularly in their contact with professionals. In the first part of the chapter, he identifies fifteen distinct functions which a professional assessment of a child may serve, apart from the purported aim of identifying the child's needs. In the second part of the chapter, he analyses in detail extracts from the assessment of two children. He uses the exchange between parent and professional to demonstrate how remote these encounters are from the mythology of professionalism that remain such a potent force in special education.

With the implementation of the 1981 Education Act the law on children with special needs includes details of how assessments are to be carried out, and from whom advice should be taken. Many professionals and parents have simply trusted that the purpose of assessing a child's needs is self-evident: you have to identify needs in order to meet them.

However, this is only one of many possible functions that assessments can serve. Other possible functions can be inferred from a variety of comments in professional files, interviews with parents, and meetings between parents and professionals, for the same group of children. This was done for a group of twenty children attending a school for children with severe hearing difficulties in 1982. The various medical, psychological and educational files were examined, with particular reference to the letters written between professionals about the children and their parents. Parents' views were recorded by taped interviews looking at their practical problems, their problems with the services and their problems in obtaining information. Various face-to-face encounters between parents and professionals were also tape-recorded with the knowledge of the participants and in my presence. In addition I kept a fieldwork diary of my experiences and any untaped conversations with parents or professionals.

Here, then, are some other possible functions of assessment. It should be stressed that the interpretation of the evidence merely suggests the *possibility* that these are functions of assessment, rather than claiming to be definitive proof that they are in these particular cases.

1 *Assessments are a means of deflating a parents' expectation of their child, which professionals may regard as unrealistic.* The possible importance to a professional of an assessment which identified the precise cause of a child's learning difficulty can be seen by a mother's reaction when an assessment of her child fails to do so.

They didn't know what was wrong with him, but he would always be like it? Now our argument was, if you don't know what's wrong with him, how do you know he's always going to be like it?

Interview with parents

2 *Assessments are a means of justifying school placements.* In this example of a child with Down's Syndrome it seems that the decision to segregate the child by special school placement has been made in the minds of some professionals *before* any educational assessment has been made.

> She is due to start at [special school] in May, and we are going to arrange for an educational assessment to be performed in the near future.

Files: paediatrician

3 *Assessments are a means of persuading parents to allow their child to be segregated by attending a special school.* Here the mother's recollection of a visit by a senior clinical medical officer to test her child [X] on the Griffiths Developmental Scale suggests that the linking of the assessment and special school placement formed part of an act of persuasion since she has just explained how she was not keen for her child to go to that school.

> [Medical Officer] assessed X which they do and he said obviously that she would need a special school.

Interview with parents

4 *Assessments are a means of justifying the involvement of a particular professional with a child.* Where professionals either have, or feel they have, little practical help to offer, assessments can arguably be seen as the primary mechanism by which a professional can maintain *any* jurisdiction over a child. Here a doctor at an assessment unit writes to a paediatrician about a child with Down's Syndrome.

> I thought I would bring to your attention the fact that she has not had a regular paediatric review.

Files: doctor

5 *Assessments are a means of justifying* any *professional involvement with a child.* One interpretation of the following comment is that there is a stock of rhetoric which can be referred to in order to justify the regular paediatric assessments which are frustrating the parents of a child [X] with spina bifida.

> Parents were rather resentful to attend the outpatients clinic frequently, so I gave them the usual explanation that X will need team work and this is the best way of allocating resources.

Files: paediatrician

6 *Assessments are a means of justifying the existence of certain services, institutions or professional roles.* In the context of a home visit by a senior clinical medical officer [MO] to assess a child [X] with multiple disabilities on the Griffiths Developmental Scale, the father [F] asks about the value of assessment at an assessment unit based within a subnormality hospital. The rationale given apparently links assessment with a justification of the existence of a series of professional posts.

> *F:* Do you think it's worth, er, X going to have/get some assessment? Your personal feeling?

MO: I . . . I think it depends on what you are looking for with assessment. Now *you* have got a very definite thing. You are concerned about this slapping [the child slapping his own head] and . . . things. And the way he responds.

F: He gets frustrated.

MO: He gets frustrated.

F: And we can't . . .

MO: And you can't find what it is that frustrates him.

F: Right, that's right.

MO: Well it could well be that they can . . . find an answer.

F: That's a good idea.

MO: But in other respects you see, I sometimes think, well . . . you're going along there [to an assessment unit based at a subnormality hospital]. You will see . . . a psychologist. Well we've got . . . you know, educational psychologists within the authority who are seeing the children in schools. You see a speech therapist there. We already have speech therapists. So . . .

F: Right.

MO: In some respects I do wonder . . . how much you do . . . get . . . There *is* good co-operation. But it's just that I wonder sometimes . . .

F: Mmn.

MO: What you are . . . Hoping for.

F: Yes.

MO: Hoping for.

Visit by medical officer

7 *Assessments are a means to explain or justify the restricting of access to certain services.* In this instance the parents of a child with disabilities for whom there was no sure diagnosis had requested that their child be transferred from an 'ESN(S) school' to a school for children with physical disabilities because the latter had the services of a physiotherapist which the former at that time did not. The medical officer had made a home visit to assess the child.

Mr and Mrs X are very anxious that X should have physiotherapy in order to enable him to walk unaided. Personally I think this is part of the general pattern of his retardation.

Files: medical officer

8 *Assessments are a means of justifying or estimating the merits of a particular developmental or psychological test.* This is one interpretation of these two comments written by the same psychologist at an assessment unit, of the same child, approximately one year apart.

Current test results correlate well with previous findings and confirm that X is functioning in the severe/moderate range of retardation.

Files: clinical psychologist

Current test results correlate well with previous findings and confirm that X is functioning in the moderate range of retardation.

Files: clinical psychologist

9 *Assessments are a means of 'proving' that the professionals have a more realistic view of the child's abilities than the parents.* This interpretation is suggested by a variety of material on different children. In the professional files parents are either 'well adjusted' or 'have not accepted' their child's handicap. Now, the visit of a medical officer to assess a child on the Griffiths test is just one of many occasions

when parents feel, to judge from their comments at interview, that it is expecting too much to think that a child will perform on demand, and under time limit, for a stranger. Because explanations of their child's performance as having been affected by mood, shyness, illness or tiredness are common and recurrent themes amongst parents, this in itself should not invalidate them, as a medical officer seems to be implying in these exchanges (at two earlier points in the transcript of the assessment quoted above under point 6), where the mother [M] speaks first:

M: The trouble with him, if he's not in the mood...
MO: He won't do it.
M: He won't do it. It's very frustrating 'cause you see...
MO: *You* know what he's capable of.
M: Absolutely and he...
MO: ...And when somebody else comes to try and measure him [MO laughs]
M: Forget it.

Visit by medical officer

F: You've caught him when he's really weary. Yes. You know.
MO: Yes, sure. I'm always doing this to youngsters.
F: Yes, well, yes.
MO: And all... well I say, well all right. All we can do is see what he does today.
F: That's right. Fair comment, yes.
MO: You know. And try to catch him at a different time another...

Visit by medical officer

The point that assessments can function as a justification for the professional's view of a child against the view held by the parents can also be inferred from the case of another child with various disabilities. The quotation from the files that follows is part of a professional report on an assessment of the child, and is followed by the views held by that same child's mother on assessments generally.

Mrs X frequently imparts meaning to X's vocalization.

Files: speech therapist

M: We put no limitations on X and we won't allow anybody else to do it either. I was accused by a doctor once of having my head in the sand like an ostrich, refusing to see certain things. Now I know as of today, he might be restricted in lots of ways. But that is today. That is not to say that he'll be that way in six months time or twelve months time or in two years time. Because six months ago we brought a child here who was lying on the floor and could do nothing. *Now* we've got a child who is almost fully mobile. So I won't allow anyone to put him in a little box and label him.

Interview with parents

10 *Assessments are a means of monitoring the relationship between parents and children to see if parents are bringing up children in ways the professionals consider to be 'appropriate'.* In this extract an educational psychologist [EP] is reporting on a home assessment he has done of a child with Down's Syndrome to a case-conference. The case-conference is a regular educational review held at the school. The parents were not allowed to attend such case-conferences at that time, but the participants knew that I was present and that their conversation was being recorded.

I sometimes wonder if mother's concentration on these cognitive things is at the expense of, in order to avoid the question of control. I mean both children were performing madly for me, and didn't seem to respond very well when mum said, you know, stop it and slow down. Particularly the boy but X as well.

Educational case conference

11 *Assessments are a means of defusing parental anger when they feel that services are not responding to the clients in the way that they should.* Following on from the child in point 7 above, the parental anger at not having their child transferred from the ESN(S) school makes itself felt to a medical officer in such a way as to lead him to pressure an educational psychologist about an assessment.

I suspect that the parents distrust me and feel that I am keeping their child away from [the school for children with physical disabilities]. If you could possibly find any glimmer of light that the boy might benefit academically from [this school] I would go along with the physical need for his transfer.

Files: medical officer

12 *Assessments are a means of protecting professionals by demonstrating that comprehensive records are kept.* This interpretation is suggested by the following example, in which the non-occurrence of an assessment is meticulously recorded in the files. From the corresponding interviews it is clear the parents dislike assessments – or rather the particular form of assessment offered which would have involved a two-week period of hospitalization, which in the parents' view has previously not only disturbed the child but led to a regression.

Unfortunately the parents did not agree to this assessment, and the case-conference, which was to have been held to discuss our findings, was therefore cancelled.

Files: medical officer

13 *Assessments are a means for professionals to comply with bureaucratic and legal requirements, real or perceived.* The evidence here refers to the old special education forms that had sections for doctors (SE2) and for educational psychologists (SE3), and which pre-date the implementation of the 1981 Education Act. But a change of forms does not detract from an argument about the possible functions of assessments in general. The practice in the county studied was for a doctor, in this case a senior medical officer from the community health services to take the major responsibility for identifying children to be categorized as 'ESN(S)' and for an educational psychologist to be largely accountable for making referrals to the ESN(M) school. Thus, for the majority of the twenty children described as ESN(S) under consideration there are comments in the files which suggest a psychologist is using a doctor's assessment to fulfil his own bureaucratic duty, and vice-versa in the case of 103 files of children attending a local 'ESN(M)' school which were also studied.

I enclose completed form SE2 in respect of X. I have not seen X myself but from the information supplied by [medical officer] would support his recommendation for admission to ESN(S) school.

Files: educational psychologist

I support [educational psychologist]'s recommendation for admission to ESN(M) school.

Files: medical officer

14 *Assessments are a means to actually* constitute *the body of knowledge which represents a particular discipline.* Just as medical knowledge generally depends (amongst other

factors) on hospitals which allow the generalities of series of cases to emerge, so both medical and psychological knowledge of children with disabilities depends on identifying certain common factors between cases. This is perhaps why the failure to ascertain any general features is worthy of a comment, as here:

> She looks as if she should have a syndrome, but I cannot recognize one.
> *Files: paediatrician*

15 *Assessments are a means of demonstrating the competence of a particular professional.* The implication of the following comments about two different children is that the professional in question can triumph in obtaining an assessment, even when the tests cannot readily be applied.

> Although the boy was hyperactive and needed firm handling I consider that these results are a true reflection of his level of development.
> *Files: medical officer*

> Once again the boy proved to be hyperactive and difficult to test. Nevertheless, I think my findings are probably a fair reflection of his ability level.
> *Files: medical officer*

The possibility that these are functions of assessment arises in analysing assessment as a social process which involves the totality of actions which the participants engage in. The developmental or psychological instrument itself constitutes only *one* part of this process. This general point has been made by writers such as MacKay (1974), Heap (1982) and Osser (1985) in contexts other than children with disabilities, but it is in contrast to much previous work on assessments which has been done by psychologists and emphasizes the technicalities of the tests themselves. The implication of this viewpoint is that there is a critical distinction to be drawn between the explicitly stated functions of assessments and their actual functions. Amongst other factors it has been suggested that what is sometimes claimed to be an assessment of educational need is actually a justification for a decision about school placement that *has already been made* (point 2, above).

This distinction between rhetoric and reality can be illustrated by reference to a case which is something of a mirror image to this point. The evidence is drawn both from the fieldwork diary and the taped conversation between a mother and a medical officer. From the fieldwork diary, the educational psychologists had explained that in the multi-disciplinary case-conferences held at the end of a two-week stay in the hospital-based assessment unit, the medical officers were the professionals who 'smoothed things over'. This would seem to have been because the medical officers stand midway between the medical, hospital-based viewpoint of assessment unit doctors and the psychological, community-based viewpoint of educational psychologists. One consequence of this seems to be that a medical officer can listen to a parent's point of view and seem to agree whilst reinterpreting what has been said for consumption by other professionals. During a home visit by a medical officer to assess a child, the mother puts forward a whole range of explanations to show why it would be inappropriate for her child to attend the hospital-based assessment unit. The mother simply did not want her child to go to the assessment unit; the child had already been once; all the tests had been done before; the child reacts badly to hospitals; teachers, not hospital staff, were the best people to assess the child; the child had had enough interruptions to an attempt to lead a normal life; the child was only just getting over a major operation. The reply by the medical officer suggests that none of the staff at the assessment unit will be confronted with these accounts.

> Yes, I quite agree with you. So you know, if the name comes forward again, they will ask me, and I will say that in my opinion he is making steady progress and there is no point in re-assessing him at the unit at present.
>
> *Visit by medical officer*

Whether the rhetoric is the medical officer's claim that he agrees with the mother, or in what he claims he will say to the assessment unit staff is not important to this particular point of the argument. What it demonstrates is the principle of a gap between rhetoric and reality over the issues of assessment.

Case studies of assessment

We can now turn to look in more detail at two case studies of assessment selected from the twenty children categorized as 'ESN(S)'.

CASE STUDY ONE

In this example a ten-year-old boy has attended the ESN(S) school since he was five. From interviewing the parents and from the corresponding files it is clear that the child is from a working-class background, typically over-represented in placements in ESN(M) schools (Tomlinson 1981). Indeed the child's brother was in the process of being placed in the ESN(M) school by the usual procedure of referral from mainstream primary school. In fact, to judge from the 103 files reviewed at that school one is struck by how often several children from the same family end up in such a special school. Furthermore, as was the case with many children categorized as ESN(M), those who come to be regarded as slow learners are seen by professionals as a product of poor home environments, specifically some form of inadequate parenting. This certainly seems to have been the case with the ten-year old in question.

> His general lack of initiative and inability to respond would probably be associated with his handling at home.
>
> *Files: educational psychologist*

The ten-year old had been denied the opportunity to start mainstream primary school because the primary teachers were unable to deal with the problem of enuresis.

> Initially I had hoped that he would be able to at least attempt the local primary school but, due to his lack of toilet training, this proved to be impracticable. X was admitted to ESN(S) school.
>
> *Files: medical officer*

At the time the child was first referred to the ESN(S) school, the local ESN(M) school did not take children below the age of seven. Far from being a decision based on educational need, the original ESN(S) placement seems to have been determined by the existing structure of local school provision, since mainstream placement was out of the question because of wetting and ESN(M) school because of age. During the course of this research the child *was* to be reclassified as 'ESN(M)' by virtue of being transferred to the appropriate school. The educational psychologist [EP] summoned the mother [M] to a meeting at the ESN(S) school to discuss the assessment and school transfer and I was allowed to be present and to tape the conversation. Below is an extract from their conversation. The small Roman numerals refer to the commentary which follows the extract.

> *EP:* [Speech therapist] came across X. I didn't know about X before then I
[i] > don't think. I'd not seen him. Came across X and thought he was much
> further ahead than all the children in the school.
> *M:* Yes.
> *EP:* Um...I saw him...very...just for sort of half an hour, and agreed that,
> you know, there looked to be a lot of promise there.
> *M:* Yeh.
[ii] > *EP:* And it did look as if he was well ahead of the others in his class.
> *M:* Mmn.
> *EP:* Um...since then, the school's been pushing him so that we can see, you
> know, whether he can take it or not. Whether he can actually, you know...
> *M:* Yes.
[iii] > *EP:* If you really plug language and, and all the rest of it...
> *M:* Mmn, yes.
> *EP:* Will he learn it? Will he pick it up? Um...I saw him again...we
> planned you know, we'd give him six months, nine months and then look
> again. Um, the speech therapist saw him again and was very pleased with
[iv] > how...how he'd come on.
> *M:* Mmn, yes.
> *EP:* Um...what are...I mean what are your thoughts about it? You're
[v] > presumably pleased with having the two...
> *M:* Well I think [inaudible]. He can't...he can't miss er...you know to
> what I thought he were. I mean it's just marvellous...I didn't realize he
> were doing so well. I mean he just comes day by day. It just goes past and
> that's it.
> *EP:* I think we're thinking he's got almost...he's outgrown the school. He's,
> he's now...he's a big fish in a little, little pond.
> *M:* Yeh, because I mean a lot of my neighbours and everything, they think,
[vi] > well he's not any...he shouldn't go to a school like that. I thought, well I'm
> not going to upset him. I'm just going to leave him the way he is. I mean if
[vii] > they want him to go, they'll let me know. And I mean this is it.
> *EP:* Well, we're thinking now...I mean he could sit on his backside for the
[viii] > next, you know, how ever many years that he'll be at school.
> *M:* Yes.
> *EP:* And he doesn't have to try very hard [laughs] to stay ahead.

[i] In fact the child had not been seen by an educational psychologist before being admitted to the ESN(S) school. This is explained by the unofficial division of labour between the medical officers and the educational psychologists, whereby the medical officers take primary responsibility for 'ESN(S)' children (see point 13 above).

[ii] From the background to this case study, which seems to suggest that the child was more typical of those labelled 'ESN(M)', it follows that a possible

account of what the psychologist is saying here is that the child in certain senses was bound to be 'ahead of the others'.

[iii] A knowledge of another case dealt with by the same educational psychologist suggests that the psychologist is systematically contradicting himself. The other case concerns a child with Down's Syndrome from the ESN(S) school, whom the mother wishes to transfer to the ESN(M) school so that the child's language will improve. When interviewed the mother had said:

> Rex Brinkworth who runs the Down's Children's Association [...] he assessed her and said, all right, perhaps she's not the most brainy of the children but she should be in an 'M' school not an 'S'. She needs pushing and her speech won't come on with children that don't speak, she's got to be with children who do speak.
>
> *Interview with parents*

A few months later I was at an educational case-conference on this child attended by the headteacher of the ESN(S) school, the class teacher, a paediatrician, a clinical medical officer and the educational psychologist but not the mother. Here is an extract from the fieldwork diary, written that same evening:

> At one point I was told to switch off the tape-recorder while the professionals discussed Rex Brinkworth and the Down's Children's Association. Amongst points made were:
>
> 1 It raised false hopes in parents.
> 2 Questions were raised about what medical or psychological qualifications he had. Whether he knew what the Griffiths Test really meant.
> 3 That he continually overstepped his educational jurisdiction.
> 4 That his own daughter was exceptional.
> 5 That children with General Quotients between 50 and 60 on the Griffiths Scale would be considered for 'ESN(M)' education, but not if Down's because the ESN(M) school had not got the language-centred curriculum to cope.
> 6 Down's Groups were mischievous if reducing educational placements to General Quotient scores.
> 7 That Down's Groups were 'ginger groups' to the educational system.
> 8 That parents groups should strike a balance between being oversubdued and misleading.
>
> When the tape was switched on again the professionals joked that I had missed the best bits.
>
> *Fieldwork diary*

Let us leave aside the issues of professionals feeling threatened by articulate lay groups, refusing to be bound by their own assessment procedures and defining how parents' groups should behave. If the ESN(M) school *really* does not have a language-centred curriculum, will the ten-year-old boy of this case study continue to progress in a context where language is not central to the curriculum?

[iv] This happened without consulting the parents, to judge from another interview with the parents in the middle of this six to nine months, when they talk as if there were no alternative to the ESN(S) school he is attending.

[v] As has been mentioned, the child's younger brother is also to transfer to the ESN(M) school, but from a local primary school.

[vi] Behind this observation are a host of considerations, including why neighbours sense something inappropriate; how intelligence need not be an important criterion of integration into a social group (Albizu-Miranda et al 1966); how standards of intellectual deviance may vary between different groups in society (Mercer 1973), and how the segregated provision of 'ESN(M)' education is a legacy of a general attempt of the elementary education system to exert social control over the working class of the nineteenth century:

> It was the introduction of state compulsory education in the 1870s that focused attention more acutely on children who were not idiots or imbeciles, but who experienced difficulty with a formal educational system. Again, state intervention in discovering these dull and troublesome children was not necessarily for their own 'good' or a recognition of their 'needs'. It was primarily to ensure the smoother running of the normal educational system.
>
> (Tomlinson 1982, p. 42)

[vii] Considering the relative lack of consultation of the parents, and the extent to which assessment of schooling requirements has been guided by factors other than educational needs, this faith in authority appears somewhat misguided.

[viii] The variety of social factors contributing to the child's situation become reduced finally to a question of individual motivation: a classic example of focusing a complex range of social problems onto an individual. In the corresponding files, the child is even blamed for factors which might well be consequences of his ESN(S) placement.

> It may well be that X is rather too fond of the helpless handicapped role...
>
> *Files: educational psychologist*

CASE STUDY TWO

The five-year-old boy under consideration here has many disabilities, including severe hearing impairment. The child's early development was punctuated with a series of major life-saving operations. The mother's view of her child at that time was that professionals were not seeing her son at his best in a home environment, but at his worst in clinical settings, as she explained to me at interview.

> You see the little boy who walked across this room right now wanting to turn [the tape recorder] on and off. [Paediatrician] has never seen that. All he's ever seen is a little boy who's got his head on his mother's shoulder and cries all the time.
>
> *Interview with parents*

The professionals' initial typification of the child as a case without potential was implicitly and explicitly acknowledged to be wrong by a medical officer.

> *M:* ... [Medical officer] came back [to the child's house]. Because he was getting all these reports about a child who didn't sound at all like the child he'd seen in the first place.
>
> *Interview with parents*

> X proved to be a much more lively and 'bright' child than when originally seen in April.
>
> *Files: medical officer*

Indeed the mother's dissatisfaction with the tendency of assessments to be used
by professionals to label a child once and for all has already been discussed at the
end of point 9 above. Against this background the child is visited at home by a
senior clinical medical officer (referred to in the following extracts as DR) for an
assessment on the Griffiths Developmental Scale. The child [X] has not long
recovered from a tracheotomy. The series of extracts from the conversation that
was taped in my presence are again commented upon at the end of the extracts:

Extract 1

DR: You know he's not the little cabbage that we ...

M: No. But that's ... He never was you know.

DR: No.

[i]   M: I mean I always knew that [laughs]. It was bringing it out.

Extract 2

[ii]   DR: X! ... X! Where is your nose? Will he ... does he know parts of the body?

M: He does, he does. According to the report I got from school. But I'm just
sitting here wondering how much of it he's been ... he hasn't got his
hearing aid on.

Extract 3

DR: If one sets a few things in front of him ... a doll, a ball, a spoon, and
things and said: 'give me the ball', would he do it?

M: Errrr ... now. They've been doing this [at school]. It's all connected with

[iii]   his hearing.

DR: Yes.

M: They were working on this for a couple of years with his hearing. And if he
sort of ... oh, again, in the mood, yes he can do it. Provided there aren't too
many things in front of him.

DR: Yes. That's right.

M: If I have about three things.

DR: Mmn.

M: But I couldn't say a hundred out of a hundred, no.

DR: No ... OK. So what is really coming through from this testing and what
you've shown me and told me is how handicapped he is on the hearing and

[iv]   speech side.

Extract 4

M: Um, are you aware that he has a paralysed right vocal chord? None of us
were until [date] when they operated on his heart [laughs].

DR: Oh!

M: And they said ... the ENT people said that that would have a lot to do
with the fact he's not talking yet.

DR: I would have thought that the hearing is more ...

M: Yes.

DR: Personally.

M: Yes.

[v]   DR: I think if you are deaf. You can't hear and therefore you can't respond.

Extract 5

M: I'm intrigued by your tests ... I'm intrigued by what ... putting shapes
together and different patterns in their correct holes. What exactly does it
tell you?

DR: What does it tell me? Well, one knows that ... you know these things have been worked out on lots of children. And we know that children of certain ages should be able to do certain things. And what one is trying to work out is, what is X's ...

M: Mental age.

DR: Mental age.

M: Right.

DR: What level he is working at in different things.

M: And what would you say his mental age was?

DR: Well the overall one that comes out is about 21 months ... I think he/well, he's undoubtedly higher – 24, 25 months on the personal-social [scale]. That's ... you know that's the way he can start to feed himself in certain things.

M: Yes.

DR: Um ... knowing parts of the body, opening the door. He's coming out at about ... just about 24 months there. Building the tower, when he got up to the eight bricks, um ... those kind of things and what ... and where he's doing with his scribbles; throwing a ball, again about 24 months. Putting the ... six shapes back in the board with ... just in the minute, is taking him to 25, 26 months. Now if he was rather more co-operative today we may have got him another month or two on.

M: Yes.

DR: But ... and then ... overall ... he's 21.5 months I'd say and his age is 65 months, so we give you a ... his mental age as a percentage of his actual age and its 33 per cent.

M: Right.

DR: And when I saw him last time it was 33 per cent.

M: So, up.

DR: So that means ...

M: He's keeping up.

DR: He's going along at the steady rate ... The first time I saw him he was 28 per cent and that was before he went to school.

M: Yes.

DR: So going to school has ... helped him along, and he's progressing
[vi] steadily.

[i] This exchange, which shows the doctor at his most insensitive, typifies two very different perspectives on assessments. That of the medical officer might be characterized as static: what levels of developmental retardation can be established at any particular time? The mother's orientation seems entirely different and dynamic: what strategies must be invoked to elicit further development? This distinction is elaborated on in the comments that follow.

[ii] From the context of the rest of the encounter it seems more likely that the doctor does not know or has forgotten the child is hearing-impaired rather than has assumed the hearing aid to be in.

[iii] To develop point [i], above, the comment of the mother here is typical of many comments made by parents when interviewed. Disabilities such as hearing impairment and other learning difficulties are continually referred to as obstacles to the child's development which must be resolved or at least addressed to enable that child to progress. On the other hand, to judge from what psychologists,

medical officers and paediatricians write in their files about the same children, learning difficulties and disabilities are conceptualized as evidence of a certain 'syndrome' or 'generalized retardation'. In other words, from the point of view of such professionals, one function of assessments is to produce evidence to substantiate their commonsense view of the child as somehow different. This point is similar to that made by Davis (1982), a medical sociologist who has studied children with disabilities and other children in a range of clinical settings by close analysis of the conversation that takes place in those clinics. Where there are 'serious doubts' about a child's development, he comments:

> Thus parents would typically 'claim' their children were progressing, that they *could* do things at home that they 'wouldn't' do in the clinic [...] children's limitations, often *demonstrated* by the doctor, served to show the parents that his typification of the child was correct.
>
> (Davis 1982, p. 24)

However, Davis does not make explicit comparisons to so-called 'normal' children who are not usually subject to such close observation and detailed testing. This points to the unstated political bias of Davis, for he actually has examples from local authority child welfare clinics with which to make comparisons. Children considered 'normal' from commonsense observations are excused failure at certain tests.

> ... 'failure' was remedied by checking with the mother that the child could normally do it and the 'failure' explained away as due to character, setting or temperament.
>
> (Davis 1982, p. 55)

[iv] This extract constitutes evidence that the professional account of the purpose of assessments being to provide information for parents about their child is somewhat misconceived. It is the mother who is the expert on her own child. She actually provides the senior clinical medical officer with his own information by herself estimating the child's level of ability so that the doctor can complete his tests. But the 'information' he then gives the mother sounds somewhat absurd. He has to be reminded that the child is deaf; he has to rely largely on the mother's information about what the child can do only to come up with the conclusion that the tests show that the child is handicapped with regard to hearing and speech.

The fact that the medical officer may write up a more technical account of his findings, which he does not present to the mother because he feels she wouldn't understand, is immaterial to the argument. This is because in all twenty cases studied the corresponding records of the developmental tests are linked *not* to an educational strategy but to one of three factors:

1 Previous expectations voiced by professionals of how the child would develop:

> These results show that whilst X is making some definite progress, nevertheless the actual rate of development is slowing down as I think one would expect.
>
> *Files: medical officer*

2 The diagnosed medical syndrome of the child:

> Her rate of development is, however, slowing down which is to be expected in this condition [Down's Syndrome].
>
> *Files: medical officer*

3 The fact of the child's placement in an ESN(S) school:

These results are almost identical with the ones reported to you [previously] and suggest that X is making very steady progress at [ESN(S) school].

Files: medical officer

[v] The information that the mother continues to provide reaches the point where the role of the senior clinical medical officer is becoming entirely upstaged and he is reduced to the defeated exclamation 'Oh!... I think' Coupled with the fact that hearing impairment, which was not an issue until the mother pointed it out, has now become an all-embracing explanation, this suggests that the explanation represents a somewhat desperate attempt by the doctor to regain some credibility. One can perhaps conclude that a hidden purpose of professional assessments is an attempt to generate a type of information that seeks to establish professional knowledge as intrinsically superior to 'commonsense' knowledge of parents, a distinction which can then be used to rationalize the involvement of professionals in the first place.

[vi] The 'knowledge' generated by assessments also provides a convenient justification for decisions made and implemented by professionals, particularly, as in this case, with regard to the history of the child's school placement. How much better the child may have fared in a different educational setting is not an issue which is allowed to appear on the agenda not only with regard to this particular conversation, but in the case as a whole.

Conclusion

This chapter has attempted to point out several issues about assessment that are not readily acknowledged by the professionals involved in such procedures. The first issue is that what professionals claim to be the reasons for assessment may not be the *actual* reasons. Thus an assessment may be put forward as taking place to establish a child's educational needs, when the assessment is really to justify a decision about school placement which has been made on the grounds of some 'commonsense' notion, for example that all children with Down's Syndrome should go to an ESN(S) school. The second issue is that there are many possible functions of assessment: to discount the parent's view of the child; to justify school placements; to persuade parents about school placement; to justify the involvement of a particular professional, or indeed any professional; to justify the existence of certain services, or restricting access to them; to establish the merits of a particular psychological instrument; to validate the professional's typification of a child; to check up on the parents; to defuse parental anger when they feel nothing is being done; to protect professionals by allowing them to compile comprehensive records; to comply with bureaucratic or legal necessities; to actually constitute professional knowledge, and, finally, to demonstrate professional competence. Thirdly, the two case studies demonstrate the existence of a whole cluster of constraints on assessment.

Case Study One suggests that the constraints in assessing the child are:

1 The practical availability of ancillary help and of the policies of local schools.

2 The informal division of labour between an educational psychologist (taking responsibility for 'ESN(M)' referral) and a medical officer ('ESN(S)' referral) presumably to reduce workloads.

Case Study Two illustrates other reasons constraining the course of the assessment. I would argue that the roles of professional assessments illustrated by this particular case study are:

1 To provide a rationale for the involvement of the medical officer with the child in the first place.
2 To reinforce the justifications for professional decisions that have already been made and implemented with regard to school placement.
3 To generate information that differentiates the knowledge of professionals from that of parents.
4 To justify the professional's typification of the child as inevitably different from 'normal'.

References

Albizu-Miranda, C., Martin, N. and Stanton, H. K. 1966. *The Successful Retardate*, Puerto Rico, Department of Health, Education and Welfare.

Davis, A. G. 1982. *Children in Clinics: a Sociological Analysis of Medical Work with Children*, London, Tavistock.

Heap, J. 1982. 'The social organization of reading assessment: reasons for eclecticism', in Payne, G. C. F. and Cuff, E. C. (eds.), *Doing Teaching*, London, Batsford.

MacKay, R. 1974. 'Standardised tests: objective/objectified measures of "competence"', in Cicourel, A. V. (ed.), *Language Use and School Performance*, New York, Academic Press.

Mercer, J. 1973. *Labelling the Mentally Retarded*, Berkeley, University of California Press.

Osser, H. 1985. 'Understanding students: teacher's problems of assessment', in Cuff, E. C. and Payne, G. C. F. (eds.), *Crisis in the Curriculum*, London, Croom Helm.

Tomlinson, S. 1981. *Educational Subnormality: a study in decision-making*, London, Routledge and Kegan Paul.

Tomlinson, S. 1982. *A Sociology of Special Education*, London, Routledge and Kegan Paul.

16 Statements of intent: an assessment of reality
Will Swann

This chapter concerns the impact of the assessment and Statement provisions of the 1981 Education Act. By examining a small number of Statements and the assessment leading up to them, Will Swann reveals a sizeable gap between the rhetoric of individualized assessment, and the reality of a series of events the main purpose of which is to categorize the child. He argues that while segregated provision exists, a means to select and allocate children will be needed. The latter part of the chapter deals with the power of parents under the Act to affect the Statement process, and concludes that strict limits to this power continue.

The objectives of the 1981 Education Act

The 1981 Education Act has been said to embody certain policy objectives, grown out of slow but steady progress towards a more rational, effective and caring system of special education. Accounts of the underlying aims of the Act vary, and thus one is presented with a problem in describing them. All accounts are inevitably interpretations. For my purposes here, I am primarily interested in official and quasi-official versions of the aims of the law. I shall use two sources in particular: first the Department of Education and Science *Circular 1/83* (DES 1983), that conveyed authoritative guidance to local authorities on the interpretation of the Act, and second, a recent book by John Fish (1985) called *Special Education: the Way Ahead*. John Fish, as Staff Inspector for Special Education at the time of the Act's development, was deeply involved in the production of the Act, and may be taken as an authority on it.

Under previous legislation,[1] pupils who required 'special educational treatment' were placed into one of ten statutory categories[2] for which separate types of provision were made. Categories include 'educationally subnormal', 'physical handicap', 'partially sighted' and 'maladjusted'. In most cases, categories were defined in terms of disability or defect. The growing opposition to this system was summarized by the Warnock Report (DES 1978). The report pointed out that children often 'suffer from' more than one disability, that the major disability was often educationally irrelevant, that the category label carried a stigma, and that categorization encouraged the mistaken view that all children with the same disability required the same kind of education. The most important argument from the Warnock Committee's own viewpoint was that categorization promoted too sharp a distinction between 'the handicapped and the non-handicapped'; abolition would, it claimed, weaken this invidious boundary.

Superseding categorization by disability was the notion embedded in the 1981

---

[1] Before 1981, special education was governed by Sections 33 and 34 of the 1944 Education Act.
[2] The statutory categories in force in 1981 were set out in the *Handicapped Pupils and Special Schools Regulations*, 1959.

Education Act of 'a child with special educational needs', defined as one who has 'significantly greater difficulty in learning than the majority of children of his age' or who has 'a disability which either prevents or hinders him from making use of educational facilities of a kind generally provided in schools . . . for children of his age'. No further legal categorization now exists. The emphasis was to be on the child's educational needs, not on his or her disability. As Circular 1/83 put it: 'The main focus should be on the child himself rather than on his disability' (para. 3).

This focus was to redefine the purpose and the extent of assessment. Assessment was no longer intended to allocate children to categories, but rather, according to the Circular, it was: 'a means of arriving at a better understanding of a child's learning difficulties for the practical purpose of providing a guide to his education' (para. 4). The DES, through Circular 1/83, also accepted that a child's needs depended not only on his or her personal characteristics but also on the nature of the environment the child was in. There was, therefore, an indirect pointer to the need to assess the child and the environment, and their interrelationships: 'The extent to which a learning difficulty hinders a child's development depends not only on the nature and severity of that difficulty, but also on the personal resources and attributes of the child, and on the help and support he receives at home and at school. A child's special educational needs are thus related to his abilities as well as his disabilities, and to the nature of his interaction with his environment' (para. 3). The hope that this new conceptual framework would blur the distinction between children with and without special needs survived from the Warnock Report. John Fish records that the Act 'sees disabilities and significant difficulties as variations in need and not as defining different kinds of children' (pp. 4–5).

The objectives embodied in the assessment and statement procedures followed closely from the new definition of the client group. John Fish writes that: 'the most significant change which has taken place in the assessment of children with disabilities and significant difficulties is from a system which placed children into categories of handicap to one based on determining individual special educational needs and specifying the means of meeting them' (p. 53). How is this to be achieved? Local authorities are to identify the children who in their view require a formal assessment by the authority. They must seek psychological, medical and educational advice on the child's needs, as well as any other advice they deem relevant. On the basis of that advice they may prepare a 'Statement of special needs'. This must specify the child's special needs, the provision required to meet those needs, the school the child is to attend, and any additional non-educational provision. Once made, the Statement has the force of law: the authority must provide what it specifies.

A critical feature of the Statement is the requirement to specify separately the provision the child requires and the school which is to provide it. The aim here was to avoid the naive equation of special provision and special school, a point on which John Fish is very clear:

> . . . special schools must now be more clear about what they offer . . . the new position where the statement is a form of contract between the local authority and parents means that such schools will need to provide defined services.
>
> (Fish 1985, p. 69)

The mechanisms and procedures of assessment were not the only new feature of the Act. It was envisaged that it would provide a new structure of control over the whole process, with parents playing a much more important role than hitherto. Under the earlier legislation, the positively asserted rights of parents were quite limited. They could request a medical examination of their child which the LEA would have to comply with if reasonable, and they could attend any medical examination. Parental involvement was a watchword of the Warnock Committee: 'the successful education of children with special educational needs is dependent on the full involvement of their parents: indeed, unless the parents are seen as equal partners in the educational process the purpose of our report will be frustrated'. The 1981 Education Act subsequently gave parents extensive new rights to be involved in the process of assessing and preparing a Statement on their child. Parents can now submit evidence as part of the assessment, and attend examinations. They must receive a draft Statement and copies of all the professional advice on which the Statement is based. They then have the right to meet officers and other professionals to discuss the draft before a final Statement is released. If they remain dissatisfied with the content of the Statement they may appeal against it to a local appeal tribunal, and if the tribunal confirms the Statement, they may, in the final analysis, appeal to the Secretary of State for Education and Science.

On the face of it, this gives parents many more opportunities to influence the nature of their child's assessment and the content of the Statement. 'Parents', John Fish confirms, 'are to have more information and be more involved in the decisions' (p. 5).

From rhetoric to reality

In order to contrast the claims made for the Act and the reality of the assessment and statement process I shall consider the cases of four children. Three of them, Andrew, Simon and Linda, have been categorized as having severe learning difficulties; they all live in one local education authority. The fourth child, Paul, comes from another LEA, and has a rare and extremely disabling skin disorder called *epidermolysis bullosa*. I acted as 'advocate' for their parents at their local appeals against the Statements.

All four children were involved with professional handicap services from birth or shortly afterwards, and this continued in the five years prior to the formal assessment for a Statement. The one common and enduring factor of all this contact with professionals was parental dissatisfaction. The conflict reached its peak in the Statement process principally because the parents wished their children to attend ordinary schools, and the local authorities decided that they should attend special schools. In Andrew, Simon and Linda's case this was a special school for children with severe learning difficulties; in Paul's case, it was a special school for children with physical disabilities.

THE STATEMENTS

The Statement process has been portrayed as involving an individualized assessment, leading to an individualized Statement of needs. To what extent did this happen in these cases? Andrew's Statement read as follows (Section I is omitted as it contains only personal details such as name and address):

II – Special educational needs
Andrew has a chromosomal abnormality causing severe delayed development. He therefore needs considerable individual attention to help develop his potential.

III – Special educational provision
A very small protective teaching environment where all learning is carefully structured and appropriate for a child with severe developmental delay.

IV – Appropriate school or other arrangements
A day school making specific provision for children with severe general developmental delay. The nearest appropriate school is _____ Day Special School.

V – Additonal non-educational provision
Regular physiotherapy (balance work) and speech therapy.
Transport.

Section II of Andrew's Statement identifies only one special need: 'for considerable individual attention to help develop his potential'. It is difficult to construe this as an account of his individual needs, for the expression applies to thousands of other children. This need is said to arise from the fact that Andrew has a chromosomal abnormality which causes 'severe delayed development'. The only characteristic named in the Statement is Andrew's biological defect; it focuses explicitly not on the child but on his disability, and in doing so contradicts Circular 1/83. Circular 1/83 was incorporated almost in its entirety into this LEA's *Notes of Guidance for Schools on the Implications of the 1981 Education Act*. These notes included the exhortation for a focus on the child not the disability. Thus, Andrew's Statement contravened local as well as national policy.

Andrew's abnormality is 'cri-du-chat syndrome'. This is a defect arising from a deletion of part of the 5th chromosome, and it is associated with mental handicap and certain physical abnormalities. If there were a one-to-one relationship between the defect and mental ability then Section II of the Statement might be justified. In fact, this is not the case. A study in America of 65 children and adults with cri-du-chat syndrome revealed a wide range of ability. Social quotients range from 6 to 85 (Wilkins *et al* 1980).[1] Andrew's defect is, therefore, no guide to his educational needs at all.

Having described Andrew as a child with 'severe delayed development', it follows that what he requires is teaching appropriate to such a child. Section III of the Statement defines this as: 'A very small protective teaching environment where all learning is carefully structured and appropriate' for such children. Here categorization is very much alive: Andrew has been allocated to a category, and is to be educated by means appropriate to it. There is no attempt to define any provision unique to Andrew. Not surprisingly, Section IV names a special school for children with 'severe general developmental delay'. This special school before the 1981 Act, catered for children categorized as ESN(S) (severely educationally

---

[1] The parallel here with the assumption that all children with Down's Syndrome are severely mentally handicapped is striking. See Booth (1985).

subnormal), and it continues to do so under a new terminology. The equation of special school with special provision remains firmly intact, so that the wording of Section III is no more than a circumlocution for 'special school for severely mentally handicapped children'.

In no sense could this Statement be described as a guide to Andrew's education. No specific goals, approaches or resources are set out. When the education officer responsible for writing the statement was asked at the subsequent appeal hearing why the statement lacked any detail, he explained that this was the job of the expert staff of the school, not of the Statementing authority.

Simon's Statement was issued at almost the same time. It reads thus:

II – Special educational needs
Simon has severe delayed development in all areas. Improvement has been made in areas of motor function and Makaton signing has been started.

III – Special educational provision
Simon needs considerable attention in a very small protective teaching environment where all learning is carefully structured and appropriate for a child with severe general developmental delay.

IV – Appropriate school or other arrangements
A day school making specific provision for children with severe general developmental delay. The nearest appropriate school is _____ Day Special School.

V – Additional non-educational provision
Particular attention is needed in the direction of activities to encourage Simon to look at the material he is handling.

Section II of Simon's Statement specifies no needs at all, but simply classifies Simon as severely delayed in all aspects of his development. The wording of Section III is virtually identical to the Section III of Andrew's statement, and also to that in Linda's Statement. This reproduction of identical phraseology reinforces the central place of categorization in these Statements. It also caused the parents of these children much concern, and was a subject of frequent discussion in meetings of the support group to which they all belong. They repeatedly challenged the authority to account for what appeared to be the mass processing of their children. In a statement to the press, a senior education officer said: 'the wording of the statements is similar, I acknowledge, but that is because the provision required is very similar'. If the 'provision' is defined as the school the children are to attend, and if we accept the LEA's view of what the children require, then the officer's statement is entirely accurate.

Paul's Statement, drawn up in a different LEA, differs in many respects from those I have discussed so far. It is, most obviously, much more detailed:

II – Special educational needs
Paul needs:
A   An infant curriculum with objectives that are clearly stated.
B   Teaching programmes which are in small enough steps for Paul to be able to succeed and which will:
    (1)   Assist the development of early literacy, numeracy and communication skills.

(2)   Allow Paul to further develop his self-help skills and assist him to achieve as much independence as possible.

(3)   Enlarge Paul's knowledge, experience and imaginative understanding in all areas of early learning but with particular regard to, for example, practical activities such as Art, Craft and Physical Education.

C   An appropriate protective school environment which offers maximum space and freedom of movement within which he can gain confidence in and through physical activity.

D   Access to appropriate technology (e.g. a computer or adapted typewriter) to assist his learning by facilitating manual dexterity.

E   Access to small group teaching with regular individual support.

F   Arrangements for monitoring his progress regularly against objectives set.

III – Special educational provision

A   A day school which provides specially for pupils with special needs associated with physical difficulties.

B   A small group setting (not to exceed a pupil teacher ratio of 1:10) – as well as assistance with the manipulation of materials when appropriate.

C   An individual teaching programme drawn up in consultation with parents, with consideration being given to how the parents can be involved in the programme.

D   Monitoring arrangements to check progress within school and review of progress not less than once a year in which the parents are invited to take full part. Consideration will be given at the annual review to the integration of Paul into a mainstream school setting according to an agreed set of criteria.

IV – Appropriate school or other arrangements
———— School

V – Additional non-educational provision

A   Availability of Borough transport.

B   Daily access to suitably qualified and experienced staff who can dress open and infected wounds when necessary.

C   Individual supervision of Paul's personal needs in respect of toiletting, dressing and to aid his movement from one position to another and from one place to another.

D   Access to regular physiotherapy with a daily programme being continued in class under the physiotherapist's supervision and after consultation with parents.

E   Access to speech therapy with a clearly defined programme which can be operated in collaboration with Paul's class teacher and after consultation with parents.

F   Access to appropriate occupational therapy after consultation with parents in order to maximize Paul's abilities.

Paul's list of needs is a lengthy one, but the striking feature is that only some of them are *special* needs in any obvious sense. For example, it would be hard to claim that any five year old does *not* need an infant curriculum with objectives that are clearly stated. Whatever the authority's intentions in writing the Statement, the end-product is a list of needs, many of which are entirely ordinary.

In Section III, we again find much more detail than in the previous examples. But although the provision is specified in some detail, it does not identify an individual service that the school is to offer this particular child. Point A is a circumlocution for 'special school for children with physical disabilities'. Points B to D then list three features of the provision in this school that are available to *all* children attending it. Thus the service is defined, but not individualized.

Let me pose three questions about these Statements. First, do they amount to individualized Statements of need and provision? In all three cases I have detailed, and in the case of Linda as well, the answer must be 'no'. Secondly, do they succeed in avoiding the categorization of these children? In the cases of Andrew, Simon and Linda, the answer must be 'no'. Categorization and labelling is much less in evidence in Paul's statement, however. Third, do the Statements succeed in defining the provision to be made for these children separately from the naming of the appropriate school? In all cases, the answer is 'no'. Finally, could these Statements be construed as guides to these children's education? Andrew's and Simon's, and Linda's which is almost identical, can in no sense be taken as guides, since they provide no useful information. Paul's comes closer to this aim, but does not achieve it. Items A, B, E, F in Section II of Paul's Statement are no more than any child would be offered. Items C and D are more specific to Paul, but they fall far short of the level of detail required by a teacher to provide an appropriate physical environment and appropriate technology.

In sum, the practice revealed by these Statements is remote from the claims made for the procedures set out in the 1981 Education Act.

THE PROFESSIONAL ADVICE

A great deal of written and oral information and opinion already existed for all four children before the formal assessment process began. By the time the Statements were prepared this had grown into a substantial file on each child, containing many reports, letters and notes of meetings. An analysis of the professional advice is revealing on two counts: first it gives us an insight into the extent to which professional practices matched up to policy guidelines, and second, it reveals the formal basis on which the education officers wrote the Statements. In doing so, they were legally bound to take into account psychological, medical and educational advice, formally part of the assessment procedure, but they were aware of much more background information.

Because of the complexity and volume of information, I shall consider only the case of Simon.

Simon was first referred to his LEA in July 1983, aged 4:3, by the Child Development Unit he had attended since he was one year old. In September 1983, the LEA wrote to Simon's parents proposing a formal assessment under the 1981 Education Act. The parents replied requesting a delay until nearer his fifth birthday, on the grounds that Simon had just been fully assessed at the Child Development Unit in July that year, and that he had just started walking and would benefit from being fully mobile before he was assessed again. They also made some comments on the form they would wish the assessment to take: that it should take place over an extended period, and that it should take place at home or at the opportunity group Simon attended part-time (this was an integrated provision for both able-bodied and disabled children run jointly by a voluntary agency and the local social services department).

The LEA agreed to the delay and acknowledged the parents' suggestions. In May 1984, they wrote again to the parents, when Simon was aged 5:0, and formal assessment began. By July 1984, an educational psychologist, doctor, nursery nurse, speech therapist and physiotherapist had written reports on Simon and in September 1984, the draft Statement was issued. Simon's parents immediately noticed the absence of the statutory educational advice, notified the LEA of this fact, and sent them a report on Simon that had been prepared by the teacher at the opportunity group who was, in fact, an ex-special school teacher, formerly employed by the LEA. A month later, at the parent's request, additional reports from other professionals based at the opportunity group and from an ordinary nursery that Simon was now also attending, were sent to the LEA.

In early March 1985, the final Statement was issued, still without any educational advice appended. In late March, the LEA wrote to the parents withdrawing the Statement, on the grounds that 'it has been pointed out to me' that the educational advice was absent. No reference was made to the teacher's report submitted by the parents. Instead the LEA sought advice from the teacher of the nursery class at the special school named on the withdrawn Statement. With this report now appended, the Statement was reissued with minor changes.

The critical advice in leading to Simon's designation as a child with 'severe general developmental delay' was that provided by the educational psychologist. He observed and tested Simon for a total of just under two hours, at the child Development Unit, at home and at the opportunity group. His assessment of Simon read as follows:

> I saw Simon with his father present, finding him an enthusiastic, well-motivated young man who was now very mobile. I heard plenty of vocalization and some recognizable words (e.g. baby; now; there). Simon tended to look at the person rather than the materials in front of him, but once the materials did engage his attention, then he often worked rapidly and successfully on tasks.
>
> I administered the Merill-Palmer Scale of Mental Tests and found Simon to achieve a mental age of 2 years and 2 months at his chronological age of 5 years 3 months. This was essentially a non-verbal result and indicated Simon to be functioning at a very limited level of general ability.
>
> Mr and Mrs A. asked me to extend my assessment, seeing Simon at the opportunity group and at home.
>
> On the 19th July I visited the opportunity group and first observed Simon in a free play situation – he tended to be rather aimless in that unstructured setting.
>
> I then observed him being taught by Mrs L. and his whole level of performance improved considerably in a very structured situation which aided his concentration and attention. Simon was very accurate in picture–picture matching and in word–picture matching, and was able to follow two-element commands. He knows the parts of his face and was able to thread large beads quickly. He was able consistently to select and name pictures from an array of 20 pictures and he could do this for each of the pictures in that array.
>
> Simon was enthusiastic, cheerful and rapid, throughout the 20 minutes session I observed and I found his skills to scatter over a 2.0–3.0 year level.
>
> I then observed Simon with the physiotherapist at the opportunity group following his activities in the balance room. He has clearly improved considerably in all areas of his motor function and although he moaned a great deal about some of the tasks required, he was able to be successful in everything.

I then saw Simon at his home with his mother and sometimes his older brother present. Clearly Simon is an extremely happy, active boy surrounded by stimulating activities at home. He played with gusto and pleasure, being completely relaxed in his natural environment. I observed no new skills however, but certainly saw the fluent utilization of those which I had observed elsewhere.

There are many points of interest in this report. Why, for example, did the psychologist choose to use a test, the Merrill-Palmer, whose first and only standardization took place in America during the 1920s and 30s, and whose reliability with children of this mental age level is very poor?[1] My central concern here, however, is the uses to which the information in the report might be put. We can distinguish two general purposes: to provide information on which to base teaching programmes, and to provide information on which to categorize the child. What information is provided on which teaching programmes could be built? Although some qualitative information is offered, it is partial and would have to be supplemented considerably. No systematic strategy appears to have been followed in collecting or reporting the information. Moreover some parts of the report seem to contradict each other. Thus, Simon's performance is said to improve considerably in a very structured situation at the opportunity group, but he plays with 'gusto and pleasure' and is 'relaxed' in his home environment.

Embedded in these qualitative observations is information from formal testing. It is on this basis that the psychologist concluded that Simon had 'a very limited level of general ability'. The relative weight of the two types of information gathered can be judged from the section of the report where the psychologist states his recommendations. This reads as follows:

Special educational needs
Simon needs considerable individual attention in a very small protective teaching environment where all the learning is carefully structured and appropriate for a child with severe general developmental delay.

Recommended facilities and resources
Particular attention needs to be directed to activities which increase Simon's need to look at the materials he is handling.

The wording of the first part of the recommendations is that which eventually appeared on Simon's Statement, and on the Statements for Andrew and Linda. Both the reports prepared by educational psychologists on Andrew and Linda also contain this paragraph. Linda was assessed by the same psychologist as Simon; Andrew by another. Thus the routinization of assessment, and the central place of categorization, went far beyond the writing of the Statements, and was manifest at the stage of professional advice. In Simon's case, only one recommendation follows from the qualitative information in the report, and it is far from clear why this recommendation has been selected from many others that could have been made. It appears, then, that the normative, test-based, information was far the most important in determining the conclusions of the report. To the

---

[1] The Merrill-Palmer Scale was first published in 1931 in America and has not been standardized since then: Stutsman (1931). Its test-retest reliability over six months at age 24 months was reported as 0.63, and at age 42 months as 0.80 by Ebert and Simmons (1943).

extent that other evidence came into play, it too may have been used to make normative comparisons.

When the draft Statement arrived without any educational advice, Simon's parents notified the LEA of this fact, and sent a report prepared by Mrs L., the teacher at the opportunity group. This teacher had had eighteen months' experience of Simon. On a number of details, her evidence challenged the conclusion reached by the educational psychologist. In particular, she found Simon's comprehension at age 5:6 to be considerable:

> During the teaching sessions I have ascertained that he can understand all that is said to him, despite his aphasia.[1] At the most I heard him say two words. He is able to colour match, picture match and pick up the picture of a specific object when asked. He can recognize most of the letters of the alphabet and place many of them on the appropriate picture beginning with that letter.

The LEA did not accept this report as the formal educational advice, but instead asked for an assessment by Mrs S., the nursery teacher at the special school named in the draft Statement. Mrs S., with no previous knowledge of Simon, observed and tested him at home for one hour and at his ordinary nursery for thirty minutes. Amongst her recommendations, Mrs S. stated that Simon should have access to 'existing integration facilities to be used where appropriate'. The only 'integration facilities' in existence were a programme of part-time integration from the special school named in the draft Statement. Thus, Mrs S. had already concluded that Simon was an appropriate candidate for her school. This conflicts with the advice given in Circular 1/83 that: 'Professional advice should not be influenced by considerations of the eventual school placement to be made for the child, since that is a matter to be determined by the LEA at a later stage' (para. 35). However, this particular paragraph was not included in the LEA's *Notes of Guidance*.

As part of their attempt to have Simon educated in an ordinary school, the parents sought a second opinion, from another educational psychologist employed by a different LEA. She assessed Simon when he was aged 6:0. Using a combination of published norm-referenced and criterion-referenced assessment instruments, she reached tentative conclusions that differed considerably from the LEA's own psychologist. One instrument she used was the British Ability Scales:

> Since his ability to name objects is very limited I tried out of interest spreading all the pictures from the Naming Vocabulary Scale of the BAS in front of Simon in random order and asking him to point to the one I named. Since generating a name for a picture and recognizing a named object are rather different skills it would be invalid to score this. Nonetheless I thought his performance was impressive – he failed only two items, 'scales' and 'compass'; had he been naming all these items his score would have been well above average for his age and I think this indicates a significant vocabulary...
>
> Because of a growing unease about Simon's difficulties, and a suspicion based on rather intangible evidence that the combination of specific language difficulty or

---

[1] Aphasia is the term generally used to refer to specific language delay or disorder.

disorder and the effects of ataxia[1] could combine to mask possible strengths I tried some age appropriate scales that did not rely on a spoken response, very lengthy instruction, or fine motor skills. Although Simon could build towers and make patterns with bricks, I could not get him to copy the block design pictures – in part this seemed to relate to his being distracted by the patterns made by the sides of the blocks. However on the Visual Recognition Scale he was able to remember and identify one and two pictures of a toy from any number of distractors and one set of three pictures with two distractors. While I tend to regard Visual Recognition as a test of a hypothetical ability that has little direct implication for programme planning, this score . . . does at least show that in one area Simon is performing like an ordinary six-year old.

Faced with this evidence, and only limited time in which to observe Simon, she concluded:

It is always difficult to differentiate general learning difficulties from the effects of such a combination of specific learning difficulties. This assessment has not done so, but it has, I believe, highlighted sufficient ordinary attainment to suggest that further investigation should be undertaken over time, and that it is reasonable at least to test out the hypothesis that Simon could respond to a programme for specific difficulties.

It is significant that two professional psychologists should arrive at such conflicting conclusions. More important for our purposes here, however, is that the fact that categorization was as deeply embedded in the mode of assessment and reporting of this psychologist as it was in that of the LEA's psychologist. They differed as to which category Simon belonged in, but both assumed that it was appropriate to classify children in categories such as 'general learning difficulties' and 'specific learning difficulties'.

It should now be clear that in Simon's case, the failure to provide a guide to education and the continued existence of categorization which were evident in the Statement were also apparent in the advice on which the Statement was based, and in advice collected in order to challenge the Statement. Categorization was also apparent in the preparation of the Statement, at two levels. First, it influenced the choice of advisers. The initial classification of Simon as having 'severe general developmental delay' led the LEA to ask for educational advice from a teacher in the relevant special school. When asked at the appeal to explain his choice of adviser, the education officer concerned stated that she was experienced with 'this kind of child'. Secondly, categorization influenced the way the advice and information was filtered and assessed in writing the Statement. The evidence from Mrs L., the teacher at the opportunity group, was available before the final Statement was written, yet it had no impact on the wording of the Statement. It is difficult to explain this except in two ways. First, we might argue that the officer who wrote the Statement had already decided that Simon had 'severe general developmental delay' and that this decision was so firmly established that contradictory information was rejected. Alternatively, it may simply be that the officer disregarded the information from Mrs L. as untrustworthy. If so, he was at odds with Simon's parents.

---

[1] Ataxia is a form of cerebral palsy characterized by unco-ordinated movements and an unsteady gait.

There is not space here to consider in any detail the professional assessments on Andrew, Linda and Paul. An analysis reveals similar processes, though the details in each case are quite different. In all cases, categorization played a central role in the assessments.

Accounting for the facts

We may assume that policy statements at national and local level are not made in a consciously insincere manner. How then do we account for the gap between rhetoric and reality that these cases present? Let me advance three possible explanations. The first is that professionals and administrators are incompetent: although not insincere in their rhetoric, they fail to understand the implications of it, and stick rigidly and inappropriately to outdated, discredited modes of action. If incompetence exists, then to a degree those who behave incompetently may be excused some or all of the blame. Education officers, educational psychologists and other professionals do not have infinite time and resources at their disposal. For example, the education officer who wrote the Statements for Andrew, Simon and Linda is not only responsible for all other Statements in an area with a school population of over 14,000, but has extensive duties outside special education as well. The time available to consider and weigh evidence is strictly limited.

A second possible explanation follows from this: namely that lack of resources is the key. Perhaps if enough administrators and professionals could be employed there would then be time to produce Statements in line with Circular 1/83. This, at best, is a partial explanation, for if it accounted wholly for the events I have described, then a sizeable injection of money would lead to all the objectives set out in the Circular being attained. This is highly improbable, for it fails to take account of the ill-pervasive influence of the structure and distribution of special educational resources within the LEA. I shall now focus on this third explanation.

Whatever the intentions that underlay the emergence of Statements, what determined their nature was the function they were to serve in decision-making. In the case of all four children I have referred to, the administrators concerned were essentially faced with an allocation decision. All their resources were located in segregated provision, and to redistribute them was either lengthy, difficult, disruptive, costly or undesirable from their perspective. They had little choice, then, but to allocate the children to segregated provision. Since they knew there would be parental resistance, the primary function of the assessment process must have been to guarantee as smooth a process of allocation as possible. As the responsible education officer in Paul's case remarked: 'this is our first appeal, and I want to make sure it's our last'.

The advisers too were equally aware that whatever they wrote might serve the function of evidence in the placement debate. In order that the assessment could serve as a guide to the child's education, the advisers would need to know not just about the child, but about *the setting the child will be in*, since a programme in an ordinary school would necessarily be quite different, and involve different resources, from a programme for the same child in a special school. But to make any assumptions about the child's eventual destination would be to pre-empt the conclusion of the Statementing process. This was precisely what Mrs S. understandably failed to avoid in Simon's case. Thus, the segregation of provision forced itself as a structural constraint on the actions of the professionals preparing advice, as well as on the officers writing the Statement.

Thus, any hope that Statements could be, at the same time, an allocation device and a guide to the child's education is forlorn, for the two purposes are mutually antagonistic, if not incompatible. But because the law requires it, the entire complex procedure ends up as an expensive way of legitimating allocation decisions.

As long as there remain separate special institutions, there will remain the problem of who to put in them. By divorcing policy on assessment from policy on integration, the Government guaranteed that in many cases the objectives of the new assessment procedures would be undermined. Only where parents and LEA are in complete accord as to where a child should go to school is it possible to envisage the Statement becoming a guide to the child's education. Where there is conflict between the parties, the Statement necessarily becomes the battleground on which the combatants fight over the child's placement.

Who controls the Statement process?

Up to 1981 the process of defining needs and provision was almost entirely under professional control. The key issue was not the relative power of parents and professionals, but which professional group should be in control. The 1970s was the decade that marked the ascendancy of the educational psychologist over medical officers (Sutton 1982). The 1981 Act is said to contain a brake on professional power through the right of parents to appeal against Statements.

In order to understand the extent of the power the Act confers on parents it is useful to compare Special Education Appeal Tribunals with another system of quasi-legal bodies: Industrial Tribunals. These exist to deal with appeals on over twenty different matters, the most common of which is unfair dismissal from employment. The constitution of Industrial Tribunals recognizes the nature of the conflicts they adjudicate by representing the different interests involved. They are composed of three members: a chairperson who must be a lawyer of at least seven years standing, and two others: one nominated by the Confederation of British Industries, and one nominated by the Trades Union Congress (McIlroy 1983).

Special Education Tribunals are asked to adjudicate conflicts, but do not recognize this in their constitution. All members are nominated by the LEA; parents have no right to nominate members, or object to any individuals nominated by the LEA. Appeal committees may be three, five or seven people, of whom a majority by one may be elected members of the local authority. Impartiality appears to rest on the claims that such a committee is not composed of the officers who drew up the Statement and may not be chaired by a member of the Education Committee. This is a tenuous argument, for in cases where the parents' wishes entail significant additional expenditure, this may directly conflict with the perceived responsibilities of a majority of the committee. Moreover, in preparing a Statement, the officers of the authority formally act on behalf of the elected members.

Andrew, Simon and Linda's appeals were heard jointly, at the parents' request, by a committee of five. Three were elected members of the authority, one of whom was also the governor of a special school. One member was a teacher governor of a special school and the other a parent governor of a special school. By any account such a committee could not be said to be neutral in deciding appeals against special school placements. A conflict of interest may exist. In Paul's case the appeal committee consisted of two elected councillors and a retired educational psychologist, formerly employed by the authority. In questioning one of the parents' witnesses, the chairman of this committee said: 'I wouldn't want you to go thinking that we in this authority have done nothing about Warnock'. However much he might attempt to be neutral, he could not avoid, at this point, identifying himself with the authority to which he was elected.

Appeal Tribunals' powers are very limited: if they side with the parents they can only ask the authority to reconsider its decision. They cannot direct the authority what to do as they can in the case of ordinary school choice appeals. In the case of Andrew, Simon and Linda, after a hearing lasting nine hours, the tribunal confirmed all three statements. In their letters to the parents, they stated that whilst they were impressed by the arguments put by the parents, they had to balance this against the fact that the authority had no integrated unit of the kind the parents had asked for their children to attend, nor could one be provided in the immediate future. However, they also recommended that the authority 'should review the whole question of integrated provision with a view to the possibility of establishing the kind of unit you would wish your child to attend'.

Shortly after the appeal, the political control of this LEA moved from the Conservative Party to the Labour Party, and a review of special educational provision was introduced. The parents hoped that this would provide an opportunity to develop integrated education for their children. After six months lengthy debate, this possibility evaporated and the parents decided to appeal to the Secretary of State. None of the three has so far received any full-time education since reaching statutory school age. At the time of writing they range in age from 6:7 to 7:3. This in itself imposes considerable pressure on the parents to conform to the LEA's wishes. They have so far refused to do so on the grounds that to concede their case would delay even further the achievement of their objectives, and that educating their children in the special school concerned would be against the children's interests.

In Paul's case, after an eight-hour hearing, the appeal committee referred the Statement back for reconsideration and recommended that a permanent place for Paul be found in a mainstream school within easy reach of his home. Nevertheless, they also said that Paul should have a further trial period (he had already had one) of at least six months before reaching a decision that his needs could not be provided in a mainstream school. The LEA accepted this decision and Paul was given a full-time place in an infant school supported by a full-time nursery-nurse. At the end of six months, Paul was reassessed and the authority decided that continued attendance at a mainstream school was inappropriate. A new Statement was issued naming two special schools as alternatives for the parents to choose from. The parents gave notice of their intention to appeal again. Although the original appeal committee provided the parents with the means to persuade the authority to change its mind, the authority's officers and professionals continued to have the power to decide whether or not Paul's attendance in a mainstream school was viable.

The distribution of power over decision-making is quite separate from the question of whether or not Paul ought to remain in an ordinary school. In cases where there is a dispute about how a child with special needs should be educated, the LEA, its officers and professionals have the final say, until the parents decide to appeal to the Secretary of State. Decisions at this level so far have favoured the LEA. Of 47 appeals to the Secretary of State under Section 8(6) of the 1981 Education Act made between 1 April 1984 and 31 March 1986, 23 were confirmed, eight were amended and 16 had not yet been decided.[1] It is not known whether the amendments made were those requested by the parents.

Conclusion

Both individualized assessment-for-teaching and parental participation in decision-making are laudable goals. Unfortunately it is clear from the analysis of these cases that the conditions to achieve them did not exist. Assessment as a guide to teaching would only be viable where placement of the child was not an issue. While there remain segregated special schools, placement will remain the crucial decision in assessment, and assessment must be predominantly a selection mechanism. In a non-selective system, or in one where placement was not in dispute, assessment could be otherwise than it was in these cases. Since segregated special education resources are always limited, there are few instances where placement in special provision is beyond question before formal assessment, and thus few instances where the selective function of assessment could be eliminated.

The doctrine of 'parents as partners' in the Warnock Report had relatively little to do with questions of the relative power and rights of parents and professionals in the education of their children, and rather more to do with recruiting parents as resources in the education of their children, pursuing goals defined by professionals. Indeed the notion of a partnership between parents and professionals depends on the assumption of shared goals. The possibility of fundamental dispute over the appropriate education of children was scarcely recognized by the Warnock Committee, and none of the appeal provisions in the 1981 Act originated from this source. In conditions where partnership is impractical, the law needs to stipulate a distribution of power. The consequences of investing too much power in the hands of parents were obviously alarming to the Government during the Parliamentary debates on the Act, and they would not accept even that special education appeal committee decisions could be binding on the LEA, for fear of the financial consequences. The exercise of parental power depends on the ability of the system of provision to satisfy all reasonable wishes. It is very far from doing so, and thus, for the foreseeable future, we may expect parental power to be strictly curtailed.

---

[1] Hansard, April 24 1985, Col 469; April 9 1986, Col. 109.

References

Booth, T. 1985. 'Down's Syndome: labels and their consequences', in Lane, D. and Stratford, B. (eds.), *Current Approaches to Down's Syndrome*, London, Holt Saunders.

Department of Education and Science (DES) 1978. *Special Educational Needs* (The Warnock Report), London, HMSO.

Department of Education and Science (DES) 1983. *Assessments and Statements of Special Educational Needs*, Circular 1/83, London, DES.

Ebert, E. and Simmons, K. 1943. 'Foundation study of child growth and development: I: psychometric tests', *Monographs of the Society for Research in Child Development*, *8*, No. 2.

Fish, J. 1985. *Special Education: the Way Ahead*, Milton Keynes, Open University Press.

McIlroy, J. 1983. *Industrial Tribunals*, London, Pluto Press.

Stutsman, R. 1931. *Mental Measurement of Preschool Children*. Tarrytown-on-Hudson, New York.

Sutton, A. 1982. 'The powers that be', Unit 8 of *E241: Special Needs in Education*, Milton Keynes, Open University Press.

Wilkins, L. E., Brown, J. E. and Wolf, B. 1980. 'Psychomotor development in 65 home-reared children with cri-du-chat syndrome', *Journal of Pediatrics*, 97, pp. 401–405.

17 The development of an integration scheme: a governor's view
David Ruebain

This chapter tells the story of the opening moves in the development of a link between a comprehensive school and a special school for children with physical disabilities. It is told by David Ruebain from his probably unique perspective as a governor of the comprehensive school and an ex-pupil of the special school. His account reveals a lack of planning by the local authority characterized in particular by the absence of any statement of the goals of the scheme. He also describes the problems he had in identifying exactly how he was to 'govern' this part of his school's activity when in fact his power was very limited. Nonetheless, David Ruebain's account indicates the way other governors might contribute to the process of integration.

Introduction

Throughout this chapter, the following abbreviations will be used. The comprehensive school and the school for children with physical disabilities will be referred to respectively as the host school and the special school and the arrangements will be called the link. All teachers and professionals are called by their professional titles.

Perhaps I ought to explain the reasons for anonymity: it is not so much to protect the characters but rather the schools and especially the link, which is still at a very formative and uncertain stage. I hope this does not seem over-cautious. I should also state that this account is presented from my own viewpoint. I must declare an interest in that I am strongly in favour of integration for all children and adults and this is bound to colour my perspectives and interpretations of the events to be described. I know that colleagues would give a different analysis and I can only promise that I have tried to be accurate. I should also state that I attended the special school as a child between the ages of two and nine.

The development of the link

During the summer of 1983, negotiations between the authority and the two schools began, on the possibility of developing a link in order to pursue a policy of integration of students from the special school. The following is an account of the development of this link, in two stages: up until February 1985 when I was appointed a governor of the host school, and from then to the present.

EVENTS PRIOR TO MY APPOINTMENT

The development of the link began with the appointment of a new Divisional Education Officer, part of whose remit was to develop integrated practice. At the

195

time, integration was a nascent issue and it seems that the experience that the Divisional Education Officer (DEO) brought with him from previous integration 'pilot schemes' helped win the appointment for him. In addition, the authority had just initiated a major review of their special needs provision which was later to call for the full and complete integration of all children with special needs, the first report to draw such conclusions. With this background, the new DEO began looking for a suitable pair of schools to develop a pilot scheme within his division and the schools chosen were selected largely because of their geographical proximity, although there were certainly other considerations. The host school had only recently shed its image as a 'dump school' and still had difficulties filling its rolls and this may have been a factor in the DEO's consideration. It has recently been designated as a community school which means that it stays open after school hours as a Community Education Centre (CEC), with some teachers staying to offer classes to the community. With such an open door policy, the host school had the ability to welcome special school students informally in the evenings through the CEC and thereby give an extra dimension to the link. Mixed-ability teaching goes right through to the fifth year in virtually all subjects and the school has a radical staff and a recently appointed, experienced and perceptive headteacher. There has been much innovation, both authority- and school-initiated, and this has been praised by HM Inspectors in their recent report. However, the staff have felt (and still feel) under considerable pressure to carry out these initiatives in addition to their existing duties and this is made all the more difficult by the industrial action which has been a major hindrance to the link.

The special school takes students with most motor disabilities, between the ages of two and nineteen, and has a roll of about sixty. Many of the staff are long-serving members and there is a relatively low turnover which may have led to a sense of inertia in some, though by no means all respects. The school had many areas of developed expertise and these will prove invaluable in the future. Adjacent to the special school and sharing its campus there is a school for delicate children, one of whose students has recently become involved in the link.

Before going on to describe some of the events connected with the link, it may be as well to mention some of the other characters involved and the roles they played in its development. Aside from those already mentioned, a key figure is the link teacher. She is responsible for the day-to-day co-ordination of the link and as an 'anchor-person' for all negotiations and developments. Unfortunately we were unlucky to have someone not wholly sympathetic to the principles of integration. I shall return to this later. The head of the special needs department at the host school and the head of the host school CEC were both very supportive and enthusiastic about the link and the former played a key role in its development. The Chairs of governors of both schools were involved at each stage and other governors also took an active interest. Various teacher union officers and representatives were involved, including a health and safety representative who assisted with overseeing the structural alterations to the host school and also the Chair of the area teachers association who played a central role in negotiating the link with the staff, more of which I shall discuss later.

To return to events prior to my involvement, the DEO began a process of consultation whereby the various issues were to be thrashed out. An initial programme of building alterations was outlined. This included the installation of ramps and special toilets, the widening of certain doors and the possibility of a lift. The discussions preceding this were, in my opinion, never really concluded properly. For example, the installation of special toilets began before a firm decision had been reached about funding for a lift, presenting the possibility of adequate toilet facilities for wheelchair-bound students who would not be able to come to the school through lack of a lift! Later on, the authority did in fact authorize finance for a lift, but this example indicates the lack of clear planning. Indeed, many 'access' questions have yet to be raised and here lies the underlying problem: the whole history of the link is characterized by a series of reactions to events rather than the generation of a plan. Fundamentally, there was no co-ordinated approach to a plan whereby all parties involved could anticipate and prepare for the many radical changes necessary for full integration to be realized. This point is one which the authority may now recognize but it was the source of many problems at the host school.

In order to introduce staff to practical examples of integration some of those involved visited other similar projects and made contact with specialists such as the Centre for Studies on Integration in Education at the Spastics Society. Host school students made an *A day in the life of . . .* video to introduce special school students to the host school and a week-long joint school trip with equal numbers of special and host school students was organized. By most accounts this was a success, since reports suggested that the host school students began to 'see the person not the disability'.

One area of major difficulty was teacher participation in the scheme's development. The host school, in line with its philosophy, had developed a relatively non-hierarchical decision-making structure with a strong input from the staff in all initiatives. There were many committed integrationists among the staff but the necessary support from the staff in general did not materialize. This has still to be resolved. (This is not to say the staff were opposed to the link, merely that they were not as committed as is perhaps necessary for a development as radical in its implications as this.)

The three factors which limited support from the staff were the ongoing industrial action, which prevented any full discussion on the matter; union hostility in the form of partial opposition derived largely through a combination of genuine concern and fears and sheer ignorance of the issues; and, unfortunately, a not very helpful introduction to the staff of the host school, about the link, by the link teacher. Some of these problems could have arisen no matter how well planned the link. Nevertheless, time and time again it was shown that, with foresight, problems could have been anticipated and at least partially prepared for.

Many of the fears were legitimate concerns about retraining, money to finance the changes etc., but some were the result of a lack of basic philosophical discussion and understanding of the social issues. For example, some teachers look upon the link as a means of curriculum provision otherwise lacking in the special school, rather than as a goal in itself with important social implications for all students. Certainly, programmes such as those of the authority's anti-racist and anti-sexist policy seem equally necessary for an issue such as integration. Along the same lines, there was, as far as I am aware, little contact with PTAs about the link in general although I have not noticed any opposition to it from parents.

I have mentioned the link teacher and the fact that she is not wholly sympathetic to the concept of full integration. I should explain my reasons for believing this and the consequences of appointment to this post. The link teacher was appointed on the recommendation of neither the host, nor the special school governing body but by the divisional office directly. I soon realized that she had a distinctly limited view of the goals of the link, at variance with my own goals and those of the headteacher at the host school. She believed that to admit more than a certain number of students from the special school would lead to a 'psychological imbalance within the host school'. Her view was honestly held and she worked hard to assist the first group of students admitted under the link, but such a post is critical in anticipating and co-ordinating the link and needs someone fully and passionately committed to full integration. Some of the problems encountered in the development may have been ameliorated had such a person held the post of link teacher.

THE DEVELOPMENT OF THE LINK SINCE FEBRUARY 1985

When I arrived in February 1985, the link was only in its second term, and numerically very limited. Four students from the special school came over for a total of eight periods per week (i.e. two periods each) in business studies, computing, biology, and design and technology. In addition though, a number came over to the CEC for drama, music and a wide range of other activities. Some of the teachers involved were positively euphoric about the effects of introducing students with disabilities whilst others took a more cautious attitude. The general impression was one of a link at a very early stage.

The governors of the host school decided to form a sub-committee to evaluate progress and provide assistance wherever possible, and I spent most of the remaining school year meeting people and trying to develop a clear picture. A great problem for myself as a governor, though by no means for the link, was the difficulty in trying to connect with the decision-making process. No matter how many people I made, and kept contact with, there were always new areas and new aspects of the link developing which I might only hear about accidentally. This is no one's fault. It highlights the problems governors have in trying to make a positive contribution and is, in any event, an extremely frustrating business.

The sub-committee resolved to do a number of things. We pressed for building alterations to begin, or conclude, as quickly as possible and despite many problems, not least in communicating with the authority's architects department, there has been some measure of achievement. We also decided to try and push for the replacement of the link teacher. There has been some success with this in that a new teacher has been appointed to work with the original one. Finally, we decided to try and produce a plan for the link in the form of a strategy of means and ends. With the publication of the authority's own report on special needs, the link was given a political 'boost' and it was with these points in mind that the sub-committee returned after the summer vacation.

At the beginning of the school year, September 1985, a further four students were added to the original four, commuting two, three or four times per week each to the host school. The building operations were now well under way and it was learnt that the authority had approved funding for a lift. The impetus was now clearly in favour of a far more extensive link and the next stage for the governors' sub-committee seemed to be to try and produce the report by meeting regularly with those closely involved. Industrial action made this very difficult and to date, we have only managed to meet with all the main individuals once. This meeting took place at the special school and involved governors of both schools, both headteachers, staff of both schools and the DEO. The sub-committee went to this meeting with the intention of proposing that an agenda be set to map out the future of the link more clearly and deliberately.

What happened was, for me, an interesting example of the operation of mutually incompatible power structures. The DEO, in effect, pre-empted the sub-committee by suggesting that it would be useful for the officers to take evidence from all the parties involved, including the sub-committee, to formulate options for the future. The sub-committee then suggested an alternative and proposed a structured series of meetings whereby the governors would produce their report, but this was rejected in favour of the authority's proposal. I do not suspect conspiracy, but the net effect of this was to shift the centre of decision-making from the governors to the authority. This may prove to be the best alternative in the long run but it was another frustrating experience and highlights a point emphasized by many governors, that it is very difficult trying to delineate one's role as a governor and to work out exactly how to 'govern', especially as one's power as a governor seems to be limited to making recommendations to the authority.

Nevertheless, I may have left the meeting perfectly happy, had it not been for one comment made by the Divisional Inspector for Special Needs. Whilst discussing some of the options open to the link, the inspector stated that there was no need to consider the practicalities of opening a physiotherapy unit at the host school since there was a perfectly adequate one at the special school – and this from someone who claims to be an integrationist! It left me rather deflated. An interesting postcript to this is that the superintendent physiotherapist at the special school has written to all governors asking for support in trying to persuade the authority to open a therapy unit in the host school, a very welcome boost from an unexpected quarter.

THE PRESENT

Building operations are now well under way and the sub-committee has made its submission to the authority, detailing its recommendations for greater co-ordination, consultation and planning and for clearly defined goals. There are plans to open up a dialogue with parents' groups and staff unions but the industrial action remains a hindrance. It remains very difficult to keep track of all discussions and developments within the schools and authority, and it is therefore very difficult to anticipate what will be required since events are so largely dependent on numerous individuals and autonomous developments.

Conclusions

It would be wholly wrong to lay responsibility for any of the problems or lack of progress mentioned at the feet of any individual. One of the lessons that the experience has taught me is that for any one ideal, there is a plethora of perspectives, many of which are incompatible with each other. Each of them generates different aims and different interests to preserve. Thus, to take a very simplified example, some of the unions felt that the most immediate concern to them was the threat of extra responsibilities without remuneration or training. This is not to suggest that everyone takes a mercenary view of everything, but unless some attempt is made to anticipate the issues raised by the introduction of a new and potentially far-reaching plan, then difficulties and obstacles will arise. Lack of co-ordination and foresight continues: more than two years into the link, it is still uncertain what exactly is to be the end result.

Without the commitment of large numbers of individuals from the DEO to individual teachers and other school staff, the link would never have got started. The link is, in many respects, a pilot scheme and lack of progress is perhaps inevitable at this stage since mistakes will be made. With the benefit of hindsight, I would make three recommendations to an authority with such a scheme in mind. First, develop clear policy directives both in general and in particular, and ensure that the discussions around them are generated at the outset. Secondly, appoint an individual or team to oversee the development, ensuring they have clear channels to all sectors of the authority with the power to influence, assist and react to even the most localized problem. Thirdly, back up the programme with resources to fund in-service training, seminars, building, transport, and all other necessary features.

18 'Firm links should be established': a case study in conflict and policy-making for integration

Will Swann

In many areas, integration has proceeded through the development of a link between a special school and one or more mainstream schools, as in the preceding chapter. This chapter gives an account of the development of one such scheme. The account focuses on the recent history of this scheme and highlights the conflicts and tensions that have arisen, and which will play a central role in the future development of policy. The chapter brings together the perspectives of the leading decision-makers, it illustrates how radically they differ and considers the causes of these differences. At the heart of the matter lie differences of philosophy and conflicts of interests which have cohered around two separate institutions.

The absence of policy in English special education is often presented as a virtue: 'policy' is something inflexible and unresponsive, imposed by bureaucrats (or worse, politicians) who know little about the real issues that face schools, who lack professional expertise and who are principally self-interested. The 1981 Education Act, which obliged local education authorities to do nothing in particular about their special educational provision, was part of a tradition of decentralized policy-making in special education. It has been described as enabling legislation, although as far as the organization of provision was concerned, it enabled LEAs to do what they could have done without it.

Many LEAs have produced policy documents in the three years since the Act was implemented. Many do not entail any radical changes in the way the local authority distributes its special educational resources. Others do; for example, a report from Cumbria proposes the closure of six special schools over the next six years.[1] A working party has recommended that all children with 'mild, moderate and specific learning difficulties' should be taught in mainstream schools, as will most physically disabled children. For those children who will remain in special schools – some children with physical disabilities, and children with severe learning difficulties – the working party wants to see links established between special and mainstream schools to facilitate integration. ILEA's recent review of special education by the Fish Committee (ILEA 1985) is generally acknowledged to be amongst the most radical set of policy recommendations to have emerged so far. Yet despite recommending that the authority should aim to meet the special educational needs of all children in the mainstream, the Fish Report limited this aim by recognizing: 'a longer term need for a few special schools to provide specific services to meet particular needs (p. 191).' For these special schools, as in Cumbria, there should be links with local mainstream provision.

---

[1] *Times Educational Supplement*, 13 June 1986, p. 10.

Establishing links between special and ordinary schools may be a positive move to increase the participation of children with special needs in ordinary schools. It may also be a line of least resistance: a way of responding to pressures for integration without posing serious threats to the lives of staff and institutions on either side of the divide. It was extensively canvassed by the Warnock Committee (DES 1978), one of whose recommendations was that: 'firm links should be established between special and ordinary schools in the same vicinity'. The Report elaborated on what these links might consist of:

> Wherever possible we believe that there should be some sharing of educational programmes between special and ordinary schools. Where this is possible, there should at least be opportunities for the pupils to share social experience on as regular a basis as possible.
>
> Arrangements for links between special and ordinary schools require very careful planning. If children attending special schools are to be enabled to receive part of their education in an ordinary school and if children with special needs in ordinary schools are to attend special school part-time there must clearly be joint planning of the curriculum and time-tables, as well as careful attention to the administrative and organizational aspects, including the dove-tailing of supporting services and the provision of transport. More than this, there must be a common basis of commitment and interest on the part of all the staff concerned if the arrangements, however faultless in form, are in practice to succeed . . .
>
> We also think that the staff in ordinary and special schools have much to gain from closer relationships. The expertise in special schools is likely to be of consider-able benefit to teachers in ordinary schools in a range of areas, particularly the following: the teaching of children with sensory disabilities; the care of physically handicapped children and appreciation of the level of achievement which can be expected of them; and curriculum planning for children with special educational needs. In addition, teachers in schools for the maladjusted should be able to offer expertise on the management of children with emotional and behavioural problems and the development of personal relations with them. Teachers in ordinary schools will need this kind of experienced help if they are to cater effectively for increased numbers of children with disabilities or significant difficulties (pp. 123–4).

Three issues are raised here: the need for administrative co-ordination, the need for 'a common basis of commitment and interest', and the need to share expertise. The Warnock Report was notably weak on practical examples of existing pro-vision from which future practice could develop, so it was never clear how readily these three needs could be satisfied, nor what the ultimate consequences of establishing links between special and mainstream schools might be.

A number of schemes existed before the Report was published, and many more have since emerged. Dessent (1984) has analysed a number of critical features of schemes whereby the special school develops as a 'resource centre' for the mainstream. In this chapter I shall describe one such 'scheme' and consider its progress and implications, through the eyes of a number of the key policy-makers involved in it.

The background

Alnwick Green is a large, modern comprehensive school in an inner city borough which falls within the bottom six English authorities in terms of social deprivation. Evesham School is the borough's special school for children with physical disabilities. It draws its seventy pupils not only from its own borough but from two neighbouring boroughs as well. Since 1972, some of Evesham's pupils have attended mainstream secondary schools. An initial link for four years with another comprehensive school grew into the link with Alnwick Green in 1976. The first link has since ceased.

At the time of writing, there were fifteen pupils with physical disabilities from Evesham who were at Alnwick Green. A further twenty pupils of second-ary age remained in the secondary department at Evesham. The fifteen inte-grated pupils spend all their timetable in mainstream classes. Like all others, they are each assigned to a tutor group. They are supported by one teacher and two welfare assistants, drawn from the staffing of Evesham School. The support teacher spends three-fifths of her time at Alnwick Green, of which half is devoted to liaison work, and half to class teaching in the English depart-ment. She advises staff regularly, and spends much time monitoring and doing administrative work, but is not involved in any support teaching. The two welfare assistants are responsible for carrying out physiotherapy under the physiotherapist's direction, helping children around school, transporting equipment, taking pupils to the toilet, and in-class support in practical sub-jects such as home economics.

The school had a lift and ramps, but its design still has many limitations. A full-scale access survey has recently been conducted by representatives of the school, the LEA and the local disablement association. This has revealed in detail the obstacles to full access to the school. A physiotherapy room with adjoining adapted toilets has recently been added, easing what were previously inadequate arrangements.

A shared responsibility

Patience Franklin, one of the deputy heads of Alnwick Green, has direct respons-ibility for children with disabilities. She is also responsible for general administration and staff development. When she took over in autumn 1982 she felt that the links between the schools were tenuous. In her view, behind the apparent success of the scheme, many children were denied access to the cur-riculum, especially in home economics, science and technology. Toilet facilities were very poor, as were facilities for physiotherapy. There were no reserved places for children from Evesham, so classes frequently rose above the NUT recommended maximum of 30, and it appeared this was the result of the addition of a child from Evesham. In a strong NUT school, this caused antagonism, particularly when staff cuts loomed. However this arrangement had initially been made at the insistence of Alnwick Green, in order to ensure that children in the catchment area were not disadvantaged by the integration scheme. Perceptions of the state of the link at this time differ however, as perceptions on many points later on were to conflict. Peter Wheeler, the borough's Adviser for Special Education described the links as anything but tenuous. There were, according to him, frequent meetings at headteacher level, and the liaison teacher spent a great deal of time maintaining communication between the two schools.

One of Patience Franklin's first tasks was finalize a policy statement agreed by the two schools and the education authority. This was completed in May 1983. It set out a philosophy of 'shared responsibility' for the children with disabilities:

> The Headteacher and staff of Alnwick Green School have day-to-day responsibility for these pupils but this responsibility is exercised with the assistance of support staff from Evesham School, and in consultation and collaboration with the Headteacher of Evesham School.
>
> (Policy document, May 1983)

Although the children would spend all their school time at Alnwick Green, they were to remain on the roll of Evesham School.

The detail of this shared responsibility was set out in the rest of the document. The roles of the support teacher, welfare assistants and physiotherapist, all of whom come from Evesham's staffing, were listed at length, as was the practice that should be followed in the use of support services, in the case of any need for adaptations and equipment, the provision of counselling, and transport. This was intended as blueprint for who should do what, with whom, when and how. Underlying all there was to be: 'a consensus model of problem solving, in which the joint case conference is crucial'.

Although the solution might look neat on paper, nonetheless it required both sets of staff to deal with the integrated children in a different way from others at their schools. Few decisions could be taken unilaterally by staff in one school, even if they could argue plausibly that such action was the most efficient means of solving a problem. Even when quite uncontentious events arose, such as a visit from a researcher, the need to inform Evesham could add, in Patience Franklin's words:

> An extra layer of work ... I've got to let somebody know straight away if we are the first to be contacted, so that there's no misunderstanding or bad feeling when they eventually get the news through from somebody else.

Staff at Evesham were equally conscious of the need to inform Alnwick Green quickly on any point concerning the integrated pupils.

Relationships with parents were affected by the arrangement. Where a difficulty occurred, such as non-attendance, Alnwick Green could handle it without too many problems until it became necessary to involve services beyond the school. If it was felt that a social worker should be involved, this had to be the social worker attached to Evesham, and it was quite possible that the child concerned would be unfamiliar to her. In these circumstances differences of view about the nature of the difficulty could easily arise, and common understanding was made more difficult by the physical distance between the two schools. In three cases over the course of one year, this problem had arisen. Patience Franklin commented on a recent case:

> We've kept the social worker informed and she of course will be involved in the work but the complication is, first of all she's working at a distance, she's not in here more than rarely. So I think it would be true to say there's a difference in perception of the situation between us. There's also I think a difference in that staff here feel more vigorous about getting the family involved, it has to be said I think that certainly the social worker at Evesham had felt there wasn't much more that could be done ... Now there is going to continue to be difficulty in following up because the

case conference will be here and decisions will be made but the social worker support will continue to be from Evesham, from somebody who isn't in here very often in regular contact with staff in the way that our school social worker is and I think it's highlighted the different perceptions of what the needs are and also perhaps a different approach to dealing with them.

These difficulties and others like them arose because one school was having to deploy resources that belonged to, and were located in another. They stemmed from the fact that the integrated children remained on the Evesham School roll. Indeed, any other child moving into Alnwick Green from any other direction who happened to have a physical disability was also placed on the Evesham roll. At the time of writing there were six such children. It was the long-standing wish of Alnwick Green staff, written into the 1983 policy document, that all the children who attended the school should be on their roll, and this was also the view of the support teacher.

Although a switch to the comprehensive's roll would ease many of the administrative problems of the scheme, this was by no means the only issue involved in this seemingly innocuous change. One of the initial motives for retaining pupils on the Evesham roll was that it provided a safety net: a pupil whose placement at Alnwick Green was going wrong could be easily moved back to Evesham. In fact this had only ever happened once in ten years, and was the result of animosity between two of the integrated pupils.

Opinions on the roll issue differed. Tim Malvern is the borough's Assistant Education Officer (Special Education). He felt that the issue was relatively unimportant: 'there are a lot of bigger fish to be chasing after'. Nevertheless, he perceived a split between Evesham, along with Peter Wheeler, the borough's Adviser for Special Education, and the management of Alnwick Green: 'Evesham would see themselves as the experts in the handling of children with physical handicap...' Certainly, Peter Wheeler saw Evesham as a centre of expertise, as the people 'who actually deal with the kids all the time'. But expertise was not an argument advanced by the Head of Evesham, Noel Garrick, for the retention of the status quo.

From Alnwick Green, Patience Franklin knew that it had been implicitly assumed that expertise lay at Evesham, but increasingly doubted the validity of this assumption:

> What's been overlooked is that the mainstream school now has a different set of expertise which is the integrating expertise and that is actually something new, and it is in most cases expertise that the specialist school doesn't have... there are a whole new set of things to learn about managing physically handicapped children in an integrated setting, which I think this school is quite far advanced along.

To Bill Shoemaker, the Head of Alnwick Green, the whole question 'totally eluded' him:

> There seems to me to be no need for them to remain there and the suggestion that they should remain on the Evesham roll negates some of the reasons why they should be here fully integrated, and for some reason somebody is trying to hold on to the strings.

But from other perspectives, there were sound reasons for keeping the integrated pupils on the roll of Evesham. Noel Garrick, the Head of Evesham, had mixed feelings about the issue. In principle he felt that: 'there should be some way of getting them into the roll of the host school'. Nevertheless, he knew that this would pose a threat to his school:

> One of the worries is that it reduces the school dramatically in number . . . twenty-five children out of a thousand doesn't mean very much on paper and in capitation terms. In a small special school, twenty-five constitutes quite a large proportion.

He knew that a large drop in numbers would not only lose the school capitation, some of which was in any case forwarded to Alnwick Green, but the number of scale posts would drop, as would the ability of the school to attract good-quality teachers.

In Garrick's view, his willingness to find a way of transferring the pupils to the Alnwick Green roll was not matched by the authority's: 'I'm certainly not speaking on behalf of the authority when I say that, in fact the authority would not uphold that view'. The authority, in Garrick's terms, referred to officers and advisers.

It was the personal view of Tim Malvern, the officer with direct responsibility for the scheme, that he 'would, on balance, go for having them on roll at the mainstream schools'. Peter Wheeler was clearly opposed to transferring the pupils to Alnwick Green's roll. In his view, if all the integrated pupils were removed from the Evesham roll, the school would cease to be viable. This would then leave the pupils who had not been integrated in a precarious position, with the possibility that they might have to be educated outside the borough. In addition, he argued, that other children would be denied the level of multi-disciplinary support that Evesham, as a specialist facility, could offer.

Thus, the roll issue was much more than an administrative problem. It had implications for the survival of Evesham as a separate institution.

Taking the cream off

Rather less than half of the pupils of secondary age who were registered at Evesham attended Alnwick Green. A careful selection policy, detailed in the 1983 policy document, was followed. The initial selection of candidates lay with the staff at Evesham. The policy document was not precise about criteria. The critical requirements were the pupil's ability to participate in and benefit from the mainstream curriculum, given the current level of support, and the pupil's and parents' willingness to move to Alnwick Green. A pupil could be put forward at Evesham by staff, parents, or the pupil himself or herself. Once a list of possible candidates had been prepared. Evesham informed the authority of the maximum number of places at Alnwick Green that might be needed, and this number was then reserved in the total intake figure for that year. The recommendations then went forward to Alnwick Green for consideration, and in the term before transfer a detailed assessment was conducted to determine the selected pupils' needs for support resources.

Those selected were the most academically able and with the least disability of Evesham's pupils. So far, no pupils who were unable to speak had been transferred. One had been proposed, and although Alnwick Green had agreed to take him, his parents decided against the move. No pupils recommended by Evesham have been rejected by Alnwick Green. On the contrary, it was Patience Franklin's view that more could have transferred:

> What has become apparent over the years is that there are children who possibly could have been integrated, but who haven't, either because the child had decided they don't want to or the parents have expressed doubt or indeed Evesham felt that the child wasn't suitable for integration. Now we are not involved in that initial process because they're not our children, and yet in a way I feel that we now have enough expertise to be able to offer an input to an assessment of whether a child is suitable or not.

The scheme began in 1976 with this selection operating at 11+. It was envisaged at the time that the necessary preparation for the demands of life at Alnwick Green could be done at Evesham. It quickly became apparent that this was not so, and a parallel scheme was started with a local junior school which eventually spread to its associated infant school. The effect of this was to bring forward the decision about integration to the early stage of primary education. If an 11+ had been operating at first, it was gradually becoming a 5+ or 7+ test of eligibility. At the time of writing, when the primary integration scheme was quite recent, a majority of the pupils integrated into Alnwick Green had been at Evesham for their primary years. The staff knew that would be less and less true in future. Simon Cox, the teacher at Evesham responsible for primary integration doubted there were any Evesham pupils not integrated into the primary school now who would 'make it' at secondary level.

The selection of the most able children from Evesham has had a massive effect on the school, as Noel Garrick made clear:

> I think it has – I get too emotional – a disastrous effect in some ways. We are losing models... we are losing a certain amount of impetus in the classroom, challenge in the classroom. I'm very much concerned about staff morale... Some years ago we had staff who joined this school, secondary subject teachers, now what they've had to do is they've had to retrain as special school teachers, rather than subject teachers. I used to do CSE Oral English. We can't do that any more; we just haven't got the children who can do it, and one reason is that we're getting more and more children who can't speak at all and those who can speak haven't the intellectual prowess... when one particular boy left, suddenly my Oral English lessons plummeted... that wonderful sparkle, the challenge in the classroom that kept the others going, had gone.

Garrick knew too that the demoralizing effects of selection was not restricted to staff. Pupils who failed to 'make it' knew perfectly well what their position was:

> There are different reactions, some children don't want to know about that anyway, they're much happier here and say, 'no thanks'. There are some children who are aware and say, 'Oh so and so's at Alnwick Green, I'd like to go there...' If you go into the classroom, if the children are capable of speaking they will talk to you, but there are two areas which they don't seem to speak much of at all, and one is integration and the other is death, and we have a fair amount of both in this school.

One option to reduce the level of demoralization amongst the remaining pupils would be to develop part-time integration, so that most if not all pupils could have some experience of the mainstream. There were practical barriers to this. Evesham was geographically isolated from other schools, and had no comprehensive school in the immediate vicinity. Part-time integration would entail difficult transport arrangements. More important was the willingness of other schools to accept pupils on this basis. Peter Wheeler and Tim Malvern were both critical of Alnwick Green's refusal to contemplate part-time integration, or to consider integrating pupils who would require extensive modification to the curriculum. Such an approach was, in fact, in line with the 1983 policy document which had stated that one criterion for admission was 'the ability of the pupil to participate in and benefit from the mainstream curriculum'. More recently, Alnwick Green had begun to widen these criteria. One pupil with muscular dystrophy and marked learning difficulties had been considered for integration but it had been decided that he was too immature and his learning problems were too extreme. The following year, Alnwick Green signalled their willingness to consider this pupil. They would provide remedial support from their staffing, and they suggested Evesham commit some of their staffing in the form of support teaching. With these resources, the boy would have a reduced four to five subject timetable, but would attend Alnwick Green full-time. Evesham, however, wanted a part-time arrangement, with the boy travelling between the two schools daily. Agreement was not reached on this case in time for September 1986.

Arguing about new provision: the consensus model

The 1983 policy document had stated that: 'an essential feature of shared responsibility is a consensus model of problem solving'. It realistically accepted, however, that consensus might not always be forthcoming, and it allocated to the authority a role as the final arbiter: 'in instances of exceptional difficulty, normally relating to placement, the authority could be required to resolve the matter'. This consensus and the role of the authority in maintaining it, was severely tested in 1984–5 over the issue of facilities for physiotherapy and managing incontinent children at Alnwick Green.

The document had anticipated the need for adaptations to Alnwick Green, and laid out a procedure. Requests were to be agreed by the Heads of the two schools in consultation with the Adviser for Special Education. The agreed request would be forwarded to the Education Officer (Development, Finance and Resources) with a copy to the Assistant Education Officer (Special Education). It would then be for these officers to decide whether or not the request could be granted.

Patience Franklin had identified the need for a number of adaptations when she took over responsibility for the scheme:

> Until recent years it was assumed by everybody, this school as well as . . . but particularly Evesham, that because the children were physically present in the rooms they were integrated, and it became clear to me that this was not the case.

Toilet facilities were inadequate in her view and there was no suitable area for changing incontinent children, no sluice, and no adapted toilet on the first floor of the school. Physiotherapy had to be carried out in a cramped converted toilet which did not guarantee privacy. This was especially important for one Muslim girl, who had to have complete privacy. In practical subjects, some rooms and equipment were inaccessible. There was, for example, no adapted area in the home economics room which could be effectively and safely used by children in wheelchairs.

The first proposal from Alnwick Green was for an extension to the existing physiotherapy room. During preliminary discussions, all sides agreed that improvements were needed, but disagreed about the scale of the exercise. Peter Wheeler, the Adviser, argued that Alnwick Green's proposal was much too expensive an option. In concert with staff at Evesham, he then suggested that the new facilities should be based in the existing medical room, with the necessary alterations. Alnwick Green eventually agreed to this, but consequently the school doctors and nurses had to make do with unsatisfactory accommodation. Relations between school and medical staff became somewhat strained. Even though the second proposal was accepted, Alnwick Green still saw themselves as having to fight for the adaptations they thought necessary. Eventually, they took the unusual step of sending a deputation direct to the Education Committee to press their case. It was eventually agreed, and the adaptations they requested were installed. The process, described by Patience Franklin as 'an eighteen-month battle' overlapped with Alnwick Green opening a second front in their campaign, for adapted facilities in the home economics room. Other smaller skirmishes had also occurred over facilities to give children access to science, woodwork and business studies.

Throughout these events, the argument from Patience Franklin and her Head, Bill Shoemaker, was that mere physical presence in a mainstream school was not enough. Their physical and curricular needs, insofar as the school had a responsibility to meet them, should be properly met. As far as Patience Franklin was concerned, there had never been a proper assessment of need. The consequences, in her view, were serious, as she graphically illustrated:

> We had a muscular dystrophy child here who needed from the word go the very kind of facilities I've spoken about, who was incontinent. We had great difficulty in lifting, very delicate, fragile child and the welfare assistant, one we had here then, managed with great difficulty. We had the toilets in the foyer, which were unsuitable; they've got very limited value for other than mildly disabled people. We had a converted lavatory up here, which had a rudimentary metal partition and an area where physiotherapy was done. This boy was basically seen to either on a couch or with a bottle, in circumstances that were not private at all.

Patience Franklin and Bill Shoemaker saw their main opponent in the 'battle' for resources as Peter Wheeler, the Adviser for Special Education, who had to be consulted in line with the agreed policy. As Franklin saw it their disagreement concerned both philosophies and priorities:

> If I were to summarize his views and he might consider this unfair, he does not perceive integration as needing that fine detail working up, they made the best of it I think, I would say. They're here, they're getting a lot out of it, if they can't actually get to the science labs or do every single lesson then they're getting enough to make it worthwhile. The borough's short of money, this isn't one of our top priorities, therefore there's not going to be a lot of support coming from that direction for what we are asking for. Now a similar point was made over the physiotherapy room, which was you're feather bedding the children, they don't need these adaptations.

Peter Wheeler did not accept this characterization of his position:

It's partially accurate. She's quite right in as much as I wouldn't want to make enormous numbers of specialized adaptations to the environment. But the approach is no less detailed, it's just a different way of working.

His approach was determined partly by his view of the long-term interests of children with disabilities, and partly by his view of how those interests should be balanced against the interests of other children. He did not believe children with physical disabilities were well served by extensively adapting their environment:

It's always seemed to me, and it's certainly an argument that I've had from the staff at Evesham, who actually deal with the kids all the time, that they're going into a world which is unadapted. You don't actually get the world adapted for physically handicapped kids. It would be nice if you did, but you don't. So it makes more sense to adapt the children to the environment, rather than the other way round.

As an example of this, he cited the provision of a specialized chair to raise a child to the requisite height, as an alternative to providing a lower bench or table. Related to this was his view, endorsed in particular by the Deputy Head of Evesham at the time, that providing purpose-built specialist facilities could lead to the isolation of the pupils with disabilities in Alnwick Green.

But the interests of the children with disabilities were not Peter Wheeler's sole concern. As he saw it, two other groups' interests were at issue: those of the able-bodied children, and those of other children with special needs. The interests of these might easily conflict:

Patience wants us to modify domestic science areas, business studies, science, craft – she'd actually like us to modify suites. If we modify an area for physically handicapped kids, we sterilize it for anyone else. Now the number of children we have requiring that level of modification at any one time is tiny.

He rejected the view that his job was to fight for the interests of the children with disabilities, if it was at the expense of others, not the least because these children were only part of his constituency:

It is my job to look after the education of children with special needs, and physically handicapped children are a tiny minority ... One of the things you have to do with mainstream schools is to actually restrain them. As soon as they get handicapped kids in – and when I say handicapped kids I mean cuddly handicapped kids – they've got their own problems of underachievement and behaviour problems – but the cuddly handicapped; there is a tremendous tendency to over-protect them. It's not difficult to say: 'Look, this year's building budget is x. My resources this year are y. There are 12,000 kids in this borough's schools. Let's just look at your underachievers: what are you doing for them? It makes very little sense in my book to spend all of your resources on this very small sector, and we're ignoring the much larger one.

Had resources been unlimited, Wheeler might have taken a different view, but this was not the case:

Ever since I came here in 1979 the context in which the service has operated has been one of over-stretched budgets, constant and growing social deprivation and the need to meet increasing burdens with a decreasing resource. At no time have we had a capital allocation for integration and the kind of bids that the school were making on the general capital budget were simply unrealistic. A bid for the kind of provision that they originally asked for lay so far outside the availability of resources that it would have stood no chance of success. Alnwick Green was our last great prestige project in the education service, and however much Bill and Patience might think the facilities are inadequate, they are light years better than those in ninety per cent of the rest of the schools in the area.

The disposition of forces in the battle was, thus, somewhat improbable. It seemed that the Deputy Head and Head of the Comprehensive School were fighting for the interests of children with physical disabilities, against the Adviser for Special Education with a conflicting view of their interests, and a wish to defend the interests of other children which appeared to be threatened.

Peter Wheeler sought an explanation for Patience Franklin's stance in her personal background:

Patience has herself got a very severely handicapped daughter. In many ways, I doubt the wisdom of involving close relatives of severely handicapped people in such an enterprise. It is almost impossible for them to retain a sense of proportion in the wake of their own quite literally traumatic experiences. They become simply too emotionally involved.

For Peter Wheeler, then, the difference of view between himself and Patience Franklin was not simply a matter of conflicting but rationally held philosophies. Clearly, Patience Franklin would not have agreed, and would wish her position to be judged on its merits. Indeed, to an extent she agreed with Wheeler:

It is true that you mustn't overadapt the physical environment because the children have got to go out into the big wide world. But there are some areas of the children's experience that must be safeguarded; they include the right to privacy and discretion about toileting arrangements.

In assessing her own priorities, she described her responsibilities thus:

The admin. (of the whole school) has to come first, because the school has to run, so my administrative duties which start very early in the morning, have to come first. Anything, unless it's a crisis, has to be postponed until I have two or three hours getting things under way. But it would be hard to say it [i.e. children with disabilities] come next, it's there all through everything.

Not only did Peter Wheeler and Patience Franklin disagree over principles, but they also disagreed about the actual extent of the combat. To Peter Wheeler the battle had been exaggerated: 'there wasn't really any resistance at all. What we did say was that it isn't our Number One priority'. In the event, he felt that the facilities at Alnwick Green were: 'about right, now'. But to Patience Franklin, almost every detail had had to be contested – even when they agreed to the proposal to adapt the medical room:

Even that degree of adaptation we've had to fight really hard with the Adviser. To get the special lavatory we've had to fight; that wasn't necessary we were told. To get a sluice we were told that wasn't necessary and we had to say 'well we do have to deal with soiled and wet clothing at times'... I felt it was a very hard battle.

In taking up their position in the debate, the staff at Evesham had to consider not only their philosophies, but also the state of their own facilities. As Bill Shoemaker, Head of Alnwick Green saw it, there was not complete unanimity:

As far as the Deputy Head of Evesham was concerned I think she believed that things could be done more cheaply and without the kind of detail we wanted to address. As far as the Head was concerned, I think he was coming down in neither camp, and I'm not sure that he was involved that much to come down in either camp.

Noel Garrick was indeed ambivalent:

Obviously we will want to support it if it's a building adaptation for our children in effect and obviously we would be churlish to turn anything like that down. The irony of the situation is that the integrating school because of the nature of this building are getting better facilities than the base school. Now that's not their fault, I mean fair enough they should fight for it and rightly too. It so happens that's a modern building and this is an old, crumbling one.

The grossly inadequate facilities at Evesham were well known to all participants. Tim Malvern, the AEO (Special) described it as 'the pits, compared to Alnwick Green'. From Patience Franklin's perspective, there was a consensus between the two schools against Peter Wheeler:

In the end the conflict was very much between the Adviser, and Evesham and Alnwick Park very much agreeing that facilities were generally very unsatisfactory at both schools. At one stage the Adviser suggested that because Evesham facilities were rather unsatisfactory, we shouldn't be asking for anything better. It seemed to me to be a complete diversion from the real issues.

The protagonist with the most fiercely expressed feelings on the state of Evesham's facilities was Peter Wheeler himself:

Evesham is a slum, in my view, and I don't mind being quoted. You can say this out loud, and put it in print and attach my name to it. It's a bloody awful school. It is disgusting. It is foul. The thing that makes it work is the damn good assistant teachers, and the fact that we had an inspired and dynamic headteacher in the school. Mary [the previous head] was there for ten years...

I've been resisting spending £100,000 at Alnwick Green because we desperately need to put reasonable incontinence facilities into Evesham. We are still operating with separate toilet booths with curtains. Why I'm not prepared to do it all at once there [Alnwick Green] is that it rules out Evesham. The only reason I haven't been agitating for more radical measures is that I want to knock the bloody place down and rebuild it.

In the face of such disagreements the authority's officers could be legitimately excused a sense of uncertainty as to how to respond. Tim Malvern, the AEO (Special Education), was the fifth person to occupy that post in seven years. The post was the most junior in the education officer hierarchy, and had been a stepping stone to greater things for many. Malvern had been an English teacher, and had spent ten months as a professional assistant before taking up his post.

He found himself in the middle of 'so many different perceptions of need'. Not only was he acutely aware of the differences of view between Alnwick Green, Evesham and Peter Wheeler, but he also had to contend with what he saw as conflicting opinions from within Alnwick Green itself. He recalled one meeting he had minuted when someone had said that there was no suitable seating for pupils with disabilities in the business studies department, so Peter Wheeler had said he could supply an adjustable chair:

So I minute that, and then he goes and has a separate word with the Head of Business Studies at some stage and she said, 'well, no, there's no problem with this particular girl . . . I'm not quite sure where they get that from, we don't need it.

Patience Franklin was aware of such inconsistencies, and saw them as arising from unreasonable expectations being placed on the staff of the school, by the authority:

The physiotherapists were asked to do something they're never usually asked to do, which is to say exactly how many couches and how much space you need, and of course amongst themselves they didn't always agree. It was quite a long process getting them to come to a consensus.

Faced with such disagreements, said Tim Malvern, 'one tends to be suspicious'.

The root of this problem may have lain with conflicting views as to whose responsibility it was to define precisely what adaptations were needed. Malvern and the officers in the development division were in no position to do the job themselves:

For somebody like myself, or indeed somebody in development division, it's terribly difficult to measure or quantify a need because you have to rely on the so-called experts, people there doing the job.

But when experts did not agree, the officers were faced with a dilemma. According to Patience Franklin, development division equated expertise with working at Evesham. This equation was a solution that also attracted Tim Malvern:

I suppose a good model would have been host school says: 'we need incontinence facilities', who are the people who are most dealing with incontinent children? Right, will you, special school, please tell us what sort of things should go into it. But again, there were differences of perception . . . one person's definition of need is another person's definition of luxury.

Clearly, the limit to this solution, from Alnwick Green's perspective, would be the extent to which staff at Evesham could be dispassionate, and possibly self-denying. Of course, the extent to which Evesham would have accepted Alnwick Green's assessment of need would be similarly limited.

Tim Malvern, like Peter Wheeler, saw his job partly as being an impartial check on overzealous bidding for resources: 'Human nature being human nature people will get what they can'. He drew an analogy with the success of the articulate middle classes in capturing state resources, and saw his task as a champion of the inarticulate in the special education system:

I actually have a bit of a thing about fairness of resources, that would be perceived as making sure everybody gets an equal amount of inadequacy. But then, I believe that it shouldn't go to the strong and Alnwick Green is a very powerful school in lots of ways. It's been given a lot of status in its time.

To Patience Franklin, this argument was as much a diversion as was Peter Wheeler's that Evesham's need for improved facilities was equally pressing. If integration was to proceed properly, it should not be botched:

I don't think we're asking for too much. I think we're asking for things that should have been sorted out years ago. I don't really think we have magnificent facilities, we have adequate facilities [for physiotherapy and incontinence]. We don't have adequate facilities in the curriculum areas. In fact the more I think about it, the more scandalous I feel it is that we pretend to integrate them, and they can't do the work ... In other areas, things have broken down because these needs have not been adequately discussed. At primary level the integration schemes [in the borough] have run into very considerable difficulties and I think that has caused a lot more ill feeling in that school than it has here.

The culmination of the 'eighteen-month battle' came when Bill Shoemaker and Patience Franklin decided to take the unusual and controversial step of taking a deputation to the borough's Schools Subcommittee to press their case. There was already one pupil at Alnwick Green who was incontinent, and two more children with incontinence problems had been put forward by Evesham. Alnwick Green believed that they faced three options: either refuse to accept these children, take them with inadequate facilities, or force the issue with the borough for adequate facilities, effectively bypassing Peter Wheeler and Tim Malvern. They chose the last of these. To Shoemaker it was: 'a direct exercise in lobbying and in ensuring that the children who were handicapped got a fair deal'. The risks were apparent, as Patience Franklin remarked: 'I think we stuck our necks out and we possibly caused quite a lot of unpleasantness by doing it'.

Tim Malvern was more irritated than annoyed by the move:

It niggles, but if part of the game is lobbying and being heard, and the more you're heard, the more chance you have of getting things happening – which is the way, I suppose, a democracy operates.

He was sceptical about the motives of the deputation: 'I'm afraid the notion of the deputation as a move because, "we only want the kids' best interests" rings a bit hollow'. In any case, he argued that the deputation changed nothing. The adaptations had already been agreed, and the most that could have been achieved would be to advance the building schedule. No resolution was passed following the deputation.

If Tim Malvern and Peter Wheeler were right in their perceptions of Councillors' understanding of and interest in special education, then Malvern's comment on lobbying is doubly relevant. On many issues, the borough's education service was highly politicized, as Peter Wheeler commented:

Special education hasn't got much of a constituency in the borough. We are currently building an Irish Cultural Centre, and a West Indian Cultural Centre. We've got all sorts of initiatives for all the trendy causes ...

In an LEA in which, according to Tim Malvern, the officers were much less powerful than in most because of the 'high profile' of councillors, special education excited no one's political passions:

There isn't a group of people who see special education as particularly significant or horrendous or whatever, and are pushing for it. It [special education] is pretty much of a mystery to most of them.

In this state of relative ignorance, and with no clear set of priorities to guide them, the Schools Subcommittee would have faced the same dilemma that Tim Malvern himself had confronted, had they been exposed in equal measure to Peter Wheeler's side of the case. In the event, the long-demanded facilities were finally installed.

Policy: the root of the problem?

One point united all the protagonists: something needed to be done about the borough's policy on special education. Their epithets varied, but the underlying message was the same: that there was no clear and agreed view of what ought to happen, and there should be. To Patience Franklin, the policy was non-existent, and on this, at least, she was at one with Peter Wheeler, who held that there was no coherent policy, just a series of practices, which changed randomly over time. Tim Malvern was less severe in his strictures:

> It's truer to say its's a bit like the British Constitution: it's non-existent in the sense that it's not written down; to say that it's non-existent is obviously untrue. I suppose if there's provision there must be policy. If you say it's patchworky and ad hoc and isn't clearly understood by everybody – and certainly it's not understood in its totality by anyone – then I'd agree.

The current irrelevance both of written documents of policy, and of the elected council's own activities to the way special education operated was revealed more in the tone of some of Tim Malvern's comments than in the substance:

> I think I can probably find a council minute which came out in response to the 1981 Act where the council probably said: 'We're for integration as far as possible' ... It's not in illuminated gold-lettering in the buildings anywhere.

Whatever policy did exist in the borough had resulted, according to Tim Malvern, from individual, and largely professional initiative. But this version of policy did no more than describe the current practice. The vital absence, which was at the root of so many of the difficulties that Alnwick Green and Evesham had faced, was the lack of any statement of what ought to happen in the future. Noel Garrick and Tim Malvern, for example, could agree that there was a policy of integration, yet this alone was quite inadequate. 'Where', asked Noel Garrick, 'do we draw the line? Is the borough saying that every child shall be integrated, or is it saying that certain children shall be integrated?' Bill Shoemaker similarly wanted, 'a statement of borough policy, which probably would contain projections of where the authority would be looking to go both in the short-term and the long-term'.

A critical issue to be resolved was the future of Evesham. Everyone knew the school could not continue for long as it was. Its geographical isolation ensured that it was virtually impossible to integrate any of the more seriously disabled pupils who had not 'made it' to Alnwick Green. The question was, would the school survive? Here, Bill Shoemaker and Peter Wheeler were in accord: both wanted Evesham to be rebuilt on a campus alongside mainstream primary and secondary schools. Peter Wheeler went further and argued for a site at the opposite end of the borough to Alnwick Green, since the latter already had facilities. The alternative was advanced by Patience Franklin and Tim Malvern. Patience Franklin could not see the rationale for a separate school, even if resited on a mainstream campus. This would, in her view, perpetuate all the problems of sharing responsibility between two institutions. She favoured, with Tim Malvern, the development of resource bases attached to a number of primary and secondary schools. Thus, at the heart of the debate about the future were the same loyalties to Evesham as an institution that had permeated the past.

But with no plan for the future, and no clearly stated direction or limits to development, something close to the rules of the market applied. Bill Shoemaker was more than willing to compete for his school's interests:

> Everybody can argue their corner and argue it most vociferously, and rightly so. What has to be determined is an order of priorities. Where people are unable to see where they fit into those priorities then they will continue to badger and push for whatever corner they've got because they can't see where the progress is going to be made.

In an expanding system, the officers might have been able to handle this. But the borough was constantly surviving by the skin of its teeth. Rate-capping was constantly on the horizon. In this climate, one should not be surprised if the officers worked on the assumption that schools in general need less than they ask for.

Patience Franklin did not even believe that schools ought to have to ask for everything. In a world where the policy framework was firmly established, the officers and advisers would be taking the initiative:

> I don't really see why the receiving school should always have to be the one to identify the needs and put the pressure on. I feel if there is expertise it ought to have been coming up here and saying: 'you really need this, you ought to be having this, you're not doing this properly'. Now that has never been the case.

In the permanent atmosphere of uncertainty that hung over Evesham and with the sense that they had already been 'run down', it would have been unreasonable to expect them to promote further integration alone. Nor would Peter Wheeler, with his own loyalty to the school, and his sense of the injustice they had suffered. Tim Malvern was in no position to play the role either; on the contrary, he expected Alnwick Green and Evesham to come to a much clearer consensus on which he could then act. As it was, he, like the elected members of the authority, was caught between the conflicting pressure and arguments of others, and his own beliefs. He had not long been in the post, and he was sceptical about his status with schools: 'it can be counter-productive for an officer, who is seen as a sort of rat carrying rabies, to suggest something'.

Nevertheless, he did see a positive role for himself as the orchestrator of the development of a coherent policy. The process had already begun in the borough. He had wanted to avoid a centrally produced document that would meet resistance when it went out for comment, and so had set up an extensive grass roots system of eight working parties, co-ordinated by a steering group of twenty. Everyone with any possible interest was invited to put themselves up for membership of working parties, and 230 had applied. It was, he said, 'going to be a nightmare to organize'. But he held out the hope that, 'because the amount of involvement at this stage will have been so great then it will be seen as a grass roots report, as opposed to a bureaucrats report'.

Whether or not consensus would be established this way remains to be seen. On the evidence of the past, it seemed unlikely. At Alnwick Green and Evesham, the issues had been sharply focused by ten years of experience, so at least open debate would be possible, and decisions would be well informed. Even so, simple involvement in the debate would not be enough. The survival of an institution, and with it the beliefs, identities, loyalties and jobs of many people would be at stake. Either one party to the debate would have to concede that their goals would not be satisfied, or power would have to be exercised in favour of one set of protagonists, or a compromise would have to be found. The latter course was improbable. The existing arrangements were already a compromise with which all sides had become disenchanted. Any new position would entail there being winners and losers. Although the protagonists themselves would probably agree as to who amongst them had lost out, there was a distinct and worrying prospect that they would never agree about whether the pupils were winners, or losers.

References

Department of Education and Science (DES) 1978. *Special Educational Needs* (The Warnock Report), London, HMSO.

Dessent, T. 1984. 'Special schools and the mainstream – "the resource stretch"', in Bowers, T. (ed), *Management and the Special School*, London, Croom Helm.

Inner London Education Authority (ILEA) 1985. *Equal Opportunities for All?* (The Fish Report), London, ILEA.

19 Parents, power and the politics of special education in a London borough

Linda Jordan

Linda Jordan is a teacher, a local councillor who chairs the Schools Subcommittee of the London Borough of Newham, and the mother of a child with Down's Syndrome. In this chapter, she tells the story of her attempt, along with other parents of children with disabilities, to introduce a policy of integration in the borough. Her chapter recounts the manoeuvring and lobbying that is the life-blood of any local political system, and the resistance that she encountered to the radical changes she wanted to introduce. Few parents have taken their campaign this far. More are likely to follow.

In September 1982 my first child, Ellen, was born. She has Down's Syndrome. During my stay in hospital the nursing officer gave me the name of a women in my area who is the local parent contact for the Down's Children's Association. I was pleased that I had this woman's phone number because I felt sure that it would be helpful to know other families with a child with Down's Syndrome. When Ellen was just a few weeks old, my husband and I took her to our first meeting of the Newham Down's Group. The group holds meetings once a month, taking it in turns at each others's houses. At that first meeting there were about eight children's parents. All the children were under five.

That first meeting was very lively; a lot of the evening was taken up with talk about education. During the evening someone explained to us that there was a new Education Act about to be implemented, which would mean that handicapped children would be able to go to ordinary schools. The main problem being discussed was: would everything be sorted out in time for their children to start at ordinary nursery schools, rather than having to go to one of the special school nurseries?

It had run through my mind in hospital that we would be meeting people who had had their children late in life, and who spent their Saturdays in the market with collecting tins for poor handicapped children. Instead, I found myself in a roomful of young, lively people who were aggressively determined that their children were going to be accepted as human beings with the same right as everyone else. I remember one mother talking in a very matter-of-fact way about her hope that her daughter would get married. I was so happy to find a group of people who shared our attitudes and feelings. As to education, I had not realized that many children with disabilities were still automatically placed in segregated schools. I had qualified as a teacher two months before Ellen was born, after being out of education since leaving school sixteen years earlier. I can, however, remember once, many years ago, reading something about handicapped children going to ordinary schools and thinking, 'of course'. When Ellen was one month old I was visited by the borough paediatrician with special responsibility for children with disabilities. She said that Ellen would be going to a school for 'severely educationally subnormal children' and that a full-time nursery place would be hers at the age of two: weren't we lucky?

In April 1983, when the 1981 Education Act was put into operation, the Down's Group felt that something should have been happening. Through one or two sympathetic professionals attached to the local parents' centre, we invited the Chair of the Schools Subcommittee to come and speak to us. She told us that although the officers of the authority had done what they had to do as far as the assessment procedures were concerned, integration had not been discussed, either by the council or its officers. In our naivety, we were devastated and gave her a really hard time. We said that we would expect discussions to take place very quickly. She agreed to put the issue on the next Schools Subcommittee agenda.

Two months later, the Subcommittee met and integration was on the agenda. The Subcommittee agreed that they supported the 'spirit' of the act and they decided to establish a working party to draft a policy statement. The working party was to consist of councillors, teachers' and parents' representatives. Newham was the first local educational authority to have parents on the education committee and it was left up to these to find parents to sit on the working party. I decided to try and get on the working party and in the event it was easy to do so as there was very little interest among parents of children in special schools. In fact, another Down's Group mother got on the working party too.

The Newham Integration Working Party first met in October 1983 and its final composition was as follows: three councillors, four teachers' representatives, a priest (who never spoke), and five parents. However, one of the parents (myself) was a teacher, all of the teachers were parents, and one of the councillors was a teacher. The working party met over a period of eighteen months, for a total of seventy hours and they were the most frustrating hours of my life. The terms of reference were to:

1 examine existing provision in the borough for pupils with special educational needs;
2 consider ways in which special educational provision could be made in ordinary primary and secondary schools to enable pupils for whom the authority will maintain statements of special educational needs to be educated with their peers;
3 consider the means by which ordinary schools may support those mainstream pupils who have special educational needs under the definition of the 1981 Act but whose learning difficulties are not sufficient to require statements;
4 consider how teachers in ordinary schools may be made more able to recognize and support pupils with special educational needs; and
5 prepare a policy statement on the integration of pupils with special educational needs in ordinary schools.

Our terms of reference seemed to me then, and still seem, quite clear: we were writing a policy document for integration. What in fact happened was that we spent those seventy hours discussing whether integration should take place at all, and the working conditions of teachers. At the first meeting I heard the most patronizing anti-handicap prejudice I have experienced. Most members of the working party and the professional advisers seemed to think that we parents were stupid and, because we wanted integrated education for our children, unable to cope with their disabilities. I was told that night that I had no understanding of the issues; that the 1981 Education Act was not about integration; that there were no children in our LEA in special schools who could possibly be integrated; that the special schools in our area were the best in the country and that people came from all over the world to see them; that we spend more on special education than any other LEA in the country; that integration would be too expensive. The one parent whose child was already at a special school was told by his daughter's headteacher, who was also on the working party, that if we had integration his daughter would have to go to a boarding school as she would never cope in an ordinary school. In fact the first meeting consisted of the parents being lectured on how wonderful the special schools in the LEA were.

I did not sleep that night. I did not know what to do. I had thought that I would be part of a group whose job it was to work out a way in which children with special needs could begin to go to ordinary schools and how those already in special schools could either be integrated or their schools develop as ordinary schools over a period of several years. I had no idea that there was going to be such entrenched resistance. I somehow imagined that because the Labour Party has always run the LEA and has been proud of its progressive educational initiatives, everyone working in it would be delighted about the possibility of taking the comprehensive ideal to its logical conclusion.

As the weeks went on, the Down's Group discussed their children's education. It was clear by now that it was not going to be easy for us to get our children into ordinary schools, and in fact one child had started at one of the special school nurseries. His parents were very unhappy about their decision, but saw it as a temporary arrangement. I felt that I needed to understand the whole area of special education and particularly the 1981 Education Act much better, so that I could argue with the other people on the working party; other members of the Down's Group felt the same. During the next year I did the Open University course E241, *Special Needs in Education*, and other members of the group attended endless meetings, conferences and courses. The Down's Group still met once a month: most of the time at our meetings was spent discussing integration.

During 1984 it became increasingly obvious to me that I would eventually have to work in a special school. I was teaching in a secondary school and enjoying it very much, but for many reasons I thought that I would have to change. I was fed up with people saying that I didn't know what I was talking about. For instance, one of the headteachers who was on the working party had said, at a public meeting, that I had no right to be advocating integration as my child was not at school and I had no idea what went on in special schools. I felt that working in a special school would make me more confident when arguing and give me a wonderful opportunity to experience the expertise I had been told so much about.

In October 1985 I started teaching at Grosvenor House School in the London Borough of Waltham Forest. This is a school for children categorized as having severe learning difficulties. I worked there for eight months and left because I was standing as a candidate in the local government elections. I did not feel that I could fit in a full-time job, council work and looking after two under-five year olds.

I really enjoyed my short time at Grosvenor House, as I have enjoyed all my teaching. For two months I covered for absent colleagues and therefore spent time in most of the classes. Working there did not change my views about integration at all. The only way in which I changed my mind was that I thought many of the children could have been integrated without too much trouble on anybody's part. I had previously thought that children who had spent many years in a special school may not be easy to integrate since they might not want to change schools.

Grosvenor House School was full of smashing people who worked very hard. Working there confirmed what I had previously believed: there is nothing wrong with special schools – they simply shouldn't exist.

In September 1984, what we thought was to be the last meeting of the working party took place. To say that relationships were at an all-time low would not be an exaggeration. We had our final discussion about the rights and wrongs of integration, and decided in an atmosphere of open hostility that the working party would have to produce two reports. The officers who had attended our meetings advised very strongly against this, but there was no alternative. Myself, three other parents and one councillor (an ex-special school teacher) decided to write a minority report which became known as *Report B*. The four teachers' representatives (all of whom were working for the LEA – three of them in special schools, two of them as special school headteachers), two of the councillors, and one parent, endorsed with some amendments a report prepared by the Director of Education, which became known as *Report A*.

The five of us who dissented met one evening the following week, and after the hell of the previous meetings, for the first time were able to discuss how integration might happen in Newham. We discussed the practical stages needed to prepare everyone concerned. We prepared a draft, met once more, and had it typed. The day we handed Report B into the Director of Education's Office I felt that I had done my finals in a degree in integration, with torturers instead of tutors.

At the next Schools Subcommittee meeting, both reports were presented. As usual, most of the Down's Group and some other parents were in the public gallery. Our case was presented by a working party member who was a parent representative on the Education Committee; the other side declined to present their case formally, saying their report spoke for itself. There was a debate. The members of the Schools Subcommittee decided that the officers should prepare a compromise document and that a special meeting of the Subcommittee be convened to discuss this issue alone.

The special meeting was barely quorate, and demonstrated the lack of interest of the elected members. The 'compromise' document was considerably closer to Report A. The parent representative on the Subcommittee, suddenly realizing that supporters of integration were in the majority, was able to make drastic amendments which amounted to a summary restatement of Report B. Halfway through the meeting, the two committee members from Report A walked out, hoping to make the meeting inquorate.

However, because no one knew exactly what constituted a quorum, the meeting continued. At the meeting of the full education committee the following week, it was decided to ratify the policy recommendations even though the meeting had in fact been inquorate. At this point we had achieved much more than we had expected, although, correctly as it turned out, we remained sceptical about the outcome.

The recommendations now had to go before the full council. But before that could happen, they had to be discussed by the Labour Group (Labour members of the council meeting separately), who had an overwhelming majority on the council.

During the two weeks before this meeting a lot happened. The local teachers' associations organized meetings of special school teachers. Parents of children at special schools, fearing that their children were on the point of being thrust into mainstream schools overnight without support and the special schools closed down, joined the opposition. There was a massive lobby of all councillors to 'Save our Special Schools'. The discussions at the Labour Group meeting were private, but the consequence was that the recommendations did not get ratified at the next full council meeting.

At the next Schools Subcommittee meeting in March 1985 there was a massive turnout. The complete Schools Subcommittee attended and the meeting had to be moved to a special room to accommodate 100-odd members of the public, made up of special school teachers, parents of children at special schools, plus a handful of integrationists.

We had not organized a lobby of our own. Partly we had not expected such a large backlash. But more importantly, we felt that integration would happen eventually and that all this commotion was just part of an inevitable process that had to be endured. We felt that we had achieved something really important by getting the issue out into the open. If we had not stuck to our guns on the working party, no one would have heard of it even now. We were just disappointed that the integrationist arguments had, in our view, been distorted.

Because so many people attended the meeting, I had become separated from my friends and I was only able to sit among rows of hostile teachers who were accusing me of being a 'dangerous woman'. To our amazement, the Chair of Schools Subcommittee, who had supported us throughout, announced that the policy recommendations which had previously been agreed by the Education Committee had been rejected by the Director of Education because they did not constitute 'good educational practice'. Instead, the way forward was for a consultation document to be prepared. She suggested that the working party reconvene in order for a document to be drafted. This would then go to governing bodies of schools and other representative organizations. It seemed at first that the Director of Education was making the policy. In reality, he does not make the decisions. If the majority party had been determined about the policy, it would have gone through in spite of the director's objections.

The working party met once more to draft the consultation document. I did not attend this meeting. As the Labour councillors would not accept anything I was prepared to put my name to, there was no point in taking any further part in the proceedings. Three of the other signatories to Report B did attend, but found themselves back to square one arguing the case for integration. The ideal of a consultation document was in any case ridiculous as there had been extensive consultation during the life of the working party. A document was prepared which pleased no one, caused more confusion, but is now the borough's policy document.

Meanwhile, our children were nearing school age, and one by one, the parents started fighting successfully by various means, to get mainstream nursery and infant places for their children. The only child in our group who had gone to a special school was transferred to a mainstream infant class in January 1986 after having gone through the 1981 Education Act procedures, a battle which lasted fifteen months. During this time my daughter was admitted to a mainstream nursery, with a Statement.

However, without a policy for integration, our children, despite their Statements, are permanently on trial, are not getting the resources they ought to have, and all of the families involved have had to make personal sacrifices in terms of time, emotion and money. Much more importantly, apart from a few exceptions, the only children being integrated are those whose parents have challenged the authority. Integration is not being offered as an option to the vast majority of children and young people with special educational needs.

My experience of being on the integration working party made me realize that the only hope of getting a proper policy of integration established is to have enough councillors who want it and who are able to convince the rest of the council of the contradictions in having policies of comprehensive education and community schools, anti-racist and anti-sexist policies and yet still segregating two per cent of the school population on the basis of their 'special needs'. With this in mind I accepted the invitation of my Labour Party branch to stand as a candidate in the May 1986 local government elections. I was elected to the council. Two weeks later I was elected as Chair of the Schools Subcommittee.

Conclusion

I believe that the only way integration will happen is either by a political decision from a government that will pass enforcing legislation, or by LEAs making a political decision to use the 1981 Education Act to end segregation. In a sense I feel relieved, selfishly, that in future, whatever happens, I will be very closely involved in the decision-making process. I will no longer experience the same frustrations of the last three years. But I also feel very angry that the attitude towards people with disabilities is such that only a minority of able-bodied people are interested in becoming involved in their liberation. I am angry at some of the arguments I have heard against integration over the last three years, especially from people who otherwise share my political views, or from people who are professionally involved with children with special needs. If anyone says to me again that double incontinence is a reason for not putting a child in a mainstream classroom I think that I may be guilty of murder. I shall never forget the proposal put forward at a working party meeting by one of the special school headteachers. A parent had said to him that one of your roots in the community is the fact that you all collect your children from the same school gates every day. His response was to suggest that the children in special schools should be bussed back each afternoon to the schools they would be attending if they were not in the special schools, so that parents could collect them there and would not feel so isolated and stigmatized. His eyes lit up as if he had just found the perfect solution.

20 The development of educational policy for deaf children

Gordon Mitchell

In the first part of this chapter, Gordon Mitchell describes the major changes that have occurred in the education of pupils with hearing impairments in the last ten years. He notes changes in the size and nature of the population of pupils, in patterns of placement, in the work of teachers of the deaf, and in methods of communication used, with an increased move towards the use of 'total communication'. In the second part of the chapter he assesses the factors that have promoted these changes. He considers the influence of LEAs, central government, parents, the deaf community and the voluntary organizations.

Introduction

The first schools for the deaf were established in Edinburgh and London (in 1760 and 1783 respectively) and the precise techniques used by early educators were often closely guarded secrets. However, one issue has dominated all others in the development of educational provision for deaf children since then – communication. Principally the debate has been about whether or not to use signs and fingerspelling in education. Two main strands of the debate developed.

One broad approach was to use a range of different forms of communication. These included speech, the use of residual hearing, lipreading, signs and fingerspelling. In some instances forms of signing were constructed in order to convey the grammar of English. It was believed that the use of the visual senses offered a way of compensating for the lack of information through hearing. It was noted that in some cases children found it easier to gain access to language and other forms of educational achievement through a form of manual communication. In some instances it was felt that the use of signs was primarily to aid the learning of reading and writing. The Victorian practice of peer tutoring or pupil instructors was also found in early schools for the deaf. This meant that there were deaf teachers of the deaf. At this early stage, deaf adult role models were available to deaf children.

The second approach was to become known as *oralism*. This reflects its focus upon oral means of communication. Traditional oralism not only insists on oral methods of communication, it explicitly claims that the use of forms of manual communication will interfere with a child's acquisition of speech. The theoretical base for this approach is to be found in the work of Thomas Heinicke working in Germany, who believed that abstract thought was only possible through speech.

The Congress of Milan in 1880 is often cited as a turning point in policy in the education of the deaf. At this meeting a resolution claiming oralism as the preferred method of teaching deaf children was agreed, which led to marked changes in communication policy in schools for the deaf across Europe (although there is recorded opposition from deaf people, see Savage et al 1981).

A second phase in the development of this debate occurred in the 1940s and 1950s. It was at this time that technology revolutionized the development of hearing aids. The development in miniaturized electronic components (perhaps ironically originating in defence associated research) meant much more powerful amplification devices that could be worn comfortably. The effect was to raise the threshold of deafness at which residual hearing became useful for speech. The belief was born that deafness and its effects could virtually be eliminated through improvements in hearing aid technology. It was assumed that it would only be a matter of time until that occurred (see Chapter 10 for a fuller discussion of hearing aids).

In many respects the 1940s are the major fulcrum for a series of policy decisions for the following forty years. Because hearing aid technology offered so much for deaf people and indeed provided access to spoken language for many, educational progress became inextricably linked to the provision of and the use of this technology. This was reflected in the fact that the most prominent academic and training centre associated with the education of the deaf was for many years to be found at the University of Manchester's Department of Audiology and Education of the Deaf.

This focus has produced the development of hearing assessment clinics with close links to local education services. It has emphasised the importance of early screening and diagnosis, the fitting of appropriate hearing aids and their careful maintenance. Trained teachers of the deaf now have considerable technical knowledge in addition to language teaching skills. But this preoccupation with technology and its application has led to a distancing from other sectors of education. This separateness has led to a very considerable specialization, and the development of a skilled teaching force. While the benefits of this are important, over-specialization can be a serious drawback. Indeed, the 1985 World Congress on the Education of the Deaf, hosted by Britain, barely mentioned ordinary curriculum issues.

Recent Policy Development

There have been four major areas in which change can be charted over the last ten years. In this section I shall describe four major areas of change. An analysis of the influences on these changes can be found later in the chapter.

POPULATION

It may seem somewhat strange to describe an increase in the numbers of children with educationally significant hearing losses at a time when the school population generally is falling. However there are two reasons for this situation. Firstly, the DES has begun to collect more accurate statistics and, secondly the effects of slight or even temporary hearing losses on educational achievement are now becoming better understood.

The number of pupils who receive attention from qualified teachers of the deaf is much greater than shown in Table 20.1: it amounts to some 31,000. This figure was established through a survey carried out by the British Association of Teachers of the Deaf (BATOD) (1983) which was conducted through LEAs.

Many of this additional number are children based in ordinary classes, but who receive additional support either in that setting or perhaps through withdrawal from class. The DES, by contrast, counts only a small proportion of this group. The size of the group who may have specific educational needs

Table 20.1   Number of deaf and partially hearing children in England by
type of provision 1974–1983

	Ordinary schools			Special schools	All schools
Year	Deaf	P-H	Total		
1974	50	2123	2173	5753	7926
1975	128	2156	2284	5994	8278
1976	261	2786	3047	5796	8843
1977	278	3138	3416	5613	9029
1978	310	3221	3531	5447	8978
1979	292	3474	3766	4193	7959
1980	382	3405	3787	4703	8490
1981	491	3365	3856	4063	7919
1982	883	5681	6564	3975	10539
1983	1116	7202	8318	3935	12253

(Source: DES Statistics)

because of temporary or slight hearing losses is even larger again: now variously
estimated at between 5 and 10 per cent of the school population (NDCS 1984).
Limited research in Manchester is now suggesting that the pattern of hearing
losses in the emerging school population is changing: there will be fewer children
with severe or profound losses, and greater numbers where deafness is associated
with other impairments.

PLACEMENT

The most informative picture of patterns of school placement is provided by the
recent BATOD survey, shown in Table 20.2. There is a clear decrease in the
proportion of the total school population at schools for the deaf, from 6.3 per
10,000 total population in 1974 down to 5.1 per 10,000 in 1983. In addition there
has been a slight decrease in the number of special schools, with school rolls
falling steadily.

The first special classes for deaf children attached to ordinary schools were
opened in Manchester and London in the 1940s. They have for some time been
known as PHUs (Partially Hearing Units) but are given other names in some
areas. In 1962, there were 40 PHUs; by 1970 this had grown to 212, and by 1982
the figure had reached 502 (Lynas 1986). We do not have access to any accurate
statistics regarding trends in the number of deaf children receiving their education in ordinary classes. We do know, however, that approximately 87 per cent of
children with educationally significant hearing losses are currently placed in the
ordinary school system.

TEACHER ROLES

The changing pattern of educational provision is also reflected in a change of
duties expected of teachers of the deaf. Peripatetic teachers appeared with the
placement of children in ordinary schools. The preschool work of some teachers
of the deaf, mostly with parents but also with infants, grew with the improvement

Table 20.2 Number of pupils with educationally significant hearing loss

	England and Wales		Scotland		Total	
	Number	Per cent	Number	Per cent	Number	Per cent
In schools for deaf and partially hearing pupils	3469	11.7	339	24.0	3808	12.2
In units for hearing impaired pupils	4049	13.6	176	12.4	4225	13.6
In local schools seen by peripatetics (including some hearing impaired pupils in special schools for other categories)	19231	64.8	761	53.8	19992	64.3
Under school age seen by peripatetics	2099	7.1	115	8.1	2214	7.1
In full time further education	818	2.8	24	1.7	842	2.7
Total	29666		1415		31081	

(Source: BATOD Statistics)

and expansion of hearing assessment and diagnostic services. Two surveys (BATOD 1977 and 1981) put total number of teachers of the deaf employed in the recent past at just under 2000 teachers. Peripatetic teachers now form approximately one quarter of the specialist teaching force. Their numbers grew from 331 in 1974 to 407 in 1983, according to DES statistics. A recent survey from NATED, the National Association for Tertiary Education for the Deaf (1986), noted that at least 75 LEAs now employ a qualified teacher of the deaf to support deaf students in post-school education. Some LEAs employ a team of support workers for this purpose.

COMMUNICATION

There have been significant changes in communication practices in the education of deaf children. This is true of approaches to language development and of modes of communication. In relation to language development the trend has been away from methods which emphasized repetition, imitation, and language form to methods which stress natural acquisition, modelling, and communicative function. The change in modes of communication is primarily a marked growth in the use of manual systems of communication. The main forms currently in use are:

1 *Signed English*: BSL signs used with additional markers to represent English language structure. This is used with speech;
2 *Signs Supporting English*: BSL signs used in English word order to support spoken English;
3 *British Sign Language (BSL)*: the visual–manual language used by a majority of profoundly deaf adults in Britain. This is currently rarely used in educational settings, but where it is it is normally part of a bilingual approach probably also using Signed English to teach English.

Figure 20.1   Number of schools reporting a change to toal communication 172–1980.

The term *total communication* is used here to include all methods which involve a mixture of manual and oral modes of communication. In the vast majority of instances schools or units report using Signed English as a formal model and Signs Supporting English for most communicative interchanges (Mitchell 1984).

An American researcher (himself profoundly deaf) on sabbatical in Britain surveyed the types of communication used in schools and units, and charted the rate of change. The changes, shown in Figure 20.1, were all from forms of oralism to forms of total communication (Jordan 1982).

At present, 57 per cent of special schools for the deaf and 9 per cent of PHUs report using total communication (Mitchell 1984). Another measure of the current use of a variety of methods of communication was gained through a very full survey of teachers of the deaf who were asked which methods they used in the course of their work (BATOD 1983). The results are shown in Table 20.3.

Changing influences on policy development

EDUCATIONAL MANAGEMENT STRUCTURES

In the times when schools for the deaf were the predominant means of provision the headteacher's views and beliefs were paramount in all aspects of school management. Although the Victorian tradition of headteacher as despot has gone, it is still the case that individual headteachers can determine school policy, subject of course, to the approval of the governing body.

The growth of maintained schools for the deaf and the subsequent development of PHUs offered greater flexibility in placement for individual children. Initially, the two forms of provision were sometimes construed as competitors for the same children. In 1970, the Middlesborough area (now Cleveland LEA) appointed a head of service who was both head of the local maintained school for the deaf and of the other specialist services in the area. This was introduced as a 'comprehensive service for the hearing impaired'. It encompassed the special

Table 20.3 Teachers using signing in the education of pupils with hearing impairments

Communication system			*Teachers using each system*		
	Number	Per cent	Number	Per cent	Number	Per cent
Signed English	184	9.1	65	34.0	249	11.2
British Signs Supporting English	73	3.6	6	3.2	79	3.6
British Sign Language	76	3.8	1	0.5	77	3.5
Makaton	38	1.9	3	1.6	41	1.8
Paget Gorman	54	2.7	20	10.5	74	3.3
Others	4	0.2	—	—	4	0.2
All signing systems	429	21.2	95	49.7	524	23.7
Total number of teachers	2022		191		2213	

(Source: BATOD, 1983)

school, PHUs, and peripatetic teachers working in ordinary classes and with preschool children. Thus a very wide range of provision was available in-county and any barriers to movement between the different forms of provision for children were reduced. This model has subsequently been replicated in a number of other LEAs.

One reason for the relatively well-developed level of educational provision for children with hearing impairments compared to other sectors of special education has been its independence with LEAs. Teachers of the deaf are marked by their specialized and additional qualifications, but more importantly the most senior teacher of the deaf has often been graded at adviser level. This has allowed two things to happen. The head of service has been in a relatively good position to secure resources, and developments have reflected the particular concerns of teachers of the deaf. The education of the deaf has remained somewhat distant from the issues current in the wider field of special education and education generally. For example, the consideration of multiculturalism and racism in education has been viewed as of only minor significance in relation to deaf children. Also while there has been some thoughtful analysis of the application of models of linguistic and cultural ethnocentrism in relation to the deaf community as a linguistic minority group (see Brennan, Chapter 26 of this volume), it is difficult to find any serious consideration emanating from educational sources.

Recently, a number of LEAs have replaced heads of service for the hearing impaired with advisers who are expected to deal with several sectors of special educational need. The prime consideration is surely financial but these changes have been given impetus through the introduction of the 1981 Education Act. This is for two reasons. Firstly it is a reflection of the fact that special education has moved higher up the education agenda, and secondly it reflects the belief that strategies to meet special educational needs have much in common despite the significant differences between groups of children. Many people involved in the education of deaf children see this trend as a straightforward attack on the quality of educational provision available to deaf children. For example, a tentative proposal of this nature in Hertfordshire at the end of 1985 led to a flurry of representations from teachers, parents and local and national agencies. The proposal was subsequently withdrawn.

PARENTAL INVOLVEMENT

It may be true, and it is certainly possible to persuade parents, that a particular form of provision – the most appropriate for their child – is only available at a residential school. It is my experience that, other things being equal, parents prefer their children to remain at home and to attend a local school. This, allied to the policy of many LEAs, has led to a large decrease in the number of residential school placements and in part has contributed to the development of units and support facilities for severely and profoundly deaf children in ordinary schools.

Parents have also begun to challenge advice about methods of communication. Arguments for or against any particular method of communication have traditionally been justified in terms of educational success. Teaching speech and language has been regarded as a fundamental aim of teachers of the deaf and therefore subject to theorizing from educationalists concerned with deaf children. Recently, parents, perhaps now persuaded that greater parental choice in these matters is possible, have challenged the primacy of these arguments. The traditional arguments given to parents of newly diagnosed deaf infants often go something like this:

> 'Nowadays, with the use of modern and powerful hearing aids, the vast majority of hearing-impaired children acquire language and learn to communicate through speech and lipreading; your child will learn to communicate rather more slowly than other children, but given time will more than likely develop oral communication skills; it is important therefore that you speak to your child just as you would your other children, but clearly and in the line of sight; using signs is a possibility, but as only a few children need to use signs it is probably better to wait and see; there may well be no need to use them, and anyway it takes time to learn; there is not really any research to prove that it's any better than oral methods, and it might even hinder speech development'.

From the narrow view of education all of the above statements are justifiable, although not precisely accurate. For instance, this position does not take account of emerging evidence pointing to the achievement gains for pupils using systematic signing (Meadow 1985, Montgomery and Montgomery 1985).

Some parents have said that the development of a good relationship with their children is of paramount importance, and that easy communication is the key. They may argue that decisions about the use of communication methods should be taken on personal and social grounds. Parents' wishes have therefore contributed significantly to the growth in the use of total communication methods in education.

The negotiation procedures in the 1981 Education Act have, in general, enabled parents to participate more fully in decision-making. In addition to enabling some families to secure their chosen provision, the Act has also fostered the development of new provision in some LEAs. These include units for profoundly deaf children in Kent and increased teacher tutorial support for individual pupils in Humberside. A case of special interest is that of Ben Fletcher who was given support in nursery and infant school in the form of a deaf native signer as a language model and tutor (see Chapters 6 and 15 of this volume).

Parental influence through local campaign groups or organizations can also be very effective. For example, the North Humberside region of the National Deaf Children's Society were successful in improving information services to parents of young deaf children and also in persuading the LEA to change its policy on total communication. Total communication is now available as an option, although only out-of-county.

DEAF ADULTS

Although there were deaf instructors in Victorian schools for the deaf, since that time the education system has developed in such a way as to exclude deaf people from being involved either in teaching or policy development. This is beginning to change. Few deaf people have been able to become qualified teachers, because of inappropriate medical guidelines, but in schools using signs deaf people are currently employed as language resource assistants and classroom aides. Deaf people are beginning to make their views on the education system known. As might be expected from people who have been excluded from rightful participation over a long period of time, some of the writings reflect considerable anger and frustration. Take, for example, an article by the Rev. Mark Frame who has been deaf from infancy, which anticipates later deaf reporters in criticizing the use of restrictive oral methods in schools. He stated:

> I may be biased – I *am* biased as a matter of fact, because I have to live with the thing that teachers theorize about – but I don't think the restricted outlook of the pure oralist is conducive to personal progress in life after school years.

(Frame 1958)

Deaf writers have begun to publish their considered and intimately informed views on a variety of topical educational issues including methods of communication used in schools, bilingualism in the classroom, integration, the contribution of different forms of school experience to the growth of personal identity, and children's rights (Hay 1977, Holmes 1981, Ladd 1981).

Two themes emerge from this wealth of opinion above all others. The first is that the use of signs in total communication approach should be encouraged as part of a more liberal and open approach to communication, and that suitably qualified deaf people have a significant role to play in this revised education system. The second concerns the respective roles of PHUs and schools for the deaf. A coherent positive policy has not yet emerged but the concerns are quite clear. There exists a strong feeling that a significant number of children have been and continue to be placed in ordinary schools either inappropriately or with insufficient support. There are particular concerns for the personal and emotional development of children in these circumstances. Closely linked to this is a growing awareness of the traditional role of schools for the deaf in the development of the deaf community. It is often argued therefore that the best practical solution to the problems, from the point of view of deaf people, is for a greater proportion of deaf children to receive their education in schools for the deaf. There are parallels here with ethnic minority groups in Britain and the difficulties they experience in achieving a form of integration which is deeper than mere physical proximity. A policy document on these issues entitled, *Raise the Standard: the Case for Improving the Education of Deaf Children*, has been issued by the British Deaf Association and is the basis of the BDA's campaigning programme.

CENTRAL GOVERNMENT

Since the 1981 Education Act there have been two major reports from the DES which have very significant implications for the nature of educational provision available to deaf children.

The first is innocuously entitled, *Provision for Hearing Impaired Children in Special Schools* (DES 1984). Some two years earlier the DES had initiated discussions on the implications of small school rolls and the need for regional and national planning to 'rationalize special school provision'. The exercise generated some concern about school closures. The process of 'consultation' which was carried out revealed resolute non-co-operation between LEAs and protection strategies from non-LEA schools for the deaf. The aim of the exercise was warmly welcomed on all sides, but the DES's own in activity in promoting planning was subsequently subjected to equally wide-ranging criticism. The Royal National Institute for the Deaf was particularly vociferous, and its discussion document received support from schools, other voluntary organizations and teaching unions. It commented thus:

> The manner in which most regions conducted their initial discussions was nothing short of farcical. The regional reports were: largely lacking in adequate statistical information; ill-informed through a paucity of appropriate consultation and repre-sentative opinion; devoid of positive commitment to co-operation between LEAs; and weak in terms of subsequent planning strategies.

This exercise might better be viewed in retrospect as a crude strategy to encourage ordinary school placements. Due to the persistent resistance of the DES to discuss the issues in terms of meeting children's needs, the exercise has in fact raised the issues of quality of education and the resources needed to achieve acceptable conditions.

The second report came from the Advisory Committee on the Supply and Education of Teachers (ACSET 1984). The report suggests a major revision of teacher training in special education generally, and made two recommendations of special significance to the education of deaf children. It first recommended the abolition of the existing legal requirement for specially qualified teachers of the deaf. Following a major campaign involving a consortium of national voluntary organizations, teacher associations and parents this recommendation was reversed.

A second recommendation was to restrict entry to specialized training courses, in this case teacher of the deaf courses, to post-qualified and post-experience teachers. Under current conditions of funding this measure will reduce the number of teachers of the deaf in training by 70 per cent. No satisfactory solution has yet emerged.

This pressure on training courses has had other effects. The four centres offering teacher of the deaf courses have been criticized in recent years for not being sufficiently responsive to the needs of schools and LEAs. It is perhaps no coincidence that the colleges have for the first time agreed to participate in a joint working party with voluntary organizations to investigate possible ways of providing training for teachers in the use of manual communication skills.

VOLUNTARY ORGANIZATIONS

The voluntary organizations see a clear role for themselves in educational developments. They are not the philanthropic bodies of yesteryear. They now assume a central role in policy analysis and development. They are well capable of offering considered critical comment and increasingly do so. The campaigning styles adopted by the organizations are relatively new and as yet not fully developed. They bring different perspectives to bear on educational issues. They represent the views of deaf people, parents and independent professionals. They are, in their way, helping to create a new partnership.

References

Advisory Committee on the Supply and Education of Teachers (ACSET) 1984. *Teacher Training and Special Educational Needs*, London, DES.

British Association of Teachers of the Deaf (BATOD) 1977. *Reports of Surveys Concerning Levels of Staffing in England and Wales and Scotland*, BATOD Association News.

British Association of Teachers of the Deaf (BATOD) 1981. *Reports of Surveys Concerning Levels of Staffing in England and Wales and Scotland*, BATOD Association News.

British Association of Teachers of the Deaf (BATOD) 1983. *Reports of Surveys Concerning Levels of Staffing and Methods of Communication Used in Schools in England and Wales and Scotland*, BATOD Association News.

Department of Education and Science (DES) 1984. Consultative Document: Provision for Hearing Impaired Children in Special Schools, London, DES.

Frame, M. 1981. 'The testimony of Mark Frame', in Montgomery, G. W. G. (ed.), *The Integration and Disintegration of the Deaf in Society*, Edinburgh, Scottish Workshop Publications.

Hay, J. 1977. 'Courtesy, humour and adjustment to a mad world', in Montgomery, G. W. G. (ed.), *Of Sound and Mind: Deafness, Personality and Mental Health*, Edinburgh, Scottish Workshop Publications.

Holmes, M. 1981. 'Integration on an equal footing: the need for deaf representation', in Montgomery, G. W. G. (ed.), *The Integration and Disintegration of the Deaf in Society*, Edinburgh, Scottish Workshop Publications.

Jordan, I. K. 1982. 'Communication methods used at schools for the deaf and partially hearing and at units for partially hearing children in the United Kingdom', *American Annals of the Deaf, 127* (7), pp. 811–815.

Ladd, P. 1981. 'The erosion of self and self identity' in Montgomery, G. W. G. (ed.), *The Integration and Disintegration of the Deaf in Society*, Edinburgh, Scottish Workshop Publications.

Lynas, W. 1986. *Integrating the Handicapped into Ordinary Schools: a Study of Hearing Impaired Children*, London, Croom Helm.

Meadow, K. P. 1985. 'Effective intervention for hearing-impaired children' in Guralnick, M. J. and Bennett, F. C. (eds.), *The Effectiveness of Early Intervention*, New York, Academic Press.

Mitchell, G. S. 1984. 'Total communication in the 80s: an overview', Proceedings of the Sign 84 Conference, Edinburgh.

Montgomery, J. and Montgomery, G. W. G. 1985. 'Differences in profoundly deaf children taught by total communication and by oral methods', paper presented to the International Congress on the Education of the Deaf, Manchester.

National Association of Tertiary Education of the Deaf (NATED) 1986. *Directory of Supported Courses and LEA Support Available to Deaf Students 1986*, High Peak College, Derbyshire, NATED.

National Deaf Children's Society (NDCS) 1984. *Discovering Deafness*, London, NDCS.

Savage, R. D., Evans, L. and Savage, J. F. 1981. *Psychology and Communication in Deaf Children*, New York, Grune and Stratton.

21 Inertia, resistance and change: educational policy for pupils with visual disabilities

Terry Moody

This chapter considers the development of national and local policies for pupils with visual disabilities. Terry Moody outlines the system of provision which became established after the second war, within which special schools predominated, and which continues to the present. Against this background, he assesses recent pressures for change and the response of the policy-makers and providers. He focuses on the role of central government and the voluntary societies. The chapter concludes with a critique of recent attempts by the DES to produce a co-ordinated plan at national and regional level. Terry Moody argues that these attempts have failed to link up provision in ordinary and special schools; instead, their main consequence is a costly and inappropriate reorganization of the special school sector.

Introduction

The Warnock Report (DES 1978) deliberately refrained from attempting to distinguish between the different special educational needs arising from different specific disabilities. No doubt this was a useful device: it enabled the committee to develop general principles for identifying and attempting to provide for special educational needs across the board; to avoid getting diverted into the minutiae of provision for particular groups, and to emphasize that classification can obscure individual diversity.

Nonetheless, we need to plan provision for meeting special educational needs rather than relying on ad hoc arrangements for each individual case as and when it arises. For this reason we need to know what kinds of needs will arise in the future and on what scale; thus, identification of particular disabilities or, combinations of disabilities, and of the special educational needs which they imply seems to be essential. (Perhaps this is more clear-cut with regard to visual disability where, although individual visual capacity varies very widely there are clearly identifiable material resources more or less specific to pupils with visual disabilities which are required. These include visual aids, tactile and auditory equipment and specific skills in the teaching of braille, mobility, and the use of residual vision.)

A possible classification of the kinds of special educational needs which arise in relation to pupils with visual disabilities is as follows. Firstly, the mechanics of the learning process (narrowly defined) are normally very largely dependent on visual methods so that pupils with visual disabilities require resources either to enhance or provide substitutes for their limited visual capacity.

Secondly, although this problem is not nearly as important as is sometimes assumed, some parts of the curriculum are dependent on vision in such a way that the subject matter may need to be substantially modified or substituted in teaching some pupils with visual disabilities. Art and physical education are obvious examples, but in almost all other subjects the content of the subject as distinct from the techniques by which it is communicated need not, and should not, be different for pupils with visual disabilities than for normally sighted pupils. Although the number of topics studied by ordinary children which are not appropriate for pupils with visual disabilities is thus very small, it may be the case that their rate of progress may differ at some stages of education from that of sighted pupils either because of the need to spend time acquiring specific skills such as braille, or because the onset of visual disability interrupts a child's schooling. There is thus a need for flexibility. It is sometimes further asserted that with pupils with visual disabilities necessarily lag behind their sighted peers in learning. There seems to be no evidence for such an assertion which cannot also be explained by the proposition that special schools, in which most children with visual disabilities in this country have received their education, set their own pace, and are not subjected to the challenge of comparison with ordinary schools.

Thirdly, the educational process more broadly conceived will be influenced by the way in which visual disability affects social interaction. Correspondingly, there is a need in providing educational facilities for pupils with visual disabilities to look to the development of social skills as well as to some of the practical skills of everyday living such as mobility. Finally, visual disabilities will give rise to the need for specific attention to medical and pastoral care within the educational context.

It follows from the above that the special educational needs of pupils with visual disabilities imply a substantial input of resources including special equipment and materials, specialized teaching skills and access to medical resources, but it is important to emphasize that young people with visual disabilities have both the capacity and the right to enjoy access to the same range and quality of educational opportunities as their peers.

The ascendancy of the special schools

The period between 1945 and the beginning of the 1970s saw the development of a pattern of provision for pupils with visual disabilities in which special schools were overwhelmingly predominant. Although this was not necessarily an intended consequence of legislation, developments following the 1944 Education Act consolidated the presumption in favour of special schooling which had been developing, but had by no means become universal, in the pre-war period. In particular, additional schools for partially sighted children were established, particularly in England and Wales, and in Scotland the last remaining scheme of integrated provision in ordinary schools, which had flourished in Glasgow before the war, was replaced by separate special school provision. By the time of the Vernon Committee's deliberations (DES 1972) a pattern of provision seemed firmly established in which the overwhelming majority of pupils with visual disabilities for whom special provision was made were educated in separate special schools.

Although in recent years there have been strong pressures for change, and important steps have been taken in the direction of more provision in ordinary schools, the structure of special school provision itself had not changed greatly as we entered the 1980s, from that which was established in the 50s and 60s. Thus it would be useful to review some of the main features of this special school system during this period.

Individual schools for pupils with visual disabilities vary widely depending not only on age range of pupils, degree of visual disability catered for and size, but also on history and local circumstances. A number of general observations can be made. The great majority of schools for the blind were, and are in the non-maintained sector, run by voluntary bodies, although there is a larger number of maintained schools for the partially sighted. All of the schools are small or very small in terms of pupil numbers as compared with the general run of ordinary schools, especially at the secondary level. They are also located geographically in a way which often reflects the exigencies of history, rather than current require-ments, giving rise to regional imbalances in the distribution of provision. Some schools are remote from major population centres.

All of the schools for the blind and some of those for the partially sighted were, and remain residential, so that the great majority of blind children and a substantial proportion of the partially sighted were boarding pupils (42 per cent in England and Wales at the time of Vernon with a gradual decline thereafter). This was an inevitable feature of special school provision given the relatively small overall numbers of pupils, but to some extent the need for boarding provision was exacerbated by the uneven geographical distribution of schools and the remote location of some.

Selection at 11-plus has characterized the special school system for blind children in England and Wales, with the two single-sex grammar schools at Worcester (boys) and Chorleywood (girls) being the only blind schools providing a substantial range of 'O' and 'A' level opportunities. There has also been an element of 11-plus selection for partially sighted children, with Exhall Grange School in Coventry operating a selective national intake together with a non-selective intake from the region. In Scotland, 11-plus selection is generally absent though pupils occasionally attend the English selective schools.

The Vernon Committee also drew attention to the prevalence of separate special school provision for blind and for partially sighted children, with only 2 out of 39 schools at the time in England and Wales catering for both groups. Formally, this pattern continued largely unchanged into the 1980s though there was increasing recognition of the need for flexibility in practice, so that by the early 80s it could be claimed that, 'the rigid barrier between schools which catered for blind pupils, and schools which catered for partially-sighted children has begun to crumble' (DES 1984, para. 7). No doubt this was partly a response by schools to falling pupil numbers, but it may also reflect a recognition of the arbitrariness of the dividing line between the two groups, the lack of corre-spondence between medical categories and educational need, and the increased availability of visual aids and techniques of training in the use of residual vision which enable some children to make some use of visual methods.

Finally, all-age provision, as distinct from a clear differentiation between primary and secondary schools, has been a dominant pattern amongst schools for the partially sighted, though not to the same extent among schools for the blind, at least in England and Wales. Again, relatively small pupil numbers have militated in this direction, in spite of trends in the remainder of the education system.

Pressures for change

We can identify a number of developments since around 1970 indicating the need for changes in policy. Some adjustments have been made gradually over the intervening period, others are currently in hand, and I consider later to what extent this is a sufficient response. Here I will look at the underlying pressures for change arising partly from the number of pupils and the range of disabilities to be catered for, partly from changes in attitudes and expectations, and partly from the need to deploy scarce resources, and the changing opportunities and constraints arising from technological developments.

DEMOGRAPHIC AND MEDICAL FACTORS

Over recent years demographic trends for the population as a whole, and medical developments affecting both the survival of children with disabilities and the prevention and treatment of visual disability, have combined to affect very substantially the numbers of children with visual disabilities, the type and severity of visual disabilities, and the incidence of additional disabilities amongst them. These changes have important implications for special educational provision. Both a decline in the school age population generally and a decreased incidence of visual disability within that population have contributed to a substantial fall amongst those whose main disability is visual.

At the time of the Vernon Report in 1972, the numbers of school-age blind and partially sighted children in England and Wales were 1,207 and 2,338 respectively giving prevalence rates per ten thousand of the school population of 1.37 and 2.66. By 1981, the figures had fallen to 975 blind and 2,098 partially sighted, i.e. prevalence rates of 1.12 and 2.41. Projections for 1987 (DES 1984) based on English figures only, suggest a further fall in prevalence rates to 0.90 for blind and 2.10 for partially sighted children. These figures exclude a substantial number of school-age children who have a visual disability, but who are not classified under this heading for educational purposes because they attend special schools providing mainly for other categories of pupil, particularly schools for children categorized as having severe learning difficulties. Data are not readily available from which to identify the trend over time in the numbers of these children, but some indication of the numbers involved may be gained from a study by Colborne Brown and Tobin (1982) who identified 686 children who were 'educationally blind' but had additional disabilities and were placed for the most part in special schools other than for pupils with visual disabilities. Since these figures relate only to those identified as 'educationally blind', we must asume that there are a substantial number of other children in these special schools with needs arising from a lesser degree of visual disability.

We should also note the increase in the incidence of additional disabilities amongst children in special schools for pupils with visual disabilities. Three schools specialize in this area together with the RNIB's Sunshine Homes which take pre-school age multiply handicapped children. The numbers here have not fallen in line with those for the visually disabled school population generally. But there has also been a marked and widely recognized increase in the numbers of (less severely) additionally disabled children in the remaining schools for pupils with visual disabilities. Again, figures enabling us to measure the increase are not available on a consistent basis, but a recent study by Westwood (1983) identified 452 children with additional disabilities out of a population of 895 children in 19 residential schools for children with visual disabilities in England, giving an incidence of just over 50 per cent.

The pattern that emerges therefore is one in which special schools for pupils with visual disabilities (other than those providing specifically for those with additional disabilities) have had to face a substantial decline in numbers. This seems likely to continue in the future and is reinforced, as we shall see, by increased integration into ordinary schools, associated however with an increasing incidence of additional disabilities which has reached a level sufficient to have major policy implications. Meanwhile we have evidence of a relatively large number of children with a visual disability, located in other kinds of special schools, for whom the input from the visual disability sector of education has been almost non-existent in the past. This raises important questions about how best to respond to their needs in the future. On the face of it, the special schools, with their increasing experience of provision for children with more than one handicap, might be a source of expertise and resources which could be directed towards this need, provided suitable arrangements for co-ordinating and financing such provision could be found.

ATTITUDES TO INTEGRATION

The proposition that educational provision for children with visual disabilities should be integrated with that for their normally sighted peers by their being educated together in ordinary schools has a history which goes back at least to the end of the nineteenth century (Jamieson, Parlett and Pocklington 1977). As we have seen, the post-war period saw the consolidation of a system of provision in which virtually all blind children and the great majority of partially sighted children for whom any special provision was made, were educated in separate special schools. It is against this background that recent debate concerning the desirability and practicability of ordinary school provision has taken place. At the same time there is, of course, a broader context, which is the enormously increased concern in recent years with the integration of all people with disabilities into the life of the community as a whole. In such an approach the scheme of educational provision is of crucial importance, not least in that it influences the formation of those attitudes towards each other on the part of people with disabilities and others which crucially affect the prospects for integration in other areas of life.

There had been renewed interest in integrating children with visual disabilities into ordinary schools prior to the deliberations of the Vernon Committee, but the report triggered off a substantial debate on the integration issue. The participants included people with visual disabilities and their organizations, special schools and voluntary bodies involved in education, such as the RNIB, and those engaged in the slowly increasing number of integration schemes. I shall not review the integration debate here in full, but some of the principal arguments are mentioned below. For further details, see DES (1972), NFBUK and ABAPSTAS (1973), Low (1983).

Consistent and closely argued support for the adoption of a large scale programme of integrated education comes from two organizations of people with visual disabilities – the National Federation of the Blind in the United Kingdom, and the Association of Blind and Partially Sighted Teachers and Students (NFBUK and ABAPSTA S 1973, 1980, 1982). They argue that integrated education is both desirable and practicable and propose a particular model of supported integration based on 'units' or 'resource centres' to be established on a permanent basis in selected ordinary schools.

The main advantages of a system of education in ordinary schools are the following. First, supported integration into ordinary schools teaches children with visual disabilities to grow up naturally as part of the normally sighted community of which they would wish, and need, to be a part in later life, and likewise engenders in other children, their teachers and parents, an appreciation and understanding of people with visual disabilities and their capacity to play a full part in the life of the school and the community. Second, it enables far more children to live at home and attend school on a daily basis than is possible with special schooling. Third, it provides a much more challenging and stimulating educational experience than can be offered in the inevitably more self-contained and inward-looking special schools, and, in particular, offers the only viable way of providing children with visual disabilities with a fully comprehensive secondary education.

The particular model of integrated provision advocated by the NFBUK and ABAPSTAS involves resource centres (including specially qualified teaching staff as well as equipment and materials) which are located in *selected* ordinary schools, each of which would be permanently geared up to teach (mostly in its ordinary classes) a number of blind and partially-sighted pupils. It aims to strike a balance between the objective that the great majority of children should live at home, and the danger that if each individual attends her/his neighbourhood school, specialized resources would be spread too thinly and schools would not have the opportunity to develop amongst their ordinary teachers the expertise and commitment that the permanently established resource centres would seek to engender. One example of the model is the provision at Castlecroft and Smestow Schools in Wolverhampton, briefly described in Chapter 9 of this volume.

Others argue in favour of provision in special schools, at least for a substantial number of children with visual disabilities (RNIB 1977). They fear a lack of adequate specialized resources and of commitment in ordinary schools, and that individual children might either be 'swamped' or over-protected there. They also argue, perhaps paradoxically, that special schools provide support and protection within which children with visual disabilities will develop the skills and attainments, and the sense of independence which will enable them to integrate into the community after they leave school. For some comments on the 'ideology' of segregated special education, see Low (1983).

Emphasis is also placed on the increased preoccupation within special schools with the problems of children with additional disabilities, but it should be noted that while this may be a reasonable argument for the continued important role of special schools, it might also imply that they should recognize the priority to be given to multiply-handicapped children, and encourage the integration into ordinary schools of those without severe additional disabilities.

The above arguments in favour of special schooling are to be found particularly amongst those involved with the special schools themselves, and providers such as the RNIB. Some people with visual disabilities also have reservations about integration, for example, the National League of the Blind and Disabled, and the Old Pupils Associations of the two selective grammar schools. As far as parents are concerned, there is some indication that, not surprisingly, parents favour the provision with which they are most familiar, at least so long as there has been *some* special provision made for their children's special needs. However, a survey in Scotland suggests that among parents who might have preferred alternative provision, there was some inclination to support the idea of units attached to ordinary schools (Buultjens 1986).

The evidence of the successful operation of well-planned integration schemes, such as those in Wolverhampton, seems likely to stimulate demand for more such opportunities. At a time when parents are being promised a greater say in educational provision, policymakers are likely to find themselves under increased pressure to make a reality of parental choice, by offering integrated provision in many more parts of the country than at present.

In spite of reservations, there can be little doubt that the climate of opinion has swung strongly in favour of integration in general, and the integrated education of people with visual disabilities in particular during the past two decades. One can perhaps characterize the outcome of the debate so far by noting that many of the critics of integration start from the assumption that it will be unplanned, piecemeal and under-resourced, whereas proponents of 'supported integration' have demonstrated the very great advantages of properly resourced and planned ordinary school provision. It is, of course, proper to draw attention to the danger that integration might be done badly or on the cheap, but perhaps the most effective way of ensuring that this does not happen would prove to be the adoption of a more positive policy of favouring good integrated practice, rather than the more negative stance. Interestingly, the Royal National Institute for the Blind has adopted an increasingly positive stance towards integration in recent years as we shall see below.

RESOURCES

Over the past decade, in particular, education authorities have been subject to increasingly stringent financial constraints which seems certain to impinge on decisions concerning special educational provision, including that for children with visual disabilities, and, in particular, on the choice between special and ordinary schooling. But such financial considerations interact in a complex way with the changes noted above in the incidence of disability and the pressure for change in methods of provision. All are agreed that integration must not be thought of as 'a cheap option'; yet, if special school provision has to include residential accommodation, as is the case for most blind and many partially sighted children, the question must arise whether resources could not be better directed towards specifically educational purposes by redeploying them in ordinary schools nearer to children's homes.

Meanwhile, the combined effect of falling roles in ordinary schools, and the more rapid decline in the numbers of children with visual disabilities in the special school system, is likely to improve the relative cost position of properly supported integration as compared with special schooling. This is because there is, inevitably, some continuing spare capacity (in physical terms at the very least) in ordinary schools, which reduces the marginal cost of accepting additional pupils from the special school system. In the special schools, many of which are in the non-maintained sector, the spreading of fixed costs over fewer pupils, plus the increased costs of providing adequately for more children with additional disabilities, means that very high fees must be charged to education authorities.

The costs of properly supported integration into ordinary schools depend to an important extent on how resources are deployed. As I indicated earlier the education of children with severe visual disabilities requires substantial expenditure. This is one strong argument for resource centres in selected ordinary schools rather than attempting provision on an individual basis in the child's neighbourhood school – although this is certainly feasible for the pupils with less severe visual disabilities (see, for example, Swann 1987). Some indication of the levels of staffing and other resources required for a good integrating resource centre are given in NFBUK and ABAPSTAS 1982. Where such resources are shared within an ordinary school by a significant number of pupils with visual disabilities, it seems unlikely that the cost per child could be as much as that of residential special schooling, given that the special school itself must provide the same facilities, plus residential accommodation, while also attempting to match the full range of ordinary educational facilities to which the children in ordinary schools will have access.

We may conclude that pressure on resources ought not to be seen as a constraint on the response of the education system to demands for integrated provision; indeed some LEAs may have been stimulated by financial pressure into looking at alternatives to special schools. However, it will be important to resist any tendency for inadequately supported integration arising either from financial constraints or from lack of proper planning, and there is a need for additional assistance with the set up costs for new schemes of integration.

Meanwhile there are a number of other areas where additional resources need to be mobilized. These include much more advice and support for parents, especially at the pre-school stage, and more provision for children with additional disabilities, both to meet the increased costs likely to be encountered in special schools for pupils with visual disabilities and in making provision for children with a visual disability currently placed in other special schools.

TECHNOLOGY

Technological developments and their applications can affect methods of teaching and learning, as well as the cost and practicability of different forms of organization. For example, Jamieson, Parlett and Pocklington (1977) noted that the triumph of braille over media such as raised print reinforced the development of separate special schooling for the blind, since the use of braille required special tuition, and it could not easily be shared by blind and sighted children and non-specialist teachers.

Braille is still, and should remain, a crucially important medium for the education of blind children, but recent technological developments have both facilitated the use of other media complementary to braille, and made the use of braille less isolating within the ordinary school classroom. Thus, on the one hand, access to information for pupils with visual disabilities is greatly facilitated by cheap and easy-to-operate tape-recording facilities, and, except for the small minority with almost no remaining sight, by a range of aids to low vision including close-circuit television devices. On the other hand, micro-computers have led to the development of systems for translating between braille and ordinary print in both directions, so that, for example, input from a braille keyboard can generate ordinary print output, or braille copy can be generated from a conventional keyboard by someone with no knowledge of the braille code; see Chapter 9 of this volume.

Such technological developments greatly reduce the extent to which the mechanics of the learning process employed with pupils with visual disabilities inhibits their capacity to interact with sighted peers and non-specialist teachers in the ordinary school. Of course, they still require specialized teaching of braille codes and of other skills and techniques, but their ability to deploy them, once acquired, in the ordinary school classroom is undoubtedly enhanced.

It follows that the need to live with this technology, and to use it in communicating with and working alongside sighted people, reinforces the other pressures for a shift towards ordinary school provision.

The policy response

This section looks at the way in which education policy for pupils with visual disabilities has developed since the early 1970s in response to pressures for change such as those outlined above.

In the 1970s central government commissioned two major reports from the Vernon Committee (1972) and the Warnock Committee (1978). The central issue with which they had to grapple was integration. Almost all of the major problems to which they addressed themselves depend for their solutions on the strategy adopted towards integration.

The Vernon Committee held back from a wholehearted commitment to integration into ordinary schools, contenting itself with recommending 'further systematic experiments' within the context of a national plan. This approach was severely criticized in some quarters (NFBUK and ABAPSTAS 1973) not least because it was argued that provision in separate special schools *necessarily* implied or strongly reinforced a number of features of the system about which the committee were unhappy, such as children living away from home from the age of 5, schools being too small to provide an appropriate range of opportunities, 11-plus selection, all-age schools, and a generally undemanding and inward-looking approach within special schools.

The Warnock Rerport recognized integration as 'the central contemporary issue in special education' (para. 7.1) and offered a wealth of recommendations designed to extend the concept of special educational needs and the scope of special education, and to integrate such provision with the mainstream of education.

However, the committee's strategy of refraining for the most part from making explicit recommendations for specific categories of handicap can be criticized. In the first place, the special educational needs of children with visual disabilities call in the main for specific kinds of human and material resources. Thus the implementation of a strategy for maximum integration could, in the case of blind and partially sighted children, have been facilitated by explicit recommendations about the kinds of resources which should be provided within integrating ordinary schools, and how these could be most effectively deployed.

A second but related problem is that in the absence of any clear indication to the contrary in the report, it might be inferred that blind children in particular fall into that category of children with 'severe or complex physical, sensory or intellectual disabilities' (para. 6.10) for whom special schooling might be required. A more explicit specification of the special educational needs of children with visual disabilities and the appropriate kinds of provision for those needs, would have pre-empted any tendency for such an interpretation.

Implementation of the kind of strategy developed by the Warnock Committee was dependent upon a combination of new laws, additional resources, and planning. The 1981 Education Act (and corresponding legislation in Scotland) included a limited presumption in favour of special educational provision in ordinary schools which, however, represented a retreat relative to the (never-activated) provisions of Section 10 of the 1976 Act. Moreover, the preceding White Paper *Special Needs in Education* (DES 1980) gave no indication that increased resources would be directed towards educational provision. Nor has there been subsequently the commitment of additional resources to special education which would be necessary to implement many of the general recommendations of the Warnock Committee.

A 'national plan' for the education of pupils with visual disabilities envisaged by the Vernon Committee seemed to be in prospect when, in 1982, the DES invited the LEAs in England to convene regional conferences to formulate comprehensive regional plans covering developments up to 1986–87, which would be incorporated into a national plan by the DES. Conferences generally included representatives of LEAs, special schools, voluntary bodies providing special education, organizations of those with visual disabilities and other specialists in the field.

The outcome of this process was the publication in 1984 of the *Secretary of State's Proposals for Future Provision in Special Schools for Children with Visual Handicaps* (DES 1984). Far from being a comprehensive national plan, the proposals were essentially for a reorganization of special school provision to take account of the need for some streamlining of the system as a result of declining numbers of pupils and the existing regional imbalance. It was proposed that all-age provision should cease; the education of blind and partially sighted children in the same special school was given qualified support.

The proposals were criticized (especially by the NFBUK and ABAPSTAS 1984) firstly, for failing to bring together the planning of future provision in special and ordinary schools. It was argued that following the 1981 Education Act, planning of special schools should anticipate much lower numbers due to the swing to education in ordinary schools. At the same time even the pattern of special schooling assumed in the proposals would involve schools too small in terms of pupil numbers to allow them to meet the Secretary of State's belief that, 'special schools for the visually handicapped should seek to offer to their pupils a curriculum which matches up to what is offered in ordinary schools' (DES 1984, para. 12). Minimum rolls were to be 30 pupils for a primary and 80 for a secondary school and a number of the schools were projected to be at or below these proposed minima.

The proposals also envisaged the continuation of 11-plus selection and the merger, (now scheduled for 1987), of the grammar schools for the blind at Worcester and Chorleywood. Critics of the merger and of continued 11-plus selection have doubted whether even a merged grammar school will maintain a sufficient intake of academically able pupils given the falling numbers of blind children generally, the increased incidence of additional handicap and the likelihood that able pupils will be regarded as particularly suited to integration. At the same time, the large-scale investment of resources in such a merger pre-empts future decisions about the pattern of provision and may jeopardize standards in the rest of the secondary special schools, while the principle of selection is as unsatisfactory in the education of pupils with disabilities as it is with other children. Perhaps the most important criticism of the planning process so far is the failure of central government to give a lead in promoting and co-ordinating schemes of integration on the ground. The efficient use of resources in providing for successful integration requires planning ahead. Moreover, the idea of a choice of educational facilities is without meaning if integrating facilities are not in existence in a wide range of localities in advance of the choice being offered. Ad hoc individual integration is inefficient in most cases, except where the degree of visual disability is slight, because resources are spread too thinly and there is likely to be an absence of continuity and commitment on the part of the ordinary schools concerned.

Nonetheless, the extent to which education authorities are implementing integration has increased significantly during the 1980s, with arrangements varying between well resourced provision for groups of blind and partially sighted children in selected ordinary schools to schemes depending on peripatetic support sometimes for partially-sighted children only. A more comprehensive approach currently under consideration in the Inner London Education Authority arises from the recommendations of the Fish Report (ILEA 1985) with its proposals for comprehensive provision for special educational needs within ordinary schools and colleges as well as the much greater involvement of people with disabilities themselves in educational provision and policy-making. Meanwhile, in the non-maintained sector, the Royal National Institute for the Blind has recently moved to a much more positive stance towards integration, although maintaining its commitment to the special schools for which it is responsible, including the selective grammar school provision. The RNIB has, for long, maintained its support for integration in principle, but in the early 80s the institute began to acknowledge a lack of practical implementation of this commitment and to take steps to fill this gap, initially by organizing seminars in 1983–84 to consider how the Institute could help education authorities involved in integration. The Institute subsequently formed an integration advisory group, carried out a survey of different kinds of provision for pupils with visual disabilities by education authorities throughout Britain, and is currently developing a package of practical measures to assist education authorities, with a shift in emphasis within its education advisory service towards support for integration.

Conclusions

Low (1983) has referred to existing educational provision for pupils with visual disabilities as being divided between, on the one hand, an 'official, comparatively self-contained, blind education system' in the special schools, and on the other hand, a more diffuse set of arrangements for an almost equal number of children, some of whom are placed in ordinary schools with varying degrees of support, while a much larger number whose visual disability is not regarded as their main handicap are placed in special schools and in other provision outside the visual disability sector.

In the special school sector, a degree of insulation from the mainstream of the educational system combined with small numbers of pupils and hence excessively small school size, has led to the retention of some features which much of the mainstream of education has rejected, such as 11-plus selection and all-age provision. Schools have been unable, generally, to match the range and standard of curriculum provision available in good ordinary schools. At the same time there is, not surprisingly, strong resistance to change, in particular to systematic moves towards integration into ordinary schools, especially within the special schools themselves and on the part of the voluntary bodies involved.

Apart from the problem of inertia and retrenchment in the special schools, the response of policy-makers to the pressures for change in the system is inhibited by the division of responsibilities between central government, LEAs and the voluntary sector. This partly explains the lack of progress in regional and national planning of provision. The need for such planning is clear, including a co-ordinated programme of integration schemes in different parts of the country, to make a reality of the idea of choice over a range of different types of provision. However, the DES's response so far has been to confine specific proposals to the rationalizing of special schools. Even here, the rationalization process will have to go somewhat further than is envisaged in the DES proposals if the remaining special schools are to continue to be viable in the face of the likely development of integration. At the same time much more attention should be paid to the changing role and functions which special schools should take on board (see the Warnock Report para. 8.18 and NFBUK and ABAPSTAS 1984). Finally, much more attention and considerably increased resources should be devoted to pupils with visual disabilities who have other disabilities as well, not only by recognizing the need for all the special schools for pupils with visual disabilities to concentrate their efforts much more in this area, but also by devising ways of ensuring an input from the visual disability sector into provision for these children wherever they are.

References

Buultjens, M. 1986. 'Parental perceptions of special educational provision for the visually impaired', *British Journal of Visual Impairment*, 4(2), pp. 65–68.

Colborne Brown, M. S. and Tobin, M. J. 1982. 'Integration of the educationally blind: numbers and placements', *New Beacon*, 66, pp. 113–117.

Department of Education and Science (DES) 1972. *The Education of the Visually Handicapped* (The Vernon Report), London, HMSO.

Department of Education and Science (DES) 1978. *Special Educational Needs* (The Warnock Report), London, HMSO.

Department of Education and Science (DES) 1980. *Special Needs in Education*, London, HMSO.

Department of Education and Science (DES) 1984. *Proposals for Future Provision in Special Schools for Children with Visual Handicaps*, London, DES.

Inner London Education Authority (ILEA) 1985. *Educational Opportunities for All?* (The Fish Report), London, ILEA.

Jamieson, M., Parlett, M. and Pocklington, K. 1977. *Towards Integration: a study of blind and partially sighted children in ordinary schools*, Windsor, NFER.

Low, C. 1983. 'Integrating the visually handicapped', in Booth, T. and Potts, P. (eds), *Integrating Special Education*, Oxford, Basil Blackwell.

National Federation of the Blind in the UK and Association of Blind and Partially Sighted Teachers and Students 1973. *Educational Provision for the Visually Handicapped: Comments on the Vernon Report*.

National Federation of the Blind in the UK and Association of Blind and Partially Sighted Teachers and Students 1980. *Response to Special Educational Needs: Comments on the Warnock Report*.

National Federation of the Blind in the UK and Association of Blind and Partially Sighted Teachers and Students 1982. *Regional Planning of Educational Provision for Visually Handicapped Children*.

National Federation of the Blind in the UK and Association of Blind and Partially Sighted Teachers and Students 1984. *Response to the Secretary of State's Proposals for Future Provision in Special Schools for Children with Visual Handicaps*.

Royal National Institute for the Blind (RNIB) 1977. *Response to the Consultative Document on the Implementation of Section 10 of the Education Act 1976*, London, RNIB.

Swann, W. 1987. 'Support for Mark: the learning experience of a six year old with partial sight', in Booth, T., Potts, P. and Swann, W. (eds), *Preventing Difficulties in Learning*, Oxford, Basil Blackwell.

Westwood, P. N. 1983. *The Future of Residential Special Schools for the Visually Handicapped in England*, Birmingham University, unpublished report.

SECTION
THREE

Liberty, Equality and Disability

22   Just waking up: the experience of epilepsy
Jenny Corbett

Jenny Corbett recounts the experience of the emergence and effects of her son Richard's epilepsy. Richard was ten when he had his first epileptic fit. He returned to his ordinary school shortly afterwards, and has continued to lead a full and active life ever since. The family's determination to treat epilepsy as an ordinary, if unwelcome, part of their lives was greatly helped by the sensible, supportive work of their paediatrician. No one handicapped Richard because of his epilepsy.

I was going up to the bedroom at ten thirty, on that March evening. It had been a surprisingly hot day and I felt physically tired. I walked past the open door of Richard's bedroom on my way to the bathroom and then immediately turned round. He was making extraordinary gargling noises and his limbs were flailing around. I stood transfixed, watching him in the throes of a classic *grand mal* fit. He had never, to my knowledge, had a fit before and I was horrified to watch his body struggling beyond control while he remained unconscious. In his first ten years Richard had experienced measles, chicken pox, mumps and endless sore throats but I had never seen him having anything as frightening as a fit. I touched his shoulder and spoke to him, willing him to recover. As he continued to shake and gargle, still unconscious, I called my husband, Mike, and we rang for the GP. It was a Sunday night and I remember feeling that accidents and domestic disasters always seemed to occur on Sunday when help was often unobtainable. Fortunately there was a GP on duty who came to the house within fifteen minutes. In the intervening period Richard had been violently sick and had soaked the bed in urine, both common features of a *grand mal* fit.

When the doctor arrived I told him that I thought Richard was having a *grand mal* fit which seemed to be on one side only, as his violent movement was restricted to one whole side of his body from his face to his feet, while the other side seemed rigid. He looked like someone who was having a stroke. The doctor was unwilling to commit himself and asked about earlier signs of sickness or fever, perhaps brought on by the warm weather. He implied that this could be a febrile convulsion and nothing to be too concerned about, but I knew that febrile convulsions were common in infants, not in ten-year olds, and I had seen pupils at the special school I taught at have *grand mal* fits similar to Richard's. I understood that the doctor did not want to distress us and wished in some respects that I was ignorant of the area and could have dissociated my experience of epilepsy in severely brain damaged children from the experience we were having with my son. Watching his shaking, unconscious body, I could not believe he would come through the experience without critical intellectual impairment.

When he arrived at the hospital, after a difficult journey which involved Mike and our neighbour, Denis, dragging Richard's heavy body onto the back seat of the car and then humping him up the stairs to the children's ward, he was still

249

unconscious and shaking violently, three quarters of an hour after I found him. The GP had suggested that we took him immediately, rather than wait for an ambulance, as speed was essential. Mike stayed in hospital with Richard as I had to wait at home with our younger son who was sleeping on, oblivious of the drama. The fit was not brought under control for another half an hour. It was 2 a.m. by this time and the locum on duty had given *diazepam* to arrest the fit, followed immediately by a lumbar puncture to test for meningitis. The discomfort of this treatment coincided with Richard's regaining consciousness, and he howled in pain. Mike had to stand by powerless to help while he heard Richard screaming and calling for us. Watching your child in extreme pain and distress is terrible.

In the first two days after his fit, Richard stayed in bed in the hospital ward and the pain of the lumbar puncture increased his discomfort which made him cry out and become hysterical in his confusion. The approach from the paediatrician, Dr Morgan, was practical and direct from the outset: 'Now, that's quite enough of that fuss. Sit up on your pillows and look at the books your Mum's brought you'.

She always talked to Richard, not to us about him. She was firm and sensible with him, encouraging him to return to a normal routine as soon as possible. She was critical of the level of drugs used to get him out of the fit, as she always used the lowest drug level required. She explained the prognosis carefully to us, without being patronizing or evasive. She suspected that he had idiopathic epilepsy, which has no demonstrable pathological cause. She also suggested, from our description, that his epilepsy was focused in one side of the brain only. Her objective now was to find the correct dose of the appropriate drug to prevent the recurrence of fits.

I had watched Richard anxiously to perceive the impact of *status epilepticus*, which prolonged and continuous *grand mal* epilepsy is called. I had heard from consultation with nursing staff at the special school that this condition was potentially very dangerous and could lead to permanent brain damage and paralysis. Dr Morgan reassured me that Richard would not be permanently brain damaged as a result of his prolonged fit, but was just in a tired and hysterical state after the fright and discomfort. I had felt very frightened and vulnerable that night and was anxious to receive professional support and guidance. It is quite different to be a rational, detached professional in a special school, advising parents on the treatment of their children, and to be the parent feeling overwhelmed by unforeseen circumstances. The treatment we experienced from the medical profession was most supportive and helpful. The GP who came out late on that Sunday night was by Richard's hospital bedside by nine o'clock on Monday morning to find out how he was progressing. His evident concern, beyond the call of duty, and Dr Morgan's consistent practical reassurance, made me realize how grateful one feels as a parent when professionals show care and consideration.

The experience of electroencephalography was a distressing one for Richard although it was not painful. It took place four days after his fit, when he should have been well over the ordeal, but the high level of drugs which he had received had left him with a painful headache and some unsteadiness. It took almost fifteen minutes to attach all the wires to his head with a gel-like substance and he grew restless and anxious during this time, despite gentle reassurance from the doctor who explained what the procedure would be. I was able to stay with Richard throughout the half-hour process and chat to him while he lay on the couch with the electroencephalogram churning out sheets of scribbles which recorded his brain waves. I could see irregular patterns within the lines which ran across the sheets of paper but we were told that it would need thorough assessment by an expert to confirm a diagnosis from the results. Confirmation of his lack of usual vigour was Richard's inability to finish a hamburger, chips and milk shake in the cafe on the way home – a sure sign that the headache and dizziness were debilitating him.

Despite the evident discomfort which Richard had felt, I was pleased to have been able to experience this medical technique which could aid diagnosis and indicate appropriate treatment. Before such facilities were available, epilepsy was more of a mystery disease, ill-understood and untreated. While there is criticism of the over-use of drugs in the treatment of epilepsy, and the adverse side-effects of some drugs, it has to be remembered that when epilepsy was untreated and misunderstood, fear and stigma of those 'possessed by the devil' persisted. While drugs can be unsatisfactory and produce additional complications, they are subject to constant evaluation and have been modified considerably over the last ten years to eliminate adverse effects and to suit the individual. The great benefit of the electoencephalogram is that it can indicate exactly what type of epilepsy is effecting the individual and can locate the specific area of the brain which is being affected.

Richard's type of local epilepsy is called *benign focal epilepsy of childhood* or *Rolandic epilepsy*, as the focus is adjacent to the Rolandic fissure in the brain. The chief characteristics are: onset at age seven to ten: males outnumbering females; fits occurring at night when the child is asleep in most instances. During a fit the head and eyes may briefly turn away from the side of the EEG abnormality, then turn back to the side of the abnormality, followed by clonic jerking of that side. The EEG abnormalities increase during sleep. Fits which occur during the day usually present with twitching on one side of the face and may show twitching of a limb on the opposite side. The face and tongue may feel numb on one side. The child is usually unable to speak for a while although aware of what others say. The typical EEG shows spike discharges in the lower Rolandic (central) area. This type of epilepsy is thought to be inherited and is not associated with brain pathology. The prognosis is very good: fits become less likely in later teens. If behaviour problems develop they are likely to be the consequence of other people's attitudes and not brain damage. Response to the drug prescribed, *carbamazepine*, is generally excellent, and allows for an unrestricted way of life.

A week after Richard had had his massive fit, he was back at school. Whilst I felt anxious at his early return to school, he seemed quite happy and eager to get into routine. Teachers knew of his fit and the diagnosis of epilepsy and were alert to any signs of his having another fit, although these were most likely to occur at night. During the early weeks back at school we were working with Dr Morgan to find the correct dose of *carbamazepine*. One morning Richard came into our bedroom pointing to his face. He was aware that one side of his body was in spasm while the other was rigid. Fully conscious, he sat on the bed until the twitching stopped. He was able to walk but could not talk: he knew what we said and what he wanted to say. He later told us that his face and tongue had been numb on one side. Another day he began to shake slightly in school assembly and dropped his hymn book. Whenever we were in the least worried, or when incidents suggested that the dose of *carbamazepine* might need to be increased, we could phone Dr Morgan, our accessible peadiatrician, at work or home, and she would give generously of her time in talking through any problems and explaining what might be useful. She was very opposed to prescribing over-large doses of drugs and preferred to err on the side of caution, adding another half a tablet if he had recorded a slight fit and letting adjustment take a gradual course rather than prescribe heavily from the onset. Her manner and approach to epilepsy had a significant effect on the way we all coped with it as a family. She always talked to Richard about his progress and his condition, making him an active participant in his treatment. Dr Morgan told him that it would help his progress if he took as much exercise as possible, rather than opting out in any way. As he was overweight, she encouraged him to diet sensibly and to take responsibility for his own medication and well-being. He knew he was tired and he should not over-exert himself. She also discouraged his habit of preferring to go to bed late! His disease was not shrouded in mystery nor was it discussed in hushed tones between professionals and parents to the exclusion of the child.

Although he was only ten at the onset, Richard has always been kept informed of his condition by Dr Morgan. Her calm reassurance to him helped us to be equally natural towards his problem and keep it in perspective. I think it was important, in adopting a normal routine, that Richard was a naturally placid, even-tempered child, who tended to take events in his stride. He had been calm in response to other problems in his life and seemed able to cope with epilepsy without fuss. However, we had to accept his inflexible, sometimes tiresome, bedtime routine. After his experience he was uneasy about the process of passing into sleep. To relax he developed a routine which included having the radio turned on low with talking or music as a background, and the bedroom door ajar to a specific angle so that he could see the hall light while lying in his bed. A break from this routine, which perhaps a holiday in another house might entail, would unsettle him. This was a minor effect of his experience and the medication seemed to cause little drowsiness or create difficulty in concentration. He was slow to wake up in the morning – but he always had been!

Another characteristic feature of Richard's personality was his introspection, which meant that he often failed to share thoughts with others. It was not until Dr Morgan asked him the day after his admission to hospital if he had experienced any earlier fits that he agreed that he had had several,

> ... but, as it seemed to happen most mornings as I was coming round after being called to get dressed, I thought it was just waking up. I used to lie there until the twitching had stopped. My face and arm used to feel funny for a few minutes but it went away. I never told anyone as I thought it was just waking up; I didn't know what it was.

It was a surprise to us that Richard had been having nocturnal fits for some time, but was unaware of their significance, and therefore had not thought to tell us. This phlegmatic approach to life, while being maddening to his parents, was probably a great protection from panic and neurosis.

Since we found Richard having that dreadful fit in March 1981, he has progressed very well. After he started on *carbamazepine*, he had several minor fits but as the dose was adjusted he had very few. His last fit was on holiday to Sydney in 1982 where exhaustion after the long journey sent him into a very brief state of semi-consciousness. Since then he has continued to take 200 mg tablets of *carbamazepine* morning and night, dropping the morning dose two years ago. At first I would ask him if he had taken his tablets every night but now, aged fifteen, he has been taking them as a routine without any supervision for some time and it is as much part of bedtime ritual as brushing his teeth. Last year he had a long talk with Dr Morgan as to when he might consider stopping taking tablets altogether. She suggested to him that it might be wise to continue to take the tablets as they had no side effects, rather than risk a recurrence of fits by dropping them during the chemical upheaval of adolescence. He was quite agreeable to this as he found taking his tablets no problem and was eager to learn to drive at seventeen if possible.

This approach was again an example of the way in which Richard was encouraged to be an active participant in his treatment. He chose to continue with medication: it was not chosen for him. His school work was progressing very well and he was coping in a selective grammar school with considerable academic success. It was apparent that the *carbamazepine* had no adverse effect on his cognitive development. He has become more active than before he was diagnosed as having epilepsy: he plays football, cricket and tennis and swims. Apart from the clear danger of swimming alone, there is no physical activity barred to him. His school knows he is on medication for epilepsy but, as he has never had a fit at school, I doubt if many pupils know of his problem. Significantly, it really is not much of a problem for Richard. He accepts it and will talk openly about epilepsy because it is something which he regards as 'just one of those things'. I am convinced that having a paediatrician who took such a practical approach to his needs has enabled Richard to regard epilepsy as a minor inconvenience rather than a tragedy.

I appreciate that Richard has been very lucky in having a form of epilepsy which has proved to respond so well to medication, and that many people with epilepsy are not so fortunate. While it has impinged so slightly on his life, it can create significant problems for other people who have difficulty in treating their epilepsy. In recent months he has been asked twice to attend examination sessions for doctors who are training to become paediatricians. He has visited the hospital in which he spent those first few uncomfortable days after having had his major fit, and has been very successful in answering all the questions which the trainees can find for him to ensure a thorough diagnosis. He entered enthusiastically into the whole procedure (encouraged by the small but useful fee) and was perfectly content to lie on the couch while they examined him and to recall the details of his experiences with epilepsy. It was almost as if he was discussing quite objectively an interesting condition of which he could offer them experience. I feel that it was beneficial for people coming into paediatrics to meet a young person with epilepsy for whom it was no significant problem. One of the most valuable lessons which our excellent Dr Morgan taught us was that the person always came before the label. It seems quite inappropriate to refer to anyone as 'epileptic': they are people first and foremost, who happen to have epilepsy.

23 The B6 Incident: pupil perceptions of integration

David Cropp

This chapter tells a story of political development among a group of adolescents with disabilities and difficulties. These pupils challenged a number of features of school life which, in their view, forced on them a disabled identity which they rejected. Equally important, they did so in a co-ordinated and politically effective manner. But their demands did not attack any fundamental features of the structure of their schooling. The pupils wanted participation on equal terms: they wanted the same rules applied to them as to all others. The did not challenge the rules themselves: indeed, their demands served to reinforce them.

Introduction

We often believe that we can predict accurately the viewpoints of adolescents, particularly those with special needs. The particular incident which I describe in this article tells us about how pupils may define their own needs. It involved thirty-five adolescents aged between eleven and seventeen, all of whom had some form of special educational need, and were placed in the Special Educational Unit attached to Bartley Green School.

The school is a six-form entry, eleven to sixteen comprehensive, though at the time of this description it was completing its final sixth form. When I became Head of Unit, I had to administer to the needs and welfare of forty-seven pupils. The Unit was staffed by five teachers and a nursing ancillary. All Unit pupils were referred through the Special Education Department of Birmingham LEA. The school has a formal catchment area as part of a consortium of local schools, but pupils being admitted to the Unit came from a wider area.

From the start Unit pupils had received part of their education integrated into mainstream classes, each pupil having their own individually designed timetable. Pupils registered within the Unit, and each Unit year had a Unit teacher acting in the role of form teacher.

The Unit was a conversion of the school's original library and staff rooms during the last phase of building on the school site. It is geographically at the heart of the main school building and is therefore not separate nor cut off from the school's physical or social structure. The Unit is not named or labelled but merely links with classrooms at both ends. It consists of a double-sized classroom (the original library), a standard-sized classroom, a half-sized classroom, an office, medical room, staff, boys' and girls' cloakrooms, and an acoustically lined room for speech therapy. Recently, an additional room has been added to accommodate the peripatetic Teacher of the Deaf now attached to the Unit. The number of pupils has risen, and the Unit now caters for up to fifty-five pupils.

One third of the intake have speech and/or language difficulties, one fifth are hearing impaired. In addition the Unit caters for pupils with a variety of physical impairments, including road-traffic accident victims; emotionally and/or physically delicate pupils including those with terminal illnesses; children who have specific learning difficulties, and children who are mildly autistic.

When I became Head of Unit the pupils participated with some degree of success in the school, with decisions on their activities, as traditionally you might expect, being taken by the teaching staff of the Unit.

This, then, is the background to what happened on one particular occasion in the Unit which had a long-lasting influence on the inter-relationships between not only pupils and teachers within the Unit, but also in the way in which the Unit functions as part of the whole-school community. It also raises the wider issue: the nature of any synthetically created or managed adolescent group, and what that group's actual potential for decision-making may be.

The B6 Incident

Shortly after my appointment to the Unit, an open letter signed by some thirty-five or so Unit pupils arrived on my desk requesting a meeting with me. Fortunately the headmaster of the school consented to the meeting taking place. Therefore, it was with some misgivings that, shortly after, in a lunch-hour, I faced these pupils in classroom B6.

SHEEP AND GOATS

Surprisingly, before any points could be raised, the status of those present was challenged by the pupils and all who had not had the courage, as they put it, to sign the letter were ejected from the meeting on the grounds that they had abrogated their right to join in any discussion or decision-making. Those who were most vociferous in their demand to stay were pressured out by the fact that nobody was going to start any meeting of any kind with them present.

GROUND-RULES

Having cleansed the assembly of non-qualifiers, the first pupil-spokesman wanted some clarification of the future of whatever might be decided, recommended, or requested during the meeting.

Unable to predict what was going to appear in the agenda, I stated that all items would be considered seriously, would be dependent on the head's view, and would be implemented if I felt them reasonable and/or possible. The principle of sanctions against those present in the meeting was then raised. I gave an undertaking that none would be invoked, and the meeting proper started.

AGENDA

Given most people's knowledge and expectations of comprehensive schools and their pupils, one might expect there to be demands for derestrictions, relaxations, and freedoms from the school-rule system. What actually came up on the agenda was somewhat different.

All forms in the school are styled according to the year number followed by form teacher initials. Historically, the separate years in the Unit had been allocated the suffix 'G' (thus: 1G, 2G . . . 5G). Agenda Item 1 was a request to change this method of identifying Unit forms, and to adopt the standard main school pattern. Quite reasonably they felt that this would establish anonymity in form group classification.

Not surprisingly, you might think, Agenda Item 2 was the subject of school sanctions and punishments. Their view was somewhat unexpected. It was that Unit pupils shoud be subject to the same system as that meted out to main school pupils. As the school had at that time a well-established report, detention, and corporal punishment system, I asked for an expansion of their reasoning behind this request. They said that if they were seen to be able to avoid the sanction system by reason of being pupils with special needs, then either they were seen as less of a person, or if appropriate the pupil subculture of the school would apportion a suitable substitute at some other time or place to make things 'fair'.

This led to the third point they wished to raise. They felt that all the Unit pupils should be required to present themselves in a school uniform which conformed exactly to the standard as laid down. The fact that in many instances pupils throughout the school did not conform precisely to the standard was not accepted as a legitimate argument by them. Their view was that while recognizing that uniform was in a sense an arbitrary aspect of school life, nevertheless the closer they conformed to it the more likely they were to be assimilated into the school environment as 'just another pupil'.

Agenda Item 4 was based on an established link between the main school and the Unit. During their fifth year a number of main school pupils were, by choice, attached to the Unit, particularly to help the less able or physically handicapped younger pupils, either in class with their work, or with mobility around the school. There seemed to be advantages for both groups, particularly in fostering an awareness of special needs, or so I believed. Without malice, the Unit pupils wished to reject their presence in this arranged side-by-side relationship, firstly because it implied a lack of independence of all Unit pupils, and secondly, as a result, a difference of status within the school. My response that their placement in the Unit was as much to help main school pupils recognize the needs of others cut no ice with the group: status was the key to the rejection of this 'help-link' scheme.

Status and independence were the themes of the fifth area of discussion. There were a number of traditional arrangements which I had inherited, and which seemed to me at first sight somewhat innocuous. But not to them. And as it turned out, they were right. One of the provisions commonly found in special school placements is taxi-transport for those pupils who by reason of distance and/or disability are unable to reach their school within a reasonable time. Some pupils lived close enough to reach school on foot or by public transport. I was now asked to extend the provision of bus passes to whoever thought themselves capable of travelling to school by public transport and could successfully convince their parents. Another arrangement which should change, they felt, concerned school reports. Main school pupils received their school reports unsealed for them to read before taking them home. Unit pupils received their's sealed, as often they had apparently less successful reports to see. Item 6 of the discussion was that this 'sealing' practice should cease, and *they* would decide if they were competent to see their own reports, whether good or bad.

Following this, the seventh area of discussion was more general and concerned their independence within the physical and social environment of the school, with the right to be able to mix freely in and out of school in the same way as every other pupil, including being able, where reasonable, to leave the school premises without escort. Previously, Unit pupils had been given a number of 'safety-privileges', such as having school lunch before the main school 'rush' started. There was now a 'restriction-for-independence' move on their part to have themselves attached to their school year groups. Thus the outward signs of separate identity, however trivial, were to be erased in favour of their being able to create their own identity within the society of the whole school.

Item 8 was based on academic 'access'. They felt they had the right to claim access at all levels and to all subjects available in the school, where they would have been placed by merit and attainment if they had been a main school pupil.

It was at this point that the discussion ended; the main grievances had been given a public hearing. Strangely, there was no demand for either a follow-up meeting, nor for a reporting back session. It was as if the expression of the wishes of the group had been a sufficient action, and the response to their requests would be considered at a different and inaccessible level.

Aftermath

While the demands of the pupils may at first seem to have been fairly mundane, the method of expressing a consensus view was quite radical, particularly when you consider that this was all taking place in a fairly typical comprehensive. Since that meeting there have been a number of evolutionary and natural changes within the Unit, most in those areas which they discussed.

Once the meeting concluded, the head of the school and the staff of the Unit were told the nature of the proceedings. Almost immediately most of the demands were implemented. The forms' numbering system was changed to match main school; in any list of forms it is now impossible to distinguish which is a Unit form. As far as is possible and reasonable Unit pupils are subject to the same range of school sanctions as that experienced by all main school pupils. The pupils in the Unit, with little prompting, presented themselves in school uniform, often impeccably dressed. No scheme to introduce main school pupils into the Unit now exists, unless these pupils themselves have some temporary special need, for example, following an operation, and on these occasions they seem to be readily accepted. Taxi provision still exists, though on a reduced level. Public transport passes are a common status symbol, almost at times a symbol of freedom, flaunted before other less fortunate or still over-protected pupils (I hasten to add, not less fortunate by reason of handicap). More often it is parental rather than pupil opposition which prevents some moving to independent travel. However, a significant number of Unit pupils travel long or double bus journeys in preference to taxi provision. Pupils read their own reports, good or bad, in the same way as main school, before taking them home. Over the past years Unit pupils have been able to take part in all main school activities, including the more physically taxing such as skiing and potholing, and in a recent sponsored walk one notable member of the Unit completed eight kilometres on crutches in one and a half hours, in company with his main school friends.

An emphasis on academic success had always been part of the ethos of the school and its Unit; the transition into sets and groups on the basis of academic merit alone now appears to be a smooth and relatively unexciting procedure within the school. For those pupils whose access to examination courses would be logistically difficult for reasons of the severity of their handicap, examination courses have been completed where the work has been serviced entirely within the Unit, and to date there has been a pass rate of more than 90 per cent (albeit mainly grades 4 and 5).

There have been more global changes in the school as well as the particular changes they requested. Because the pupils of the Unit found that sensible and thoughtful discussion appeared to bring positive gains without any retribution, individual pupils began to use this to re-examine their own position. Previously, dissatisfaction or frustration was expressed merely through negative behaviour. Consequently, they gained when they used this new tactic in the school at large. The strategy was obviously worth maintaining. It has also had an effect on the way we, as staff, behave with our pupils, because as most of us recognized, negotiation could resolve most moments of difficulty. A recent example was a pupil who thought through how to leave the Unit and integrate completely into the main school, a process which had to be as carefully considered by her form teacher.

Pupils now also perceive, even if dimly, that they are to a certain extent in control of their own destiny. If you control your own destiny in an environment which will save rather than destroy you if you make an error of judgement, then you are released from any fear of the unknown, and far more likely to take calculated risks, and thereby discover your strengths. The Unit therefore changed from being a group that feared what it faced, to a group that appeared to accept the challenge presented by their disabilities or difficulties.

As a result pupils from the Unit began to achieve a greater status from main school staff and pupils alike; instead of using their disability or difficulties as an automatic excuse for their inability to meet a challenge, they would make the attempt if nothing else.

Now, when pupils of the Unit feel they have a position to justify, then they exercise their individual right to negotiate with their teacher or with the Head of Unit. One irate pupil who thought her view had been wrongly rejected, took it further by negotiating direct with the headmaster, somewhat to his surprise. This attitude does appear to be transmitted to newcomers who never experienced that original meeting. A pupil recently moved from a situation where she was close to suspension and a possible psychiatric referral, and within the course of one school term began to recognize that a pattern of negotiation and decision-making seemed to benefit her.

This new found social success has of course had an academic 'fall-out'. Most schools work towards some form of academic success. Pupils had in the past been unsure as to how to respond to the possibility of failure but are now less afraid. Similarly, as staff, we are more prepared to be optimistic. Levels of integration have now risen. In the first three years approximately 40 per cent of pupil time is contact in integrated lessons, in years four and five this rises to an average of approximately 65 per cent of pupil time. As Head of Unit I feel more at ease negotiating placements when I can recognize that a pupil is making positive decisions at the same time.

It may of course have not simply depended on one single meeting with Unit pupils. Certainly I had only recently been appointed as Head of Unit, and change was in the air. Maybe the Unit had now outgrown these limits, and the pupils (not the teachers!) had recognized that change was necessary.

Certainly the consensus politics of the Unit turns the very idea of 'special needs pupils' on its head, as Unit pupils often have an almost tangible feeling of elitism in the school. When Unit pupils express a point of view now, they do so predominantly about things which affect them as a pupil of the school, not as a pupil with special needs: their concerns relate to the general quality of academic life. It is expressed reasonably, and thoughtfully, and as a result I think it is accepted precisely because the attitude that goes with such an expression presents no threat.

Conclusion

In the introduction, I stated that this episode raised the issue of the potential for decision-making of a synthetically created adolescent group. I believe that what occurred in this particular meeting needed a number of key factors in place:

1 There had to be a sense of 'change needed': that is, the group perceived a set of goals which they were frustrated from reaching.

2 The chance of gain outweighed any risk of possible sanctions: that is, they perceived that their new Head of Unit was unlikely to invoke sanctions as a result of their actions.

3 The gains, if achieved, would be tangible: that is, each member of the meeting would make actual gains in their day-to-day life.

The actual demands made were achieveable alternatives, not merely critical of the existing system. Above all it shows that given scope to design change this particular group were able to do it. Recently the Unit (*not* the teachers of the Unit) decided to organize a coach trip to Slimbridge Wildfowl Trust and to adopt a duck. The project was suggested by one of the youngest members of the Unit, who had not experienced the meeting, but who is clearly learning the gain of decision-making, and the subsequent freedoms that are offered.

What I have described here is a single event and its consequences in the on-going existence of a Special Education Unit. It was important because it was the result of the spontaneously generated actions of a group of adolescents with special needs who clearly felt the need to change their world, who found a successful strategy for doing it, and who as a result managed to deflect the Unit onto its present course where pupils can have a much more open and honest relationship with each other and with staff, and a much greater potential for individual decision-making.

24 Progress with humanity?: the experience of a disabled lecturer

Jenny Morris

Dr Jenny Morris teaches Housing, Sociology and Social Policy at Tottenham College of Technology. On the day that she signed her contract for this post, in June 1983, she fell off a wall onto a railway line while trying to rescue a child. She is now paralysed below the waist. She is a single parent with a two and a half year old daughter. In this chapter, she tells of her encounters with other people's reactions and attitudes towards her and her disability.

Being a disabled college lecturer is a paradoxical situation in terms of the status that I am accorded by other people. To be disabled is to be classified as belonging to one of the most 'vulnerable and deprived' groups in society, particularly if your disability is very visible as mine is. It is assumed that such a severely disabled person is unemployed and is dependent on others. Other assumptions are also part of this general image of a disabled person: poverty, lack of ability, lack of mobility, lack of control over one's life. To be a college lecturer, on the other hand, is to be defined as a professional, someone with above average educational qualifications and above average earnings, someone in control, articulate and autonomous.

It is difficult, if not impossible, for people to reconcile the two images. To some extent, they only manage to deal with the fact that I have this contradictory position by ignoring my disability. I thus become an honorary able-bodied person, in the way that many women holding high-status positions become honorary men.

However, I say this now from the position of having been back at work for some time since breaking my back. The initial reaction was to me as a disabled person and my status as such was made very clear when Haringey Council's first response to my disability was to declare my newly acquired contract of employment void, as I had not turned up for work on the first day of term. I was, at that point, just learning to use a wheelchair, having spent nine weeks flat on my back in bed. Haringey is, of course, an equal opportunities employer; its motto is 'Progress with Humanity'. And this was the first lesson that I learnt from my new status. The negative assumptions and views held about disabled people are of such strength that there is many, many a slip between intention and implementation. It's like racism and sexism. The discrimination is deep within people's subsconscious and permeates our social institutions.

I relied on another social institution, my trade union, to fight Haringey's discrimination which they did very effectively and successfully. Yet I have subsequently found out that it was the principle of the matter which primarily motivated the union. After all, if my contract was void then so was that of any teacher who had 'flu on the first day of term in a new job. Most of the individuals

260

involved in putting pressure on Haringey to keep my new job open for me assumed in fact that I would never be able to take it up.

Before I started work at the college, I went in a couple of times to discuss my timetable and to see if there were any problems with accessibility. I was lucky in that the department in which I work is in an accessible building and that various measures had been taken the previous year to enable a bridging course for disabled students to be held there. The alterations that had been done for these students were, however, quite inadequate, and this was another lesson I learnt. Unless you have disabled people involved in making such adaptations then they won't be the right ones. There was an unnecessary lip to the ramp into the building which made it almost impossible for those who can't do a 'wheelie' (flipping your wheelchair onto its back wheels) to get up the ramp; the entrance doors were very heavy and there hadn't even been a handle put on at a lower height; rails had been put into the students' wheelchair toilet in every place except the one required; the lift panel was too high and most wheelchair users wouldn't be able to reach the emergency button, or the buttons for the upper floors. All these things are important physical details which increase our dependence on other people and illustrate how the environment can handicap us. The necessary commitment could do so much to minimize our disability.

It took a year since I first got into the college to talk about what alterations were required – nine months since I started work – for a staff wheelchair toilet to be provided. Every time I asked about progress I was made to feel as if I was asking for something which was a great deal of trouble. Indeed, my first reaction on learning that the alterations had finally been done was to be incredibly grateful and to think of writing a 'thank you' letter. However, I didn't, as I felt that this would be falling into the trap that had been set to make me feel as if I really had no right to ask for such alterations to be done and that if they were done it was as a very big favour. If education authorities and their employees acted as if disabled people have the right to be students and employees, then the adequate provision of the necessary adaptations would follow automatically and we wouldn't be put in the position of pleading for our exceptional circumstances.

Other changes in attitudes are required when alterations to the physical environment are involved. There are many different types of disability and each individual is affected differently. So it's no good a local authority thinking that just because they have put in a ramped access for a wheelchair user that that is the end of their responsibility for adapting their buildings. What if the next employee or student can walk but has very weak hands? They will then have to make adaptations to the door handles. What if the next person is partially sighted? They may have to paint a white line on the steps or staircases.

Furthermore, an individual's abilities may change over time and thus necessitate further adaptations. If a local education authority is truly committed to equal opportunities for people with disabilities they will need to be continually responsive to new demands.

To get back to people's attitudes to me. Generally, I find there is a combination of total insensitivity to the difficulties which I experience and paradoxically, at the same time, a classification of me as 'unable'; there is a failure to see that being unable to walk means exactly that, and not 'unable' generally. I am handicapped by various physical obstacles, but these obstacles can be got round given the willingness of people to help. It is just this willingness which is lacking on so many occasions. People offer help when I am doing things which *don't* require help. I am considered so 'unable' that when I do everyday things like getting out of my car, strangers rush over in a panic of concern. Yet if I am confronted by a couple of steps, their reaction is not to ask me if I would like to be carried up but to assume that yet another place is barred to me. I should mention that I am not a daunting prospect for being lifted up and down stairs; my wheelchair is very light and I weigh under 8 stone.

So many people's attitudes to disabled people are dominated by the assumption that we are alien to 'normal' society, that we don't belong, that we are an embarrassment, an eyesore that shouldn't be allowed out. The problem with being disabled and a college lecturer is that I don't fit into people's expectations of a disabled person.

As I mentioned, I am treated by some work colleagues as an 'honorary able-bodied' person, now that they have got over the strangeness of me being there at all. Yet this being treated as an equal is very much on the surface. Scratch this surface and you find the fear and contempt which underlies much of the discrimination against people who don't measure up to what we consider to be 'normal'. This attitude has come out recently over my having to park my car in a way which blocks other cars because someone else has parked in the disabled driver's space in the college car park. One member of staff threatened to cut my car brakes at the same time as saying to other members of staff how sorry he feels for me. This particular incident has confirmed my view that the patronizing pity expressed for disabled people is conditional on our fulfilling the passive dependent role expected of us.

The second type of reaction I experience at work is from those who I come across as I go through the building who do not realize that I am a lecturer there. Thus I get patronizing remarks in the lift, or someone points out that I shouldn't be using the staff toilet, or someone tries to push my wheelchair out of the lift on the third floor under the misapprehension that I am one of the disabled students who are based there.

I do find this reaction very difficult to deal with as I am not normally one to worry about status. Since joining the group of third-class citizens, however, I am more concerned with making as much of my professional status as possible just because it means people do behave a bit more as if I'm a human being if they realize what job I do.

The third type of reaction is from the students that I teach. When I go into a room to teach I am not someone in a wheelchair but a teacher and someone who enjoys teaching at that. You might have thought that when I came back to work after being disabled I would have worried about students' reactions to me. Not a bit of it. When I go into a room to teach, it is the only time apart from with a very few close friends, and with my daughter, that being in a wheelchair is completely irrelevant.

The fourth type of reaction is limited to one member of staff. For months after I went back to work I sensed that there was something very different about this particular woman's reaction to me. I don't always get on well with her so it wasn't so much that there was a sympathy between us, rather that I sensed she had a basic acceptance of me which is lacking in most people. I thought I was imagining it until I discovered that her brother-in-law is a paraplegic and then I realized that she did indeed have a basic acceptance and an assumption that I was a perfectly competent teacher and human being, because her previous experience led her to expect this of me.

This is one of the most important lessons I have learnt. People's expectations of us are formed by their previous experience of disabled people. If disabled people are segregated, are treated as alien, as different in a fundamental way, then we will never be accepted as full members of society. This is the strongest argument against special schools and against separate provision. If everyone, in their childhood and adulthood alike, and at some time during their daily lives, came across people with all sorts of disabilities, then those disabilities would cease to be so frightening and threatening. They would, instead, be recognized for what they are, as handicaps to our functioning, not negations of us as people.

25 Speaking for ourselves: self-advocacy by people called mentally handicapped

June Statham

In this account of the work of a group of 'self-advocates', June Statham describes how some people who have been categorized as 'mentally handicapped' have challenged that label. The people involved in this group have all attended special schools, and several have lived in mental handicap hospitals. Over a number of years they have worked together in ways that many other groups of 'ordinary' people would envy, to develop their self-confidence and independence. They are collectively challenging the routine oppression they encounter from professionals and public alike.

We want the chance to speak. To speak about different things what we need to talk about, like about the word 'handicap' and being treated like children and about night classes for people who can't read and write. We want people to listen to us.

(Marion)

The most important thing is to be independent. To be your own boss. To be treated like a normal person and a citizen and to have your rights.

(Gary)

Marion and Gary are part of an increasing number of people in Britain who have been labelled 'mentally handicapped' who are now beginning to speak up for themselves and for their rights. Self-advocacy has been a growing movement in this country and others for some time amongst adults with physical and sensory disabilities, but is a fairly recent development amongst those with learning difficulties. Self-advocacy in this context had its beginnings in the mid 1970s in America, and *People First* groups were established in many states over the following decade. In 1984, the Washington People First group held an international conference which was attended by nine British self-advocates, including Gary and Marion, together with several professionals in the role of supporters. On coming back to England the group decided to set up a London-based People First group, and held their first meeting in October 1984.

The trip to the States was not however the beginning of the road to self-advocacy for people like Marion and Gary. Many of those who went to the American conference had already been meeting together for some time to learn the skills and the confidence that would enable them to speak out about their feelings and their rights. Several had been attending classes at the City Lit, one of London's Adult Education Institutes, which runs speaking and discussion classes as part of their Creative Education courses for people with learning difficulties. Others were members of a group called the Participation Forum, which meets every Tuesday morning at the offices of the London division of MENCAP, the Royal Society for Mentally Handicapped Children and Adults.

In November 1985, there were nine regular members of the Participation Forum. Marion, Gary and Tony have been involved since the group was set up at the end of 1981, as an off-shoot of a meeting of representatives from Adult Training Centres organized by MENCAP. Bernard, Kenny, Lorraine, David and George have all been coming for three years or more, and Julie joined eighteen months ago. Most of the group are in their late twenties and thirties. All have in the past been labelled 'mentally handicapped', some have Down's Syndrome, and all have experienced some kind of special schooling. Some members have spent part of their adult lives in hospitals, but they now live in a variety of different situations in hostels, with their parents, in group homes or in a flat. Most spend some of their time at an Adult Training Centre, fitted around their other activities and commitments. The Tuesday morning 'talking session' has become a regular and important part of their lives.

The tenth member of the Participation Forum is John, a professional, who has also been involved from the start. At first he ran the group on a voluntary basis, but for the past two years has been funded by MENCAP. His role in the early meetings was a fairly directive one, but as the group developed skills and confidence the balance changed and he was able to organize and direct it less. Now, as Lorraine says, 'John helps to guide us along, but he doesn't tell us what to do. We all know each other, and we all talk out'.

At a typical meeting, the group decide between themselves at the start of the session what they will discuss. This particular Tuesday there is a full agenda. John is asked to report back on a meeting he attended the previous week. Someone asks for details of the People First open day to be held at the weekend. David and George have seen a television programme about a proposed reduction of staff at the tube stations and want to talk about it. Transport is a particularly important issue for them, since both used to live in a hospital and have only learnt how to get about on public transport since moving out to a hostel. They can now find their way around London on buses and tubes and are justifiably proud of their achievement. 'We know all the stations, where to get off and where not to get off. We learnt it by heart. We got our own heart and we learn it. We joined it all together' (George). The group discusses the proposed cut in staff at tube stations and feels this would make it harder for many people with disabilities to travel. Together they work out a letter of complaint to London Regional Transport, and John agrees to write it and send it.

The next item is Gary's suggestion for a training course for people with learning difficulties, so they will be able to organize and speak for themselves. There is an increasing amount of training materials and courses in self-advocacy for professionals, but he wants one for consumers, to be organized largely by themselves. 'It will be for consumers, but it will be more professional!' John asks what other members of the group think, and what they would like to see such a course contain. The quieter participants want it to be about helping people to speak, 'getting their ability out of them' as George puts it. Gary's particular concern is for people to learn how to organize and set up groups, and how to have meetings and elect officers like the American People First groups have done. He bears the brunt of the administrative work for People First, and wants others to learn the skills so they can share the responsibility and so that the movement can grow. They decide to invite other self-advocates across the country to a meeting to swap ideas about a training course. John reminds them that some people will probably need supporters to help them to travel to the meeting, but that doesn't necessarily mean they can't hold the meeting alone.

The discussion moves on to training centres. Marion has put 'raising money' on the agenda and she starts to tell the group about her centre's fund-raising for children in Ethiopia. John asks how the new trainees' committee is working at her centre, and gradually Marion starts to talk about an issue that is obviously worrying her, the level of violence and aggression at the training centre. 'There's all this trouble with fights. Fighting with chairs. It makes me ill. It happens every day'. John asks if the others have the same problem at their centres. Kenny says they used to, 'but then our committee told them if they do it they will have their wages stopped or will be banned from the centre. They all stopped it'. The group discuss whether that would work as a strategy at Marion's centre. She thinks not, because the parents would complain. Kenny agrees. 'If they banned them for six months their parents would complain to Council and Welfare'. Gary is against punitive measures. 'They should learn how to control themselves. Not someone else controlling them'. The discussion broadens to include other incidents like people having money stolen or fires being started in the centres. Gary says:

> ... it could be to do with conditions at the centre, what it looks like. What kind of food they get there. It's hygiene standards as well. Being too crowded. That's some of the things that could have made the people that work there behave like that.

They don't come up with an immediate solution to Marion's problem, but speaking about it seems to have helped.

The Participation Forum is a strong, cohesive group. They have been meeting together for four years now and provide each other with a high level of encouragement and support. When two members were waiting for months to move from a hostel to a flat, the others prevented them from becoming discouraged. David and George's training centre announced that it intended to introduce charges for attendance and to lower the already minimal wages, and the group as a whole dictated a letter of protest to the Social Services Department. They help each other and encourage the less articulate or confident members to speak. Tony describes how Lorraine was nervous when she spoke in public for the first time, 'but we all pushed her to make sure she does it and you see her now, she talks like no one's business!' As the newest, Julie, leaves the meeting, Lorraine says 'goodbye love, and thanks for talking'.

The group has had a big effect on their lives. 'People listen to me more. It's changed me in a lot of ways. I used to have a lot of tempers but I don't get hardly any tempers now. I can say what I want now' (Tony).

After the meeting Marion, David and George stay behind to work out with John the details of a talk they are going to give to a group of medical students later that afternoon. Marion takes notes. John suggests various topics they might want to discuss, such as the difference between living in a hostel and a hospital, and the others add suggestions of their own. 'We could tell them about the committees at our centres'. 'About not liking the H [for handicapped] on bus passes'. 'How we went to America and about People First'. John tries to make sure that George will get a chance to speak by suggesting that the other two ask him questions. 'He's got lots of interesting ideas, but he's very quiet and polite and doesn't speak as easily as you do'. John accompanies them to the hospital, but leaves before they give their talk.

Speaking at meetings, to professionals, parents, students and also to other consumers of services like themselves, is something that the members of the Participation Forum have been doing increasingly over the past couple of years. It is a skill they have developed through coming to the group, through gaining confidence from discussing issues amongst themselves and from the support they provide for each other. For the first two years or so they very rarely had visitors and felt happier talking on their own. More recently they have felt secure enough to allow a wide range of people to sit in on their meetings, including parents, GLC and DHSS staff, student teachers and a *Guardian* financial page writer, who produced an article on the group's feelings about allowances, benefits and spending their own money. They have organized two conferences called *Speaking for Ourselves* and *Have we a Future?*, with the help of John, MENCAP and the City Lit, who videotaped the events. The conferences were aimed at spreading the word about self-advocacy to both professionals and consumers, and the videotapes capture the sense of excitement and emerging control over their lives felt by members of the audience as they come to the front to speak into the microphone for the first time, or join in small discussions to share with others in the same position their feelings about work, education, or the way they have been treated by society.

> People call us nasty names or treat us like kids because they're frightened. They don't know what we're like or what we can do ... We're labelled, called mongol, makes me feel not wanted ... Lots of us could live on our own with a bit of teaching and help. Then others could get out of hospitals and live where we are now ... Tell them not reading and writing doesn't mean you're stupid.

A common reaction from the professionals who hear the self-advocates speak is that they are not typical, and that, 'ours aren't like you, they couldn't do what you are doing'. Self-advocacy is a new movement amongst people called mentally handicapped, and those involved are bound to be pioneers who can probably express their views particularly well. But their ability and confidence in speaking up for their rights is something that they have learnt over fairly long periods. The members of the Participation Forum, for instance, spent several years meeting together and exploring ideas in a safe environment before they felt able to speak out in public. They have discovered ways of helping themselves to do this. George is shy and quiet, so the others need to make space for him and he has had to learn to speak louder. Lorraine finds it easier to answer questions directed at her by someone like John, than to speak directly to an audience. Gary described how he sat with a less experienced speaker and held his hand in order to give him the confidence to talk. John feels that the 'ours couldn't do it' attitude of some professionals is a way of avoiding the issues raised by self-advocacy. The fact that the groups of students he works with can communicate so well should be taken not as an argument that they are atypical but as an example of what people can do given the time and encouragement to learn.

> It means that you have to be prepared to spend a long time helping people to build up the confidence and the skills. This group has been meeting for three or four years

now. But that's a small amount of time in someone's lifetime, to learn skills that will stand them in good stead for life.

(John)

The self-advocates themselves know that speaking out is a skill that has to be learnt.

Self-advocacy is about speaking your mind, like I'm doing now. Not to be frightened, just go out and say what's in your mind. There's just one thing that's got me doing it, coming here. This group at MENCAP.

(Tony)

You wouldn't throw someone in and make them speak to a lot of people. You'd help them to talk. Meet in small groups and get confidence.

(Gary)

Eileen, who goes to one of John's speaking classes at the City Lit and is also a People First member, gets annoyed when professionals say 'ours couldn't' about the people with whom they work.

It's always the same when we do talks, they always say that. It makes me angry because I know they can, it might just take a longer time.

Eileen thinks it is important that they go back again to groups they have visited, to provide continuing encouragement and support. 'It's no good just going once and then you don't know how they get on'. She also prefers talking to consumers rather than to professionals. 'Because it's about their lives, it's more important to them. The professionals can just go home afterwards'.

The self-advocates see their movement as being for all those who have been labelled mentally handicapped, and not just the most articulate.

It's not just for those that can speak out well. There are other ways, like acting and sign language and music and art. And these are all ways of speaking up for People First.

(Gary)

They are concerned that no one be excluded. The People First group uses pictures in their newsletter and shares ideas like drawing shopping lists, to include those who are, in Gary's words, 'hard of reading'; they are campaigning on transport and access issues to include those who have physical disabilities, and members have visited hospitals to share their ideas with those who have more severe learning difficulties. One member attending his first People First meeting spoke on behalf of his more severely handicapped friend back at the hospital, and was encouraged to bring the friend to the next meeting and help him become involved.

The kind of issues which the self-advocates discuss, both among themselves and in public, are: housing, transport, schooling, leisure facilities, work and money, labelling, the word 'handicap'. In all these areas they want greater independence and control over their lives. In housing this means more hostels, flats and group homes, and support for people to move from one to the other. 'We need hostels for helping people to leave their hospitals and new group homes to get people out of hostels' (Gary). David and George both moved from hospitals to hostels. 'I didn't like the hospital much. I didn't like the rules there. You get told off. Like children. Now I live at the hostel with David. You have keys, but you have to tell them when you go out' (George). 'The hostel is more better than the hospital. There's more things to do and you meet more people' (David). Tony used to live at home with his parents but moved out to a hostel and then to a flat, where he does his own shopping and cooking. He shares with two other men, and a member of staff has a separate flat in the building.

> The staff come in every now and then to see how we're getting on, not all the time. They mainly come in when they want to or if they hear a big row and think we can't sort it out. I tell them to go away and say if we want you we'll get you. They butt in when they shouldn't. They wouldn't like it if you did it to them.
>
> (Tony)

Julie, Kenny, Marion and Gary live with their parents, and Lorraine has recently moved from a hostel to a flat. 'It's better on my own, I prefer it. I can go out when I want, I don't have to come back at a certain time' (Lorraine).

Many people with learning difficulties have spent a large part of their youth living in residential special schools. The memories of this group were mostly negative; memories of boredom or fear, of endless regulations like having to go to bed at seven o'clock, of not seeing enough of their parents and family. Lorraine was the only one who had enjoyed her schooling. She went to a small residential school 'for mentally retarded children' from the age of four to sixteen, and liked the sense of family that was lacking in her holiday visits to foster parents or children's homes. She still goes back to the annual reunion, and remembers fondly the long walks and shopping expeditions on Saturdays, the swimming lessons and the coach trips.

> We didn't do 'O' levels or 'A' levels. You couldn't in that sort of school. But we had a really good time. I wouldn't have liked to go to an ordinary school. I'd be far behind. I wouldn't be able to keep up.
>
> (Lorraine)

Julie did go to an ordinary school and had found it hard to keep up, but hadn't wanted to go to a special school.

> I went there because I couldn't do the lessons in the junior school. All I could do was cookery and art and craft. I couldn't do anything else because they were too hard for me. No one gave me any help. I would rather have stayed if they had helped me but I had to move on.
>
> (Julie)

Gary is in favour of integrated education too. 'There should be extra helpers. It means the teachers will have to have different education. They will have to learn'. Tony went to half a dozen different boarding schools, the last one of which he described as being 'like Colditz'.

> The worst thing is you're stuck there for months on end. You work there, you sleep there. I didn't like it. They just put me there. I'd like to have gone to an ordinary day school. Your parents can come and pick you up at the end of the day and take you

home, and when you're older you can find your own way there and back. I only went
to an ordinary school for a year, and then they said boarding school is more suitable
for him, he's a handicapped person.

(Tony)

David received little education in the school attached to the hospital where he
lived. 'I went to a school in the hospital grounds. From nine till half past ten in the
mornings. But I can read now, I can tell the numbers on buses'. He felt that
school should 'teach you education'. George adds 'how to get about and use real
money'. David says they've recently stopped having further education classes at
his and George's training centre. 'They're packing it up now because they've cut
it back. The teacher left. We asked for another teacher at the meetings but they
say they can't do it' (David).

Eileen's centre has also cut back on education classes. 'I don't get anything
now at the ATC. I've really got a good brain and I just can't use it'. Her
experiences of schooling have left her frustrated, and with strong views on
segregated education:

> I went to an ordinary school till I was nine. The headmistress didn't have no time for
> me. They said I was damaged in my brain and sent me for tests. The tests didn't
> show anything wrong but I still got sent to an ESN school. My mother fought it, she
> went to the County Hall, but I still had to go. They said it was for a short time but
> once I got there they didn't bother any more. I couldn't go back. It was horrible. I
> could have learnt a lot but I didn't get any education, nothing at all. I felt I missed
> out on everything that was going on. They shouldn't have special schools. They
> shouldn't even have special classes in ordinary schools because that's just the same.
> Like in one school there was a class called the Lower Class and all the Down's
> syndrome children were in that class. There's hundreds of people with Down's
> syndrome, hundreds of people with a disability, and they're probably brighter than
> anybody else. You're saying, 'you're Down's so you should be shut away' and that's
> not right. There's a little girl in the nursery [a nursery class for Down's syndrome
> children where Eileen is a helper] and they say she has to go to a special school, but
> we've fought it and the court has just said she can go to an ordinary school.

(Eileen)

Eileen doesn't like the term 'children with special needs' either. 'It's all the
same. It's still a label. It's still saying you're handicapped. We don't want any
label, we're just ordinary people'. Her dislike of the term 'mentally handicapped'
is shared by most of the people it is used to describe. 'It's cruel and hurtful and
doesn't tell people what we're good at. We want them to take the "H" off the bus
passes and put a star or some kind of mark on it instead. We don't like it because
we're not handicapped' (Marion). 'If you're called a handicapped person, if
people see you in the street with a pass they say "don't go near him or her because
look, they've got a pass"' (Tony). The term 'learning disabled' has been
suggested as an alternative, but they are not sure that it is any better. 'It's still
saying you're handicapped'. It is a complicated issue, and all too easy to reject a
label for oneself by transferring it onto another category of people. One person
objects to the 'H' on the bus passes because, 'we're not handicapped. We're real
high grades. We're not in wheelchairs'. Another says she didn't want to go to live
in a particular residential village because 'a lot of them were mongol or backwards children. I don't like the word "handicap", but a lot of them were'.

Most self-advocates feel that labels like 'handicapped' affect the way that society treats them, and hope that if the labels are changed, then maybe people's attitudes will change too. Most have had bad experiences of being mocked or ridiculed in the street. 'I've been taken the mickey out of by people in buses, and by some girls at the school down the road. They call you handicapped and mental and all that. It's not very nice. I just ignore it, take no notice. If you let them see you're worried they'll carry on' (Marion). Several members of the Participation Forum are planning to go into schools to talk to the pupils there. 'Because if we tell them, they'll understand what we're talking about. If we don't do that they'll keep taking the mickey out of us all the time' (David). George agrees, and adds that 'you've got to remember that you're the speaker'.

Work and money is another subject that occupies the group. Most attend an Adult Training Centre for all or part of the week, and receive up to £4 a week in wages on top of their social security benefits. 'We want workplaces that teach you to do a proper job with proper wages' (Gary). 'It's somewhere to go, something to do' (David). 'They don't treat you as adults, they treat you as children. They make you do painting or drawing' (Kenny). They have explored various channels for making their views known. Marion has been involved in staff selection at her centre: 'there were three of us at the centre who was picked to interview Diane with the staff. Next time it will be another three'. Eileen tried going on strike when her centre reduced their 'wages' to 69 pence per week:

> I said I wasn't going to do the work. They made me sit out in the corridor because I wouldn't work. Mostly I slept and read comics. It was very boring. Nobody else would go on strike, they were all afraid. I sat in the corridor for three weeks, and then I started going to classes (at the City Lit) instead.

> (Eileen)

Many Adult Training Centres have set up committees so that the trainees have some say in what goes on at their centre. These meetings between staff and students are a form of self-advocacy, since they are a place for trainees to express their views, but they often involve a conflict of interests for the professionals, caught between their desire to encourage student participation and their role as managers of the centre who have to deal with the ensuing criticisms. Some Boroughs, like Hillingdon which runs David and George's centre, have begun to use outside advisers instead of centre staff on these committees in an attempt to avoid this problem. In a sense, groups like the Participation Forum and the Creative Education classes at the City Lit are not true self-advocacy either, since they are a part of an organization (MENCAP and Adult Education respectively) and are led, in however non-directive a fashion, by a professional. However John sees these groups as part of the self-advocacy process, allowing students to learn the skills that enable them to organize for themselves and to set up groups like People First.

> When the London People First was being set up, the self-advocates wanted to be able to belong to this group (Participation Forum) as well. They saw it as a similar process to people learning the skills to move from a hospital to a hostel and then to a group home.

> (John)

People First uses people like John as an adviser, called upon only if they feel it is necessary. At the Open Day to celebrate the first anniversary of the setting up of the London and Thames People First, there are many of the same faces. Marion is behind the registration desk, helping people to write their names and addresses on a piece of paper as they arrive. Alice is selling T shirts, with messages like 'People First' and 'Label Jars not People'. Another stall offers publicity material and a newsletter, and there is a display of all the letters Gary has received over the past year inviting him to speak to various groups and conferences. Gary is President of People First, and stands at the microphone to give an introduction.

> This is the first anniversary of People First in London. It's an organization for people who are self-advocates and who want to speak up for their rights and put new ideas forward and have a better position. It's for people who've been labelled mentally handicapped, though we don't like that word. We call them 'friend' or 'people with learning disabilities' or we call them by their name, which is the proper way of introducing somebody.
>
> (Gary)

He describes how People First of London was set up by the nine people who had been to the American conference, and has now grown to about fifty members, including a supporters group, 'for the people we call professionals. But instead of the professionals running the organization it's the advocates running the organization'. Gary is an accomplished speaker, getting his audience's attention, putting them at their ease, introducing humour into his speeches. He studies the news on television, 'to see how they do it, and to pick up ideas'. He tells his audience that they will be split up by area in order to have small group discussions after lunch. 'There's a South-East London group, a North London group and lots more, so you can meet with people from your area'. A West Indian woman in the audience asks, 'have you got a Jamaica?' Gary says no, 'but you could set one up'. Someone else in the audience tells her that, 'we've not got a Jamaica, but we have got a Jamaica Road'. They go off into their small groups, and at the end of the day several new local branches of People First seem likely to be set up.

The self-advocacy movement is spreading rapidly. Groups have been started in Holland and Australia as well as America and Britain, and an increasing number of local groups are springing up around the country. People First has just sent its information leaflet to all the schools and hospitals in the London area attended by adolescents with learning difficulties, hoping to bring over-sixteen years olds who are still in full-time education into People First. They plan to hold the next international conference in London, in 1988. They want to set up training courses to help more people speak out for themselves. The interest in self-advocacy amongst both professionals and consumers is such that the founder members of People First are inundated with requests for information and invitations to speak and are having to learn to say 'no', often to the professionals who have held that power over them in the past.

Self-advocacy has given them greater control over their lives, but sometimes they can feel like it has taken over their lives as well.

> I can't sleep sometimes because I'm always thinking about it. Even when I play pop music to relax and forget, it's still in my brain. It's not a one-day thing. You can't say, 'I'll do it today', and then tomorrow you forget. It's all the time.
>
> (Gary)

It is a commitment to improving the world, not just for themselves but for all those who have been labelled handicapped.

> I'd like us to go forward towards a better independence and a better life for handicapped people. We'd like to think that if a child is born in the future that might be called handicapped, it will have a better life than we've had. We don't want pity, we want a future.

(Gary)

Further reading

Williams, P. 1982. *We Can Speak for Ourselves*, London, Souvenir Press.

26 British Sign Language: the language of the Deaf community

Mary Brennan
illustrated by Martin Connell and Linda Hurd

In the first part of this chapter, Mary Brennan provides an insight into the elegant complexities of British Sign Language, the language of the Deaf community in Britain. For many years, Deaf people have found their language systematically devalued and attacked in ways that resemble other political attacks on languages, such as the banning of Gaelic under the British administration of Ireland. Now, at least, professionals in deaf education have, through their organizations, recognized BSL as a full language. But in the second part of the chapter, Mary Brennan finds continued resistance to incorporating it into the education of deaf children. She considers the recent expansion of varieties of manually-coded English, and concludes that they are less effective means of communication and learning for Deaf people than BSL. She makes positive suggestions for a bilingual education system based on BSL as a native language for deaf children.

Introduction

The title of this chapter incorporates a number of assumptions which are not totally shared either by the general public or by many professionals concerned with deaf people. The two major assumptions which we shall examine in this chapter are that there is in Britain such an entity as *the deaf community* and that within this community the major form of communication is a highly complex linguistic system, directly comparable to other human languages and known as *British Sign Language (BSL)*. The two assumptions are intricately bound up with each other. In examining the notion of 'the deaf community' we are inevitably forced to examine its language and vice versa. As we shall see, the existence of both the deaf community and its language has implications for the education of the deaf child: implications which have too often been ignored by those responsible for that education. The kind of findings reported here require the attention not only of linguists and social scientists, but of policymakers from government departments down.

The Deaf community

To the outsider, a 'deaf' person is someone who suffers from the particular biological disadvantage of hearing impairment. It is little more than stating the obvious to say that being deaf means not being able to hear properly. The hearing person is also likely to take it for granted that the degree and type of deafness must be of considerable importance to the deaf person and must indeed be an essential part of her/his identity. It may come as something of a surprise then to learn that

274

many deaf adults are surprisingly ill-informed about the nature of their deafness and, what is more, exhibit relatively little interest in becoming more knowledgeable about it. Why should this be so?

The answer seems to be that the concept of oneself as a 'deaf' person has much more to do with language and community than it has with gross statements of hearing impairment. However, stressing the notion of community does not imply that the whole of the hearing impaired population can be thought of as constituting a recognizable grouping. Membership of the deaf community typically involves a kind of conscious opting in: a conscious choice and commitment (Kyle and Woll 1985). Although in everyday colloquial language, we may use the adjective 'deaf' both of a person who has acquired some form of hearing loss in old age and of someone born deaf, most people intuitively recognize that there is a major difference between these two groups. It is unlikely that members of the second group will see themselves as 'deaf' rather than as 'hearing' people, belonging to a hearing community who have to find ways of coping with their hearing loss within the hearing world. People who are born with a hearing loss are much more likely to choose to belong to the recognizable cultural grouping we describe as the Deaf community.

Baker and Cokely (1980) have contrasted what they term 'clinical-pathological' definitions of the deaf community with those which are 'cultural' in nature. Clinical-pathological definitions focus not only on audiological factors but on certain suggested negative consequences, such as difficulties of communication and learning, as well as purported psychological problems. The overall impression is of impairment, disability and deficiency. In contrast, the cultural perspective sees the deaf community as a minority cultural grouping, with its own language, history and values.

The American linguist Carol Padden (Padden 1980), herself a full member of a Deaf community, uses the simple device of the difference between upper and lower case 'd' to separate out two notions of the deaf person:

a 'deaf' person would be someone with some kind of hearing loss;

a 'Deaf' person would be someone who espouses Deaf cultural values.

It is fascinating to observe that this artificial device within the written English forms of the word 'deaf' is mirrored in the language of the Deaf community itself. There are several different signs within British Sign Language translatable by the adjective 'deaf'. One of the most frequently used is shown in Figure 26.1. Here the index and middle finger, extended from the closed fist, make contact with the right ear. This may be seen as a fairly neutral sign, equivalent to the lower case notion above and suggesting that the person concerned has some form of hearing loss.

A contrasting sign is shown in Figures 26.2 and 26.3. These can be treated as two variants of the same sign. In the first case, the full flat hand contacts the right ear and then makes a firm twisting movement to contact the mouth. This version is sometimes given the English translation of 'deaf and dumb'. The version shown in Figure 26.3 has the full flat hand twisting towards the right ear in a sharp movement. Often the head is turned away to the left and cheeks are puffed out to show emphasis. One possible translation would be 'really deaf'. Although hearing people might interpret the forms shown in Figures 26.2 and 26.3 as relating to

Figure 26.1   deaf.

physical deafness, the connotation of these forms within the Deaf community has little to do with medical definitions of hearing loss. The use of such forms indicates that the person referred to is recognized as being a full member of the Deaf community. A corollary of this is that the person is a 'real signer', that is, a user of BSL. Actual degree of hearing loss is quite immaterial. However, significantly perhaps, these forms are rarely, if ever, used for hearing native users of BSL. In almost ten years of observation and research we have never observed such usage.

This brings us to the question, 'Who are members of the Deaf community?' Most typically, we can expect members to be: profoundly deaf people who have either been born deaf or who have become deaf before the age of five (Kyle and Woll 1985); people who use BSL as their first or best language; and people who share specific Deaf-oriented cultural values.

We could regard someone who complies with all three criteria as being in a sense most typical. In practice, degree of physical deafness is less important than the use of BSL and espousal of Deaf values. Deaf people who, in some circumstances at least, make use of hearing aids, frequently see themselves, and indeed are accepted, as full members of the Deaf community. Even Deaf people who have sufficient hearing to communicate by telephone – something quite outside the experience of the profoundly deaf person – may be recognized as a full community member. It is the common language which, as Schlesinger and Meadow (1972) have noted, 'provides the basis for group cohesion and identity' (see also Brien 1981). This does allow hearing people, particularly hearing children of Deaf parents, to be seen as members of the Deaf community. However, there is some doubt as to whether even such hearing people who can be recognized as native signers ever penetrate to the 'core' of the Deaf community.

Figure 26.2   Deaf (sometimes translated as 'deaf and dumb').

In a detailed discussion of the nature of Deaf community and culture, David Brien draws attention to the crucial significance of what might be called the 'cultural' view of deafness proposed here:

> The contrast in orientation (between the cultural and the clinical-pathological) is obvious. The cultural provides a way to call into question the deeply entrenched view that profound deafness is to be automatically associated with disability, and thereby, inability. In a society which sought to accommodate rather than assimilate

Figure 26.3   Deaf (sometimes translated as 'really deaf').

difference, to maximize potential rather than reify differences as unacceptable, the position of deaf people would indeed be different.

(Brien 1981, p. 6)

The extent to which this cultural perspective has, or more accurately has not, permeated the traditional deaf professions, will be discussed in the final section of this chapter. We turn now to what Brien pinpointed as the 'catalyst' for a change towards a cultural perspective, namely work on human sign language and in particular the sign language used in Britain, British Sign Langauge.

British Sign Language (BSL)

It does not come as any surprise to hearing people to learn that Deaf people communicate by means of a sign language. However, most of us have not thought very deeply about what kind of a communication system this might be. There is, for example, a widely held misconception that there is a single, universal sign language, comprehensible to deaf people throughout the world. When hearing people are informed that Sweden has its own sign language, America another, Britain another and so on, they often ask, in some bewilderment, why this should be so. Thus despite accepting without question that there are numerous different spoken languages in the world, hearing people are usually surprised at the variety of sign languages. This is possibly because they have not fully recognized that sign languages are genuinely comparable to other human languages.

BSL is a *visual-gestural* language and both elements of that description are crucial to an understanding of this communication system. It is a language which is perceived by the eye and it therefore exploits forms of patterning which are easily visible. It is produced in the form of gestures which occur in space and in order to understand BSL fully we need to understand something about the specific forms these gestures take and the use which is made of the so-called signing space.

THE WORDS OF BSL

We can begin to understand the nature of linguistic gesture if we look firstly at the individual sign, that is, the unit which corresponds most directly to the spoken word. The notion of *linguistic gesture* is important here. We can all use gestures to communicate if necessary. Indeed most of us use gesture as an accompaniment to speech. Some gestures have communicative significance, but they rarely have specific meanings. Others may take on generalized meanings such as the thumbs up sign, the victory V sign and the alternative V sign with its obscene connotations. The gestures have one thing in common with the linguistic gestures of BSL: they can be described very precisely.

In Figure 26.4, you can see some examples of individual signs of BSL. The hands in each sign have different configurations. In NAME the handshape used has the index and middle finger extended from the closed fist; in CHEAT the hand is closed into a fist and the thumb is extended; in BIRD the thumb and index finger are held parallel to each other and in FAR both index finger and thumb are extended but held at right angles to each other. The gestural words of

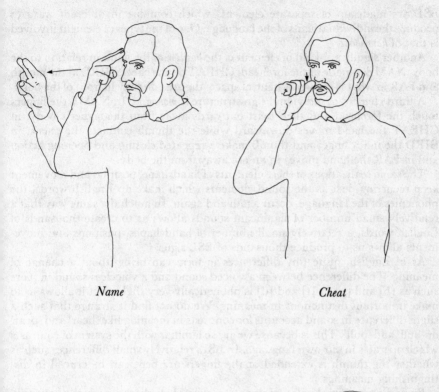

Name

Cheat

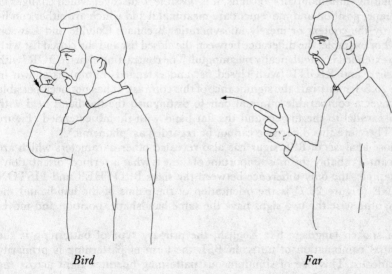

Bird

Far

Figure 26.4

BSL are made up of separate elements which combine in different ways to produce the individual signs of the language. One of the types of element involved is that of *handshape*.

Another significant kind of element is the *position* of the hand in relation to the body. NAME is made at the forehead; CHEAT on the cheek; BIRD at the mouth and FAR in what is known as neutral space: the area directly in front of the body.

A third element of individual sign structure is *movement*. In NAME the fingers touch the forehead and then twist outwards away from the signer's body; in CHEAT the hand moves downward while the thumb contacts the cheek; in BIRD the index finger and thumb make a repeated closing and opening action and in FAR the hand moves in an arc away from the body.

The same realizations of these elements of handshape, position and movement keep recurring, just as the sound elements which make up English words, the phonemes of the language, occur again and again. In much the same way that a relatively small number of significant sounds allows us to create thousands of English words, a relatively small number of handshapes, positions and movements allows us to produce thousands of BSL signs.

As in English, quite tiny differences in form can bring about a change of meaning. The difference between a voiced sound and a voiceless sound in pairs such as [b] and [p] or [t] and [d] is phonetically very slight, but it allows us to make important distinctions in meaning. We do not find it strange that such a slight difference in sound accounts for contrasts in meaning like 'bear' and 'pear' or 'bull' and 'pull'. This is because we are so familiar with the system of contrasts which operates in our own language. In BSL, relatively small differences such as whether the thumb is extended or the fingers are bent can be crucial in distinguishing meanings.

By finding 'minimal pairs' of signs, it is possible to discover which changes in handshape, position and movement are meaningful and which are either conditioned by the context or merely idiosyncratic (Brennan, Colville and Lawson 1984). For example, the difference between the closed fist and the closed fist with thumb extended is linguistically meaningful. The contrasting signs YOUR (with closed fist) and RIGHT (with closed fist and extended thumb) as shown in Figure 26.5 demonstrate the significance of this contrast. It has not been possible to discover a comparable minimal pair to distinguish the flat hand held with thumb parallel to the fingers and the flat hand with thumb extended (Figure 26.6). Therefore this difference cannot be regarded as 'phonemic'.

A close analysis of BSL signs has also revealed other parameters which are significant. Probably the most important of these is what is termed 'orientation'. For example, the only difference between the signs BROTHER and PISTON ENGINE (Figure 26.7) is the orientation of the palms of the hands and the fingers, otherwise the two signs have the same handshape, position and movement.

In a spoken language like English, the primary type of patterning is the sequential combination of units; in BSL the form of patterning is primarily simultaneous. This use of simultaneous patterning operates right across the language, whether we are talking of word structure or grammatical structure. At word level, it simply means that at whatever point we choose to examine the sign, we can describe it in terms of the parameters established above. However, signs

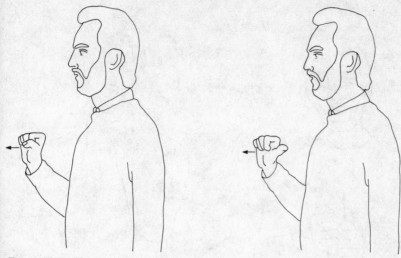

Figure 26.5   Your   Right.

do have some sequential structure as well. Recent studies in America suggest it is possible to recognize sign equivalents of syllables (Liddell 1984). Whether this is the case or not, the interaction of simultaneous and sequential patterning has much to offer in terms of clues towards a greater understanding of human languages in general. This issue is discussed further below in relation to grammatical structure in BSL.

Pictorial signs

Are signs merely pictures in space? The account given so far of individual sign structure focuses on the seemingly arbitrary structural elements which combine together to form BSL signs. So if signs are pictorial, then they are very different from the somewhat idiosyncratic pictures that hearing individuals tend to create if they are asked to present meanings through gesture. Moreover, it is a simple

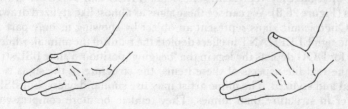

Figure 26.6   'Non-phonemic' contrast.

Figure 26.7   Brother   *Piston Engine*

matter of observation to discover that hearing people who do not know sign language usually have no idea at all what signers are conversing about. This is not really surprising: hearing people do not expect to be able to understand a conversation in Mandarin Chinese or Polish if they do not already know these languages. Nevertheless there is something in the intuition that most of us have that gestural language is potentially able to show greater links between form and meaning than spoken languages.

The extent to which sign languages show a link between form and meaning is one of the most controversial issues in sign language studies today. There are many more links between form and meaning in BSL vocabulary than can be discerned, say, in English. However these links are not all of the same type. Some signs of BSL can be regarded as *iconic-pictorial*. They provide some kind of picture in space of what they represent. The signs TREE and HOUSE are typical examples (Figure 26.8). We can see these signs as almost like stylized drawings or images. Often iconic signs represent an object by showing us only part of that object: the sign ELEPHANT in effect depicts the trunk of the animal, while one of the signs for DOG depicts the legs in the 'begging' position. While BSL structure mirrors the real life aspects of these items, the structure of the signs is highly controlled and stylized. The mime artist may use similar devices, but BSL signs are tighter in structure than mimes. They tend to be more compressed, both spatially and temporally, than equivalent mimes. Moreover, they also use handshapes, positions and movements which may be used completely arbitrarily in other signs.

Some signs are related to their meanings by *conventional* associations of meaning, rather than by inherent links. In BSL, the closed fist handshape with thumb

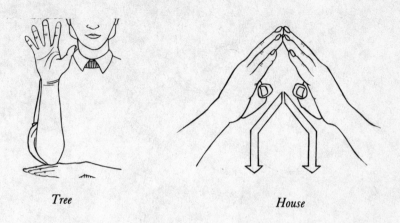

Tree   *House*

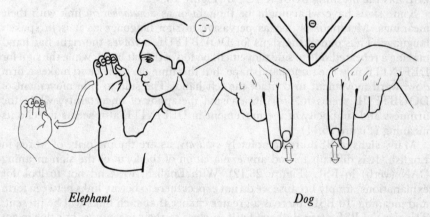

Elephant   *Dog*

Figure 26.8

extended is generally associated with meanings which are connected with notions of 'goodness'; the handshape in which the little finger is extended from the closed fist is linked with 'badness'. Thus the thumb up version is used in GOOD and PRAISE, while the little finger version is used in BAD and CRITICIZE (Figure 26.10). Of course, there is nothing intrinsically bad about the little finger; it is purely a matter of convention that this association is made in BSL. In American Sign Language (ASL) such a convention does not operate: the ASL sign for

Figure 26.9   Suspicious (BSL) or Imagine (ASL).

IDEA and IMAGINE make use of the little finger handshape. A similar form in BSL has the meaning SUSPICIOUS (Figure 26.9).

Some signs have what might be thought of as a *metaphorical* link with their meanings. Metaphor is just as pervasive in sign language as it is in spoken language. Thus one of the signs for DOUBTFUL involves the right flat hand making a repeated side to side movement on top of the left hand, while the sign for DEFINITE uses the same handshape, but this time the right hand makes a firm downward movement to contact the left hand. The side to side movement of DOUBTFUL seems to provide a visual metaphor of uncertainty, while the firmness and simplicity of the movement in DEFINITE also seems to echo its meaning (Figure 26.11).

Many signs of BSL are completely *arbitrary*, as are the majority of words in English. It is difficult to find any explanation of the form of the sign meaning CAN (verb) in BSL (Figure 26.12). With English, we tend not to look for explanations, simply because we do not expect there to be any links between form and meaning. In BSL, there is a greater chance that such links will be present. The signs of BSL often do have built-in clues to their meanings, but this is not always the case. Moreover, it is possible to describe BSL signs in a purely structural way, just as we can in English.

Expanding BSL vocabulary

Just as English has ways of expanding its vocabulary to meet new needs, so does BSL. One of the most productive ways is by means of compounding. Many compounds are formed simply by combining sequentially two separate words of the language to create a new word with a new meaning. THINK and GRASP combine together to form the new compound UNDERSTAND; SAY plus TALK produces RUMOUR (Figure 26.13).

Good

Praise

Bad

Criticize

Figure 26.10

Doubtful

Definite

Figure 26.11

However, BSL is able to do something which is much more difficult, although just about possible to imagine, in spoken language. BSL can combine two separate meaningful signs together *simultaneously* rather than sequentially. This is because we have two hands and can therefore express one sign with one hand and another sign with the other hand. The telephone device for deaf people known as 'Vistel' which makes use of a keyboard, an electronic print-out and a telephone is represented in BSL by means of a simultaneous compound. The left hand uses the handshape normally used in the sign TELEPHONE, but instead of being

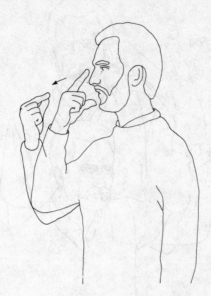

Figure 26.12 Can

place at the ear, the hand is placed in front of the body. The right hand, fully open with fingers spread, is placed under the left hand and the right hand makes a side to side movement with fingers flickering (as in typing). Thus with one hand the signer represents the telephone receiver, which during telephone communication of this kind is fitted to a location on top of the keyboard, and at exactly the same time, represents the action of typing with the other hand. Similar examples of simultaneous compound signs include PERSON plus LEGS, giving us JUMP DOWN ONE'S THROAT, and PERSON plus SCISSORS, producing BAR-BER. (Figure 26.14). The presence of *simultaneous compounds* in BSL stresses the way in which the language exploits its medium to full advantage.

THE GRAMMAR OF BSL

It would take rather more than a few pages, or indeed a few books, to describe the grammatical structure of BSL. Like any other natural human language, BSL has a highly complex and efficient grammatical system. Here it is only possible to give a hint of the nature of BSL grammatical structure. In order to give a sense of the rather specialized use made of spatial-gestural features, the focus will be on those aspects of structure which are not quite so familiar to English speakers. Every grammatical device or feature so far found in BSL has some equivalent in some spoken language of the world, albeit expressed in a different medium.

Non-manual features So far I have concentrated almost entirely on the *manual* signs of BSL, but there are other equally important non-manual elements. Such elements can include movements of the head, eyes, mouth, cheeks, shoulders and trunk.

Understand

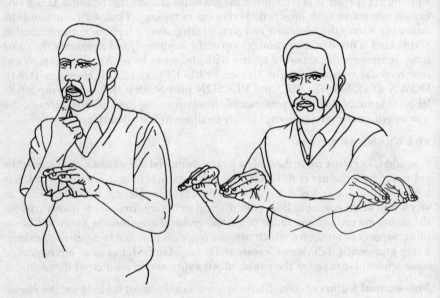

Rumour

Figure 26.13

Vistel   *Jump down one's throat*

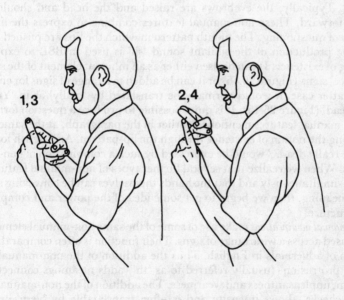

Barber

Figure 26.14

Figure 26.15   'sh' in 'Yes, he is really dead'.

Very often we are dealing with the simultaneous articulation of several non-manual gestures. In some cases, a combination of specific features expresses one particular linguistic function; in other cases, each feature expresses a different function. Yes–no questions in BSL are expressed by means of non-manual features. Typically, the eyebrows are raised and the head and shoulders are pushed forward. These non-manual features combine to express the linguistic function of questioning. The mouth pattern in which the lips are pushed forward as in the production of the sibilant sound 'sh' is used in BSL to express the meaning of existence. It can be used either as an inherent element of the so-called 'existence' signs (Figure 26.16) or it can be added to a range of signs for emphasis. In the latter case, it would normally be translated by 'really' as in 'Yes, he is really dead' (Figure 26.15). It is quite possible to produce a question form, using the non-manual features mentioned earlier in the paragraph, at the same time as expressing the notion of existence through the lip-pattern. An English form such as 'Is he really dead?,' would be expressed by such a combination of non-manual features. When we realize that several further types of non-manual feature could operate simultaneously and that the hands themselves can be conveying separate bits of meaning, then we begin to get some idea of the power and complexity of BSL structure.

Non-manual modifications make use of some of the same non-manual elements and can be used across a wide range of signs. Their function is often comparable to the function of adverbials in English. Thus the addition of the non-manual feature 'tongue protrusion' (usually referred to as 'th') adds meanings connected with boredom, unpleasantness and weariness. The addition of the non-manual feature 'puffed cheeks' shows intensity and is often translatable by 'very' or 'really' (Figure 26.15). Again the simultaneous use of such modifications allows the signer to pack a great deal of information into a very short space of time.

Non-manual features also indicate questions, negatives, topic-comment structures, conditional clauses, sentence boundary markers, and turn-taking markers.

Figure 26.16 *'sh' + existence verb*.

Research on some of these areas is still at an early stage and there is little doubt that, despite our increasing awareness of the role of non-manual features in BSL, we may, as yet, be underestimating their role in the language.

Manual Modifications (Inflections) The study of manual modifications in American Sign Language has led the American linguists Edward Klima and Ursula Bellugi to compare ASL with Latin, insofar as both languages are highly inflected (Klima and Bellugi 1979). BSL also makes use of regular changes in the movement parameter of manual signs which in turn result in systematic changes of meaning.

Directional verbs in BSL illustrate the way in which changes in movement bring about changes in meaning. These verbs make use of modifications to the direction and/or orientation of the sign to provide information concerning the subject and object of the verb. The sign EXPLAIN can be produced so that the movement is made away from the signer, in which case the meaning is 'I explain to you' or towards the signer as in 'You explain to me'. Here the only change of movement is that of direction. In the sign CRITICIZE there is a change in both direction of movement and orientation of the hands. The two closed fist hands with little fingers extended and palms facing each other move away in a circular action for the meaning 'I criticize you': for the meaning 'You criticize me', the palms face towards the signer and the movement is also towards the signer. There are several different categories of directional verbs (Brennan and Colville 1984). Not all verbs can be modulated in this way. The learner of BSL has to learn the relevant classes of verbs and the specific changes involved just as one has to learn specific conjugations in Latin.

There are several other types of inflectional change associated with BSL verbs. One group allows us to express certain types of temporal meaning. In English, we are very used to the idea that the verb phrase can express *tense*: the verb itself is able to give us some information as to when an event took/takes/will take place. Such information is often supported by other carriers of meaning, particularly adverbials such as 'tomorrow', 'in three hours time', 'in 1066' and so on. In BSL, this kind of information is usually given through adverbials alone.

However, BSL does express what is known as *aspectual* meaning within the verb, something which English does not do to the same extent. *Aspect* is a less familiar grammatical category for speakers of English than tense. It is concerned with what we might think of as a temporal perspective. It allows us to look at the same event from different points of view in respect of time. We can see the event as completed, ongoing, just about to start, just about to finish, happening again and again, happening gradually and so on. Most of these aspectual choices are made in BSL by modifying the verb. It is again the movement parameter which allows us to express these choices. The sign COME can be made with short movements to express the meaning of coming regularly or habitually; a slower, repeated movement would express the idea of the same activity happening again and again and again. To express the meaning 'It gradually became dark', the sign DARK is produced with a slow movement (Figure 26.17); to express 'It got darker and darker and darker' the movement is made in several short steps. A sign may be held in its starting position to indicate that the action was just about to take place but did not. Again, not all verbs can take the same aspectual inflection. A detailed grammar of the language would specify the categories of verbs and the inflections they may take.

Location BSL is a spatial language. The signs are made in space and it is possible to exploit this fact grammatically. BSL does this by using the location of signs in space to express relationships among signs. Signs can be localized in space in a number of different ways: by articulating the sign at a particular point in space to the right of the signer, at head height, to the left of the signer and so on; by pointing to specific locations, and by using eye gaze to indicate particular locations. The points in space are then made use of in the choice of movement inflections in directional and other categories of verbs.

As well as providing the basis of subject–object relationships, spatial location can also be used to refer to the physical location of objects or people. Meanings such as 'beside', 'in front of', 'under' and so on can be expressed easily by selective use of space. The language also has what may be thought of as a conventionalized set of locations allowing for the expression of pronouns. It is also possible to use space in a metaphorical way to express more abstract

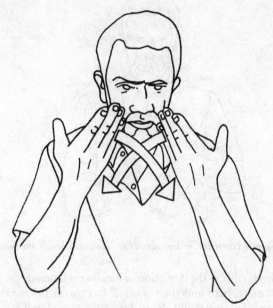

Figure 26.17 It gradually became dark.

relationships. Thus two individuals who are seen as being unequal can be placed so that one is higher than the other in space. BSL exploits such possibilities but in a highly structured manner.

Classifiers One set of signs which has received much attention in recent years has been the group known as 'classifiers'. There are, in fact, many languages of the world which are described as 'classifier languages'. Perhaps the best known of these is Chinese. Many classifier languages require the use of classifying words in numeral and/or demonstrative expressions. Lyons (1977) quotes Mandarin Chinese 'san ben shu', meaning 'three books', in which the word 'ben' is a classifier for flat object. BSL also has signs which classify objects into categories or groups. Indeed 'flat object' is one of the groups expressed in the way. Other categories include 'round object', 'narrow object', 'long thin object' and so on.

Classifiers play an important role in BSL, although this role is not identical to the use of classifiers in a language such as Chinese. One important function of classifiers in BSL is to act as 'pro-forms', i.e. to stand in place of other signs. If we were describing a journey in a car, we would not constantly repeat the sign CAR, but would replace this sign with what is known as a vehicle classifier. This is made with the flat hand held so that the palm is facing left and the fingers are pointing away. The use of the classifier form allows greater flexibility and allows noun and verb functions to be expressed simultaneously: 'the car went up the hill' will be expressed by a single sign using the vehicle classifier and an appropriate handshape.

Figure 26.18   Vehicle classifier + legs classifier 'He stood beside the motorbike'.

Classifiers also facilitate the depiction of locative relationships. If we had been talking about a motorbike and then wanted to express the meaning 'He stood beside the motorbike', we could do so by using two classifiers: the flat hand representing the vehicle and the so-called legs classifier (Figure 26.18). Their position in signing space mirrors their real-life physical relationship. We are able to express all of the information expressed in the English sentence in a single moment of time. The spatial medium and the potential for simultaneity inherent in a gestural language allow this compression of time. The language has adapted to the medium in which it is expressed.

Implications

While the above account has only been able to hint at the full complexity and richness of BSL as a language, it perhaps gives some insight into the way in which BSL structure has evolved to suit the medium in which it is expressed. While there is increasing acceptance of the linguistic status of BSL, both among professionals linked with deafness and the wider public, there remains resistance to the obvious implications of this linguistic standing.

Fifteen years ago, the name BSL was unknown in the professional literature. So-called 'deaf communication' was at worst regarded as primitive and inhuman and at best inadequate and ungrammatical (see Brennan 1976 for further details). Traces of such views, quite strong in some cases, can be found within certain groups and institutions today. Usually, rejection of BSL is couched in rather more liberal and humane terms, but it is often a very practical rejection nonetheless. There have, of course been important steps forward, but we need to examine how far these steps have taken BSL, the Deaf community and, in particular, deaf children.

THE DEAF COMMUNITY

Within the Deaf community itself there is little doubt that research on BSL and the increasing acceptance of BSL as a language has led to a new sense of self-identity. Since the mid-1970s awareness of BSL has increased beyond all recognition. It is almost impossible now to open a copy of the *British Deaf News* (the journal of the British Deaf Association) without seeing a reference to BSL. Campaigns have been mounted by the British Deaf Association (BDA), the National Union of the Deaf, the Deaf Broadcasting Association and other groups to give more practical recognition to BSL within education, the media, and community services. Such organizations play a central role within the Deaf community. The BDA is probably most important in this respect in that it has been part of Deaf culture for over one hundred years. In recent years the BDA has taken on a more direct campaigning role in support of the Deaf community. The newer organizations were founded to fight specifically for Deaf rights. Recognition by Deaf people of the linguistic status and worth of their own language has by no means been automatic. It is important to understand why this should be so. Almost invariably the answer lies in the attitudes inherent within the education system and the pervasive influence of hearing professionals on parents of deaf children and ultimately on deaf children themselves.

Even today, BSL is largely excluded from schools. Many teachers regard it as an acceptable 'playground' language, without recognizing that such a description inevitably gives BSL a lower status than English. In other schools, there remains a wholly negative attitude to the language. Of course, there are important exceptions. However, those teachers and headteachers who do fully accept BSL as a language have to fight the ignorance of local authorities, government officers and the medical establishment. In such contexts, it is not surprising that many deaf people still grow up feeling that their language is a grossly inadequate means of communication, despite the evidence which they, as it were, perform before their very own eyes every day of their lives. It says a lot for the Deaf community, and particularly individual leaders within that community, that they have been able, in recent years, to largely counteract such feelings through information and discussion.

EDUCATION

For many years, BSL was excluded from the education of deaf children. In most textbooks on education it was not even mentioned at all. However, in 1982, the British Association of Teachers of the Deaf put out a policy statement which, while recognizing BSL as a language in its own right, argued that

> The use of British Sign Language, recognized as a language in its own right distinct from English, is not recommended for use in an educational setting, since the identified goal of education is the development of understanding of the English language.

We thus have the ironic situation that BSL, which was once rejected because it was not a proper language, is now rejected because it is. Why should a language which is highly efficient and which deaf children have the potential to acquire without difficulty be rejected by professionals associated with deaf people?

The answer may be connected primarily with the vexed question of whether BSL or English can more appropriately be regarded as the *native language* of deaf children. It seems fairly obvious that the term 'native language' is normally used to refer to the language which the child can acquire naturally; the language used by the child's family; and the language used by the larger community to which the child belongs.

For most children those criteria coincide. For others this is not the case. Many children in Britain belong to families in which a language other than that of the wider community is used for daily interaction. Such children typically grow up using the home language within the context of the home and possibly within a specific community and cultural grouping, but are generally required to use English as the main language at school.

The child who uses Panjabi at home and English in school could be compared with the deaf child who is born to deaf parents and who, while using BSL fluently at home, is required to use English in school. However, there is one crucial difference: while English is accessible to the child using Panjabi, it is *not* directly accessible to the deaf child, at least not in its spoken form. Those who suggest that children from different ethnic and linguistic minorities are faced with a disadvantage in the English-dominated school system must recognize that deaf children of deaf parents are doubly disadvantaged. They are not allowed to use a complex linguistic system which they have already mastered, either as the medium for learning or as a support to their learning of English. Whatever arguments are used for denying children the use of BSL in schools, it is abundantly clear that teachers who ignore the child's competence in BSL are failing to exploit an incredibly rich source for further linguistic and cognitive development.

What then of those other deaf children who have hearing parents? These children constitute by far the larger group of deaf children, comprising approximately ninety per cent of the population of deaf children. What is their native language? The language of home and of the wider community is clearly English. In that sense, it would seem to be their native language. However, deaf children typically do not, and usually cannot acquire English in the normal way at the normal rate. Even those teachers who espouse 'natural oralism' and argue for a less structured approach to teaching English to deaf children, freely admit that there is a 'waiting' period involved before the child begins to produce language. This waiting period may continue well into the primary school years, long after the solid core of English structure has been acquired by the hearing child. The physical fact of profound hearing loss makes English, or indeed any spoken language, an impossible native language for the deaf child. David Crystal (1985) comments that the notion of 'native language' has the implication 'that this language, having been acquired naturally during childhood, is the one about which the speaker will have the most reliable intuitions...' (p. 204). In fact, the lack of such 'native intuitions' about English is one of the continuing difficulties for deaf adults in using English. To claim that English is the native language of the deaf child, when the child struggles to have mastery over its structures and is constantly hampered by the lack of an intuitive awareness of its patterning, goes against the accepted usage of the phrase. In this sense, 'natural acquisition' is an essential criterion in relation to the concept of native language.

Deaf children of Deaf parents demonstrate all too clearly that Deaf children have the same potential to acquire language at the normal time and normal rate as hearing people. The only difference is that this language must be one which is expressed in a visual-gestural medium. BSL is just such a language. However, opponents of the use of BSL point out what at first sight seems to be an insuperable difficulty: that the hearing parents of deaf children are not themselves fluent in the language and indeed have probably never even heard of BSL. What chance is there of a deaf child of hearing parents being exposed to BSL if the parents themselves do not know or use it? This is a reasonable question and must be examined fully. However, on closer examination, we realize that we are dealing with an essentially practical problem rather than an inherent theoretical difficulty.

PARENTS OF DEAF CHILDREN

Hearing parents of deaf children are in a particularly vulnerable position in that they are 'at the mercy' of the experts as so many of them can testify. The experiences recounted by Lorraine Fletcher (Chapter 14 of this volume) and Rikki Kittell (1982) demonstrate all too clearly the unwillingness of most medical professionals and many educationalists and psychologists to provide information on either BSL or the deaf people who use it. Indeed Rikki Kittell points out that it was the absence of Deaf people from these professional groups that made her and her husband somewhat suspicious of the expert advice they were being given. Of course, in the past there was some excuse. No major research on BSL was carried out until the late 1970s, although work on other sign languages, particularly those of Sweden, Denmark and the USA should have alerted professionals to the linguistic richness of BSL. Now that such research is available where does it leave parents? Unfortunately, in practice, it leaves them not much further forward.

As a proponent of early exposure to BSL, I see the following as a kind of 'ideal' scenario. Early after diagnosis the parents are given detailed information about the communication potential of their child. (Note that the stress is as much on potential, and thereby genuine possibilities, as on problems.) This would involve liaison with a professional team which would include at least one core member of the Deaf community fluent in BSL. The parents would be offered an appropriate range of services, including high-level audiological help, but would also be introduced to the concept of early acquisition of BSL leading to functional bilingualism. The parents would be offered intensive training in BSL, by trained Deaf people, and home visits involving Deaf people capable of interacting with the child and family in an appropriate variety of BSL. Such a policy would allow normal interaction to take place between parents and child; it would give the child direct access to a full linguistic system, thus allowing the child to acquire the system at the normal rate and finally, it would provide a solid base on which to build learning English. Not only is such a situation virtually unknown in Britain, it is an ideal which relatively few professionals seek to attain. What then are the arguments against such an approach?

Perhaps the first major argument is that it is not possible for hearing parents to learn BSL and certainly not at the rate which would be required to, as it were, 'keep up with the child'. Possibly the source of this argument is the genuine difficulty which many people have experienced when trying to learn to 'communicate with deaf people'. This rather loose general terms has been used here deliberately because it is only very recently indeed that genuine attempts have been made to teach BSL to hearing people. In the past, hearing people went along to sign classes and were taught individual signs of the language. They were not taught the grammar of the language, and were usually taught a very selective vocabulary. Indeed, in many cases those teaching 'sign communication' may themselves have been unaware of many aspects of the language (see Colville 1981 for further discussion of the teaching of BSL).

It is not surprising then that many hearing people never seemed to get beyond the most rudimentary steps in learning to communicate. The development of such initiatives as the British Sign Language Training Agency based at Durham University and supported by the BDA, is helping to change the whole approach to the teaching of BSL. The BSLTA has a Deaf director, Mr Clark Denmark, and is committed to training Deaf people themselves to teach their own language. The statement that hearing people cannot learn BSL is founded then on previous practice, which has little to do with current research and methodology.

Moreover, there are probably no local authorities in the country which provide full-scale support for parents to learn BSL. In a few cases, MSC programmes or similar schemes have been initiated by individual teachers, units or schools in order to make it possible for deaf people to be fully involved. However, it is difficult for such programmes to provide the continuity and intensive training which is required. It is not impossible for hearing parents to learn BSL, but like most other educational ventures it is foolish to imagine that good results can be achieved 'on the cheap'.

However, even if we imagine a perfect training system, hearing parents may well differ in the standards which they achieve. Is there any way around such a situation? There would seem to be two elements which provide a kind of fail-safe device for the children of such parents. Firstly, the involvement from an early stage of Deaf people who are fluent in BSL is crucial. In such a way the children will have regular exposure to the language in all its richness. An associated bonus is that the children will grow up aware of, and familiar with Deaf people. Even today there are headteachers who think it inappropriate for deaf children to have any contact at all with the adult Deaf world. Such contact is important for both parent and child. It removes unnecessary fears and ignorance about Deaf adults and the community to which they belong.

The second element which comes to the rescue of those hearing parents who do have genuine difficulties in learning the language is the extremely exciting finding from sign language acquisition research that deaf children can acquire sign language features even when exposed to a relatively poor model. While this may seem odd, it fits in with other findings from other areas of linguistic work. It is well known that teachers and parents have observed very young deaf children producing forms not presented to them by any adult, and yet which are very close to aspects of BSL structure. Perhaps the most obvious example of this is the significant use of location by deaf children. Deaf children can also be seen to modify signs, both manually and non-manually, in ways that are comparable to, although not always identical with, modifications used with BSL itself.

SIGN SYSTEMS

Deaf adults themselves rarely use only BSL, although this is generally the preferred language when communicating with other members of the Deaf community. Obviously Deaf people also live in the wider hearing world and have had to devise ways of communicating with hearing people. Some may do so by using a second language, English. However, the number of profoundly deaf people who can, or choose to use spoken English alone as an efficient form of communication is very small indeed. As in other contexts where two mutually unintelligible languages co-exist side by side, a 'pidgin' language has developed. The best way to think of this is that it contains grammatical features common to both languages. The term 'Pidgin Sign English' (PSE) emphasizes the fact that two separate languages are involved: a sign language (in our case BSL) and English. There are several important points to be aware of when considering Pidgin Sign English. Firstly, it is much more variable in structure than either BSL or English. An individual deaf person may vary the extent of BSL features within Pidgin Sign English according to the likely degree of understanding of such features by the person being addressed. Similarly, the Deaf person may use more English-like patterning, such as English word-order, and English function words, especially if the addressee is known to be unfamiliar with BSL. The forms of PSE used by hearing people tend to be more English-oriented, although this will again depend upon the person's own fluency in the two separate languages and the needs of the addressee. PSE has evolved naturally and is not an artificially created sign system. While the term PSE is not regularly used by Deaf people, most members of the Deaf community are fairly comfortable with this form of communication.

Deaf people tend to take a somewhat different view of the artificial sign systems which have been developed. These are systems which are aimed at expressing English through a visual-gestural medium. Thus the aim is not simply communication, but communication through English. The term *Signed English* is often used to describe such a system, although there are many different forms of Signed English being used in schools today. (Another generalized term is *Manually-Coded English*. The term *Signed English* is used here because it is current among teachers of the deaf.) In some cases, individual schools have simply developed their own systems; in other cases groups of schools have come together to agree on a system. Perhaps the best known in educational circles is that developed in England by the 'Working Party on Signed English'. This has been published in two volumes under the title *Signed English for Schools* (1984, 1985). As in most other Signed English systems, the vocabulary of the system is taken from BSL. However, additional created signs are used in order to convey exact English patterns. *Communication Link*, published by Beverly School for the Deaf also specifies a number of artificial sign additions to be used to convey past tense endings, the 'ing' participle, etc. The proponents of Signed English systems usually require that the system be used simultaneously with spoken English. Indeed it is one of the operating principles set out by the Working Party on Signed English that signing is made simultaneously with good, clear speech and that the pace and rhythm of communication aimed at is that of normal speech: so that pupils have the best opportunity to develop towards normal speech.

(Working Party on Signed English 1984, p. 16)

While such an approach is understandable in the context of teaching English, it inevitably means that Signed English is a very different kind of system from BSL. Although it may serve a useful purpose within the educational setting, it is questionable whether it can ever be as efficient, either as English alone (for hearing people) or BSL alone (for Deaf people). Why should this be so? The answer lies in the way that BSL, like other sign languages, has developed forms of patterning which suit the visual-gestural medium. While all of the sign languages so far analysed differ in their grammatical and lexical patterning, they all use complex facial and bodily movement, as well as hand movement, to express linguistic meaning. All use spatial location in a meaningful way, all exploit direction and movement parameters to express modifications of verb meaning and so on.

Such forms are at times compatible with some forms of Signed English; in other cases they are in conflict. It may be possible to use the appropriate directional movement for a verb such as 'help', depending on the particular subject–object relations being expressed. However, the BSL mouth pattern 'sh' expressing the notion of existence cannot be used if Signed English requires the simultaneous expression of some form of the verb 'to be'. Of course, the attitude towards the use of such BSL forms varies both according to the policy espoused by a particular school and the individual approach of the teacher involved. The Working Party on Signed English appears to take a very positive approach to the use of BSL forms and argues that

those wishing to gain skill in using Signed English should have a basic knowledge of British Sign Language before studying Signed English in detail (p. 8).

However, some of the operating principles outlined by the working party inevitably reduce the possibility of exploiting BSL patterning to the full. Thus Principle 7 states that:

a sign is used for each word or morpheme spoken (and that a single sign is not used to represent a phrase): so that pupils are more easily able to relate the signs to spoken and written language (p. 20).

This is the kind of principle which will be interpreted differently by different people. However, taken at face value it seems to mean that the Signed English version of 'get up' would require two separate signs for the words 'get' and 'up', although there is a single sign in BSL which corresponds directly to this meaning. The BSL form, which makes use of two classifier handshapes, suits the medium more directly.

There are numerous similar examples which could be quoted. The information intended by the phrase 'carried on' in a statement such as 'He carried on walking' would be expressed in BSL by a specific modification to the movement of the sign WALK. The sign sentence would thus require two signs at the most (the pronoun is not always made explicit if it is already clear from the context who is doing the walking). Presumably most teachers would not use the BSL sign for CARRY in this context as it would be visually-semantically incorrect; yet not to do so would seem to violate Principle 7. Even the use of a sign such as CONTINUE along with WALK, while making more visual-semantic sense, would ignore the potential for internal modification inherent in BSL verbs.

While the aim of presenting English in a signed form is a reasonable one for *some* educational purposes, there are difficulties precisely because a language which has developed structures appropriate to the spoken medium is being transfered to the visual-gestural medium. What this often means, in practice, is a 'manual' medium, as the non-manual possibilities of the visual-gestural system are usually only used to a limited degree.

CHILDREN'S USE OF SIGNED ENGLISH AND BSL

The whole reason for using Signed English systems is to help the child to use and learn English. It is highly unlikely that anyone inside or outside education could oppose such an aim. Not only is English the language of the wider hearing world in which the child must live, but it is also a language which, unlike BSL, has a well-established written form. Access to the written word is just as essential for the deaf child as it is for the hearing child. Yet standards in reading and writing of English by profoundly deaf children have been notoriously low (Conrad 1979). However, recent research brings into question whether Signed English alone is the answer.

As indicated earlier, some research suggests that deaf children exposed to Signed English forms *re-fashion* these forms so that they become more like BSL. It is as if they have a deep-seated intuition as to what kinds of structures suit the visual-gestural medium. They seem to do easily and naturally what the hearing adult learning BSL finds difficult to accomplish. In the case of the adult, the difficulty presumably lies in the fact that initial language learning has taken place via the spoken medium: the spatial-visual qualities of the gestural medium have to be explicitly learned.

Evidence of this re-fashioning and re-creation of gestural input by the child comes from a range of research in Scandinavia, France, Britain and America (Ahlgren 1984; Bouvet 1982; Wickham 1984 and Supalla 1986). The most recent research by Supalla examined the language use of young deaf children exposed to a Signed English system called SEE2 used in the USA. Supalla found that although none of these children was exposed to American Sign Language, the results showed 'the powerful nature of a tendency to organize signed languages in terms of spatial principles, even where there is no adult sign model who provides such an input' (Supalla 1986, p. 14–15).

Thus, in practice, Supalla found that children always used spatially modified verb forms even though their teachers never did so and even though they had never been exposed to such models in other contexts. However, Supalla also found that the children did not all use exactly the same spatial devices. Just as all sign languages of the world exploit spatial devices, but vary in the particular forms that such devices take, so these deaf children exploited spatial possibilities, but in different ways.

What does this mean, in practical terms, to the teacher or the parent of a deaf child? Primarily, it means that even if the input to the child is 'inadequate' compared to full BSL, the child will adapt towards a BSL-like version. Thus in the very early stages of acquisition, the parent who is trying to use BSL, but is tending towards a more English kind of signing should not worry too much. The child will almost inevitably use more BSL-like structures. Of course, to use the actual structures of BSL, exposure to BSL in use is necessary and this is where the role of Deaf adults and Deaf children of Deaf parents can be crucial.

For the teacher these findings may seem at first glance to have somewhat negative implications. They certainly bring into some question the efficiency of Signed English as a communication system. It is important to stress that this does not mean that some form of Signed English should not have some role in the teaching of English. Of course, it is extremely useful to have some way of making the detail of English grammatical structure available to the profoundly deaf child. What we need to question is whether it really makes sense to use Signed English as the major form of communication within the school and the home, when there is a far more efficient system available and easily acquirable by the child. It seems strange that we should choose the less efficient system to teach the deaf child physics or maths or biology. It is even stranger that we should insist on this being the form of ordinary daily interaction. It is as if we were condemning the child to an eternal language lesson. Proponents of such an approach have provided virtually no rationale as to why BSL should be ignored in this way. Instead there is merely repetition of the fact that English is the language of the wider community and therefore must be acquired. It is time that those of us in education took a much closer look at how we can make the most of BSL, not only for the child's personal and general educational development, but for learning English. We know that Deaf people are very keen indeed to learn English well (Kyle and Allsop 1982). However, they also wish to have the freedom to use BSL. These two objectives can be compatible and mutually supportive, rather than contradictory.

BILINGUALISM AND MULTI-CULTURALISM

It is surprising to note that the debate on multi-culturalism and bilingualism has only surfaced relatively recently within deaf education. Yet it does not take a great effort of the imagination to relate the situation of Deaf people to that of other linguistic minorities living in Britain. The claim that schools have participated and continue to participate in a system that discriminates against such minority groups (Nixon 1985) is regrettably true of the deaf educational system. As within mainstream education, there is no suggestion that such discrimination is intended or even recognized. However, now that Deaf people themselves are becoming more aware of their rights and we have more evidence on which to base new and more radical methodology, we need to be prepared to reconsider current policy and practice. John Wright has established a set of criteria for evaluating work within multi-cultural schools. Profoundly deaf children find themselves in a variety of educational settings, therefore the precise criteria may not apply in all cases. Nevertheless several of these principles could serve as a helpful guideline to those seeking to provide a full, non-discriminatory education for deaf children:

- Bring minority languages into the learning situation for utilitarian, not tokenist reasons.

- Integrate the work stimulated by minority language/books/tapes/ workcards etc. with the mainstream of class activity.
- Provide within the classroom the opportunity of developing and refining the skills of bilingualism – translation and interpretation – not only of language but of cultural experience.
- Preserve and defend the minority group student's rights to choose for her/himself the balance of minority and majority group language and culture which best meets the desired identity of the individual.

(Wright 1982, pp. 19–20)

It is just such a positive approach to the language and culture of the deaf community which has been put into practice by Miranda Llewellyn-Jones and her colleagues in a Nottingham unit:

BSL is treated as the primary language and English as a second language to be taught after the primary language has become firmly established. The particular bilingual model chosen is that of developmental interdependence: the development of skills in a second language is a function of skills already developed in a first language.

(Llewellyn-Jones 1984, p. 7)

The Nottingham work is being closely monitored and the results to date appear to give strong support for this approach. The success of the scheme seems to be linked with two main factors: the use of profoundly deaf people as major members of the team and the recognition of the importance of finding a bridge between BSL and the written form of English. Llewellyn-Jones and her team have developed an approach called 'sign literacy' which allows the child to read and write a code for Sign Language, prior to learning the written system of English. This allows the child to make a link between the two systems – in effect, to see the point of learning to read and write.

The work of Llewellyn-Jones and other innovative teachers allows BSL to be used in a positive way to help the child achieve English literacy. At the same time, both languages are respected and valued. Perhaps the irony of a purely Signed English approach is that the child may well be able to 'read' an English text, using the appropriate sign forms, without understanding a word of it. If, on the other hand, a child uses appropriate BSL-like 'translations', then we are able to recognize that the child has made progress.

In a recent presentation (Tulloch 1985), Kay Tulloch, a classroom teacher from Garvel Centre for the Deaf in Greenock, demonstrated how children in her group could differentiate between the somewhat erratic meanings of English words such as 'put', 'went' and 'get' by using a range of BSL signs and BSL modifications. Thus different signs or modifications would be used to express the meaning of 'went' in the following examples:

She swallowed hard and her eyes *went shiny*.

'Now,' gran *went on* as she started to mix all the things together.

I *went round* all the classrooms.

Slowly the afternoon *went by*.

The use of a single sign for 'went' in such examples would not demonstrate understanding. Similarly the child who expressed the whole sentence, 'All the time Patrick was hopping up and down on my shoulder', by using a single sign, made with the legs classifier performing a repeated movement on top of his left shoulder, showed absolutely clearly that he was reading for meaning.

Rather than dismissing BSL as a 'playground' language, teachers such as these are recognizing both the potential of BSL itself and the linguistic potential of each deaf child.

Conclusion

Although more linguistic and educational research is clearly required, there is nevertheless sufficient evidence at this very moment to bring into question the absence of BSL from most of our schools.

Of course, the notion of 'mother-tongue' or 'community language' teaching remains controversial within mainstream education, especially after the findings of the Swann Report (DES 1985). Nevertheless, the special situation of deaf children requires that we give urgent consideration to their needs. Even if we simply adopted the recommendations of the Swann Report in relation to other community languages, this would mean that bilingual resource persons (Deaf people using BSL and English) would be used in the classroom; BSL as a minority language would be included in the secondary curriculum and examination boards would be actively considering offering examinations in this language. So far there is little evidence that the relevant educational authorities are taking such action. Moreover, the special situation of deaf children, whereby BSL is the only feasible first language, should encourage us to move beyond the findings of the Swann Report to initiate more radical alternative provision for deaf children.

Research findings on BSL and other sign languages should encourage us to re-think established positions. BSL has evolved to meet new needs: let us hope that the professions and the professionals can do the same.

References

Ahlgren, A. 1984. 'Sign language development', paper presented at the SIGN 84 Conference, Edinburgh.

Baker, C. and Cokely, D. 1980. *American Sign Language*, Silver Springs, Maryland, T.J. Publishers.

Bouvet, D. 1982. *La Parole de l'Enfant Sourd*, Paris, Presses Universitaires de France.

Brennan, M. 1976. *Can Deaf Children Acquire Language?*, supplement to *British Deaf News*, February 1976.

Brennan, M. and Colville, M. D. 1984. *Final Report to Economic and Social Science Research Council*.

Brennan, M., Colville, M. D. and Lawson, L. 1984. *Words in Hand: A Structural Analysis of the Signs of British Sign Language* (second ed.), Edinburgh, Moray House College/Carlisle, BDA.

Brien, D. 1981. 'Is there a deaf culture available to the young deaf person?', paper presented to the National Council of Social Workers with the Deaf.

Colville, M. D. 1981. 'The influence of British Sign structure on communication teaching techniques', in Woll, B., Kyle, J. and Deuchar, M. (eds.), *Perspectives on British Sign Language and Deafness*, London, Croom Helm.

Conrad, R. 1979. *The Deaf School Child*, London, Harper and Row.

Crystal, D. 1985. *A Dictionary of Linguistics and Phonetics* (second ed.), Oxford, Basil Blackwell.

Department of Education and Science (DES) 1985. *Education for All* (The Swann Report), London, HMSO.

Kittell, R. 1982. 'A parent's perspective', paper presented to Parent-Teacher Group, Ayrshire, Scotland.

Klima, E. and Bellugi, U. 1979. *The Signs of Language*, Cambridge, Mass., Harvard University Press.

Kyle, J. G. and Allsop, L. 1982. 'Communicating with young deaf people: Some issues', *Journal of the British Association of Teachers of the Deaf*, 6, pp. 71–9.

Kyle, J. G. and Woll, B. 1985. *Sign Language: the Study of Deaf People and their Language*, Cambridge, Cambridge University Press.

Liddell, S. 1984. 'THINK and BELIEVE: sequentiality in ASL signs', *Language*, 60, pp. 372–399.

Llewellyn-Jones, M. 1984. 'Aspects of bilingualism', paper presented at the SIGN 84 Conference, Edinburgh.

Lyons, J. 1977. *Semantics* (Vol. 2), Cambridge, Cambridge University Press.

Nixon, J. 1985. *A Teacher's Guide to Multicultural Education*, Oxford, Basil Blackwell.

Padden, C. 1980. 'The Deaf community and the culture of Deaf people', in Baker, C. and Battison, R. (eds.), *Sign Language and the Deaf Community*, Silver Springs, National Association of the Deaf.

Schlesinger, H. and Meadow, K. 1972. *Sound and Sign: childhood deafness and mental health*, Berkeley, University of California Press.

Supalla, S. 1986. 'Manually Coded English: an understanding of modality's role in signed language development', abstracts from *Theoretical Issues in Sign Language* Conference, Rochester, New York.

Tulloch, K. 1985. Presentation on 'Reading and Sign' at Parents' Course, Gourock, Scotland.

Wickham, C. 1984. 'The Nature of Total Communication', paper presented at SIGN 84 Conference, Edinburgh.

Working Party on Signed English 1984/5. *Signed English for Schools* (Vols. 1 and 2), London, WPSE/RNID.

Wright, J. 1982. *Bilingualism in Education*, Issues in Race and Education (11 Carleton Gardens, London N19 5AQ).

27   Being with Sam: four children talk about their classmate

Will Swann

Chapter 1 describes how Samantha Hulley, who has severe and multiple disabilities, attends an ordinary primary school and is shortly to join a comprehensive school. This chapter provides a brief glimpse of the responses of other children in her class to Sam. Readers may wish to read Chapter 1 first to gain an idea of Sam's personality, interests and abilities. What these children say in response to adult questioning is often surprising. They challenge our own ingrained notions of 'handicap', so much so that at times it is difficult to find a way of talking with them that does not force them to use the categories of their interviewer – categories which may be remote from their own.

Sharing classroom life with a classmate with severe, multiple disabilities is a rare experience. Many of Sam Hulley's class have known her since the infants school she and they attended. I talked to four of her classmates about their relationship with her and how they saw her. Chris, Lindsey, David and Maxine were chosen by their class teacher principally because she felt they would have a lot to say. They are not representatives of their class, but their general attitude to Sam is not atypical.

I wanted to know how they described Sam and how they thought about her. It would be naive to imagine that they would describe her as just another classmate. The very fact that I wanted to talk to them about her guaranteed this would not happen. But what words would they use to talk about her? Would the idea of handicap occur, or would their descriptions be more individual and specific? I began with Chris, almost inviting a stereotyped description:

> *WS:* What sort of person is Sam?
> *Chris:* Well, she has her times, sometimes. When this new lady [Sam's new welfare assistant] came to look after her, she was crying 'cos she wanted her mum, 'cos it's like being with a stranger, and taken away from your mum and dad. So, really, she wasn't used to her. But she's getting used to her now. But she still has her times . . . But she's OK. She's nice, you know. Once you get used to her you think, you know, more of her.

I was interested in the characteristics of Sam that were uppermost in their minds, and with David tried another way to get at these:

> *WS:* David, suppose somebody came up to you who'd never seen Sam before. How would you describe her?
> *David:* Kind . . . frightened . . . nice.
> *WS:* What about you, Lindsey?
> *Lindsey:* Well, she sometimes cries 'cos she likes her dad. She gets Gil [her special teacher] or Ann [her welfare assistant] to help her with what she does.
> *WS:* What's the most important thing about Sam for you, Maxine?

Maxine: Well, Sam gets along alright but when we first saw Sam with Ann, she sort of wanted to go home and kept wanting to go to the door. But 'cos Ann was looking after her she wouldn't let her, so Sam felt as if Ann didn't like her, so she started crying.

Of all the facts about Sam that they could have mentioned, this seemed an improbable list. None of them seemed to consider it important enough to list any of the dramatic differences between themselves and Sam. I decided to force the issue:

WS: Do you think of Sam as someone very different from you?
All: No...not really.
Chris: Well, first time you think so, but once you get to know her it's OK. You just think of her as a normal person.
David: She was when she started coming into our class at first.
Chris: It was hard, it was hard to get used to it, but once you got used to it, I liked it myself. I think it gave more...it would be boring if there wasn't anyone, you know...like I think it's more adventurous with people like that.

Chris and David acknowledged that they had had to overcome some initial difficulties in their relationship with Sam. Had these difficulties persisted, and if so what exactly caused problems?

WS: Do you ever find Sam a bit difficult?
Maxine: When she's in a mood, yes.
Chris: When she don't want to do things.
David: When she wants to go out and we can't let her because she's not allowed out, she's got to stay with Gil.
Chris: Yeah, one day when it was wet play, Gil went downstairs and Sam wanted to go and get some coffee, 'cos she likes drinking it, but Helen and me was trying to say 'No, Sam, you can't do it', and she kept going out the door.
Lindsey: At one point, we were in the hall, because Gil had gone into the staff room and Mrs MacKay [the headteacher] had a visitor and Sam kept thinking that Gil was in Mrs MacKay's office and she kept opening the door, and we kept having to say, 'No, Sam', and trying to keep her away.

When problems arise, then, they were partly caused by matters that could affect anyone. These children also knew that difficulties could arise because at some times they acted as Sam's supervisors, rather than just her classmates. Their relationship with her was not always equal. Such inequality was not an enduring feature. When they described their work in and out of the classroom with Sam, they were keen to stress the value of Sam's work. They neither disparaged her efforts, nor was there a hint of a patronizing tone in their comments.

WS: What sort of work does Sam do in the classroom?
Chris: She does the same thing as us. She has her own book to stick her art in. And she does the things we done, and they're just as good as we could do.
David: Better.
WS: Can you give me an example?
Chris: Yeah, like the hessian. [This episode is described in Chapter 1. Sam and Gil were working together at a table with a group of children. All of them were making collages of trees by sticking wool onto hessian.] She was sticking these things on, and the people that was with her didn't have any ideas and Sam just stuck 'em down and she came up with quite a good thing.

Maxine: And then everyone else copied.

Lindsey: When we're doing ordinary work she gets out her picture cards and things.

WS: What are these picture cards?

Chris: You get food and things like that and the play shops... I saw Gil, she was putting out coins and she made her get... find the coin like... There's 20p. And she would find it for Gil. And when you go to the shops with Sam she gives out the money to the shopkeeper. [Shopping trips are a daily part of Sam's education. Several children go with her each day.]

WS: Maxine, tell me what happens on a shopping trip.

Maxine: Well, Sam sees us, and she thinks: 'Oh good, some children are around me; now I won't have to start screaming if I don't go the right way I want to'. 'Cos we go to different shops sometimes. And we push her sometimes, and when you get to the shops, Sam looks around to see what she wants and then tells Gil or Ann.

Chris: She done signs. Like 'Hardware', she'd be putting her hand out. That was a new one.

Lindsey: Miss Madden [the class teacher] asked us to get something, and we got something else, and we were half-way back and Sam kept using signs, and she reminded Gil that we had to get the thing.

WS: Can Sam talk? Can she use words?

All: No.

Maxine: She can say dad and mum.

David: She's learnt a lot since she came here.

Maxine: She's trying to say some words, but it doesn't actually come out.

WS: But she can still say things to you.

Lindsey: Yeah, she can do signs. Like 'door' and 'knock on the door'. She does that when she wants to go home.

WS: How much do you think Sam understands?

Maxine: All of it.

David: Most of the time.

Having asked them earlier about the difficulties of being with Sam, I went on to ask them to recall episodes when they had particularly enjoyed Sam's company.

Maxine: Well sometimes when Gil goes to get her coffee Sam says in signs: 'Can I read you the story?' and Sam really likes that.

David: I like it when she goes to Astonbury Wood with us last week.

Lindsey: Once when Gil was getting her coffee, we had a mat out in the hall, 'cos it was too cold to go to the shops and we were pretending. Sam was pretending that the mat was an island and she kept pushing us off into the sea – onto the floor, that was the sea.

Many of their comments take the form of short stories about episodes with Sam. This particular quality about their description of Sam means that they seldom resort to generalities. Ideas which might not readily fit together into lay or professional conceptions of 'mental handicap' merge without difficulty in these children's minds. It presents no contradiction to them that Sam should be taught to discriminate coins yet should also use art materials more creatively than they do. They regularly imputed ideas and motivations to Sam which she may or may not have had. Both Maxine and Lindsey do this repeatedly. The fact that Sam does not say words does not lead Maxine to conclude she has nothing to say. When Lindsey describes the rough and tumble of a pretend game, she brings Sam right into it, and assumes that she too thinks of the mat as an island. Their sense of Sam as someone whose mind was limited only by her body was evident throughout our conversation.

When I asked them how Sam should be treated by others, David said, 'treat her normally' and Chris and Lindsey took up the theme:

Chris: Yeah, because some of them just shout down thinking that she's, you know, deaf, but she isn't, she can . . .

Lindsey: She'll understand everything you say, but she can't . . .

They were also worried about the effect of older children's ignorance, when she moved to secondary school:

David: Yeah, because there'd be people a lot older than Sam. They might start thinking: 'Oh, she's stupid, or something'.

Maxine: And she isn't.

Lindsey: No.

The discussion then moved on to their reflections on how others ought to treat Sam, on their attitudes to the idea of special schooling for Sam, and what her future held. I wanted to know if they expected the rest of the world to respond to Sam as they had come to, or whether they believed she would have difficulties born of other people's ignorance and inexperience. If so, were these problems surmountable? I asked them to imagine Sam was moving to another part of the country and another ordinary school.

WS: Do you think they would treat Sam normally . . . to begin with?

David: Not to begin with, no.

Chris: Because some people were calling her names, and I really felt, you know, that's horrid. It was from our class and I though that was terrible.

Lindsey: Because when Sam was coming downstairs – because our classroom's upstairs – and we were having dinner with her, some people were standing at the bottom and shouting, 'Come on, Sam', as if she could go faster. But she can't.

WS: What do you do when that happens? Do you just ignore it or say something, or what?

Maxine: Say something.

WS: What do you do when that happens, Maxine?

Maxine: Well, if I was in Sam's situation, and somebody said that to me, I'd just, well, I'd go downstairs and then I'd think that I would tell them something like: 'you should have more consideration'.

Chris: And give them help, help to, you know, understand that Sam's just like us.

They were all aware of the existence of special schools, although one of them, Lindsey, was possibly confused as between special schools and children's homes. Even though they clearly accepted Sam's role in their own classroom, this did not mean that they would necessarily hold any views on the more general desirability of mainstream or special schooling. It was at this point that my own notions of categories of children crept into the conversation, when I referred to 'children like Sam'. Up till now, such an expression was rare in their own talk. It could not be assumed that in using it they would refer to 'children with mental handicaps'. They might equally have been referring to themselves or any other child. It may be a sign of the necessarily unequal distribution of power in this conversation that my presupposition was not challenged. It may also be a sign of how tenuous their conception of Sam may be, and how sensitive to adult redefinition.

WS: Now, there are teachers who actually think that children like Sam shouldn't be in ordinary schools. They should be in special schools.

Maxine: No.

David: I think they get more help with ordinary children.

Chris: Yeah, 'cos it helps them more, I think.

David: Makes them feel confident.

Maxine: Because if they go out and see somebody ordinary like us, they'd think: 'Well, I'm going to do something stupid, because I'm not like that and I don't have to . . . I can't do the things they do, and I don't know what they do . . . and things like that.

WS: How does being in an ordinary school make Sam more confident?

Chris: 'Cos she could see other people doing things and then she'll have more . . . more . . . you know . . . I can do it, as they can. And then she'll forget about what she is and then she might . . . can do better things.

Their sense that Sam was well placed in an ordinary primary classroom was very strong, although they were fully aware that this depended on the presence of Sam's welfare assistant and special teacher. They did not believe that she could participate successfully without this support. What then would happen at a secondary school? At nine and ten years old, they still had another four terms before they would transfer at eleven, so their answers to this question necessarily depend on whatever knowledge of life in a secondary school they have amassed.

WS: Do you think she'll be able to go to a secondary school?

Lindsey: It might be a bit difficult to get around from classroom to classroom.

David: Kids would laugh at her, some of them.

Chris: Yeah, my friend he . . . only on little things they get picked on, like he wears a tie, and he's the only one and he gets picked on about that.

WS: Now, that's a problem; do you think it's a problem that can be solved?

Chris: I would think it can be solved.

Lindsey: She'll be OK.

WS: So is it just a question of time?

Chris: Yeah, it's time.

Maxine: But meanwhile, in that time, Sam might be getting more upset and more, because they're picking on her and she can't pick on them back, like we do pick on people.

WS: Should Sam still go to an ordinary secondary school all the same?

Chris: Yeah.

David: I think so.

Lindsey: I think it could help her a bit more, because she would get a lot more attention than if she's in a special school, 'cos they'll be all the same . . . as her.

Lindsey's final comment is particularly difficult to interpret. Does she mean that distinctiveness will bring attention in an ordinary school? She also appears to have shifted to the use of the term 'same', without specifying the way in which the children in a special school would be the same as Sam. Is this a hint of a category system in her thinking similar to the one my own comments revealed, based on disability as the criterion of classification?

At the end of the conversation I asked what they thought Sam could do when she grew up. Their answers conformed to their sense of Sam as an essentially capable individual who would find a job suited to her abilities and disabilities, and who might also get married. Their reservation here did not concern whether anyone would want to marry Sam, but whether or not anybody would be prepared to devote themselves to caring for her as much as she would need. Although they introduced the idea of employment, I was responsible for bringing marriage into the conversation. Our joint construction of 'normality' may indicate the barrier that Sam will find hardest to climb, and we will find hardest to dismantle. Lindsey's final comment may presage a sense that their ideas were utopian, and might not survive the transition to adulthood.

WS: What do you think will happen to Sam when she grows up?
Maxine: Well, she should get a good job really, 'cos she's quite bright.
WS: What job do you think she could do?
Maxine: Well, shopkeeping, things like that.
Chris: Yeah, she's good at that, taking... giving the coins to them. She's good at that.
WS: Do the rest of you think she'll have a job?
Lindsey: Yeah, she should have one.
Chris: She could do things like sitting down. That'd be the best for her. You know, things that you could do sitting down.
Maxine: Secretary.
Lindsey: Sam's Dad's hoping she'll get a private apartment when she grows up and then... 'cos she's got three brothers, and they're hoping that they'll help her, when she grows up.
Chris: It'd be better, because it might be... if she gets used to being with people, then she'll never get in a home. You've got to start thinking earlier, and getting her used to it.
WS: Do you think she'll get married?
David: Don't know.
Chris: You don't know.
WS: You don't know. Does anybody think she will, or she definitely won't?
David: I don't think she will.
Maxine: Hopefully she will.
WS: OK. Now David think's she probably won't but Maxine thinks she will. Maxine, what sort of person do you think she would get married to?
Maxine: Well, somebody who's got caring consideration for her.
David: Somebody who'd be prepared to take the responsibility.
WS: David, why do you think she won't get married?
David: Because I doubt any husband would be prepared to look after her that much.
Chris: Yeah but I think if another disabled person would help, and they came together then that'd get... they could help them like, they could help them in a way, and the other one can help the other.
WS: I see.
Lindsey: 'Cos when you grow up you see things in a different way.

List of contributors

Terence Bailey is Adviser for Special Education for the London Borough of Enfield

Juliet Bishop is Research Fellow in the Deafness Research Group at the Department of Psychology, Nottingham University

Tony Booth is Lecturer in Education in the School of Education, Open University

Mary Brennan is Lecturer in the Department of English, Moray House College of Education, Edinburgh

Harry Cayton is Director of the National Deaf Children's Society

Jenny Corbett is Senior Lecturer in Special Education at North East London Polytechnic

David Cropp is Head of the Special Education Unit at Bartley Green School, Birmingham

Siân Downs teaches at Birdsedge Infants School, Kirklees

Simon Dyson is Health Education Officer for Leicestershire Health Authority

Ann Elsegood is a primary school teacher

Janis Firminger is Co-ordinator of The Access Centre at Hereward College of Further Education, Coventry

Annette Fletcher is a teacher working as a sign-language assistant at Birdsedge Infants School, Kirklees

Lorraine Fletcher is Ben Fletcher's mother. She is also a nursery teacher

Doreen Furby is Advisory Teacher for the Physically Handicapped in the London Borough of Enfield

Susan Gregory is Senior Project Officer, Department of Psychology, Open University. She was formerly Research Fellow in the Deafness Research Group at the Department of Psychology, Nottingham University

Bobby Hulley is Samantha Hulley's mother

Tom Hulley is Samantha Hulley's father and tutors in disability for a number of institutions

Linda Jordan is a teacher, and a local councillor who chairs the Schools Subcommittee of the London Borough of Newham. She has a daughter with Down's Syndrome

Sandra Madden teaches at Burydale Junior School, Stevenage

Ann Markee is a physiotherapist

Gordon Mitchell is Education and Employment Officer at the Royal National Institute for the Deaf

Terry Moody is Lecturer in Political Economy at Glasgow University. He is active in organizations of people with visual disabilities

Jenny Morris is Lecturer in Housing, Sociology and Social Policy at Tottenham College of Technology

Gil Parsons is a school-based home-tutor in Stevenage

David Ruebain is a Govenor of a large urban comprehensive school

Tim Southgate is Head of Ormerod School, Oxford

June Statham is a freelance writer, and roofer and thatcher

Andrew Sutton is Honorary Research Fellow in the Department of Psychology, Birmingham University.

Will Swann is Lecturer in Education in the School of Education, Open University

Tom Vincent is Senior Lecturer in the Institute of Educational Technology, Open University. He was Director of the 'Computing and the Blind' Project

Julian Watson is Head of Castlecroft School, Wolverhampton

INDEX

ability, xiii, 9–10, 17–18, 49–50
ACCESS Centre, 74, 82, 91
adolescents (views,) xxii, 234–9
Advisory Committee on the Supply and
    Education of Teachers (ACSET),
    232
advocacy, 181
    self-advocacy, xxii, 264–73
Ahlgren, A., 301
Akós, K., 114
Albizu-Miranda, C., 173
Allsop, L., 302
Alnwick Green School, 202–17
Amanda (in Andrew case study), 32, 38
American Sign Language, 153, 283, 301
Amerind, 6
Andrew (case study) 181, 182–3, 185,
    187, 192
Andrew Taylor (case study), xiv, xvii,
    31–40
anti-racism, 23, 197, 223
anti-sexism, 23, 197, 223
aphasia, 187
appeals tribunals, 191–3
assessment (special needs), 131, 148, 150
    appeals, 191–3
    constraints, xxi, 170–77
    parental role, 164–78, 181, 193–4
    policy aims, 179–91 passim
    professional advice, 185–90
    see also categorization; statementing
    procedure
Association of Blind and Partially Sighted
    Teachers and Students, 239, 241,
    242, 243, 245
Association of Paediatric Chartered
    physiotherapists, 130
ataxia, 188–9
Aubrey, C., 118
Auditory fatigue, 109

B6 incident, 254–9
Baker, C., 275
Bartley Green School, 254–9
BBC Electronic Notepad, 90
Beaton, Adrian (teacher), 36–7, 38

Bellugi, Ursula, 291
Ben (case study), xv, xx, 53–72, 152–63
Bernard (case study), 265
Beverley School for the deaf, 299
bilingualism, xx, 53, 58–70, 158, 162–3
    multiculturalism and, 302–4
Birdsedge School, 53–72, 159–61, 163
'blind education system', 245
blindness, see visual disabilities
Boese, R., 154
Booth, T., xiii, xiv
Borthwick, Mary (teacher), 34
Bouvet, D., 301
Braille, xxi, 93–5, 96, 98, 99, 101–3,
    241–2
Brennan, M., 154, 279, 292, 294
Brien, David, 276–8
Brinkworth, Rex, 172
Britain (conductive education) 121–6
British Ability Scales, 188
British Association of Teachers of the
    Deaf, 225–6, 227–8, 231, 295
British Deaf Association, 231, 295, 298
British Sign Language, 154, 155, 159, 161
    bilingualism, 53, 58–70, 158, 162–3
    deaf community and, xv, xix, xxii, 152,
    274–8, 295
    forms, 227, 228
    implications, 296–304
    Makaton, 5, 6, 183, 228
    Training Agency, 298
    vocabulary/grammar, xxii, 278–94
Brown, J. A., 182
buildings (access), 10, 17, 35, 197, 203,
    208–9, 261
Burydale School, 3, 4, 10–12, 15
Buultjens, M., 240

CAD/CAM, 85
Cannon Communicator, 17, 111
Carbin, C., 154
Carl (case study), 135, 136, 140
Carpenter, Philip (teacher) 35, 36
Castlecroft School, 92, 101, 239
categorization, xviii, 179–80, 183, 185,
    187, 189–90

314

R